Economic Woman

In this remarkable book, Frances Raday uses the innovative concept of 'economic woman' to expose the foundational flaws in modern economic policies and realities which belie the promises of women's universal human right to equality. Bringing together an unparalleled richness of data from many countries in the world, she once again demonstrates the incisiveness and originality of her analytic perspectives, revealing the many ways in which the invisibility of 'economic woman' facilitates and perpetuates economic inequality. This is a book which must be read.

– ***Sandra Fredman***, *Rhodes Professor of the Laws of the British Commonwealth and the USA at Oxford University, Fellow of the British Academy and Honorary Professor of Law at the University of Cape Town*

Raday's highly readable, sobering and incisive critique of women's economic status under neo-liberal capitalism in varying contexts is an urgent reminder that human rights and governments play a vital role in reversing inequality today. She argues persuasively that reducing gender inequality is central to this task, rather than a byproduct. Her call for utilizing universal human rights norms and strategies in the economic sphere, based on understanding both the intersectional diversity of women's lives, as well as their shared burdens like care giving, provides a framework for going forward. Economic Woman should inform and inspire belief that things can be better and action to make it so.

– ***Charlotte Bunch***, *Distinguished Professor, Rutgers University, and Founder, Center for Women's Global Leadership*

In a first-class feminist analysis of women's virtual exclusion from economic policy-making forums and their severe disadvantage in opportunities and rewards, Raday targets global neo-liberalism's pervasive violations of women's human right to equality, despite women's increased participation and contribution.

– ***Alda Facio***, *Costa Rican feminist jurist, writer, teacher and international expert in gender and human rights in Latin America; expert member of HRC Working Group on DAW; and founding member of the Women's Caucus for Gender Justice at the International Criminal Court*

The author introduces the concept of economic woman and makes her visible in duality with and in opposition to the exclusive model of economic man. Economic man has epitomised neo-liberal capitalism, which embraces competition and maximisation of profit, resulting in a steep increase in economic inequality. The book demonstrates that women's inequality is a crucial factor in economic inequality, which cannot be fully understood without relating to women's situation, and that economic woman cannot thrive in the conditions of economic inequality created under global neo-liberalism.

Emphasising the international human rights guarantees of women's right to equality in all fields of life, the author documents woman's increased participation in political, public, financial and corporate institutions, employment and entrepreneurship, with some women reaching high profile positions. Nevertheless, using global data, she reveals that economic woman lags behind, with a severe economic power deficit, an unfulfilled promise of equal employment opportunity, a gendered impact of poverty and barriers to gender equality in the family. The book analyses the trap of women's increased burden of breadwinning in the context of discriminatory laws and practices, infrastructural failures and policy gaps, which preempt achievement of gender equality in economic life.

The book is intended for the general reader, academics, students, policy makers and NGOs. It shows economic woman at a global crossroads between a universal paradigm of gender equality and pervasive barriers to equal economic opportunity. The author demonstrates that tackling gender inequality, restoring welfare priorities and reducing economic inequality are inextricably linked. Human rights and governments have a vital role to play in addressing them all, to create a sustainable economic infrastructure for the lives of women and men.

Frances Raday is Director of the Concord Center for International Human Rights Law at COLLMAN. Her career combines academic research and teaching with human rights activism. She has acted from 2000 to 2018 as a UN independent human rights expert, first on the CEDAW Committee and subsequently as a Special Rapporteur for the Human Rights Council. She has litigated cutting-edge human rights cases on issues of women's right to equality in political, economic and religious contexts; TU freedoms; migrant and OPT workers' rights; human rights education and more. She has submitted expert opinions to courts in the UK and Brazil regarding the right to abortion, and in the US regarding inventors' patent rights. Raday is Professor Emerita, Hebrew University, Lieberman Chair for Labour Law; Honorary Professor, University College London; and Doctor Honoris, University of Copenhagen. She is the author of numerous books and articles in the academic and the popular press on international human rights law, labour law, religion and human rights, and feminist legal theory.

Routledge Frontiers of Political Economy

Economics for an Information Age
Money-Bargaining, Support-Bargaining and the Information Interface
Patrick Spread

The Pedagogy of Economic, Political and Social Crises
Dynamics, Construals and Lessons
Edited by Bob Jessop and Karim Knio

Commodity
The Global Commodity System in the 21st Century
Photis Lysandrou

Uncertainty and Economics
A Paradigmatic Perspective
Christian Müller-Kademann

Discourse Analysis and Austerity
Critical Studies from Economics and Linguistics
Edited by Kate Power, Tanweer Ali and Eva Lebdušková

A Macroeconomic Analysis of Profit
Andrea Carrera

The Dark Places of Business Enterprise
Reinstating Social Costs in Institutional Economics
Pietro Frigato and Francisco J. Santos Arteaga

Economic Woman
Gendering Inequality in the Age of Capital
Frances Raday

For more information about this series, please visit: www.routledge.com/books/series/SE0345

Economic Woman

Gendering Inequality in the Age of Capital

Frances Raday

Routledge
Taylor & Francis Group
LONDON AND NEW YORK

First published 2019
by Routledge
2 Park Square, Milton Park, Abingdon, Oxon OX14 4RN

and by Routledge
605 Third Avenue, New York, NY 10017

First issued in paperback 2020

Routledge is an imprint of the Taylor & Francis Group, an informa business

British Library Cataloguing-in-Publication Data
A catalogue record for this book is available from the British Library

Library of Congress Cataloging-in-Publication Data
A catalog record for this book has been requested

ISBN 13: 978-0-367-72943-1 (pbk)
ISBN 13: 978-1-138-18902-7 (hbk)

Typeset in Bembo
by Apex CoVantage, LLC

To Uri, who was my true partner; to our children, Natalie, Gilead, Leanne and Dana, who have been so precious in my dual life of caring and career; and to our darling grandchildren, for whom I wish a more equal world.

Contents

List of illustrations xii
Abbreviations xiii
Acknowledgements xv
Preface xvi

Introducing Economic Woman 1

1 Conceptualising economic woman 3
2 International human rights law 12
3 Cross-cutting issues 18
4 Outline of the book 27

PART I
Economic Power 43

1 Economic leadership 45
2 Entrepreneurship 61
3 Women's economic power deficit 69

PART II
The Sale of Human Capital 87

1 Female labour force participation (FLFP) 91
2 Promotion and gender pay gaps 95
3 Informal work 100

4 Sexual harassment at work 104
5 The pension gap 107
6 The third and fourth industrial revolutions 109
7 Maternity and gendered care responsibilities 113
8 Domestic workers 122
9 The unfulfilled promise of equal employment opportunity 126

PART III
Gendered Poverty – Revisiting the Feminisation of Poverty Paradigm 147

1 The incidence of poverty 149
2 Abuse of women's bodies and dignity 153
3 Development and human rights agendas for reduction of poverty 161
4 Tackling gendered poverty 169

PART IV
Family Economics 181

1 Women's right to equality in the family – historical development 183
2 A spectrum between traditionalist and modernist families 186
3 Women's investment in the family and women breadwinners 192
4 Family caregiving 195
5 The economics of biological motherhood 199
6 Matrimonial property 201
7 Dissolution of marriage 204
8 Inheritance 207
9 Maintenance and custody 209

10 International human right to equality in the family – transformation and backlash 210

Concluding Chapter – Economic Woman at a Crossroads 223

1 Reflections 225

Index 233

Illustrations

Figures

5.1 The management power line 56
6.1 Early-stage entrepreneurship activity, by industry, sector and gender 63
14.1 Where fathers get the most paid parental leave Weeks of paid parental leave that can only be taken by the father* 117
17.1 Proportion of people living in extreme poverty, by sex and age, 2009–2013 151
18.1 Percentages of women, men, girls and boys who are victims of trafficking 155
24.1 Minutes of unpaid work per day for the population aged 15–64, over the period 1998–2009 196

Table

8.1 Labour force participation rate by sex (per cent) and gender gap (percentage points), 1997–2021 92

Abbreviations

CEDAW	Convention on the Elimination of all Forms of Discrimination Against Women
CEO	Chief Executive Officer
EU	European Union
FAO	Food and Agriculture Organization of the United Nations
FLFP	Female Labor Force Participation
GDP	Gross Domestic Product
GEM	Global Entrepreneurship Monitor
GR	General Recommendation
HRC	Human Rights Council (United Nations)
ICCPR	International Covenant on Civil and Political Rights
ICESCR	International Covenant on Economic, Social and Cultural Rights
ICT	Information and Communication Technologies
IHRL	International Human Rights Law
ILO	International Labour Organization
IMF	International Monetary Fund
LFP	Labour Force Participation
MDGs	Millennium Development Goals
NGO	Non-Governmental Organization
OECD	Organisation for Economic Co-operation and Development
OHCHR	Office of the High Commissioner for Human Rights (United Nations)
OIC	Organisation of Islamic Cooperation
OXFAM	Oxford Committee for Famine Relief
SDGs	Sustainable Development Goals
SMEs	Small and Medium-Sized Enterprises
UDHR	Universal Declaration of Human Rights
UK	United Kingdom
UN	United Nations
UNDOC	United Nations Office on Drugs and Crime
UNDP	United Nations Development Programme
UNGA	United Nations General Assembly
UNICEF	United Nations International Children's Emergency Fund

UNIFEM	United Nations Development Fund for Women
US	United States
VAW	Violence Against Women
WEF	World Economic Forum
WGDAW	Working Group on the issue of Discrimination Against Women in Law and in Practice
WHO	World Health Organization

Acknowledgements

In the writing of the book, my immeasurable thanks go to Shai Oksenberg, who as chief researcher and academic editor has been my constant companion and has contributed both intellectual stimulation and professional precision, which have made the writing a delightful shared journey.

For their much appreciated professional comments on the drafts of various parts of the book, I want to thank my colleagues and friends, Sylvia Bijaoui, Avinoam Cohen, Benson Honig, Zvi Trigger, Naomi Weiner and Josh Gilbert. For their encouragement and literary editing, I warmly thank Dahlia Scheindlin, Susie Gilbert and my daughter Leanne Raday. For indispensable institutional support, I am most grateful to Orna Ben Naftali. My gratitude goes to Yaara Mordecai for her very helpful research assistance.

For background work on this research during my time as a member of the UN Working Group on the issue of Discrimination Against Women in Law and in Practice, I am indebted to the other members of the group, Alda Facio, Kamala Chandrakirana, Eleonora Zielinska and Emna Aouij, whose personal and regional perspectives so enriched my understandings. I wish to thank my colleagues, Sandra Fredman, Mayra Gomez, Efrat Herzberg Drucker, Ama Marston and Sharon Offenberger, for their excellent work on background papers at the early stages of my formulating the annual report to the Human Rights Council on women's economic and social lives. I am particularly grateful to the professional staff of the UN Office of the High Commissioner for Human Rights, Bernadette Arditi, Frederica Donati, Nathalie Stadelmann and Hannah Wu, whose wide knowledge of the UN system and critical contribution to the work of the experts was invaluable.

I wish to express my gratitude for the financial support for this publication, generously provided by the Minerva Center for Human Rights, Law Faculty of the Hebrew University of Jerusalem, the Research Fund of the Research Authority of the College of Management Academic Studies, Rishon Lezion, Israel; and the Emil Zola Chair for Human Rights.

Finally, thank you to the Editorial staff at Routledge.

Preface

In writing this book, I have tried to grasp the realities of economic woman in the era of neo-liberal globalisation. This involves looking at a polarised spectrum of extreme differences in economic women's situations between regions, countries, cultures, religions, economic classes and individual families. At one end of the spectrum are women who are equal to men in economic achievement; and at the other, women who are subject to male guardianship, deprived of autonomy and access to resources or economic opportunity. Despite this dramatic polarisation, the feeling is that women share a common language. There is a commonality in the way women feel the long history of silencing, marginalisation and subjection to patriarchal power and gender-based violence. And there is a commonality in their awareness of the centrality of the role of caring in their lives and of the difficulties of fulfilling that role in economic environments which are usually non-supportive and in community or family environments which are too often patriarchal. It is this commonality that I have attempted to address in my work and my writing, seeking the enforcement of women's universal human rights, in the conviction that this can make a contribution to women along the entire spectrum.

It has been my work as an independent expert in the United Nations which brought home with greater immediacy just how important it is to relate to women's human rights on a global level. The universal human rights regime, introduced in the Universal Declaration of Human Rights in 1948 in response to the horrors of 20th-century wars and devastation of human lives and values, became and has remained the key to a decent society globally. In this context, the shift of perception and change of paradigm regarding women's equality with men has been central and revolutionary. Indeed, equality between women and men is an absolute precondition for the viability of the entire human rights ethos.

In 2000, I was appointed as a member of the Convention on the Elimination of all Forms of Discrimination Against Women (CEDAW) Committee. The Committee is tasked with monitoring the implementation of state parties' obligations under the Convention, and we received enormous amounts of detailed information from governments on the basis of which we made our concluding observations on progress made in advancing women's rights and eliminating discrimination, on one hand, and ongoing violations, on the other. We were in contact with international and national women's organisations, whose representatives brought us shadow reports with critical comments regarding the facts on the ground. It was encouraging to see that the CEDAW requirements were being translated into legal edict in many states, such as the setting up of national machinery for advancing women and legislation to prohibit domestic violence. However, even in those countries which adopted anti-discrimination legislation and policy, there was a frustrating gap between legal edict and implementation of women's right to equality. Participating in the Committee was an enormously enriching experience, with 23 experts, almost all women, from all regions, and there was wide agreement amongst us on the universality of women's human rights, including on issues which were controversial in some countries, cultures or religions, such as reproductive rights, polygamy, child marriage, prostitution and marital rape. The expert members, NGOs representatives and, sometimes discreetly, female members of the governmental delegations concurred in a common understanding that women's rights are universal and indivisible and that discrimination cannot be justified on grounds of conservative cultural and religious beliefs.

In 2011, I was appointed to become a special rapporteur of the Human Rights Council as a member of the expert Working Group on the issue of Discrimination Against Women in Law and in Practice (WGDAW). The role of the special rapporteurs is to keep the Council informed on human rights developments on the ground, as the 'eyes and ears of the Council' in all states. The WGDAW was composed of five regional experts for Africa, Asia Pacific, Latin America and the Caribbean, Russia and Eastern Europe, and Western Europe and Other Countries. The work of the Group was compelling. In our work, we made country visits and observed the situation of women on the ground, at first hand, dividing our time between government representatives and NGOs or academic researchers. We also conducted communications with governments regarding allegations by women's organisations of discrimination against women. As the first Group to be appointed on the issue of discrimination against women and empowerment of women, we were mandated to set an agenda to advance these goals in cooperation with the CEDAW Committee, UN Women and other UN mechanisms and agencies. Building on the important work already done, we set out four thematic areas for our reporting to the Council: political and public life, economic and social life, family and culture, health and safety. Of these topics, we found that the least reported upon in UN policy papers was the area of economic life, possibly because the topic is so complex and the data so challenging to collect and analyse. After drafting the report on economic and social life, I was convinced of the need to continue to examine the way in which international human rights policy on equality has affected women's economic situation in the light of neo-liberal capitalism.

Leading up to my UN involvement, my commitment to promoting universal human rights stems back to the diverse threads of my life and experience. I grew up with my older sister in a liberal family in the North of England. My father was a doctor who greatly supported the move to a national health service, my mother a law graduate. Growing up as a Jewish child just after World War II in Europe, I became aware, through precocious reading, of the horrors which can result from racial hatred and have lived with the conviction that it is an absolute individual responsibility not to cause suffering and also, as a bystander, not to tolerate cruelty. The promotion of universal human rights in general and women's human rights in particular became the theme and aim of my own academic and activist work.

I studied law at the London School of Economics (LSE). I was one of two females out of a law class of 60 students to graduate. I loved the LSE for its vibrant political debates and its diverse international student body from all corners of the world. This environment, with its multicultural student body, was a natural environment for a vision of universalism. I qualified as a barrister-at-law, which involved the archaic procedure of eating a set number of dinners at the Inns of Court. On passing the professional exam in 1964, I attended the required final dinner at Grey's Inn. According to protocol, each of the new barristers had to make a short after-dinner statement and, to my surprise, when my turn came the whole room of men started stamping their feet and shouting "on the table, on the table," while the judges on the high table smiled on benignly, giving me little choice but to cooperate and climb up in my black lawyer's gown and high-heeled shoes onto the table amongst the wine glasses. I instinctively made a speech, which was in retrospect my first ever feminist speech, saying "this must be the only profession in the world in which women stand above men at its commencement and beneath them thereafter."

As a researcher at the British Institute of International and Comparative Law, in London, I worked with Lord Denning, who was the Master of the Rolls in the Court of Appeals, known for his highly creative judicial decisions, and conservative and gallant in his social persona. Pub lunches were often alone, as I was not allowed with my colleagues into the Men's Only rooms, in which they frequently ate. At the age of 22, I took up an appointment at the University of East Africa in Dar es Salaam, Tanzania. My focus was entirely on problems of racism and postcolonialism. Though I was one of only two women members of faculty at the university – the other was Gloria Young Sing, a professor of political geography from Trinidad – I was scarcely aware of gender issues or feminism. I was a member of a group of academics who met weekly to discuss ways of incorporating socialist analysis into the postcolonial educational system. We presented a new university agenda to the president of Tanzania, Julius Nyerere, who generously came to the campus to meet us. He was a remarkable man and a charming interlocutor. He complimented us on our "wonderful work" and told us, with mild irony, that after we all went back to our countries of origin and successfully introduced the program there, he would certainly consider it for Tanzania.

In the years to come, I took up an appointment at the Hebrew University in Jerusalem. I married Uri, who worked as a senior civil servant in the Israeli parliament. During the years when our children were growing up, my working life included writing for long hours into the early hours of the morning when they were asleep. The move into writing and teaching in the Hebrew language had not made my working life any easier. However, as a career mother, I felt more comfortable in the Israeli context than some of my colleagues felt in England at that time. Israeli society could still, in the 1960s, chalk up important social achievements to its credit. The status of women in the parliament, the government, the army and the law profession was relatively high, in terms both of prestige and numbers, compared with the United States and much of Europe at that time. Furthermore, social attitudes facilitated the integration of salaried work and motherhood in a way paralleled only in the Scandinavian countries and the Soviet bloc. Golda Meir was one of the first women prime ministers globally, women constituted nearly half of university graduating classes and about one-fifth of doctoral graduates.

Nevertheless, these breakthroughs did not prevent discrimination and stereotypes in the labour market, and, significantly, lurking in the Israeli ethos, there were two attributes of Israeli society which were acting to hold women's progress back: the central importance of the military and the religious personal status regime, Jewish, Muslim and Christian. In 1975, I gave the first course in the Hebrew University on the legal situation of disadvantaged groups in Israel, particularly women and the Arab minority, and the following year gave the first seminar on the legal regulation of women's status, uncovering the discriminatory aspects of the Israeli reality. I experienced discrimination with the delays in promotion common amongst women academics everywhere but was finally appointed to a full professorship. In 1986, I established the Legal Center of the Israel Women's Network, with nine young volunteer lawyers, which promoted progressive feminist legislation: equal employment opportunity, equal retirement age, protection against domestic violence, equal rights in non-transferable matrimonial property, prohibition of sexual harassment and, in 1992, affirmative action for appointment of women to government company boards. From 1975, I acted as lead counsel in a number of labour union cases, in Palestinian social security rights and in feminist litigation. The feminist cases have included challenging dismissal of an employee for complaining of sexual harassment, early mandatory retirement for women, employment discrimination in promotion and segregation of women in public spaces on religious grounds. In these cases, it has been inspiring to represent women who decided to fight the discrimination they experienced. It was a shock to uncover the depths of prejudice against women plaintiffs in general and older women in particular, amongst employers and government officials whom I confronted.

From the start of the 21st century, in my work as an independent expert in the framework of the UN, I have found a site for integrating my more fragmented experience and knowledge of women's situation in the different geo-social contexts where I have worked. In this widely sweeping overview, I encountered the global reach of progress and of backlash in women's human rights and the urgent need for the recognition, enforcement and promotion of women's universal human rights and gender equality in law and practice. My overlapping work in international human rights law, labour relations and feminist theory converged in my writing of this book, focusing on the way in which neo-liberal capitalism has impacted economic woman. I set out to uncover the ways in which neo-liberal theory and practice, with its assumed neutrality and objectivity, disregards women's realities of stereotyping, discrimination, gender-based violence and disparate caring responsibilities; to show how far the surging economic inequality of neo-liberalism is interrelated with gender inequality in a symbiotic relationship in which each augments the other; and to explore the extent to which international human rights law and policy provide solutions. I am publishing this book in the hope of making a useful contribution to the work of the many committed women and some staunch male allies who are working to establish an equal playing field for economic woman.

Frances Raday, 2019

Introducing Economic Woman

Economic Woman – Gendering Inequality in the Age of Capital aims to identify and address the situation of economic woman in the age of increasing economic inequality. It questions the significance and effectiveness of the 20th-century recognition of women's universal human right to equality in the context of economic policies and realities.

1 Conceptualising economic woman

'Economic woman' in contradistinction to 'economic man'

The concept of economic man dominates the theoretical and policy discourse of the economic sphere. Economic man is characterised as the rational decision-maker who maximises profit. He is motivated by self-interest and competition.[1] The mythology of this rational economic creature has neglected to take account of the realities of a gendered dichotomy, in which the welfare of economic man has been supplied by invisible woman. Katherine Marcal cleverly exploded the myth in her book *Who Cooked Adam Smith's Dinner?*[2] in which she recounted that Adam Smith himself, the iconic founder of the hidden hand of the market, lived with his mother who provided for his daily needs. This dichotomy is based on a gendered construct which imprisons both women and men and which is critically revisited throughout this book. We need to redefine economic woman on her own terms and not merely as the invisible shadow of economic man, like Adam's mother . . . or as Adam's rib.

The macroeconomic agenda, which has attained global reach in the age of capital, is neo-liberal capitalism. The system of neo-liberal capitalism has made market forces, competition, and profit a paradigm of economic ideology with deregulation and privatisation its ritual.[3] This system has spawned extreme inequality throughout the global economy. It is my aim to trace the importance of gendering the discourse on economic inequality. This brings us to examine the interaction between two kinds of inequality: economic inequality and women's inequality. The blunt fact is that the neo-liberal system of global capital is the product of an almost sole monopoly of men while women are the primary victims of its harms. These observations do not deny the realities of the exploitation or victimisation of men together with women, in which they may be considered equal, but point to the additional burdening of women in multiple contexts, as the pawns of neo-liberal capitalism.

The term 'economic woman' is used to modify 'economic man.' It is an assertion of the female economic presence and an insistence on making her visible. In 2011, Robin West wrote a seminal paper on the abstract character who emerged from the economic analysis of law, 'economic man,' and contrasted him with 'literary woman,' whom she regarded as "at least beginning to operate as a check on the excesses of economic man run wild."[4] She regarded literary woman as the interdisciplinary cousin of economic man. Literary woman reaches empathetic competence through the metaphor and narrative of literature and holds tremendous moral promise. Economic woman is the real life version of literary woman, contending with the construction of neo-liberal capitalism by economic man, attempting to negotiate her existence within its confines and building her power to change it.

Economic woman is part of a duality with economic man and her invisibility facilitates the biasing of economic policy. This invisibility induces blindness to the full range of injustice produced by burgeoning economic inequality. Gender inequality is not external to economic inequality but rather an intrinsic aspect of it. It is powerful men as the hegemony of the economic system who gain the most from the perpetuation of economic inequality. It is those women who are members of patriarchal families, unpaid carers, low paid workers and objects of sexual exploitation and violence who pay the greatest price, and they are still in a majority, despite equality gains made.

The right to equality and women's economic progress

Women's 20th-century gains on the road to equality have left economic woman trailing far behind in leadership and participation in determining economic policy. The discrepancy between the progress made in girls and women's education, labour force participation and political representation, in law and practice, vis-à-vis their absence from the corridors of economic power is startling.

Women's right to equality, as a latecomer in the development of the rights of man, which originated in the period of the Enlightenment, has been the most revolutionary achievement of the human rights idea in the 20th century. At the start of the 20th century, women set out, with few exceptions, from facing deprivation of the right to vote, patriarchal disposition of family property, lower levels or non-existence of girls' education, the prevalent view of women as secondary in employment without entitlement to equal wages, and women's exclusion by law from entry to higher education and the free professions, on the grounds that they were not 'persons' for this purpose. In 1948, women's right to equality was entrenched in the Universal Declaration of Human Rights (UDHR) and was codified as international human rights law in a series of treaties,[5] culminating in the Convention on the Elimination of All Forms of Discrimination Against Women (CEDAW) in 1980[6] and the Beijing Declaration and Platform for Action in 1995.[7]

Women's emancipation has been significantly realised in the political system, with women in all countries acquiring the right to vote and the right to hold political office. Achieved in the space of just over 100 years,[8] the autonomous participation of women in political power is a stunning transformation, starting out from their total exclusion, except for a handful of women who ruled in various cultures as a result of their family status as daughter, wife or widow of a ruler. The gendering of democracy globally has been recognised as an established fact. Women may still hold far from half of the reins of power, but globally they have made a significant entry into the realm of political decision-making.[9]

In the book, I am concerned to elucidate the equality progress of economic woman during this period of political emancipation. Many of those who see the title of this book may initially regard it as redundant in a golden new age of opportunity for women. In the economic sphere, too, women's right to equality has been established as a human rights imperative. In some aspects of economic life, the results have been impressive. The goal of equal education for girls has been widely achieved, globally. Women's labour force participation has increased significantly. Women have entered the corporate world and the free professions and are visible as lawyers, doctors and scientists. Women's right to equality has produced dramatic shifts in law and practice regarding women's right of access to resources, including financial assets, land and earned income. These shifts were introduced in the developed world over the past century and more recently are the site of change in the developing world. Some women have become powerful leaders in economic institutions, both public and private. Angela Merkel is regarded as the economic arbiter for Europe; Christine Lagarde is the managing director of the International Monetary Fund; and successful businesswomen such as the Chinese Zhou Qunfei, the world's richest self-made woman, are becoming highly visible. These women represent fulfilment of a potential, extolled by Sheryl Sandberg in her 'Lean In' campaign, which exhorts women to use their own capabilities to break through the glass ceiling. All these achievements and more do indeed evidence the strides made globally to transform women's and girls' expectations and to open up their right to equality in economic opportunities.

Nevertheless, in terms of participation in macroeconomic decision-making, whether in parliament, government or boardroom, economic woman has lagged far behind political woman, leaving an almost total monopoly of male control over the macroeconomic agenda. While women's participation in parliaments is 23.5% and in government 18.3%, their participation in economic portfolios in government is around 3% and at the pinnacle of corporate governance between 0% and 6%.[10] Alarmingly, the World Economic Forum concluded in 2017 that, at its current rate, while the global *overall* and political gender gaps won't be closed for a century, the global economic gender gap will not be closed for 217 years.[11]

From socialism to neo-liberalism

The agenda for women's equality was set in the 1970s when the dominant economic ideologies were socialist, whether democratic socialist or communist. The capitalist West was seeking managed capitalism, in the welfare state, and the communist block was imposing state ownership and regulation. Under both ideologies, to varying extents, the concept of state responsibility for provision of an infrastructure for families and care had a place. The policy of the welfare state was to correct, within the market system, the bargaining weakness of members of socio-economically disadvantaged groups, including maternity protections for women.[12] In the communist regimes, women and men were required to work, while employment and childcare were provided by the state apparatus. At the international level, social and economic rights were introduced in the UDHR alongside political and civil rights and the two were elaborated in the twin treaties of 1966.[13] The whole of the human rights regime, including social and economic rights, rests on the non-distinction principle which prohibits discrimination on the grounds of birth or other status, such as race, colour and sex.[14]

With the global embrace of neo-liberalism since the 1980s, the commitment to social and economic rights has been degraded. Neo-liberalism is a throwback to liberalism before the era of welfare economics and was, in the 1990s, also adopted, for instance in the Soviet bloc, as an antidote to communism. We can identify liberalism as having been the source of commitment to individual autonomy and liberty. In its historical evolution, liberalism introduced a new concept of equality, which in the course of time established one of the sources for women's right to formal equality. Implicit in the move from status to contract was the recognition of the contractual autonomy of each of the sides of the new bargaining system for determining rights. The resulting message was formal equality. Members of groups previously deprived of legal capacity were to be permitted to become arbiters of their own fate. Even though, in its origins, liberalism contained the seeds of women's equality, it did not lay the foundation for their social and economic welfare. On the contrary, it left women as the weaker members of the market economy exposed to considerable economic and social hardship.[15]

The ideological challenge of neo-liberalism since the end of the 20th century is relevant primarily in the context of social and economic rights. Neo-liberalism, as did liberalism, promotes the political and civil right to liberty. It also promotes equality as regards birth identity, ensuring equality of formal capacity and opportunity to enter into contractual transactions in economic markets. Hence, there is no conflict between the non-distinction principle and the neo-liberal agenda. Indeed, formal equality constitutes both a condition precedent for efficiency and competition and, in the area of employment, increases the pool of available labour and thus reduces the wages and labour costs. Ex contra, neo-liberalism does not support the redistributive character of social and economic rights in general, or the transformative character of substantive equality for women, in particular. It is fundamentally opposed to ensuring social and economic rights by state intervention rather than by the market.[16]

Social and economic rights require the mitigation of inequality by state intervention to improve the conditions of the weaker members of society, while neo-liberalism condones inequality where it occurs as a result of market function. The inequality of neo-liberal capitalism is manifestly demonstrated as regards women. Women, though they have achieved a large measure of equality in the democratic process, have been largely excluded from positions of economic power and decision-making in the institutions of the neo-liberal economy. Furthermore, the inequality characteristic of the neo-liberal economy impacts women more severely than men, in the distribution of resources, the rewards for the investment of human capital, the infrastructure for care and the alleviation of poverty. And, in turn, women's inequality sustains and exacerbates economic inequality in general.

Economic inequality – gendering the discourse

My claim is that women's inequality is a crucial factor in economic inequality: economic inequality cannot be understood without relating to women's situation; and economic woman cannot thrive in the conditions of economic inequality created under global neo-liberalism.

The facts on inequality are well known and frequently brought up in the media and social networks. Wealth is substantially more concentrated than income[17] and hence wealth inequality is far greater than income inequality. According to Oxfam, globally 42 people own the same wealth as the bottom 3.7 billion people.[18] And according to the World Inequality Report 2018, in China, Europe and the United States, the top 10% owns more than 70% of the total wealth, the bottom 50% owns less than 2%, and the middle 40% ("the global wealth middle class") owns less than 30%.[19] Inequality in wealth has been growing since the 1980s. At the global level, represented by China, Europe and the United State, the top 1% share of wealth increased from 28% in 1980 to 33% today, while the bottom 75% share hovered around 10%.[20] Wealth inequality is posed to continue increasing and it has been predicted that by 2030 the top 1% will own between half to two-thirds of global wealth.[21] As regards income, according to the World Inequality Report 2018, in 2016, the top 10% earned 37% of the total national income in Europe; 41% in China; 46% in Russia; 47% in the United States and Canada; around 55% in sub-Saharan Africa, Brazil, and India; and 61% in the Middle East.[22] Income inequality has, since the 1980s, increased rapidly in North America, China, India and Russia and moderately in Europe. In the Middle East, sub-Saharan Africa and Brazil, income inequality has remained stable at extremely high levels.[23] In many emerging economies and countries transitioning from undemocratic rule, inequality increased dramatically, for example, wealth and income inequality in Russia and China and income inequality in South Africa.[24]

Theorists and commentators are divided between those who regard inequality as a natural and inevitable aspect of free markets and regard the accumulation of wealth as having an automatic trickle-down effect which will eventually improve the lot of the poorest off[25] and those who regard the geometrically progressing increase of inequality as undesirable and amenable to change through policy measures. This book adopts the latter approach, as it has been developed in the work of Thomas Piketty and other economists, including Amartya Sen, Joseph Stiglitz and Paul Krugman who all received Nobel Prizes in the Economic Sciences.[26] Hence, I will take it as a given that increased economic inequality is in itself highly undesirable and that it is feasible to mitigate economic inequality through policy change.

Thomas Piketty has become the iconic advocate for the war on inequality. His book *Capital in the Twenty-First Century* has documented increasing wealth and incomes for some and stagnation for the rest.[27] Piketty identifies the increasing importance of inherited wealth along with the mockery of equal opportunity in education and earning capacity as undermining of democracy, in what he terms "patrimonial capitalism." Other writers who are committed to the idea that inequality is damaging the fabric of human society site the various ills of current political choices and the options for correcting them. For instance, Joseph E. Stiglitz, in *The Price of Inequality: How Today's Divided Society Endangers Our Future*, emphasises that inequality is a matter of political choice and is not an inevitable outcome of economic laws.[28] Focusing on the United States economy, he shows that moneyed interests compound their wealth by stifling true, dynamic capitalism, crippling growth, trampling on the rule of law and undermining democracy. Kate E. Pickett and Richard G. Wilkinson, in *The Spirit Level: Why More Equal Societies Almost Always Do Better*, documented the pernicious effects of income and wealth inequality within rich countries as eroding trust, damaging physical and mental health, reducing life expectancy, generating violence, producing lower educational achievements and injuring child well-being, including teenage pregnancies.[29] Anthony B. Atkinson, in his book *Inequality: What Can Be Done?*, proposes 15 steps to reduce inequality, including tackling monopolies, encouraging trade unionism, restraining the highest pay levels, progressive taxation and child benefits to keep children out of poverty.[30] Other policy measures which have been indicated as ways to increase state revenue include ending tax evasion and avoidance and ending bank bailouts.[31]

In discussing the ills of economic inequality, mainstream commentators have not, however, analysed economic woman's situation as being central to the issue of economic inequality as such or its solutions.[32] Piketty, in his monumental book, does not examine the gender dimensions of inequality in patrimonial capitalism, although he employed a term which in itself indicates their relevance. Indeed, Eleonora Marx, the daughter of Karl Marx, had, in the 19th century, asserted that inequality between men and women did not just favour or support capitalism it made capitalism possible: "This was not clever economics or the natural law of markets; it was the unnatural law of patriarchal commodity capitalism."[33] There is a need for gender analysis of the escalating inequality in patrimonial capitalism, which is a global determinant of our times. The inequality between women and men is a persistent factor in the maintenance of patrimonial capitalism and in the economic inequality which it generates. In examining the impact of patrimonial capitalism on the globally accepted paradigm of women's right to equality, I will, inter alia, explore the impact on women's equality, in law and practice of the increasing importance of inherited wealth and the mockery of meritocracy and equal opportunity in the earning of income, which were demonstrated so clearly by Piketty.

There have been feminist researchers and activists, prominently amongst them Diane Elson, Ruth Pearson, Shahra Razavi, Naila Kabeer, Nancy Folbre, Sylvia Chant and other researchers in the field of Gender and Development (GAD) and feminist political economy, some of whom established the International Association of Feminist Economics in 1992, and have made an outstanding contribution to exposing the male bias in various aspects of economic theory, the development process and in national budgeting.[34] The groundbreaking work of these pioneers in the field of feminist economics is a springboard for addressing the current discourse on extreme inequality from a feminist policy and human rights perspective, and their work is referred to throughout this book.

Neo-liberal policy has exacerbated economic inequality globally, between countries and within countries. The impact is often borne disproportionately by women, as will be shown throughout this book. Women suffer from increased unemployment, deteriorating working conditions and social insecurity, while relatively few women enjoy the benefits of global neo-liberalism in high skilled jobs in employment, trade and investment markets.[35] Many women are in part-time, flexible and informal sector work, which typically lacks health, pension and other work-related benefits. The shift away from state-regulated trade and investment to market-led development has swept away the protections of public employment and has undermined a major source of regulated employment for women. It was initially claimed that globalisation brought benefits to women in the global south because it opened up job opportunities. It was hence revealing to hear at the Women's World Studies Conference in South Korea, in 2005, that of the 49 women presenting abstracts on the issue of globalisation, there were almost exclusively accounts of its negative impact. Amongst the harsh manifestations of neo-liberal globalisation in the developing world are the highly exploitative export processing zones, in which women constitute a large majority of those employed.

Neo-liberalism creates market conditions which make women's equal opportunity in economic and labour markets in theory axiomatic but in practice unattainable. There is no direct denial of women's right to equality and, indeed, there is a conceptual requirement of equal opportunity. However, there is a refusal to acknowledge differences resulting from gender stereotyping or to accommodate special needs arising from biological aspects of women's reproductive role. Accordingly, the neo-liberal approach opposes creation of conditions which integrate childbearing and family care functions into the economic model. It opposes imposition on the state of the costs of social services which facilitate parental participation in the public sphere and thus enables caregivers (mostly women in current realities) to implement their right to equality of opportunity in public life and in economic and labour markets. In her well-known book *The Invisible Heart: Economics and Family Values*, Nancy Folbre explores the market and the individualistic competition that it engenders, and argues that the necessary care of elders and children is not provided in the market, yet is still absolutely necessary for society.[36] Historically, women have provided this care, whether as non-market work or low-paying market work. Neo-liberal privatisation and reduction of public services also has a disparate impact on women, who not only lose the benefit of the service themselves but also frequently have to replace the lost service for dependent family members. There is a convergence in the challenges for economic woman in the developing and the developed worlds. Concurrently, in both the developed and the developing world, individual women's economic responsibility and paid employment has expanded, while time investment for the care of children or other dependents has increased as a result of diverse factors, including urbanisation, disintegration of the extended family, privatisation and increased costs of care services.

Intersectionality

Although there is a shared core experience and reality relevant to womanhood in the global economic arena, there are also highly significant intersectional differences in the way women experience economic opportunity, oppression, exploitation and poverty. These are influenced by a women's socio-economic status and/or caste, ethnicity/race, indigenous or minority status, colour, language, culture, religion or belief, political opinion, national origin, marital and parenthood status, age, health status, disability, urban/rural location, refugee or migrant status, or if she is lesbian, bisexual, transgender or intersex, a survivor of trafficking or living in armed conflict. These intersectional differences and others exist between countries and cultures and within them. Migrant and refugee women are often beyond the reach of even those safety nets which may be available to women in general since, as femina sacra, they may fall altogether outside the umbrella of social responsibility.[37] Women with privileged biographies have educational and career opportunities which women who are in lower-income groups do not have. Extreme variations between traditionalist and modern legal and social systems, regarding equality for women and girls in the family, directly impact their economic opportunity and potential.[38] Thus, economic women are spread along traditionalist, religious, cultural and economic divides.

Nevertheless, despite these vast differences in situation and attitudes, women's core experience of patriarchy is like the roots of a tree and its trunk, while the intersectional differences are like the branches and leaves spreading in multiple directions. Women in all their diversity share a common core situation in their economic lives. They share a history of patriarchy, which has expressed itself in all fields of life in traditionalist family laws or customs, less access to resources, lower pay, exposure to gender-based violence and a greater burden of unpaid care responsibilities. Patriarchy has ongoing pervasive manifestations globally, although of greatly varying intensity. All of these constitute a substantively greater and more persistent barrier to women's and girls' economic opportunities throughout their life cycle than they do to those of men and boys. Their impact on women and girls is entrenched in cultural attitudes and stereotypes, and they form an intrinsic part of the subjection of women to male power in the family and the economy.[39] So long as women as a group are disadvantaged in the socio-economic infrastructure and in discriminatory stereotypes, it is necessary to focus on women as a group and, as a start, to level up their situation to that of men.

The feminist author and activist, bell hooks, while critiquing the biases in Western feminism, expressed the universality of global feminism:

> Radical feminist work around the world daily strengthens political solidarity between women beyond the boundaries of race/ethnicity and nationality. . . . "It is a feminism that recognizes individual diversity, and freedom, and equality, defined through and beyond north/west and south/east dialogues." No one who has studied the growth of global feminism can deny the important work women are doing to ensure our freedom. . . . The goal of global feminism is to reach out and join global struggles to end sexism, sexist exploitation, and oppression.[40]

The agenda of securing equality for women in economic life has been critiqued as a feminist choice which brought with it the double burden and the second shift, giving women a harder and lesser life.[41] It would be more realistic and accurate to see the feminist endeavour as a mechanism to cope with and to challenge those changing facts of life rather than heralding them into existence. It has been the demise of the family wage, unemployment, urbanisation, industrialisation and the decline of the welfare state which has, variously, induced many women to engage in wage labour. Neo-liberalism has entrenched the impact of these changes on families and individuals. Feminism is an essential movement to secure equality and a good life for all women in the face of these economic changes, which feminism did not play any role in creating. Feminist thinking is crucial to maximise women's autonomy to make choices within this economic scenario and to ensure that their economic opportunities are not restricted as a result of stereotypes, discrimination or lack of a facilitative infrastructure for families and care. Beyond equal opportunity within the neo-liberal realities, feminist analysis is essential to challenge the economic policy which has generated these changes in a way which addresses and eliminates gender inequality, reduces economic inequality and creates an environment which is conducive to the flourishing of women and men in their families and communities.

2 International human rights law

The analytical framework for the book is international human rights law (IHRL) and, in particular, women's human rights. IHRL provides a strong normative framework for requiring states to guarantee women's right to equality in all aspects of her life, including her economic life. This includes CEDAW's prohibition of discrimination against women by private actors, including transnational corporations, companies and employers. As elaborated and applied by international human rights experts, IHRL provides a frame of reference regarding the international consensus on women's universal and indivisible right to equality and a resource for civil society organisations working to achieve the establishment and enforcement of women's right to equality.

Furthering the cause of women's right to economic equality under IHRL is useful also for advancing the cause of mitigating economic inequality in the distribution of resources, which is an issue that has not yet been directly and explicitly addressed in IHRL. The Special Rapporteur on extreme poverty and human rights, Philip Alston, has said:

> A world in which the richest 1% owns 48% of global wealth, and in which this imbalance continues to accelerate, is obscene. Extreme inequality should also be seen as a cause for shame on the part of the international human rights movement. Just as global economic institutions have eschewed human rights, so too have the major human rights groups avoided tackling the economics of rights.

He adds that, although international economic actors like the World Bank, the International Monetary Fund (IMF), the World Trade Organization (WTO) and the Organization for Economic Cooperation and Development (OECD) have begun to speak about the negative consequences of extreme economic inequality, they do not factor human rights into their policies and programs.[42] Radhika Balakrishnan, James Heintz and Diane Elson, although conceding that "the human rights framework stops short of declaring a particular distribution of income or wealth as fair or just," maintain that there is an implicit obligation for states to take steps to move towards a more just distribution of income where economic inequality impedes the realisation of human rights.[43]

Samuel Moyan has, on the other hand, been sceptical as to the capacity of the human rights movement to address market fundamentalism and achieve redistribution from the rich to the poor and concludes: "If a global welfarism is ever to be brought from the realm of the ideal, where it is currently exiled, it will need to be championed not only as a program but also by a movement."[44] However, I would respond that, although achieving social change through law as such, including IHRL, is not enough in itself, it is an essential part of the fabric of social change. It has "the potential to mobilise movements, to influence political debate and, perhaps, to contribute to social change."[45] As Rosa Brooks has emphasised,

> at a moment when left wing politics, feminism, and liberalism are all floundering, unable any longer to inspire a new generation that worries about wars and jobs and the environment, the discourse of international human rights offers us a new and potentially transformative way to conceptualise the world's many injustices. As feminist scholars, judges, and lawyers, this is an opportunity we cannot afford to pass up.[46]

Thus, as said, success in implementing women's right under IHRL to economic equality can be a stepping stone on the road to reducing economic inequality in the distribution of resources.

State obligation to ensure women's right to substantive equality

Women's right to equality was codified in the Universal Declaration of Human Rights in 1948, became binding treaty law in the International Bill of Rights in 1966 and was elaborated in CEDAW in 1980, regarded as an international bill of rights for women.[47] Women's rights were recognised as human rights in the Vienna Declaration and Program of Action, which stated that "the human rights of women and of the girl-child are an inalienable, integral and indivisible part of universal human rights."[48] This was followed by a global commitment, in the Beijing Declaration and Platform for Action in 1995, to achieve equality, development and peace for women worldwide.[49] Gender equality was adopted in the MDGs and the SDGs as a stand-alone goal and also mainstreamed into other goals.[50] The guarantee of gender equality has found widespread expression in national constitutions and legal systems, with many states enacting specific legislation prohibiting sex discrimination in various fields of life, including the workplace and the family.

CEDAW has been ratified by almost all the world's 193 UN member states, with only six states not ratifying, notably including the United States.[51] It is significant that CEDAW is openly committed to the goal of eliminating discrimination against women and does not assume a guise of gender neutrality. In its preamble, the Convention recognises that "extensive discrimination against women continues to exist . . . [and creates] an obstacle to the participation of women, on equal terms with men, in the political, social, economic and cultural life of their countries." It also expresses, in its preamble, awareness of the need for a change in the traditional roles of men and women to achieve full equality between them.

CEDAW introduced a concept of equality for women which has remained radical even after 30 years, in part as a result of its own language and in part because of its progressive interpretation by the CEDAW Committee. Embracing all aspects of women's lives – political, public and diplomatic; economic, employment and rural; educational; health; marriage and family; and protection against violence, including domestic violence – CEDAW has imposed an obligation on state parties to ensure substantive equality for women. CEDAW provides a strong basis for the transformative change required to secure women's rights to equality in their families, full access to resources, equal conditions for the sale of their human capital and proper participation in economic policy making.[52]

The overall object and purpose of the Convention is to eliminate all forms of discrimination against women with the view to achieving women's *de jure* and *de facto* equality with men. Formal equality is achieved if policies are merely gender neutral, while substantive equality is concerned with the effects of equality policies and takes into account the need to correct prevailing inequality. Of crucial importance in the economic sphere, CEDAW requires states to eliminate discrimination by private as well as public bodies.[53] CEDAW's requirement of substantive equality potentially covers *de jure* most, though not all, of the issues raised in this book but, even where the issue should be considered to be covered by CEDAW, there are enormous gaps in identifying violations and in implementing *de facto* equality in opportunity or results.

The central feminist claim made in criticism of CEDAW is that it is assimilationist and shackles women to the male model as the dominant norm.[54] Much has been written about the problem of a legal agenda which requires women to claim equality with a male comparator, which thus precludes the kind of transformative change which would allow women to participate in social and political institutions on their own terms and in accordance with their own realities.[55] A second and equally important claim is the intersectionality claim, according to which there can be no one expression of feminism which is indistinguishably applicable to women of different ethnicity, cultural or class identity.[56] It is claimed that CEDAW largely treats women as a homogenous group.[57] A postmodernist claim is made that the very retention of the category of womanhood in CEDAW is essentialist and neither accurate nor effective; that it has not achieved the broad transformative equality promised and cannot do so as long as "the harms it addresses focus solely on 'women' as a group."[58] These criticisms of CEDAW are not justified either on the basis of the language of the treaty or its application by the CEDAW Committee, the Working Group on the issue of discrimination against women in law and in practice (WGDAW) and other international mechanisms. The issue of intersectionality is constantly addressed by all of them.[59] And the claim of essentialism in the attempt to advance women as a group cannot be justified in the face of ongoing discrimination against women as a group.[60]

As regards transformative equality, the CEDAW Committee and the WGDAW[61] have constantly reiterated that "a purely formal legal or programmatic approach is not sufficient to achieve women's de facto equality with men, which the Committee interprets as substantive equality. In addition, the Convention requires that women be given an equal start and that they be empowered by an enabling environment to achieve equality of results."[62] Most particularly, when applying the right to equality to economic and social spheres of women's lives the commitment to substantive equality is crucial. The idea of substantive equality is to move beyond the mere removal of formal legal barriers to access by women to all spaces, institutions and resources and to make sure that the access is on an equal playing field, taking account of the gendered burdens and invisible barriers which women face at access point. Furthermore, CEDAW incorporated the need for temporary special measures to accelerate *de facto* equality for women.[63]

Sandra Fredman has addressed the complexity of the concept of substantive equality through a four-dimensional approach: redressing disadvantage; addressing stigma, stereotyping, prejudice and violence; enhancing voice and participation; and accommodating difference and achieving structural change.[64] All these aspects of substantive equality must and will be incorporated in critiquing the extent to which equality has been achieved in the various aspects of women's economic life. They are also pertinent to examining the policy directives for change. The aspects of substantive equality which are relevant vary from issue to issue. Thus, for instance, redressing disadvantage and addressing stigma, stereotyping, prejudice and violence are requisite in order to facilitate women's equal access to all spaces, institutions and resources. Enhancing women's voice and participation are essential to creating a critical mass of women in economic policy forums and in contributing to the development of gender-responsive policies. Accommodating difference and achieving structural change are crucial in the integration of women's different reproductive and physiological needs into both macro and micro socio-economic programs.

As this book will show, chapter by chapter, women's disadvantage stems not only from formal discrimination but also from the mismatching of the socio-economic infrastructure and macroeconomic policy to the male-female duality of humanity. This is a duality which stems from women's and men's differing life trajectories and experiences, resulting from various combinations of gender stereotypes, cultural environment and socialisation, gender hierarchies in the family, patriarchal edicts of religious communities and sexual and reproductive characteristics. This duality may be considered to lie along a spectrum rather than being a binary division, but it represents a functional dichotomy between the vast majority of men's and women's lives. The mismatching of the socio-economic infrastructure and macroeconomic policy to male-female duality stems, in no small part, from the near invisibility of women and the near monopoly of men in the evolution of the neo-liberal policy that marginalises the welfare and care concerns which are more heavily weighted in women's agendas than in men's.

Conservative backlash

While international human rights conventions, which nearly all countries have ratified, guarantee women's universal right to equality, a profound backlash is being advanced by an alliance of conservative political ideologies and religious fundamentalisms. The WGDAW reported in 2017 that

> The continuing rise of fundamentalisms of all kinds and openly misogynistic, racist, xenophobic and populist voices, including Governments, is of grave concern to the Group. Efforts to re-entrench patriarchal understandings of sex, gender and family into the law point to important questions about sustaining progress and ensuring that good practices continue to be possible in fraught contexts.[65]

Recognition of and concern about backlash was adopted by the Human Rights Council,[66] even though, it must be said, the Council had itself adopted, by majority vote, resolutions which feed into that very backlash against women's right to equality.[67] The immediate target of the backlash, at both the international and the country levels, has been directed to restoring traditional values and protection of the family. Resolutions of the Human Rights Council calling for restoration of traditional values in the interpretation of human rights and protection of family values omitted to reassert the right of women to equality.[68] In the face of this assault on the universalism of women's human right to equality, the independent experts of the international human rights mechanisms and many civil society organisations have repeatedly asserted that freedom of religion cannot justify discrimination.[69] In a statement on the 30th September 2014, the Special Procedures mandate holders of the Human Rights Council called on the Council to ensure that in all future resolutions, concept notes and reports on the issue of the family, the right to equality between women and men, as well as between girls and boys, within the family must be explicitly included as a fundamental human right. However, the Council subsequently adopted lesser language endorsing the importance of women's equality in the family not the right to it.[70]

IHRL remains a strong and unambiguous foundation for the obligation of states to respect, protect, fulfil and promote women's human right to equality in all aspects of their lives. Although the backlash, initiated in the UN by a lobby of conservative states with a traditionalist religious agenda, represents a threat, the book rests with conviction on the universalist edict of gender equality in IHRL.

Economic justifications in support of realising women's equality

Throughout the research for the book I encountered alternative arguments put forward to justify the quest for equal economic opportunity for women. These include, broadly speaking, the business case, the development case and the 'economic' case, which are fully discussed in Part I of the book.

The business case maintains that women should be promoted to corporate leadership because it results in increased profits. It has evidence to support it but also has its detractors.

The human development case relies on research that shows that the amount of influence women have over the decisions in the household has a positive impact on the nutrition, health care and education of their children.[71] The World Bank and other researchers present evidence on the many ways in which women's development and the reduction of gender inequality lead to more rapid economic growth, improved labour productivity and healthier children.[72] Women usually invest a higher proportion of their earnings in their families than men.[73] A study in Brazil showed that the likelihood of a child's survival increased by 20% when the mother controlled household income.[74] This correlation between human well-being and women's equality is relevant to the unique contribution that women's equality brings to the economic policy table.

The 'economic' case shows that women's economic inclusion and gender parity is critical to a nation's ability to thrive: a recent study by McKinsey found that if women participated in the economy identically to men it would add up to $28 trillion, or 26%, to annual global GDP by 2025.[75] Another recent study found that by improving gender equality in the European Union, GDP per capita in the region would increase by 6.1% to 9.6% by 2050, which amounts to 1.95 to 3.15 trillion euro.[76] In other countries it has been assessed that equal female labour force participation would significantly increase GDP: raising the female labour force participation rate to country-specific male levels would, for instance, raise GDP in the United States by 5%, in Japan by 9%, in the United Arab Emirates by 12% and in Egypt by 34%;[77] in India, GDP could rise by 8% if the female/male ratio of workers went up by 10%.[78]

These other cases for advancing women's economic equality are important in that they provide supportive evidence regarding the positive impact of women's equality and the correlation between improved GDP and human development indices, and allegedly also corporate profit. However, any such attempt is instrumentalist and it is in no way necessary to prove cause and effect in these outcomes of women's equality in order to justify the IHRL imperative of equality for women, which is a stand-alone goal.

3 Cross-cutting issues

Throughout this book, I explore how far the guarantee of women's right to equality has encompassed economic woman. How has the right to equality shaped, in law and in practice, women's equal participation in determining the economic policy which frames their lives, equal economic opportunity and remuneration, equal protection from the disparate impact of poverty and equal rights in the family? Through all aspects of women's economic lives runs the thread of three cross-cutting issues to which intermittent reference will be made in the relevant contexts. These cross-cutting issues are access to resources, unpaid care and violence against women.

Access to resources

Women's equal access to ownership and control of resources is crucial for equality between men and women and for their empowerment in economic decision-making at all levels. Resources include financial assets, credit facilities and land. Financial assets and credit facilities are a prerequisite for education and training, entrepreneurship and for acquiring land or a home. Land ownership may be crucial as a productive resource particularly in agriculture. Land is the basis for industrial development, particularly in the extractive industries but also in building and tourism. It may also be used as collateral for credit in commercial transactions. In a market economy, lack of access to resources has a severely debilitating impact.

Women's lack of access to resources is intrinsically related to inequality in the family and dependence on male family members. Since the late 19th century, there has been a global trend to universal legal recognition of married women's right to own and manage property, and international human rights law requires states to ensure women's right to equality in matrimonial property, although it has not explicitly mandated equality in inheritance rights. These issues will be fully discussed later in Part IV, which addresses the economy of the family.

There is a serious lack of systemic sex-disaggregated data regarding access to resources in general. Nevertheless, experts report a serious gap in men's and women's levels of ownership of property and demonstrate it in specific aspects of property ownership particularly in relation to housing and land. For instance, the HRC Special Rapporteur on adequate housing has said that, although in many countries women's rights to land are legally protected, in practice women are socially and economically disadvantaged and face *de facto* discrimination in housing, land and inheritance rights.[79] And the UN Food and Agriculture Organization (FAO) observed that women face a serious gender gap in access to productive resources.[80]

The most significant available data regarding women's access to resources has focused on land ownership. It was reported that women own only 1% of the world's land,[81] however, this assessment is contested as being below the real levels of women's land ownership. A survey of 34 developing countries by the FAO puts the percentage of women's land ownership at 10%, and according to Thomson Reuters Foundation, it is under 20%.[82] In Russia, too, it is said that land ownership is the domain of men, and women are not owners.[83] What is clear is that women own and control far less land than men, and the land they control is often of poorer quality and their tenure is insecure.[84]

Women's access to land is, in many cultures, barred by custom, which regards land given to women as 'lost to another family' in the event of marriage, divorce or (male) death, justifying the deprivation of rights from the woman by arguing that men will provide for women's financial security.[85] In some countries, widows are subject to 'property dispossession' or 'property grabbing,' in which relatives of a deceased husband, claiming customary rights, dispossess the widow and her children from property accumulated during the marriage, remove the widow from the family home and then ignore their concomitant customary responsibility to support the widow and children.[86] In China, although the marriage law gives fully equal property rights to men and women, the administration of the divorce law requires division of property in the family home according to registration, and, as a result of family custom, even when the wife's family buys the home, it is usually registered in the name of the husband.[87] In Latin American countries, Deere and Leon researched the gender distribution of land in five countries and found it to be 'extremely unequal' with women rarely representing more than one-quarter of the landowners. They attributed this to several factors: male preference in inheritance, male privilege in marriage, male bias in both community and state programs of land distribution, and gender bias in the land market.[88] In sub-Saharan Africa, research shows significant gender gaps, not only in land ownership, but also with regard to other land rights, such as plot management and the rights to sell or use the plot as collateral.[89]

Land is a primary productive resource particularly in rural and agricultural settings. FAO data show that women are concentrated in subsistence farming for households and are largely excluded from modern contract farming, which gives preference to cash production over subsistence agriculture. Their lack of secure control over land is a contributory factor in disqualifying them. Hence, the result of the fact that women do not own the land they cultivate is that instead of being owner-producers, they are virtual squatters on the land and work as informal or unpaid family workers or as agricultural employees. It is calculated that closing the gender gap in agriculture would generate significant gains for the agriculture sector and for society. If women had the same access to productive resources as men, they could increase yields on their farms by 20 to 30%. This could raise total agricultural output in developing countries by 2.5 to 4%, which could in turn reduce the number of hungry people in the world by 12 to 17%.[90] Another assessment indicates that the total agricultural outputs in Africa could increase by up to 20%, if women's access to agricultural inputs was equal to men's.[91]

As regards the extractive industries, tourism and building development, it has been well documented, especially in Africa and in Latin America,[92] that the phenomenon of land grabbing for these purposes, by states and by private corporations, is impoverishing women even more than men. The destruction of subsistence agriculture impacts women harshly, removing the food security of the dispossessed women and the family members in their care. Industrial and commercial concerns which take over the land may be required, in the terms of their concessions, to pay compensation to the local population and to provide employment opportunities. Women frequently do not benefit from either. The compensation goes to the landowners who are in the majority of cases the male members of the family, and the new jobs generally go to men. On a WGDAW visit to Peru in 2014, civil society organisations reported that women displaced by extractive industries in the Andes were often left with no choice but to leave their communities and go into towns, where their only means of supporting themselves and their children was through prostitution.[93]

There is an urgent need to collate sex-disaggregated data as regards women's share in property of all kinds: financial resources, credit, ownership of bank accounts, access to housing and land, share of matrimonial property and of inheritance. Existing data is patchy but indicates a serious gender gap. The lack of access to resources is a primary handicap for women's economic empowerment.

Unpaid care

Empirical studies clearly show that, globally, women bear the heavier share of unpaid care work. In 2017, the World Economic Forum assessed that, globally, men do only 37% of the unpaid work that women do (originally reported as 34% for OECD countries).[94] Additionally, the ILO showed that, when both paid work and unpaid work are taken into consideration, women work longer hours per day than men with a gender gap of 73 minutes per day in developing countries and 33 minutes per day in developed countries.[95]

Women's care responsibilities in the family are reinforced by gender stereotypes, and their contribution of unpaid care to the economy is made possible by the force of these stereotypes. The economic significance of gendered roles in reproduction and caregiving has been well established in the feminist literature. Diane Elson for instance, has emphasised the interdependence of the 'productive' economy and the 'reproductive' economy,[96] which she describes as monetary and non-monetary respectively:

> The ability of money to mobilize labour power for 'productive work' depends on the operation of some non-monetary set of social relations to mobilize labour power for 'reproductive work.' These non-monetary social relations are subordinate to money in the sense that they cannot function and sustain themselves without an input of money; and they are reshaped in response to the power of money. Nevertheless, neither can the monetary economy sustain itself without an input of unpaid labour, an input shaped by the structures of gender relations.[97]

Elson has further described how "macro-economic policy considers only the monetary economy, ignoring the non-monetary economy, in which women perform most of the work."[98]

Women's income-generating opportunities in their adult lives are reduced because they are characterised by the duality of production and reproduction with a gendered burden of unpaid care. Hence their income-generating slice of life is marked by the concurrence of economic opportunity with childbearing and caring responsibilities. The pressures of combining work with childrearing are infinitely increased in the neo-liberal age, where the demands of the economic market are unrelenting, requiring long hours at work, daily travel from home, long-distance travel for work, relocation and rescheduling in accordance with the needs of the employing enterprise and job insecurity which may entail constant readjustment of home management. Families are under increasing stress in attempting to bring in adequate income for family units, with the economic exigency of two-earner families, while at the same time providing the caring facilities essential for children and other dependent family members.

There are two separate aspects of the reproductive: the biologically determined aspect of maternity, which includes pregnancy, birthing and breastfeeding, and the care-giving aspect, which is a parental function whose allocation as unpaid work to women is a gendered social construction. International human rights law has addressed the barrier of reproduction to women's equal opportunity in the context of formal employment, requiring paid maternity leave, which has been adopted by almost all countries, with the notable exception of the United States. However, many women, in both developing and developed economies, are in informal or precarious employment or running small and medium-sized enterprises and do not enjoy the benefits of paid maternity leave. As regards the unpaid work of caregiving, undertaken mainly by women, international human rights law has not required states to provide childcare services or to reimburse payment for care services as recognised tax deductions, as discussed in Part II on the sale of women's human capital.

There has, rather, been individualisation of care responsibilities which now devolve heavily on families, usually on mothers. In developed countries, the individualisation is a result of the reduction of social services, care services and social security benefits. Few states provide comprehensive childcare along the lines of the Scandinavian model. Indeed, austerity policies in the Western countries have reduced existing funding for care services in many of the countries which used to provide it. In the developing world, the individualisation is a result of massive urbanisation entailing break-up of community and extended family support for childrearing. Furthermore, in countries with a formerly socialist system, such as China and Russia, state planning in their newly market-oriented development has been replaced by privatisation, affecting both the labour market and the provision of state services. Concurrently, in both the developed and the developing worlds, individual women's economic role of providing for self and family has been increased in scope and intensity.

Anne-Marie Slaughter created a storm in the American and international feminist community with her article 'Why Women Still Can't Have It All.'[99] She had spent her career in academia: as a law professor and then as the dean of Princeton's Woodrow Wilson School of Public and International Affairs. She says:

> Both were demanding jobs, but I had the ability to set my own schedule most of the time. I could be with my kids when I needed to be, and still get the work done. I knew that I was lucky in my career choice, but I had no idea how lucky until I spent two years in Washington within a rigid bureaucracy, even with bosses as understanding as Hillary Clinton. . . . My workweek started at 4:20 on Monday morning, when I got up to get the 5:30 train from Trenton to Washington. It ended late on Friday, with the train home. . . . I was entitled to four hours of vacation per pay period, which came to one day of vacation a month. . . . In short, the minute I found myself in a job that is typical for the vast majority of working women (and men), working long hours on someone else's schedule, I could no longer be both the parent and the professional I wanted to be.

Anne-Marie Slaughter readily recognises that her dilemma of choice is one for the most privileged: choice between a flexi job in academia vis-à-vis round the clock commitment to an employer's needs, with a high salary, domestic help and, she emphasises, encouragement from her husband. She represents one of the small percentage of women who have entered into the highest skill and income bracket of employment or entrepreneurship, and these women live at an ever-widening gap from their cohorts, as we will see in the book.

In contrast, most women who are engaged in economic activity outside the home are in a harrowing work and care schedule, without the supportive infrastructure she describes. They do not have flexi hours, adequate childcare support or domestic help and often do not have spousal encouragement or support. In the developed and the developing economies, there is a convergence in the disparate numbers of women who are working outside the reach of labour protection, have no rights to maternity protections and have no access to affordable childcare. Some women take their children with them to work.

I myself have watched women who sell produce at the market in Kinshasa spend their working day with their children in carrier-slings on their backs. In order to work, some parents are tragically forced to leave their children without supervision. In the visit of the expert WGDAW to Peru, we were told by mothers from the Amazon region who had taken up jobs in the mines for the family's economic survival that they had been forced to leave their young children to fend for themselves in their home villages, only to return months later and find their children emotionally and physically devastated. The advent of the migrant working woman epitomises this form of vulnerability, particularly in the sphere of domestic work. In the Philippines, since the 1970s, the government has promoted labour exportation as a strategy for relieving poverty and alleviating the national debt. A tenth of the population now works abroad, supporting nearly half of the country's households and leaving some nine million Filipino children missing a parent. In the past decade, three-quarters of these overseas foreign workers have been women who have been semi-permanently separated from their children.[100]

Care of dependents is an issue for humanity. It is largely carried out by women as an unpaid or underpaid activity. Caring is also nurturing and hence cannot be entirely outsourced or mechanised, and, indeed, many women and men do not want it to be so. However, total outsourcing is a far cry from making provision for families to cope with those aspects of caring which should clearly be funded by the state in order to allow women, like men, to combine family and economic activity outside the home on an even playing field. Failure to provide a solution including a social protection floor for care condemns caring to oblivion or women's equal economic opportunity to delusion.

Violence against women

Violence against women (VAW) creates a barrier to women's economic opportunities throughout all private and public spheres, beyond the family and the workplace, affecting women in educational institutions, in the street, public transport, informal work settings and in political and corporate activities. VAW in any of these various sites is likely to result in blocking economic opportunities or achievements of the women and girls who are its direct victims. Beyond its immediate victims, the likelihood of exposure to VAW has a ripple deterrent effect. The restriction of women's and girls' economic opportunities as a result of VAW was most recently brought into the glare of the media in the #MeToo movement. Although both in feminist theory and human rights policy, VAW has been on the agenda since the 1970s, the #MeToo movement has brought about unprecedented global awareness of VAW in the public and economic spheres.[101]

There has been widespread articulation of the need to eliminate VAW in international human rights mechanisms and in national legislation and policy.[102] Nevertheless, the phenomenon of VAW is persistent and shockingly widespread in all regions of the world.[103] According to the World Health Organization (WHO) data from 2013, one in every three women worldwide has experienced gender-based violence, either sexual or physical intimate partner violence or sexual non-partner violence.[104] The declared resolve of the international community to eliminate VAW has been focused on domestic violence, violence in conflict situations and sexual harassment in the workplace.[105] While all of these are essential loci in which VAW must be addressed, there are wider implications of VAW in the economic sphere, which have been largely neglected.

Outside the workplace, women are exposed to sexual harassment in the public arena, including service institutions, public transport, 'street harassment,' cyberbullying and pornographic advertising, producing a fear factor that curtails their freedom of movement and occupation and equal opportunity to participate in public, political, economic, social and cultural life. Several studies highlight that women are frequently targeted for sexual harassment by suppliers or service providers pressuring them for sexual favours.[106] Over 50% of female respondents to an international poll said they avoided public transport and spaces because they feared harassment: 70% of them thought that streets were the most unsafe places, and 78% thought sexual violence was increasing.[107] Public transportation, which women must use not only to get to work but also to educational institutions, shops or to access services, indeed often poses one of the greatest threats, with international media reporting horrifying cases of gang rape on public transport, including the 2012 gang rape and murder of a female medical student on a bus in Delhi (India) that produced public demonstrations and international concern.[108]

A systemic and extreme example of violence that prevented women from freely accessing economic opportunities, affecting among other things their transport to their workplaces, occurred in Ciudad Juarez, Mexico, in the 1990s and early 2000s and was the subject of international investigation and of an optional protocol decision of the CEDAW Committee. Over a period of years, there were systematic murders, abductions and rapes of hundreds of women, especially young women, who lived in extreme poverty and were employed in the Maquilas (export processing zones). The Committee found that the systemic violence was rooted in a culture of violence and discrimination, based upon women's alleged inferiority, that had developed specific characteristics marked by hatred and misogyny.[109] The brilliant Latin American writer Roberto Bolanyo, in his book *2666*, gave a searing commentary on the violence inflicted on these young women, with vivid expression of the faceless tragedy of the loss of their lives as they struggled to emerge from family poverty through their work in the Maquilas.[110]

The CEDAW Committee in its General Recommendation No. 35 in 2017 recommended that public spaces must be made safe and accessible to all women and girls, including by providing adequate physical infrastructure, with lighting, in urban and rural settings, particularly in and around schools.[111] Yet, though there are some examples of good practices,[112] state legal systems have largely failed to address the harms caused by sexual violence and harassment women face on the street and on public transport. Indeed, as demonstrated in the data from the World Bank's "Women, Business and the Law" 2016 report, only 18 of the 173 economies examined have enacted laws on sexual harassment in public spaces.[113]

A major area of concern regarding sexual violence and harassment is the education system, which constitutes the portal to economic opportunity. The international agenda on education for girls, adopted in the MDGs, has reached a high level of equality in girls' school enrolment.[114] Nevertheless, VAW creates a barrier for girls' attendance at educational institutions. Gender-based violence in schools, or fear of it, can have profound consequences on students' participation, achievement and continuation in school, particularly for girls, and may influence parents' decision to keep their girls out of school.[115] There is global evidence of gender-based violence in and around schools,[116] yet, the World Bank's 'Women, Business and the Law' 2018 report shows that of 189 economies, 65% don't have specific legal provisions addressing sexual harassment in schools.[117] Moreover, even if specific laws exist, they are often not implemented or enforced, and the reporting and accountability mechanisms are often weak and do not protect victims' privacy and rights.[118]

In higher education institutions, women students across the globe experience high levels of sexual violence on campus.[119] In China, a 2017 survey conducted by the Guangzhou Gender and Sexuality Education Centre, found that more than 69% of Chinese university student respondents, mostly women, had experienced some form of sexual harassment, although less than 4% had reported it.[120] On college campuses in the United States, the violence against women students has been designated a rape culture. The 2015 documentary movie 'The Hunting Ground' provides an exposé of rape crimes on college campuses, their institutional cover-ups, and the devastating toll they take on students and their families and, reports that, while 20% of female college students in the United States experience sexual violence, about 80% of attacks go unreported, and their perpetrators typically suffer no consequences.[121] The prevalence of VAW on campuses undermines women's confidence as regards their safety in the public space at a crucially formative stage of their careers.

Growing cyber VAW is threatening women's equality of access to economic opportunities. A 2015 report released by the UN Broadband Commission reveals that this is a growing global problem with potentially significant economic and societal consequences.[122] The research that is available suggests that women are disproportionately the targets of certain forms of cyber violence compared to men.[123] Online harassment that systematically targets women – including 'gender trolling' – is a manifestation of patriarchal culture that threatens women's ability to function in the public sphere. Misogynistic posts can have a cumulative and silencing result that chills women's freedom of speech, assembly and access to information and to jobs. Despite the severity of the threat, only 26% of law enforcement agencies in 86 countries surveyed in 2015 by the UN Broadband Commission were taking appropriate action.[124]

In the economic marketplace, VAW is commercialised and disseminated in forced prostitution, trafficking and pornography. These are highly gendered issues and are sui generis because of the nexus between these industries and VAW.[125] The profits which accrue in these industries are derived from VAW or from the portrayal of it. They contribute to the perpetuation of VAW in antithesis to the declared human rights agenda of eliminating it. Only as regards trafficking have the economic implications of these industries been addressed in international human rights law.[126]

Prostitution has a global dimension and has been assessed to involve around 40 to 42 million people, 75% of them between 13 and 25 years old, and most of them migrants.[127] They are mainly women and girls and the johns are mainly men.[128] Women and girls tragically constitute 71% of all detected trafficking victims and women and girls constitute 96% of the persons trafficked for sexual exploitation.[129] The European Parliament's Women's Rights Committee in 2004 assessed that the illegal sex industry is estimated to turn over more money annually than the total of all military budgets in the world.[130] The ILO in 2014 assessed the revenue from human trafficking for commercial sexual exploitation to be $99 billion and pointed out the very high profit margins where trafficking is for sex: sexual exploitation earns 66% of the global profits of human trafficking and slavery-like conditions.[131]

Pornography is an industry which feeds off the appetite for violent sexual abuse of women.[132] In this I am referring especially to hard porn, which by definition portrays extraordinarily violent sexual acts and represents domination and subjection of women. (I am not referring to consensual eroticism based on equality and mutual respect amongst participants.) Hard porn can only be described as the commodification and commercial profiteering from misogyny and from the most brutal levels of violence against women. It has been described as "predatory corporate capitalism" which "has moved in a few decades from a lucrative underground business with ties to organised crime to a huge corporate-capitalist industry that operates openly."[133] The porn industry is a massive gold mine with a $97 billion intake annually.[134] It was reported in 2016 that internet porn constitutes approximately 12% of the internet.[135] Pornhub, the most travelled porn site in the world, had approximately 28.5 billion visits in 2017.[136]

A shift of focus to include the economic aspects of VAW is essential to address its persistence not only in conflict but also in times of peace. Measures must be taken to secure women's safety not only in the workplace but also in the public space, in services, streets and transport. Educational institutions at all levels must be secure spaces in which girls and women are not subjected to sexual violence and harassment. The policies adopted to address the VAW industries of prostitution, trafficking and pornography must be directed to providing economic alternatives to the women who are abused in them and to removing all economic incentives for those who profit from them.[137]

Economic policy has belied the declared international commitment to eliminate VAW. Neo-liberal and austerity policies have reduced budgets which provided supportive socio-economic frameworks for women's and girls' lives, thus exposing them to increased levels of VAW.[138] Liberal policies have facilitated the commercialisation of VAW through the prostitution, trafficking and pornography industries, which normalise and commodify the abuse of women's sexuality and bodies and increase the levels of VAW. The economic realities of VAW should be recognised and factored into all economic policy making.

4 Outline of the book

The book addresses the question as to which women and how many women have broken through the glass ceiling or which women and how many women have been left behind and where the future trends are taking us. In the context of the right to gender equality and on the basis of the available data, I discuss differences in the positioning of women and men in the age of neo-liberal capitalism from two angles: the disparate impact of neo-liberal economic policy on women and the role, if any, played by women in the formulation of macro-economic policy, which determines the quality of their lives.

The difficulties I have encountered in the attempt to look at the gendered impact of global neo-liberalism lie both in the paucity of systematised sex-disaggregated data and the focus of much of the data which is accessible on the developed economies of the OECD. However, the difficulties in accessing the data are also the result of the dispersed sites of women's economic realities: the labour market, formal and informal work, unpaid care work, political and corporate economic policy forums, entrepreneurship, property ownership and management, credit facilities, educational institutions and families. The data and assessments on which I draw in the book are therefore far from comprehensive or systematic and are sometimes conflicting. They do, I hope, provide enough ground for seeking a tentative hypothesis as to women's global economic situation, the convergence between the global south and the global north, the increased burden of combining work outside the home with unpaid care, the growing wealth and income gaps between women themselves, the very low level of women's participation in economic policy forums and the gendered impact of poverty.

Part I addresses women's economic power. It peruses the available data to show what is the level of women's representation in political and in corporate forums for macroeconomic policy making and their extremely low percentage presence at the pinnacle of economic power. It examines the declared commitment of economic leaders to provide equal opportunity in the corporate world and their reliance on the business case for promoting women up the corporate ladder. Alongside this declared commitment it examines the lesser opportunity of women on company boards, in the C-suite, as CEOs and as entrepreneurs and the barriers to women's advancement in all these areas of economic power.

It examines the nexus between the near male monopoly in formulating macroeconomic policy and the substantive import of the policy produced, with its concentration on profit and competition and its neglect of gender-responsive issues such as welfare and care.

Part II takes a wide view of the different contexts in which women work for the profit of others. It critiques the increase in women's labour force participation, emphasising that participation does not mean equality or power. It pays special attention to the productive and reproductive, the formal and informal, and the paid and unpaid arenas of women's work. It will critique the adequacy of international labour law and human rights law in its mandating of equal employment opportunity, prohibition of discrimination and sexual harassment, equal wages for work of equal value and maternity rights. I discuss the problem of enforcement of equality rights for women employed in the formal labour market and the need to reach and cover a large and growing mass of women in informal or precarious employment in the global south and in the global north and to cover migrant women, especially domestic workers; to provide solutions for gendered care responsibilities of working parents; and to secure greater equality in working women's pension benefits. I also take a look at the various analyses and predictions which are being formulated regarding the impact of the third and fourth industrial revolutions on women's future work opportunities.

Part III revisits the paradigm that poverty is feminised. It examines the information on women's poverty which can or cannot be extracted from international surveys based on the income of households, the impact of patriarchy on women's share of household resources and the effect of the care burden on women's poverty. Beyond the incidence of poverty for women, I examine the gendered impact of poverty on women and girls. Beyond the ravages of physical deprivation and social exclusion suffered by both women and men in poverty, I focus on the qualitative difference of abuse and deprivation in gendered poverty. Women and girls suffer the impact of poverty even more harshly than men because of the increased sexual abuse of their bodies and dignity in violence, prostitution and trafficking; because of the barriers to reproductive health care; and because of the denial of essential nutrition and sanitation in pregnancy, lactation and menstruation.

Part IV reviews the development of an international consensus as to women's and girls' right to equality in the family and the conservative and religious backlash to the universality of this right. It examines the impact on women's and girls' family lives of patriarchal traditions of religious or customary law as compared with the modernist transformation in secular legal systems. I explore the entitlement to economic equality of individual members within households, foremost amongst them women and girls. I look at the family as the primary economic unit which shapes and determines the economic status and potential of women and girls: the investment of women's and girls' human capital in the family, as unpaid workers and as breadwinners, the economics of biological motherhood, and women's entitlement to the resources of the family, through their share of matrimonial property including inheritance.

Women's experience of economic inequality is, as will be shown, even more extreme than that of men. This is true because of the lesser returns on the sale of their human capital, because of their greater unpaid care-giving function, because of their harsher experience of poverty and because of their lesser power within the family. Furthermore, the inclusive rhetoric of equality has opened the door to women's economic participation as workers but has not established their power in the institutions of economic policy determination. Addressing economic equality through a gender perspective entails examining not only the impact of inequality on women but also women's potential for making the kind of transformative change which will reduce inequality for them, their families, their communities and the macroeconomy nationally and globally. The participation of a critical mass of women in policy making in economic institutions, from the family to the boardroom, will promote inclusion of a gendered experience of economic exigencies into the templates of macro and microeconomic planning. The importance of women's participation in macroeconomic policy making is qualitative not merely quantitative, bringing with it not only a realisation of their right to equality but also a recognition of the gendered duality of human experience and judgement.

Notes

1 For a general explanation, see John Black, Nigar Hashimzade and Gareth Myles, *A Dictionary of Economics* (4th edn, Oxford University Press 2012); Min Zhang, Zhenggang Chi and Jing Luo, 'Information Economic Man Assumption: Concept Definition and Comparison' (2018) 3(1) *Asian Business Research* 41.

2 Katrine Marcal, *Who Cooked Adam Smith's Dinner? A Story of Women and Economics* (Pegasus Books 2017).

3 See, in general, Heidi Gottfried, *Gender, Work, and Economy: Unpacking the Global Economy* (Polity 2012) 262–263. Though some critics, for example Thomas Piketty, *Capital in the Twenty-first Century* (Arthur Goldhammer tr, Harvard University Press 2014), seem to regard capitalism as such as being the author of these phenomena, I choose to relate to neo-liberal capitalism and not to capitalism in general, as this can include managed capitalism and the welfare state.

4 Robin L. West, 'Economic Man and Literary Woman: One Contrast' (1988) 39 *Mercer Law Review* 867.

5 The Universal Declaration of Human Rights, UNGA Res 217A(III), 10 December 1948, UN Doc A/810 (1948) (UDHR); International Covenant on Civil and Political Rights (entered into force 23 March 1976) 999 UNTS 171 (ICCPR); International Covenant on Economic, Social and Cultural Rights (entered into force 3 January 1976) 993 UNTS 3 (ICESCR).

6 The Convention on the Elimination of all Forms of Discrimination Against Women (entered into force 3 September 1981) 1249 UNTS 13 (CEDAW), www.un.org/womenwatch/daw/cedaw/text/econvention.htm.

7 'Beijing Declaration and Platform for Action,' adopted at the Fourth World Conference on Women at Beijing, China, 4–15 September 1995, www.un.org/womenwatch/daw/beijing/pdf/BDPfA%20E.pdf.

8 The global process started sporadically with national suffrage in countries such as Sweden in the 18th century and New Zealand in 1893, continued in countries such as the

United Kingdom in 1918 and the United States in 1920, and, finally, was achieved in countries such as Switzerland in 1991 and Saudi Arabia in 2015.

9 To this must be added the caveat that the deviation in this statistic is between over 50% of women in the parliaments of Rwanda, Cuba and Bolivia and about 10% or less in over 25 countries, including Hungary, Japan and a number of states in the African and Asia Pacific regions. See Inter-Parliamentary Union, 'Women in National Parliaments,' *Inter-Parliamentary Union Website*, 1 June 2018, http://archive.ipu.org/wmn-e/classif.htm.

10 See Part I of the book.

11 The World Economic Forum benchmarks in its 2017 Global Gender Gap Report 144 countries on their progress towards gender parity across four thematic dimensions: Economic Participation and Opportunity, Educational Attainment, Health and Survival, and Political Empowerment. The Economic Participation and Opportunity sub-index contains three concepts: the participation gap (the difference between women and men in labour force participation rates), the remuneration gap (ratio of estimated female-to-male earned income and wage equality for similar work) and the advancement gap (ratio of women to men among legislators, senior officials and managers, and the ratio of women to men among technical and professional workers). The estimations on closing of the gender gap is across the 106 countries covered since the inception of the report. See World Economic Forum, 'The Global Gender Gap Report 2017,' 2017, viii, 5 and 25, http://www3.weforum.org/docs/WEF_GGGR_2017.pdf.

12 Such as employees, protected tenants and consumers. See P.S. Atiyah, *The Rise and Fall of Freedom of Contract* (Oxford University Press 1985).

13 UDHR (n 5); ICCPR (n 5); ICESCR (n 5). However, in spite of the prevalent welfare philosophy in post–World War II Europe and post–New Deal United States, social and economic rights were downgraded as being merely a concession to the Socialist Eastern bloc countries and were neglected in mainstream human rights discourse until the last quarter of the 20th century, regarded as second-generation rights.

14 UDHR (n 5) art 2.

15 Carole Pateman, *The Sexual Contract* (Stanford University Press 1988).

16 Jack Donnelly, *Universal Human Rights in Theory and Practice* (2nd edn, Cornell University Press 2003) 48–49, 200–203.

17 World Inequality Lab, 'World Inequality Report 2018,' 2017, 198, https://wir2018.wid.world/files/download/wir2018-full-report-english.pdf.

18 Oxfam, 'Reward Work, Not Wealth: To End the Inequality Crisis, We Must Build an Economy for Ordinary Working People, Not the Rich and Powerful,' Briefing Paper, January 2018, https://d1tn3vj7xz9fdh.cloudfront.net/s3fs-public/file_attachments/bp-reward-work-not-wealth-220118-en.pdf; Katie Hope, '"World's Richest 1% Get 82% of the Wealth", Says Oxfam,' *BBC News*, 22 January 2018, www.bbc.com/news/business-42745853.

19 World Inequality Report 2018 (n 17) 198.

20 Ibid.

21 Michael Savage, 'Richest 1% on Target to Own Two-thirds of All Wealth by 2030,' *The Guardian*, 7 April 2018, www.theguardian.com/business/2018/apr/07/global-inequality-tipping-point-2030; Dominic Frisby, 'Wealth Inequality Is Soaring – Here Are the 10 Reasons Why It's Happening,' *The Guardian*, 12 April 2018, www.theguardian.com/commentisfree/2018/apr/12/wealth-inequality-reasons-richest-global-gap.

22 World Inequality Report 2018 (n 17) 9–11.

23 Ibid.

24 Ibid. 16, 106, 113 and 145.

25 For example, F.A. Hayek, Ludwig von Mises, Milton Friedman and others.

26 Piketty (n 3); Amartya Sen, *Inequality Reexamined* (Harvard University Press 1992); Joseph E. Stiglitz, *The Price of Inequality: How Today's Divided Society Endangers Our Future* (W.W. Norton & Company 2012); Paul Krugman, *"Confronting Inequality" They Say, I Say with Readings* (2nd edn, W.W. Norton & Company 2009) 322–341.

27 Piketty (n 26).
28 Stiglitz (n 26).
29 Richard G. Wilkinson and Kate E. Pickett, *The Spirit Level: Why More Equal Societies Almost Always Do Better* (Allen Lane 2009).
30 Anthony B. Atkinson, *Inequality: What Can Be Done?* (Harvard University Press 2015).
31 The Center for Economic and Social Rights (CESR), 'Human Rights in Tax Policy,' *CESR*, accessed 4 August 2018, www.cesr.org/human-rights-taxation.
32 Although some do refer to the relevance of women's equality to certain aspects of economic equality, see, for example, Wilkinson and Pickett (n 29).
33 Rachel Holmes, *Eleonora Marx: A Life* (Bloomsbury Publishing 2014) 313–333.
34 See, for example, Shirin M. Rai and Georgina Waylen (eds), *New Frontiers in Feminist Political Economy* (Routledge 2014). See also Marilyn Waring, *If Women Counted: A New Feminist Economics* (HarperCollins 1990).
35 Report of the Expert Consultation, 'Priorities in Follow Up to the Ten-year Review and Appraisal of Implementation of the Beijing Declaration and Platform for Action,' 31 October–3 November 2005, paras 33–36, www.un.org/womenwatch/daw/meetings/consult/10-review/.
36 Nancy Folbre, *The Invisible Heart: Economics and Family Values* (The New Press 2002).
37 Giorgio Agamben, *Homo Sacer: Sovereign Power and Bare Life* (Stanford University Press 1998).
38 See Part IV of the book. See also, for example, Moran Kushnir, 'I Thank My Good Fortune That I Wasn't Born a Woman in India,' *Haaretz*, 15 June 2018, www.haaretz.com/world-news/asia-and-australia/.premium.MAGAZINE-i-thank-my-good-fortune-that-i-wasn-t-born-a-woman-in-india-1.6174594.
39 Rebecca J. Cook and Simone Cusack, *Gender Stereotyping: Transnational Legal Perspectives* (University of Pennsylvania Press 2010); Rikky Holtmaat and Jonneke Naber, *Women's Human Rights and Culture: From Deadlock to Dialogue* (Intersentia 2011).
40 bell hooks, *Feminism Is for Everybody: Passionate Politics* (South End Press 2000) 47. See also Chandra Talpade Mohanty who calls for comparative feminist studies that are inextricable from studies of (anti-)globalisation and of capitalist exploitation, and which focus on the revolutionary potential in the common struggles of women worldwide without dismissing the privileges that only some women are afforded. Chandra Talpade Mohanty, *Feminism Without Borders: Decolonizing Theory, Practicing Solidarity* (Duke University Press Books 2003).
41 Sylvia Hewlett, *A Lesser Life: The Myth of Women's Liberation in America* (William Morrow & Company 1986).
42 Philip Alston, 'Extreme Inequality as the Antithesis of Human Rights,' *Open Global Rights*, 27 August 2015, www.openglobalrights.org/extreme-inequality-as-the-antithesis-of-human-rights.
43 Radhika Balakrishnan, James Heintz and Diane Elson, 'What Does Inequality Have to Do with Human Rights?' Political Economy Research Institute Working Paper Series 392, August 2015, 30, www.peri.umass.edu/publication/item/687-what-does-inequality-have-to-do-with-human-rights.
44 Samuel Moyn, 'Do Human Rights Increase Inequality?' *The Chronicle of Higher Education*, 26 May 2015, www.chronicle.com/article/do-human-rights-increase/230297.
45 Stephanie Palmer, 'Feminism and the Promise of Human Rights – Possibilities and Paradoxes' in Susan James and Stephanie Palmer (eds), *Visible Women – Essays on Feminist Legal Theory* (Oxford: Hart Publishing 2002) 115.
46 Rosa Ehrenreich Brooks, 'Feminism and International Law: An Opportunity for Transformation' (2002) 14 *Yale Journal of Law & Feminism* 345, 361.
47 UDHR (n 5) preamble and art 2; ICCPR (n 5) art 3; ICESCR (n 5) art 3; CEDAW (n 6).
48 Vienna Declaration and Programme of Action, A/CONF.157/23, 12 July 1993, para 18, www.ohchr.org/en/professionalinterest/pages/vienna.aspx.
49 Beijing Declaration and Platform for Action (n 7).

50 United Nations Millennium Goals, 'Goal 3: Promote Gender Equality and Empower Women,' *Millennium Development Goals and Beyond 2015*, accessed 22 September 2018, www.un.org/millenniumgoals/gender.shtml; United Nations Sustainable Development Goals, 'Goal 5: Achieve Gender Equality and Empower All Women and Girls,' *Sustainable Development Knowledge Platform*, accessed 22 September 2018, https://sustainabledevelopment.un.org/sdg5; High-level Political Forum on Sustainable Development, '2017 HLPF Thematic Review of SDG 5: Achieve Gender Equality and Empower All Women and Girls,' 2017, 4, https://sustainabledevelopment.un.org/content/documents/14383SDG5format-revOD.pdf.

51 The six countries include the United States, Iran, Somalia, the Pacific Islands, South Sudan and Sudan.

52 CEDAW (n 6); Frances Raday, 'Gender and Democratic Citizenship: The Impact of CEDAW' (2012) 10(2) *International Journal of Constitutional Law* 512.

53 CEDAW (n 6) art 2(e): "State obligation extends to the private sphere as well as the public sphere: states must take all appropriate measures to eliminate discrimination against women by any person, organization or enterprise." This obligation is an obligation on the state party to exercise due diligence to prevent discrimination against women by non-state bodies.

54 See, for example, Rosa Brooks, 'Feminist Justice, at Home and Abroad: Feminism and International Law: An Opportunity for Transformation' (2002) 14 *Yale Journal of Law & Feminism* 345.

55 For a comprehensive analysis of the assimilation model, see Vanessa Munro, *Law and Politics at the Perimeter – Re-evaluating Key Debates in Feminist Theory* (Hart Publishing 2007) 14–40; for the arguments used to show that CEDAW relies fundamentally on a comparison between men and women, see Dianne Otto, 'Women's Rights' in Daniel Moeckli, Sangeeta Shah and Sandesh Sivakumaran (eds), *International Human Rights Law* (Oxford University Press 2010) 345, 354–355.

56 Kimberly Krenshaw, 'Demarginalizing the Intersection of Race and Sex: A Black Feminist Critique of Anti-discrimination Doctrine, Feminist Theory and Antiracist Politics' (1989) *University of Chicago Legal Forum* 139.

57 Otto (n 55) 357.

58 Darren Rosenblum, 'Unisex CEDAW or What's Wrong with Women's Rights' (2011) 20 *Columbia Journal of Law and Gender* 98, 193.

59 For instance, the CEDAW Committee has taken cognisance of the importance of intersectionality regarding women migrant workers in General Recommendation 26, older women in General Recommendation 27 and on the basis of "factors that affect women such as race, ethnicity, religion or belief, health, status, age, in particular adolescent girls, class, caste, sexual orientation and gender identity" in General Recommendation 28. See Committee on the Elimination of Discrimination Against Women, 'General Recommendation No. 26 on Women Migrant Workers,' CEDAW/C/2009/WP.1/R, 5 December 2008, https://www2.ohchr.org/english/bodies/cedaw/docs/gr_26_on_women_migrant_workers_en.pdf; Committee on the Elimination of Discrimination Against Women, 'General Recommendation No. 27 on Older Women and Protection of Their Human Rights,' CEDAW/C/2010/47/GC.1, 19 October 2010, https://www2.ohchr.org/english/bodies/cedaw/docs/CEDAW-C-2010-47-GC1.pdf; Committee on the Elimination of Discrimination Against Women, 'General Recommendation No. 28 on the Core Obligations of States Parties Under Article 2 of the Convention on the Elimination of All Forms of Discrimination Against Women,' CEDAW/C/GC/28, 16 December 2010, https://www2.ohchr.org/english/bodies/cedaw/docs/cedaw-c-2010-47-gc2.pdf.

60 See also discussion in Raday (n 52).

61 In 2011, the Human Rights Council appointed the Working Group on the issue of Discrimination Against Women in Law and in Practice (WGDAW). The mandate of the WGDAW includes preparation of a compendium of best practices for elimination

of laws which discriminate, directly or indirectly, against women; to develop ways and means to eliminate discrimination against women in law and practice; and to make recommendations on reform and implementation of law to promote gender equality and the empowerment of women, with reference to the realisation of the Millennium Development Goals (the mandate was formulated prior to the Sustainable Development Goals). The mandate expressly directs the WGDAW to work in close coordination with CEDAW and other treaty bodies. This agenda clearly allows for an agenda of transformative and not merely formal equality. See OHCHR, 'Working Group on the Issue of Discrimination Against Women in Law and in Practice: Introduction,' *OHCHR Website*, accessed 10 October 2018, www.ohchr.org/EN/Issues/Women/WGWomen/Pages/WGWomenIndex.aspx.

62 Committee on the Elimination of Discrimination Against Women, 'General Recommendation No. 25: Article 4, Paragraph 1, of the Convention (Temporary Special Measures),' 2004, para 8, https://tbinternet.ohchr.org/_layouts/treatybodyexternal/Download.aspx?symbolno=INT/CEDAW/GEC/3733&Lang=en.

63 CEDAW's Article 4 introduced the concept of temporary special measures. The CEDAW Committee has clarified that states must use temporary special measures where they are necessary to achieve *de facto* equality. Temporary special measures can be of great importance in closing the gap between the right to equality and its realisation in the economic sphere. See CEDAW (n 6) art 4; CEDAW GR 25 (n 62); Hanna Beate Schoepp-Schilling, 'Reflections on a General Recommendation on Article 4(1) of the Convention on the Elimination of All Forms of Discrimination Against Women' in Ineke Boerefijn, Fons Coomans, Jenny Goldschmidt, Rikki Holtmaat and Ria Wolleswinkel (eds), *Temporary Special Measures: Accelerating de facto Equality of Women Under Article 4(1) UN Convention on the Elimination of All Forms of Discrimination Against Women* (Intersentia 2003) 15. There is a wide spectrum of different types of temporary special measures, which may be roughly graded in terms of the extent of intervention in the field of activity targeted. Starting from the more interventionist to the less interventionist, the different kinds of temporary special measures are quota systems, selective allocation of resources, affirmative action or preferential treatment and reporting requirements for goals and timetables. The author has more fully analysed the theories of social justice underlying temporary special measures in Frances Raday, 'Systematizing the Application of Different Types of Temporary Special Measures Under Article 4 of CEDAW' in Ineke Boerefijn, Fons Coomans, Jenny Goldschmidt, Rikki Holtmaat and Ria Wolleswinkel (eds), *Temporary Special Measures: Accelerating de facto Equality of Women Under Article 4(1) UN Convention on the Elimination of All Forms of Discrimination Against Women* (Intersentia 2003) 35. Under quota systems a numerical target is set for the appointment or advancement of women in a designated institution to positions in which they are underrepresented. Quotas are best suited to participatory representation in policy making regarding distribution of resources. Selective allocation of resources should be directed to facilitating women's entry into activities in which there are barriers to their participation, such as programs for women's entrepreneurship. Affirmative action or preferential treatment should be applied to promotion to positions in the job hierarchy where women are underrepresented, shifting the burden of proof, where the male and the female candidate have equal or substantially equal qualifications, in order to overcome stereotypes and prejudices. Reporting requirements for goals and timetables are a useful means of motivating institutions to recognise and correct discriminatory patterns of acceptance, training, remuneration and promotion of women and have been employed, often with success, to reveal wage and promotion disparities.

64 Sandra Fredman, 'Substantive Equality Revisited' (2016) 14(3) *International Journal of Constitutional Law* 712.

65 WGDAW, 'Report of the Working Group on the Issue of Discrimination Against Women in Law and in Practice,' A/HRC/35/29, 19 April 2017, para 21, www.ohchr.org/Documents/Issues/Women/WG/A_HRC_35_29_AEV.docx.

66 Human Rights Council, 'Elimination of Discrimination Against Women and Girls,' Human Rights Council Thirty-fifth session, A/HRC/35/L.29, 19 June 2017, http://ap.ohchr.org/documents/dpage_e.aspx?si=A/HRC/35/L.29.

67 Frances Raday, 'Recent Developments in the UN Human Rights Council: Traditional Values and Women's Right to Equality in the Family,' *Oxford Human Rights Hub*, 2 September 2015, http://ohrh.law.ox.ac.uk/recent-developments-in-the-un-human-rights-council-traditional-values-and-womens-right-to-equality-in-the-family/.

68 Ibid. This is discussed in detail in Part IV.

69 Ibid.

70 Ibid.; Frances Raday, 'The Family Agenda: Promoting Traditional Values in the Human Rights Council,' *Oxford Human Rights Hub*, 8 January 2015, http://ohrh.law.ox.ac.uk/the-family-agenda-promoting-traditional-values-in-the-human-rights-council/.

71 See, for example, United Nations International Children's Emergency Fund (UNICEF), 'The State of the World's Children 2007: Women and Children: The Double Dividend of Gender Equality,' 2006, www.unicef.org/publications/files/The_State_of_the_Worlds__Children__2007_e.pdf; World Bank, 'World Development Report 2012: Gender Equality and Development,' 2012, Washington, DC: World Bank. © World Bank. https://openknowledge.worldbank.org/handle/10986/4391 License: CC BY 3.0 IGO. More generally, Wilkinson and Pickett, when examining measures of the percentage of women in the legislature, the male-female income gap and the percentage of women completing higher education to make an index of women's status, found that more equal countries do significantly better in reduced inequality. Wilkinson and Pickett (n 29) Chapter 4: Community life and social relations.

72 World Development Report 2012 (n 71). See also Janet G. Stotsky, 'Gender Budgeting: Fiscal Context and Current Outcomes,' International Monetary Fund (IMF) Working Paper, 2016, 3, www.imf.org/external/pubs/ft/wp/2016/wp16149.pdf.

73 According to some sources, women invest 90% compared to only 30% to 40% by men. Tae Yoo, 'Why Women Make the Best Tech Investments,' *World Economic Forum*, 20 January 2014, www.weforum.org/agenda/2014/01/women-technology-world economy/; Clinton Global Initiative, 'Empowering Girls and Women,' accessed 17 May 2018, www.un.org/en/ecosoc/phlntrpy/notes/clinton.pdf; Plan UK, 'Because I Am a Girl: The State of the World's Girls 2009 – Girls in the Global Economy: Adding It All Up,' Executive Summary, 2009, 9, www.ungei.org/resources/files/BIAAG_Summary_ENGLISH_lo_resolution.pdf. See full discussion in Part IV. See also Derek Thompson, 'Women Are More Responsible with Money, Studies Show,' *The Atlantic*, 31 January 2011, www.theatlantic.com/business/archive/2011/01/women-are-more-responsible-with-money-studies-show/70539/.

74 OECD, 'Women's Economic Empowerment,' Issues Paper, DAC Network on Gender Equality (GENDERNET), April 2011, 6, www.oecd.org/dac/gender-development/47561694.pdf.

75 Excerpted from 'The Power of Parity: How Advancing Women's Equality Can Add $12 Trillion to Global Growth,' McKinsey Global Institute, September 2015, www.mckinsey.com. Copyright © 2018 McKinsey & Company. All rights reserved. Reprinted by permission.

76 Organization for Security and Co-operation in Europe (OSCE), 'From Commitment to Action,' Second Gender Equality Review Conference, Austria, 2017, 19, www.osce.org/secretariat/377602?download=true.

77 Katrin Elborgh-Woytek, Monique Newiak, Kalpana Kochhar, Stefania Fabrizio, Kangni Kpodar, Philippe Wingender, Benedict Clements and Gerd Schwartz, 'Women, Work, and the Economy: Macroeconomic Gains from Gender Equity,' IMF Staff Discussion Note: Strategy, Policy, and Review Department and Fiscal Affairs Department, September 2013, 4, www.imf.org/external/pubs/ft/sdn/2013/sdn1310.pdf.

78 OECD (n 74) 7. However, I question in Part II whether the raising of FLFP is in and of itself a measure of women's *de facto* economic equality.

79 OHCHR, 'Women and Adequate Housing: Report by the Special Rapporteur on Adequate Housing as a Component of the Right to an Adequate Standard of Living, and on the Right to Non-discrimination,' E/CN.4/2006/118, 27 February 2006, para 9, www.ohchr.org/EN/Issues/Housing/Pages/WomenAndHousing.aspx.
80 FAO, 'The State of Food and Agriculture 2010–2011,' 2011, 3, www.fao.org/docrep/013/i2050e/i2050e.pdf.
81 UN Women, 'Realizing Women's Rights to Land and Other Productive Resources,' 2013, 3, www.unwomen.org/-/media/headquarters/attachments/sections/library/publications/2013/11/ohchr-unwomen-land-rights-handbook-web%20pdf.pdf?vs=1455.
82 Monique Villa, 'Women Own Less than 20% of the World's Land: It's Time to Give Them Equal Property Rights,' *World Economic Forum*, 11 January 2017, www.weforum.org/agenda/2017/01/women-own-less-than-20-of-the-worlds-land-its-time-to-give-them-equal-property-rights/.
83 Stephen K. Wegren, Alexander Nikulin, Irina Trotsuk and Svetlana Golovina, 'Gender Inequality in Russia's Rural Informal Economy' (2017) 50(2) *Communist and Post-Communist Studies* 87.
84 The State of Food and Agriculture (n 80) vi, 23.
85 UN Women (n 81) 2.
86 Committee on the Elimination of Discrimination Against Women, 'General Recommendation on Article 16 of the Convention on the Elimination of All Forms of Discrimination Against Women (Economic Consequences of Marriage, Family Relations and Their Dissolution),' CEDAW/C/GC/29, 30 October 2013, para 50, https://tbinternet.ohchr.org/_layouts/treatybodyexternal/Download.aspx?symbolno=CEDAW/C/GC/29&Lang=en.
87 WGDAW, 'Report of the Working Group on the Issue of Discrimination Against Women in Law and in Practice: Mission to China,' A/HRC/26/39/Add.2, 12 June 2014, para 26, www.ohchr.org/EN/Issues/Women/WGWomen/Pages/CountryVisits.aspx.
88 Carmen Diana Deere and Magdalena Leon, 'The Gender Asset Gap: Land in Latin America' (2003) 31(6) *World Development* 925, www.amherst.edu/media/view/92212/original/gender%20asset%20gap.pdf.
89 Vanya Slavchevska, Ana Paula De La O Campos, Chiara Brunelli and Cheryl Doss, 'Beyond Ownership: Women's and Men's Land Rights in Sub-Saharan Africa,' Working Paper No. 15, Global Strategy, 2016, 3, http://pubdocs.worldbank.org/en/170131495654694482/A2-ABCA-Slavcheska-et-al-2016-Beyond-ownership-working-paper.pdf.
90 The State of Food and Agriculture (n 80) 42.
91 OECD (n 74) 7.
92 Saturnino M. Borras Jr, Cristóbal Kay, Sergio Gómez and John Wilkinson, 'Land Grabbing and Global Capitalist Accumulation: Key Features in Latin America' (2012) 33(4) *Canadian Journal of Development Studies* 402.
93 WGDAW, 'Report of the Working Group on the issue of Discrimination Against Women in Law and in Practice: Addendum – Mission to Peru,' A/HRC/29/40/Add.2, 26 June 2015, paras 69–70, http://ap.ohchr.org/documents/dpage_e.aspx?si=A/HRC/29/40/Add.2.
94 World Economic Forum, 'The Global Gender Gap Report 2016,' 2016, fn 27, http://www3.weforum.org/docs/GGGR16/WEF_Global_Gender_Gap_Report_2016.pdf.
95 International Labour Organization (ILO), 'Women at Work: Trends 2016', 2016, XV, https://www.ilo.org/wcmsp5/groups/public/---dgreports/---dcomm/—publ/documents/publication/wcms_457317.pdf.
96 Gottfried (n 3) 31–32: "Reproductive work involves those activities aimed at social provisioning and daily care for human beings, including 'caring, feeding, clothing, teaching, and nurturing individuals.' . . . A subset of reproductive work specifically centers on care producing affective relations, nurturance and healing that enhance workers' capacities to labor and release labor's productive capabilities (labor power). In essence, these activities are necessary to enable workers to be productive in society."

97 Diane Elson, 'Micro, Meso, Macro: Gender and Economic Analysis in the Context of Policy Reform' in Isabella Bakker (ed), *The Strategic Silence: Gender and Economic Policy* (Zed Books 1994), quoted in Joan Acker, 'Gender, Capitalism and Globalization' (2004) 30(1) *Critical Sociology* 17, 25.

98 Ibid.

99 Anne-Marie Slaughter, 'Why Women Still Can't Have It All,' *The Atlantic*, July/August 2012, www.theatlantic.com/magazine/archive/2012/07/why-women-still-cant-have-it-all/309020/.

100 Rachel Aviv, 'The Cost of Caring: The Lives of the Immigrant Women Who Tend to the Needs of Others,' *The New Yorker*, 11 April 2016, www.newyorker.com/magazine/2016/04/11/the-sacrifices-of-an-immigrant-caregiver.

101 The movement, starting in Hollywood, went viral after American actress Alyssa Milano called on Twitter for women who have been sexually harassed or assaulted to write 'Me too' to raise attention to the magnitude of the phenomena. The response from around the world reached over 1.7 million with the hashtag #MeToo and Facebook indicated that during the first 24 hours 4.7 million users around the world published more than 12 million posts, comments and reactions on #MeToo. Time magazine's 2017 Person of the Year recognised the #MeToo movement as 'Silence Breakers' who inspired women to speak out about harassment. See Jody Heymann and Rachel Vogelstein, 'Commentary: When Sexual Harassment Is Legal,' *Fortune*, 17 November 2017, http://fortune.com/2017/11/17/sexual-harassment-legal-gaps/; Andrea Park, '#MeToo Reaches 85 Countries with 1.7M Tweets,' *CBS News*, 24 October 2017, www.cbsnews.com/news/metoo-reaches-85-countries-with-1-7-million-tweets/; Stephanie Zacharek, Eliana Dockterman and Haley Sweetland Edwards, 'Time Person of the Year 2017: The Silence Breakers,' *Time Magazine*, 2018, http://time.com/time-person-of-the-year-2017-silence-breakers/?xid=homepage.

102 In 1980, CEDAW did not expressly incorporate a prohibition of violence against women, but the CEDAW Committee went on, starting from 1989, to categorise VAW as sex discrimination and a violation of CEDAW. See Committee on the Elimination of Discrimination Against Women, 'General Recommendation No. 12: Violence Against Women,' Eighth session, 1989, http://tbinternet.ohchr.org/_layouts/treatybodyexternal/Download.aspx?symbolno=INT/CEDAW/GEC/5831&Lang=en; Committee on the Elimination of Discrimination Against Women, 'General Recommendation No. 19: Violence Against Women,' Eleventh session, 1992, https://tbinternet.ohchr.org/Treaties/CEDAW/Shared%20Documents/1_Global/INT_CEDAW_GEC_3731_E.pdf; Committee on the Elimination of Discrimination Against Women, 'General Recommendation No. 35 on Gender-based Violence Against Women, Updating General Recommendation No. 19,' CEDAW/C/GC/35, 14 July 2017, https://tbinternet.ohchr.org/Treaties/CEDAW/Shared%20Documents/1_Global/CEDAW_C_GC_35_8267_E.pdf. See also Frances Raday and Shai Oksenberg, 'The Impact of Violence Against Women on Women's Economic and Social Life: Background Paper,' 2014, www.ohchr.org/EN/Issues/Women/WGWomen/Pages/ESL.aspx; Christine Chinkin, 'Violence Against Women' in Marsha A. Freeman, Christine Chinkin and Beate Rudolf (eds), *The UN Convention on the Elimination of All Forms of Discrimination Against Women: A Commentary* (Oxford University Press 2012) 443. It should also be noted that in 2010 the CEDAW Committee adopted GR 28, which emphasised that Article 2 of CEDAW is not limited to the prohibition of discrimination against women caused directly or indirectly by states parties, but also imposes a due diligence obligation to prevent discrimination by private actors. See CEDAW GR 28 (n 59). Further international calls for the elimination of VAW were adopted: in 1993, the UN General Assembly adopted the Declaration on the Elimination of Violence Against Women, UNGA Res 49(1993), 20 December 1993, UN Doc A/RES/48/104 (1993). In 1995 the Beijing Declaration and Platform for Action called to prevent and eliminate all forms of violence against women

and girls and set this issue as a strategic objective. Beijing Declaration and Platform for Action (n 7). In 1998, the Rome Statute of the International Criminal Court categorised rape, sexual slavery, enforced prostitution, forced pregnancy and enforced sterilisation, in international armed conflict, as a war crime. Rome Statute of the International Criminal Court (entered into force 1 July 2002) 2187 UNTS 90 (ICC Statute), art 8 (2) (b) (xxii). The UN Security has, since 2000, issued a series of eight resolutions on women, peace and security focusing on sexual violence in conflict and post-conflict settings. UN Women, 'Poster: Security Council Resolutions: Women Peace and Security,' *UN Women Website*, accessed 11 October 2018, www.unwomen.org/en/digital-library/publications/2017/1/poster-security-council-resolutions. In 2011, the Council of Europe Convention on preventing and combating violence against women and domestic violence (Istanbul Convention) was opened to signature by any non-EU member states (although it is a European Convention). Council of Europe, *The Council of Europe Convention on Preventing and Combating Violence Against Women and Domestic Violence* (November 2014), ISBN 978-92-871-7990-6, www.refworld.org/docid/548165c94.html; Council of Europe, 'Chart of Signatures and Ratifications of Treaty 210,' *Council of Europe*, accessed 13 October 2018, www.coe.int/en/web/conventions/full-list/-/conventions/treaty/210/signatures?desktop=true. In 2015, the SDGs established a target to eliminate all forms of violence against all women and girls in the public and private spheres, including trafficking and sexual and other types of exploitation. United Nations Sustainable Development Goal 5 (n 50) Target 5.2.

103 CEDAW GR 35 (n 102) para 6.

104 World Health Organization (WHO), 'Global and Regional Estimates of Violence Against Women: Prevalence and Health Effects of Intimate Partner Violence and Non-partner Sexual Violence,' 2013, 2, http://apps.who.int/iris/bitstream/handle/10665/85239/9789241564625_eng.pdf;jsessionid=B153C1D671B964796A33A5EC447DC0B4?sequence=1.

105 Sexual harassment in the workplace is further discussed in Part II of the book.

106 UN Women, 'Progress of the World's Women 2015–2016: Transforming Economies, Realizing Rights,' 2015, 92, http://progress.unwomen.org/en/2015/pdf/UNW_progressreport.pdf.

107 World Association of Girl Guides and Girl Scouts, '#Girlsareunsafe Everywhere, Make Harassment Stop,' *World Association of Girl Guides and Girl Scouts*, 15 March 2018, www.wagggs.org/en/news/girlsareunsafe-everywhere-make-harassment-stop/.

108 Niharika Mandhana and Anjani Trivedi, 'Indians Outraged over Rape on Moving Bus in New Delhi,' *India Ink, The New York Times*, 18 December 2012, https://india.blogs.nytimes.com/2012/12/18/outrage-in-delhi-after-latest-gang-rape-case; Anne F. Stenhammer, 'UN Women Condemns Gang Rape of Delhi Student,' statement by Anne F. Stenhammer, Regional Programme Director, UN Women South Asia, *UN Women*, 20 December 2012, www.unwomen.org/en/news/stories/2012/12/un-women-condemns-gang-rape-of-delhi-student. See also the horrific case of the 2013 rape and murder of a 13-year-old girl on an overnight train in Thailand – Thomson Reuters Foundation News, 'Rape and Murder of 13-Year-old Spark Debate in Junta-ruled Thailand,' *Reuters*, 9 July 2014, http://news.trust.org//item/20140709074826-usra8/.

109 Committee on the Elimination of Discrimination Against Women, 'Report on Mexico Produced by the Committee on the Elimination of Discrimination Against Women Under Article 8 of the Optional Protocol to the Convention, and Reply from the Government of Mexico,' CEDAW/C/2005/OP.8/MEXICO, 27 January 2005, www.refworld.org/docid/4a54bc0e1a.html.

110 Roberto Bolanyo, *2666* (Natasha Wimmer tr, 2nd edn, Picador 2009).

111 CEDAW GR 35 (n 102) para 36.

112 Following the 2012 gang rape and murder on public transport in Delhi, the Indian government took steps to increase the criminal penalties for sexual offences. BBC, 'Explaining India's New Anti-rape Laws,' *BBC News*, 28 March 2013, www.bbc.com/news/world-asia-india-21950197. The French government recently unveiled measures to curb sexual harassment in public transportation after a poll in which 100% of women surveyed said they had been confronted with the problem. Measures include introducing an emergency telephone number to report harassment and the creation of an app to geo-locate reported incidents. World Bank Group, 'Women, Business and the Law 2016: Getting to Equal,' 2015, 23, Washington, DC: World Bank. © World Bank. https://openknowledge.worldbank.org/handle/10986/22546 License: CC BY 3.0 IGO. See also Henry Samuel, 'Paris Launches "Shock" Poster Campaign Against Sexual Harassment on Public Transport,' *The Telegraph*, 5 March 2018, www.telegraph.co.uk/news/2018/03/05/paris-launches-shock-poster-campaign-against-sexual-harassment/; Angelique Chrisafis, 'France Plans On-the-Spot Fines for Sexual Harassment in Public,' *The Guardian*, 21 March 2018, www.theguardian.com/world/2018/mar/21/france-plans-on-the-spot-fines-for-sexual-harassment-in-public. A number of countries, including India, Brazil, Japan and Egypt, have introduced women-only carriages on buses and trains in an attempt to provide women safe transportation. Radhika Sanghani, 'These Countries Tried Women-only Transport: Here's What Happened,' *The Telegraph*, 26 August 2015, www.telegraph.co.uk/women/womens-life/11824962/Women-only-trains-and-transport-How-they-work-around-the-world.html. To serve equality aims, this must, of course, be an option for women and not a sex-segregated space which excludes them from shared areas. Canada offers a good example, prohibiting the harassment of an individual in the provisions of goods, services, facilities or accommodation customarily to the general public. See Canadian Human Rights Act, RSNS 1989, c 214. Municipalities can also make the streets safer with infrastructural changes. Public spaces should be full of people, especially at night, and so should be designed to facilitate various forms of activities which will encourage people to remain in the area. There should be formal surveillance and access to help, including security guards, public telephones and surveillance cameras, prominently displayed, so that potential predators are deterred from attacking. UN Women has been working since 2010 through its Safe Cities and Safe Public Spaces global flagship initiative to transform public spaces in 27 cities around the world. The municipality of Quito in Ecuador, for example, has amended a local ordinance to strengthen action against sexual harassment in public spaces. In Cairo, Egypt's Ministry of Housing, Utilities and Urban Development adopted women's safety audits to guide urban planning, and Port Moresby's National Capital District in Papua New Guinea has taken steps to improve women's safety in local markets, including budget allocations which ensure that the needs of women and men are taken into account across different municipal departments. UN Women, 'Creating Safe Public Spaces,' *UN Women Website*, accessed 9 October 2018, www.unwomen.org/en/what-we-do/ending-violence-against-women/creating-safe-public-spaces; UN Women, 'Safe Cities and Safe Public Spaces: Global Results Report,' 2017, www.unwomen.org/-/media/headquarters/attachments/sections/library/publications/2017/safe-cities-and-safe-public-spaces-global-results-report-en.pdf?la=en&vs=45. Technology has come to play an increasingly important role in making women safer on the street. Brazil, for example, has promoted the use of cell phones by women in low-income communities to map faulty infrastructure or services or areas with lack of lighting and to connect them with police stations that specialise in VAW. This enables the women to establish action plans to prevent and respond to violence. Raday and Oksenberg (n 102).

113 Women, Business and the Law 2016 (n 112) 23. See also World Bank Group, 'Women, Business, and the Law 2014: Removing Restrictions to Enhance Gender Equality,' 2013, 8, London: Bloomsbury. © World Bank, https://openknowledge.worldbank.org/handle/10986/20528 License: CC BY-NC-ND 3.0 IGO. For further reading regarding

harassment of women in public spaces, see Cynthia Grant Bowman, 'Street Harassment and the Informal Ghettoization of Women' (1993) 106 *Harvard Law Review* 517.

114 Target 3.A called to "eliminate gender disparity in primary and secondary education, preferably by 2005, and in all levels of education no later than 2015." See United Nations Millennium Goal 3 (n 50) Target 3.A. In 2015, it was reported that gender disparity has narrowed substantially at all levels of education since 2000 and that the developing regions as a whole have achieved the target to eliminate gender disparity at all levels of education. The United Nations, 'The Millennium Development Goals Report 2015,' 2015, 29, www.un.org/millenniumgoals/2015_MDG_Report/pdf/MDG%20 2015%20rev%20(July%201).pdf.

115 UNESCO, 'School-related Gender-based Violence in the Asia-Pacific Region,' 2014, 28–29, http://unesdoc.unesco.org/images/0022/002267/226754E.pdf.

116 Nearly half (48%) of students surveyed, in grades 7 to 12 in schools in the United States, experienced some form of sexual harassment in the 2010–11 school year, and the majority of those students (87%) said it had a negative effect on them. The survey found, in line with previous research, that girls were more likely than boys to be sexually harassed. See AAUW, 'Crossing the Line: Sexual Harassment at School,' 2011, www.aauw.org/research/crossing-the-line/. In sub-Saharan Africa countries, gender-based violence towards both male and female students was found to be common at schools. Field studies in seven African countries indicated that in Ghana, 75% of children cited teachers as the main perpetrators of violence in school; in Senegal, the figure was 80%. In the Latin American region, school-based surveys in Chile, Costa Rica, Panama, and Peru, found that between 5 and 40% of adolescent girls reported experience of sexual abuse and in some countries in Latin America, the sexual coercion was by teachers. See Plan International, 'A Girl's Right to Learn Without Fear: Working to End Gender-based Violence at School,' 2013, 28, 30, https://plan-uk.org/file/plan-report-learn-without-fearpdf/download?token=HMORNNVk. Several small studies from Bangladesh, India, Nepal and Pakistan provide examples of inappropriate sexualised behaviour by teachers towards girls, with several reports of teachers raping school girls in India and serious sexual abuse by teachers in Nepal. UNESCO (n 115) 25. See also regrading prevalence rates: Wellesley Centers for Research on Women and Development and Training Service, Inc. (DTS), 'Unsafe Schools: A Literature Review of School-related Gender-based Violence in Developing Countries,' 2004, www.wcwonline.org/vmfiles/unsafe_schools_literature_review.pdf; United Nations General Assembly (UNGA), 'In Depth Study on All Forms of Violence Against Women: Report of the Secretary General,' A/61/122/Add.1, 6 July 2006, 42, https://documents-dds-ny.un.org/doc/UNDOC/GEN/N06/419/74/PDF/N0641974.pdf?OpenElement. The most extreme form of VAW in schooling is violent opposition to girls' attendance, which persists in some countries amongst some fundamentalist religious groups. See A Girl's Right to Learn Without Fear, ibid. 29. In this context, the story of Pakistani young girl Malala Yousafzai is a lesson and an inspiration. Malala, a school girl under the rule of the Taliban, advocated for girls' rights for education. She survived an attempt to assassinate her life, which provoked national and international support for her and her cause. Malala received the Nobel Peace Prize in 2014. Malala Fund, 'Malala's Story,' *Malala Fund Website*, accessed 9 October 2018, www.malala.org/malalas-story.

117 World Bank Group, 'Women, Business and the Law 2018: Protecting Women from Violence,' 2018, http://pubdocs.worldbank.org/en/289441522241133897/WBL-fact-sheet-protecting-women-from-violence-FINAL-PDF.pdf.

118 A Girl's Right to Learn Without Fear (n 116) 23.

119 In a 2012 European Union survey of 21,516 women students regarding their experience of sexual violence and harassment during their studies at higher education institutions in five EU countries – Germany, Italy, Poland, Spain and the UK – some of the key findings were: 29.9% to 47.3% of women students were forced to engage in sexual acts, 47% to 68% were sexually harassed verbally and 41% to 58% were subjected to

stalking. Of the perpetrators, 96% to 97% were males of whom 40% to 60% were fellow students and approximately 7% higher education institution staff. See It Stops Now. Ending Sexual Harassment & Violence in Third Level Education (ESHTE), 'A Review of Data on the Prevalence of Sexual Violence and Harassment of Women Students in Higher Education in the European Union,' 2017, 3, www.itstopsnow.org/sites/default/files/2018-02/ESHTE%20A%20Review%20of%20Data%20on%20Prevalence%20of%20SVH%20of%20Women%20Students%20in%20Higher%20Education.pdf.

120 Viola Zhou and Sarah Zheng, 'Chinese Students Use #MeToo to Take Fight Against Sexual Harassment to Elite Universities,' *South China Morning Post*, 16 January 2018, www.scmp.com/news/china/society/article/2128341/chinese-students-use-metoo-take-fight-against-sexual-harassment; Lily Kuo, '#Metoo in China: Fledgling Movement in Universities Fights Censorship,' *The Guardian*, 18 April 2018, www.theguardian.com/world/2018/apr/18/metoo-in-china-fledgling-movement-in-universities-fights-censorship.

121 The Hunting Ground, 'The Facts of The Hunting Ground,' *The Hunting Ground Film Official Website*, accessed 9 October 2018, http://thehuntinggroundfilm.com/the-facts/; US Department of Justice Office of Justice Programs and Bureau of Justice Statistics, 'Rape and Sexual Assault Victimization Among College-age Females, 1995–2013,' Special Report, December 2014, www.bjs.gov/content/pub/pdf/rsavcaf9513.pdf. The victims are afraid to have their identities disclosed and the colleges downplay and dismiss reports of campus sexual assault, caring more about their public image than the safety of their students. The survivors of the attacks set up a network of survivors and organised a legal campaign against the colleges. Their activities inspired new laws to combat sexual violence on campuses and also a backlash by students who have been accused, as evident from the advertising of a legal office which specialises in countering campus disciplinary proceedings: "The Department of Education makes rules that schools have to follow when someone on campus says that they have been sexually assaulted or raped. Campus rape allegations can trigger a strong reaction from the Department of Education. We have successfully represented students who have been accused of sexual assault on campus. By diligently investigating the facts and navigating the University procedures, you can take dramatic steps to protect your future and your good name." See Kaiser Dillon Plic, 'Campus Disciplinary Defense,' *Kaiser Dillon Plic: When Your Future Is on the Line*, accessed 10 October 2018, www.kaiserdillon.com/practices/campus-disciplinary-defense/.

122 UN Women, the United Nations Development Programme (UNDP) and The International Telecommunication Union (ITU), 'Cyber Violence Against Women and Girls: A World-wide Wake-up Call,' 2015,_ www.unwomen.org/~/media/headquarters/attachments/sections/library/publications/2015/cyber_violence_gender%20report.pdf?v=1&d=20150924T154259. See also European Institute for Gender Equality (EIGE), 'Cyber Violence Against Women and Girls,' 2017, http://eige.europa.eu/rdc/eige-publications/cyber-violence-against-women-and-girls.

123 See, for example, Maeve Duggan, 'Online Harassment,' *Pew Research Center*, 22 October 2014, www.pewinternet.org/2014/10/22/online-harassment/; European Union Agency for Fundamental Rights, 'Violence Against Women: An EU-wide Survey,' 2014, 104, http://fra.europa.eu/en/publication/2014/violence-against-women-eu-wide-survey-main-results-report.

124 UN Women, 'Urgent Action Needed to Combat Online Violence Against Women and Girls, Says New UN Report,' *UN Women Website*, 24 September 2015, www.unwomen.org/en/news/stories/2015/9/cyber-violence-report-press-release.

125 There is irrefutable evidence that prostitution, whether through trafficking or not, is pervaded by VAW. As Melissa Farley notes, "Women in prostitution are frequently raped and physically assaulted. . . . Clearly violence is the norm for women in prostitution . . . payment of money does not erase all that we know about sexual harassment, rape and domestic violence." Melissa Farley, 'Prostitution Is Sexual Violence,' *Psychiatric Times*, 1 October 2004, www.psychiatrictimes.com/sexual-offenses/

prostitution-sexual-violence. The overwhelming physical and psychological harm to those in prostitution is clinically noted and well documented. See, for example, Melissa Farley, 'Prostitution and the Invisibility of Harm' (2003) 26(3–4) *Women & Therapy* 247; Melissa Farley, Isin Baral, Merab Kiremire and Ufuk Sezgin, 'Prostitution in Five Countries: Violence and Post-traumatic Stress Disorder' (1998) 8(4) *Feminism & Psychology* 405.

126 See further discussion on trafficking in Part III of the book.

127 European Parliament Study, 'Sexual Exploitation and Prostitution and Its Impact on Gender Equality,' 2014, 6, www.europarl.europa.eu/RegData/etudes/etudes/join/2014/493040/IPOL-FEMM_ET(2014)493040_EN.pdf.

128 There are surprisingly no reliable sex-segregated global statistics but this fact is common knowledge.

129 United Nations Office on Drugs and Crime (UNDOC), 'Global Report on Trafficking in Persons 2016,' 2016, 1, 27, www.unodc.org/documents/data-and-analysis/glotip/2016_Global_Report_on_Trafficking_in_Persons.pdf.

130 Marianna Eriksson, 'The Consequences of the Sex Industry in the European Union,' European Parliament (2003/2107(INI)), 9 January 2004. Incorporated into the report ofThe European Parliament, Committee on Women's Rights and Equal Opportunities, 'Explanatory Statement' section, 15 April 2004, www.europarl.europa.eu/sides/getDoc.do?pubRef=-//EP//TEXT+REPORT+A5-2004-0274+0+DOC+XML+V0//EN.

131 ILO, 'Profits and Poverty: The Economics of Forced Labour,' 2014, 15, www.ilo.org/wcmsp5/groups/public/---ed_norm/---declaration/documents/publication/wcms_243391.pdf.

132 Gail Dines, *Pornland: How Porn Has Hijacked Our Sexuality* (Beacon Press 2011).

133 Walter DeKeseredy and Marilyn Corsianos, *Violence Against Women in Pornography* (Routledge 2016) 25 and reference there.

134 NBC News, 'Things Are Looking Up in America's Porn Industry,' *NBC News*, 20 January 2015, www.nbcnews.com/business/business-news/things-are-looking-americas-porn-industry-n289431/.

135 DeKeseredy and Corsianos (n 133) 15.

136 Gail Dines, '"Choking Women Is All the Rage": It's Branded as Fun, Sexy "Breath Play,"' *The Guardian*, 13 May 2018, www.theguardian.com/commentisfree/2018/may/13/choking-women-me-too-breath-play.

137 The approach adopted by the European Council on trafficking could be the model for this approach to all three industries. It suggests that countries should consider criminalising the use of the services of the victim. It also adds that the proceeds of the criminal offences relating to trafficking should be confiscated and that the resulting assets might be used to guarantee compensation for victims or measures or programs aimed at social assistance. Council of Europe Convention on Action Against Trafficking in Human Beings (entered into force 16 May 2005), CETS 197, art 15, 19 and 23, www.refworld.org/docid/43fded544.html.

138 Evan Stark and Eve Buzawa, *Violence Against Women in Families and Relationships* (Praeger 2009) 114–119; CEDAW GR 35 (n 102) para 7. On the WGDAW's country visit to Spain, we were told that a severe cut back of the funding in almost all the provinces following the financial crisis had resulted in the closing down of shelters for victims of domestic violence but that the shelter in the Andalusian province had remained open and functioning as a result of a policy decision of its feminist president. WGDAW, 'Report of the Working Group on the Issue of Discrimination Against Women in Law and in Practice: Mission to Spain,' A/HRC/29/40/Add.3, 17 June 2015, para 76, www.ohchr.org/EN/Issues/Women/WGWomen/Pages/CountryVisits.aspx.

Part I

Economic Power

Wealth and income inequality have harsh implications for women, given their thin representation at the pinnacle of the economic hegemony and their heavier concentration lower on the value chain. Since the 1980s, macroeconomic policies and corporate and financial governance, at the international and national levels, have, as said in the Introduction, produced a dramatic increase in inequalities of wealth and incomes. Personal wealth inequality has been on the rise in most countries with higher rates of return on capital than average economic growth.[1] Income inequality has increased dramatically in North America and Asia; moderately in Europe; and stabilised at an extremely high level in the Middle East, Africa and Brazil.[2] The gendered repercussions of economic inequality call for greater attention to the need for policy interventions to empower women, both in participation in economic decision-making and in the substance of policy.

In analysing the current situation, there is a dearth of systematised data. Mapping the extent of women's power at the macro level of economic policy making is a difficult task, as the locus of economic power is highly fragmented, spread over a diversified institutional canvas: international agencies, parliaments, governmental bodies, corporations, entrepreneurial actors and cooperatives. It is considerably more challenging than charting women's political participation through numbers in executive and legislative bodies or their formal employment status through labour market participation figures and wage returns. The best that can be done is to present a collage of women's activities in various sectors of economic power in decision-making. The picture that I will show emerging from this collage is one of severe underrepresentation of women and a severe lack of gender-sensitive policy-making mechanisms throughout the centres of economic power.

Women have not yet achieved significant access to macroeconomic power in the political, corporate and financial worlds. Although there are growing numbers of women who have broken the glass ceiling into economic leadership and power, they are still a small minority and have not reached a critical mass of economic policy makers which can influence policy at the macro-level. Women hence play almost no role in formulating the neo-liberal economic policy which has adversely impacted their lives.

Economic policy making has not prioritised the issue of gendered impact. This holds true for both public and private bastions of economic power. Women's empowerment in economic leadership is, although an essential condition for mainstreaming and promoting gender-sensitive policy, not, in and of itself, a sufficient condition. Adoption by all policy makers of a gendered perspective in macroeconomic policy is essential. This entails integrating a dual world view of men's and women's life experiences and differing socio-economic needs. It requires the addressing of issues such as the integration of the care economy, regulation of the informal labour market, improving the regulatory conditions for small and medium-sized enterprises (SMEs), the economic potential of education for girls, the costs of violence against women and of restrictions on women's reproductive health and rights. It would highlight the non-sustainability of extreme inequality, both general and gendered.

Focus on the particularly low level of women's participation in economic policy making is a newly emerging area. In 2014, the WGDAW drew attention to this as an area of pervasive discrimination against women which had been largely neglected in the UN agenda on business and human rights.[3] Many of its recommendations on the subject were incorporated into that year's Human Rights Council's Resolution on 'Elimination of Discrimination Against Women,' in which the Council called upon institutions of global economic governance and business to promote women's equal access to decision-making positions and processes.[4]

Analysis of the reasons for women's underrepresentation in economic decision-making is of course part of the general understanding of the patriarchal framework of society and pervasive discrimination in appointments and promotion within institutions. However, we must address the particular challenges in this crucial area of economic policy making as regards both the exceedingly low numbers of women participating, specifically at focal points of economic power as compared with other areas of decision-making, and also as regards the lack and even delegitimisation of gender-sensitivity in the substance of economic policy and in organisational behaviour. This delegitimisation of gender-sensitivity is consonant with a premise that economics is an objective science which is blind to irrelevant characteristics such as race and gender. In both the arena of economic leadership and of entrepreneurship, the discriminatory results belie the theoretical egalitarian premise.

1 Economic leadership

Economic leadership is dispersed through the political establishment and the financial and corporate worlds. The mélange of public and private leaders at the World Economic Forum annual meeting in Davos demonstrates this graphically. In the political establishment, the level of women's participation does not guarantee an equivalent or proportionate level in the wielding of economic decision-making power within the political institutions. Nor, indeed, is the level of women's political participation necessarily an indicator for the level of their economic leadership at the corporate level. In the Nordic countries, women have long achieved as much as 40% in political and public representation, but as of 2014 only 3% of 145 Nordic large-cap companies had a female chief executive.[5] In Germany, too, led by Angela Merkel, whose cabinet was 35% female in 2014, only 7% of the executives among its top companies were female.[6] This disconnect has been observed conversely in China, in a research finding that there is a significant positive correlation between economic development and the economic status of women in China, with women well represented in senior management but not between economic development and the political status of women, where women are severely underrepresented at the top levels of central government.[7]

Hence, we shall look at women's politically-based economic power and their corporate-based economic power separately.

Politically based economic power

Political leadership is key to macroeconomic policy making and there is a crucial deficit in political women leaders' economic power. Women leaders in parliaments and governments lag severely behind in economic decision-making positions, at the international and national levels.

The near universal inclusion of women in the vote and in parliamentary membership has been hailed as the gendering of democracy or the cosmopolitanisation of feminism, "albeit in a slow and sporadic way."[8] Nevertheless, it is important to note that the gendering of democracy is still far from complete. The global average for women members of national parliaments, reached its highest-ever level in 2017 at 23.5%,[9] which still averages less than a quarter of legislators. The introduction of gender quotas in the political arena has been indicated by the CEDAW Committee and the WGDAW as a required method for achieving *de facto* equality for women's parliamentary representation and removing structural barriers that women face in the electoral process. Quota systems have been introduced by law in a growing number of countries, particularly countries with low levels of economic development, and have resulted in higher levels of political representation of women, with spectacular success for example in Rwanda, which reached a level of around 60% of women members of parliament after a genocidal civil war devastated the country.[10]

As regards top leadership in government positions, women are visible but remain scarce. According to UN Women, as of October 2017, worldwide there were 11 women serving as Head of State, and 12 serving as Head of Government, and as of January 2017, the number of women globally who were government ministers was 18.3%.[11] Lack of financial resources may play a part in keeping women out in the political election process for leadership positions. For instance, in its visit to the United States in 2015, the WGDAW noted that the potential for women political candidates has been severely curtailed by their virtual exclusion from the funding networks for candidates' election campaigns, which are dominated by men.[12]

Furthermore, it is abundantly clear that still in our times discriminatory stereotypes against women in power play a very significant role in keeping highly qualified women out of top political office. Women who reach positions of power are frequently exposed to misogynistic attacks both by political leaders and the public. The misogynistic campaign in 2016 against Hilary Clinton as presidential candidate in the United States is a pertinent example.[13] Another example is the brutal misogynistic backlash in Australia against Prime Minister Julia Gillard, who reacted to this onslaught in the Australian parliament in 2012 by calling on the leader of the opposition, Tony Abbott, to resign.[14]

Even those women who have achieved political power lag behind in economic decision-making positions, at the international, governmental and parliamentary levels. At the international level, we find Christine Lagarde, who after being the first women in any of the G8 countries to be a Finance Minister (in France), also became, in 2011, the first woman to head the International Monetary Fund (IMF), breaking the previous male monopoly and furthermore surviving in the position despite a corruption prosecution against her in France. As the head of the IMF and again at Davos in 2018 she advocated that empowering women can be an "economic game changer."[15]

In international economic institutions leadership, Lagarde remains one of the few exceptions rather than the rule as regards women holding powerful economic power positions. In 2016, the number of women in the international financial and trade institutions remained thin on the ground. The IMF had only one female executive director out of 24 and six female alternate executive directors out of 30.[16] The World Bank has never had a female president and had four female executive directors out of 25.[17] The WTO, although 45% of its professional staff were females, noted that the number of women chairing WTO bodies, panels and working groups is considerably lower than that of men.[18] And the World Economic Forum (WEF) had one woman out of nine members of the managing board and 17 women out of 49 members of the executive committee.[19]

At the governmental level, women prime ministers are, of course, endowed with formal power to direct economic policy. However, at the ministerial level, where women constitute 18.3% of all government ministers globally, their inclusion does not usually endow them with economic decision-making power: the most common portfolios for women ministers are environment, natural resources, energy, social affairs, education, family and women's affairs, with very few women ministers for finance and budget or economic affairs.[20] In 2017, UN Women and the International Parliamentary Union (IPU) reported that out of 1,237 portfolios in 186 countries women held only 38 portfolios in finance, budget, economy and development, which amounts to about 3% of ministerial positions in direct economic decision-making.[21] In Canada in 2015 and France in 2017, where gender-parity cabinets were appointed to the delight of feminists, their delight was tempered by the fact that the women ministers were appointed to portfolios with inferior resources and power.[22]

A few of the women ministers have expressly advanced gender-sensitive policies. An example is Ngozi Okonjo-Iweala of Nigeria, who served as Nigeria's Finance Minister twice (seven years in total) between 2003 and 2015. She also served as a managing director in the World Bank (2007–2011) and was considered a strong contender for presidency of the World Bank. As the finance minister of Nigeria, Okonjo-Iweala pursued pro-growth and anti-corruption policies.[23] Additionally, she introduced programs particularly focused on women and girls: a cash transfer scheme to poor households to encourage girls' enrolment in schools; gender-sensitive budgeting; mobile phones for women for purchase of subsidised seeds and fertilisers; and business opportunities for women as subcontractors on public-works projects.[24]

Only around 10% of the governors of national central banks and monetary authorities and 10 to 15% of the members of central bank boards are women.[25] The world's two premier central banks are the U.S. Federal Reserve and European Central Bank (ECB). Of the two, the Fed's board and senior managerial positions have consistently had more women, and Janet Yellen became the Fed's first female chair in 2014. Her performance was highly rated as perhaps the most successful chair in modern history, steeply reducing unemployment without incurring inflation. However, she was also the first chair not to be re-nominated for a second term (by President Trump).[26] The ECB has not had more than one female member of the six members of the executive board at any given time and in some years, has had an all male board.[27]

There was a most unusual phenomenon in Israel in 2016 in which women held the most senior positions in public and private finance: Governor of the Bank of Israel; Deputy Governor of the Bank of Israel;[28] the Supervisor of Banks; Accountant General of the Ministry of Finance; Head of the Israel Antitrust Authority; the Supervisor of the Capital Market, Insurance and Savings; and three of the CEOs of Israel's five big banks were all women. 'Lady Globes' set out to discover how this unique financial female ecosystem came about and attributed it primarily to the fact that legislation had set an annual salary cap for senior executives in banks and financial corporations, thus discouraging highly competitive people (characteristically, men) from competing. A further reason was that senior women tend to bring in more women: "[a]lthough women are seen as more competitive and hostile towards each other, the reality is that women in senior positions lean more towards hiring talented and highly capable women for key posts."[29]

In parliamentary roles, the IPU reported that women often have a reduced presence in parliamentary finance and economic committees. It is probable that women's lower representation in finance and economic contexts are determined by stereotyping and lesser opportunities provided by their political parties and parliamentarian colleagues.[30]

The reasons for requiring a higher level of women's representation in economic policy-making are compound. Women's right to participate on equal terms with men is an essential emanation of gender equality as a matter of opportunity, process and visibility. Their presence in economic forums is important symbolically and as role modelling for women and men in society. It is also an important component of the gendering of economic policy in practice, which must be based not only on women's participation but also on a policy premise of gender duality promoting a gender-sensitive perspective. A gender-sensitive perspective implies an equality agenda and an emphasis on including health, education, housing, water supply, sanitation and public transport, as women are more directly affected by failure to provide these social goods than men, both because they have greater need of the social safety net and because they are predominantly the carers for dependent family members.[31]

There are indicators that a critical mass of women in economic decision-making can promote agendas which are more gender-sensitive. As regards gender issues, the impact of a critical mass of women in parliament and in parliamentary committees for initiating a gender-sensitive agenda is indicated in IPU research, which reports that women in parliaments work across party lines through parliamentary women's caucuses and champion gender equality laws and issues which affect women such as the elimination of gender-based violence, parental leave and childcare.[32] Hence, the participatory deficit of women parliamentarians in those political forums which determine economic distributions undermines their power to implement a gendered policy effectively.

Confluence of the two goals of women's economic empowerment – political leadership and gender-sensitive policy – was well demonstrated in Iceland, where Jóhanna Sigurðardóttir, the country's first female prime minister, elected after the country's financial crisis, engaged in a process of recovery which avoided the ravages of austerity policies on women's human rights and welfare. The history of women's rights and gender equality in Iceland dates back to the mid-19th century, with women gaining equal access to education and the same inheritance rights as men. For the fifth consecutive year, Iceland ranks as the most advanced country in gender equality, according to the World Economic Forum. In 2008, Iceland suffered a dramatic drop in its economy and currency following the collapse of its banking system. The collapse came in the wake of a substantial increase in spending related to consumption and the real estate market.

The post-crisis government, which was elected in 2009, consisted of four men and five women, including the first female prime minister. Women represented 42.9% of the Althingi, the Icelandic parliament. Thus, female representation in the post-crisis government peaked. In December 2008, the Icelandic parliament established a Special Investigation Commission (SIC) tasked with investigating and analysing the processes leading to the collapse of the three main banks in Iceland. The SIC report to the Althingi in 2010 concluded that the main cause of the failure of the banks was the rapid growth of the banks, their size at the time of the collapse and high risk borrowing and investment. The governmental SIC analysis, issued by Thorgerdur Einarsdóttir and Gyða Margrét Pétursdóttir, respectively professor and assistant professor of gender studies in the faculty of political science at the University of Iceland, found that the causes for the financial collapse were heavily gendered, that all the main players in the collapse of banks were men and that women were in a minority in politics, business, and companies' boards of directors, the media, bank owners, borrowers and the recipients of grants. It also stated that men, who were the main players in the collapse, had acted in the context of a masculine culture which was highly competitive and encouraged risk-taking. The intense and highly gendered public debate following the crisis led to a governmental decision to create a "Gender Equality Watch" to ensure that the crisis would not undermine prior achievements in gender equality. Its role was to evaluate the ongoing impact of the economic situation from a gender perspective with the objective of ensuring that actions taken to strengthen the economy would reflect gender equality principles.[33]

Despite the acknowledged outstanding success of this feminist economic regime in overcoming the financial collapse while maintaining social and legal gender equality mechanisms, in the subsequent 2013 elections the electorate returned the prior conservative party to power.

Support for women's participation in economic leadership and for a gender-sensitive agenda was graphically imprinted at the WEF 48th annual meeting in Davos in 2018, through the appointment of seven female co-chairs for the annual meeting. Women's economic empowerment was a key theme of the meeting, including advocacy for promotion of women in the political and corporate worlds.[34] There may be room for scepticism as to whether women's economic empowerment was indeed mainstreamed into all 400 sessions at Davos. However, the appointment of the seven female co-chairs is, at the very least, an important symbolic development.

The Icelandic experience and the WEF's 2018 adoption of a women's economic empowerment agenda represent a sea change in the awareness of the policy implications of appointing women to economic office. Anecdotal evidence has told us that where women's political leadership has in the past endowed them with economic decision-making power, their gender-sensitivity in policy measures was not inevitable. Margaret Thatcher's economics as prime minister of the United Kingdom in the 1970s introduced neo-liberal ideology and its ritual of privatisation, with global reach, fuelling the increase in economic inequality and reducing public services on which more women are dependent than men. She also declared that working women's return home would be a solution to the unemployment problem. Post-Thatcher, women's caucuses and civil society organisations globally have articulated the expectation that women in politics must pay attention to the gendering of economic policy and promote a gender-sensitive perspective.

Press Conference: Meet the co-chairs of the Annual Meeting 2018 of the World Economic Forum in Davos, January 23, 2018 (from the left: Fon Mathuros Chantanayingyong, head of Media, member of the Executive Committee, World Economic Forum; Erna Solberg, prime minister of Norway; Chetna Sinha, founder and chair, Mann Deshi Foundation, India; Ginni Rometty, chair, president and chief executive officer, IBM Corporation, United States; Christine Lagarde, managing director, International Monetary Fund (IMF), Washington DC; Isabelle Kocher, chief executive officer, ENGIE, France; Fabiola Gianotti, director-general, European Organization for Nuclear Research (CERN), Geneva; and Sharan Burrow, general secretary, International Trade Union Confederation (ITUC), Brussels).

The corporate world

Integrating women leaders and ensuring gender-sensitive policy are important not only in the political sphere but also in the corporate world, including private and public corporations. Economic governance is generated not only *de jure* by political decision-making in international institutions, parliaments and governments but also *de facto* by the activities of economic and financial corporations at the transnational and national levels. Corporate governance directly impacts the conditions under which people work and live. The corporate sector creates and defines jobs, produces growth, sets parameters of income distribution and affects the social and environmental conditions of the communities in which they function. This applies in differing degrees of intensity to large corporations, SMEs and cooperatives.

Large corporations and wealthy individuals also have a direct impact on the economic policy decisions of the political branches of government. From campaign contributions to big philanthropic donations, big business is setting the agenda in an ever more blatant way.[35] In a political world in which corporate investment decisions greatly influence decision-makers, the corporate lobby has immense pull. Furthermore, the increased mobility of corporations has resulted in the amassing of political power vis-à-vis host states. The facts underlying this political power are obvious: in 2000 the wealth of the top 200 companies surpassed the economies of 182 countries.[36] In 2016, the NGO Global Justice Now, comparing government revenue to corporate turnover, ranked 69 corporations and only 31 countries amongst the top 100 global economic entities.[37] The impact of corporations on the policy agendas of states has been blatantly formalised and exhibited in multilateral international trade agreements, which include investor-state dispute settlement systems that allow arbitrators to require states to pay compensation to foreign investors in cases where public interest measures, including environmental protection, human rights and health measures, are adopted which adversely affect the investors' profit margins in deals concluded under the agreements.[38] The direct policy impact of large corporations, where they subordinate social welfare interests to corporate profit agendas, has a disparate impact on women, threatening social services on which women are more intensely reliant than men.

Despite moves, in IHRL and in many legal systems, to remove formal legal barriers from women's participation in all sectors of political and public life, the barriers to women attaining high-level leadership positions in the corporate world persist. The World Bank showed in its 2016 Report on Women, Business and Law, that of the 173 economies covered by the report, 155 maintain at least one barrier for women seeking opportunities that does not exist for men. The laws listed include restrictions on married women registering a business, travelling outside of a country, owning land and other productive assets, opening a bank account, inheriting family property and taking a job without a husband's or male guardian's permission.[39] Such serious legal barriers are mostly prevalent in countries with religious personal law which retains traditionalist patriarchal norms and systematically undermines women's social and economic autonomy.

Women candidates for high-level positions face negative stereotyping and lack of promotion opportunities. They lack confidence, which is not unconnected to the objective barriers they face. Women executives are, like women in political life and in the workforce, disadvantaged by their care commitments, as will be discussed in Part II. Women in senior management still take on more of the housework,[40] and they are significantly more likely to be in dual-career family relationships than men at the same levels.[41] Most corporate culture is still extremely non-accommodating for family life. Betty Yuen the VC of CLP Power Hong Kong said that "stereotyping, bias, and brutally long working hours are discouraging our women executives from reaching for the top. . . . Family-friendly policies are crucial so that our female professionals can shine in the different stages of their lives."[42] Furthermore, the lack of a corporate culture which regards family life as a legitimate demand on the time schedule of corporate players puts women at a disadvantage not only as regards maternity leave, which unlike childcare leave is necessarily female, but also as regards unpaid care commitments for children and other dependent family members, which are still largely carried by women.

In the existing family-hostile corporate environment, there are women who do all they can to prevent care commitments from interfering with their career advancement. There are examples of women executives taking extremely short periods of leave such as the two weeks, out of the 16 weeks maternity leave granted by Yahoo, taken by Yahoo CEO Marissa Meir, who was much criticised for setting this as a role modelling example.[43] The prominence of Marissa Meir made this a talking point, but it should be looked at in proportion as it is clearly not unusual for women far lower down on the supply chain to forego maternity leave in order to hold on to their jobs or to keep their small or medium-sized businesses running. Furthermore, senior women are far better placed to pay for replacement care services, and this must in fact ameliorate their situation in comparison with lower-paid women.

There is some evidence that the millennials, both female and male, seek a much greater work-life balance.[44] The CEO of Facebook, Mark Zuckerberg, for instance, took two months paid paternity leave.[45] It is increasingly accepted that the best way to advance women in corporations is to be family friendly and allow all parents to combine their careers and their family lives. It is further said that this would also serve the business case, as it would attract both male and female talent.[46] This line of thinking should not mislead us to thinking that men and women executives are symmetrically situated in their roles as parents. Where men choose to take time out for parenthood, it is celebrated as progressive role modelling. When women have children, it is a matter for public debate and concern as to whether they can possibly juggle the two roles without either being a neglectful mother or a failed executive.[47]

Negative stereotyping in the corporate world, as in the political world discussed previously, restricts women's executive opportunities. "Sex role stereotypes" describe a "normative or statistical view regarding appropriate roles or behavior for men and women."[48] Furthermore, they generalise and attribute to all women the caring obligations which are frequently but not always born by women, and they legitimise a corporate lifestyle which ignores the care obligations of men or women. The more deeply these stereotypes and priorities are entrenched in corporate culture, the less will women have the opportunities or the confidence to advance to the senior levels of management for which they are qualified.

A seminal case on stereotyping at the highest level of executive promotion was decided in the United States Supreme Court in 1989. Ann Hopkins was denied partnership at Price Waterhouse in spite of the fact that she was clearly well qualified, having outperformed her male co-workers in bringing in clients. Amongst the reasons given for rejecting her appointment was that she had an abrasive personality and was said to be aggressive, foul-mouthed, demanding and impatient with other staff members. During her evaluation, a written comment made by a firm partner stated that what Hopkins needed was a "course in charm school." The head supervisor of her department told her that to increase chances of promotion she needed to "walk more femininely, talk more femininely, dress more femininely, wear make-up, have her hair styled, and wear jewelry." The lower courts had found that this was a form of reverse stereotyping based on gender. The Supreme Court held that the gender stereotyping could constitute illegal sex discrimination.[49]

A quarter of a century later, Sheryl Sandberg in her 2013 book *Lean In: Women, Work, and the Will to Lead*, attributed much of women's failure to reach top leadership positions in North America to lack of confidence and self-censorship.[50] A key finding in the "Women in the Workplace 2016" report, produced by Sandberg's Lean In organisation in cooperation with McKinsey & Company, is that women are somewhat less interested than men in becoming executives.[51] However, women's lack of confidence in the executive context does not exist in a vacuum. The report itself concludes that women are not getting equal feedback from their employers, even when they are asking for it, and they have less access to the mentoring and sponsoring of senior leaders,[52] which are an important element of the ability to climb up the ladder.

The continuing existence of both direct and reverse gender stereotyping in companies in the United States is also overwhelmingly evident in the report itself: women who negotiate for promotion or pay, "are 30 per cent more likely than men who negotiate to receive feedback that they are 'intimidating,' 'too aggressive,' or 'bossy.'"[53] Thus women who compete on the basis of the male model of competitive confrontation are excluded for not conforming to the feminine stereotype, while women who do conform to a feminine stereotype are unlikely to make the grade for highly competitive leadership roles.

Gender stereotyping expresses itself in institutional segregation of women in corporations. The ILO has identified 'glass walls' within hierarchal structures that reproduce occupational segregation by creating subtle barriers and making career pathways different for women compared to men. It has observed that certain jobs, particularly service occupations, are still deemed 'suitable' for women, while men are considered to be more apt for others, such as management and decision-making.[54] This kind of segregation channels women in corporate C-suites to personnel and financial management rather than economic planning and development positions.

Lesser opportunity: company boards, senior management and CEOs in large corporations

Women remain significantly underrepresented in the corporate pipeline. At entry level, fewer women than men are hired, and this remains the case despite women's high achievements in education. At every rung of the corporate ladder, the representation of women further declines.[55] Although women are breaking into these enclaves, corporate leadership in company boards and senior management of large corporations is dominated by men. Within large corporations, it is generally acknowledged that, although women's representation is increasing on company boards and in senior management, a severe gender gap remains with respect to top leadership.[56]

Company boards: Emerging policy to increase women's representation in economic leadership has largely focused on quotas for women on boards. On corporate boards, women's representation remains low: various assessments between 2015 and 2017 show women's board membership globally ranging between 12% and 15%.[57] Europe is leading the way with an average representation of women in the boardroom standing at 24.4% at the end of 2015, an 80% increase over the previous six years.[58] Norway (over 40%), France and Sweden (over 30%) have the highest percentage of women serving on boards.[59] Regionally, countries in Latin America and in the Asia Pacific region, other than Australia, have progressed the least,[60] with Japan being the lowest with 1.6% in 2014, rising to 3.5% in 2016.[61]

Although there are still company boards around the world that are entirely composed of men, this has changed in the past years[62] and, in a survey of 4,218 global companies, 73.5% were found to have at least one female director. Nevertheless, this number drops to just 20.1% for boards with at least three women.[63] This is significant, as research shows that three women or more are needed to create a 'critical mass' of women at the board level in order to allow women to contribute a gender perspective effectively.[64]

Mandatory gender quotas for membership of corporate boards have been introduced in several countries.[65] Most of the countries with quota requirements are in Scandinavia and Western Europe (Iceland, France, Norway, Israel etc.) but some are in Africa (Rwanda) and Asia (India, Malaysia). The quota requirements may variously apply to government companies, publicly listed companies or companies with assets or employee rosters above a designated minimum.[66] The number of members of each sex which companies, governmental or publicly listed, are required to appoint to boards varies between a minimum of one member or a fair representation requirement (Israel) to 40% (France, Norway).[67] The failure to fulfil quota requirements may result in sanctions such as fines on the company (Italy), withholding of all directors' fees until the situation is rectified (France) or judicial enforcement mechanisms (Israel).[68]

Critics argue, however, that mandatory quotas result in tokenism rather than being an agent of structural change. They argue that they are not resulting in women achieving power in the boardroom. There are extremely few female chairs, and the proportion of women heading the board generally ranges from zero to a few per cent.[69] Moreover, a recent study in the United States that covered 1,800 company boards found that women and minorities were paid about 3% to 9% less than their 'non-diverse' white and male counterparts on the boards.[70] However, some of the earlier critics, such as ILO and also Christine Lagarde, seem to have revised their earlier scepticism, and Credit Suisse, extremely critical in its 2014 report, sings the praises of quotas in its 2016 report.[71] There have been some attempts to increase the number of women on boards by non-mandatory targets,[72] for example, voluntary corporate measures, such as the 30% Club in the United Kingdom and the 2020 Women on Board in the United States,[73] have sought to achieve gender diversity on boards.

Despite the great strategic importance of board membership in appointing the CEO and setting out the overall strategic direction of the company, the increased presence of women on boards has not yet had a demonstrable impact on gendering corporate policy. Women's numbers on boards have not reached a critical mass, they are seldom appointed chair and they have not had a demonstrable impact on the promotion of women along company pipelines.[74] Hence, this is still a work in progress.

Senior management: Credit Suisse, in its 2014 survey of more than 3,000 companies across 40 countries in all major sectors, found that women constituted only 12.9% of senior management. In contrast, Grant Thornton, in its 2016 International Business Report based on interviews with senior executives from 36 economies, suggested that rates of women in senior management, often referred to as the C-Suite, which includes chief executive officer (CEO), chief operating officer (COO) or chief finance officer (CFO), managing directors or partners, are slowly increasing globally, currently reaching 24%.[75] The extreme divergence in the numbers can be explained only by different methodologies and samples.

A further discrepancy is in the regional assessment. Credit Suisse in 2014 showed North America and Europe as having the highest percentage of women in senior management globally. In contrast, Grant Thornton, in 2016, assessed the G7 countries as lagging behind and indicated that Eastern Europe topped the list, with ASEAN (Association of Southeast Asian Nations) as another region in which there are more women than the global average in senior management, with 34% of senior roles held by women.[76] Credit Suisse in its 2016 report found that emerging Asia and China had the highest numbers of female

CFOs and business unit heads and attributed this to the political heritage in the region:

> Equal access to education under communist rule in China has helped to build skill sets more equitably compared to other emerging markets while the number of female political leaders across the region has also provided role models and served to break down stereotypes.[77]

It is clear that coordinated data is needed in order to understand the global and regional trends regarding women in senior management in general. However, there is agreement that even where women have attained increased numbers in high-level management positions, they have done so mainly in human resources, finance and administration, public relations and communications, and corporate social responsibility. The participation of women in top management thus tends to be skewed towards areas of less influence and with lower promotion opportunities, a phenomenon referred to as 'glass walls' within hierarchal structures that reproduce occupational segregation and perpetuate subtle barriers.[78]

There is also vertical segregation with a 'management power line' where the lowest female representation is at the CEO level, growing gradually as we move down toward business management and operational roles, CFO and strategy and finally shared services.[79] Women do not

> receive the same opportunities, feedback, mentoring and training as their male counterparts . . . along the "pipeline" – from graduation to recruitment, to the first assignment or project, and to lower level and middle level management. Research shows how women continue to "drop out," thus shrinking the candidate pool of women for top jobs.[80]

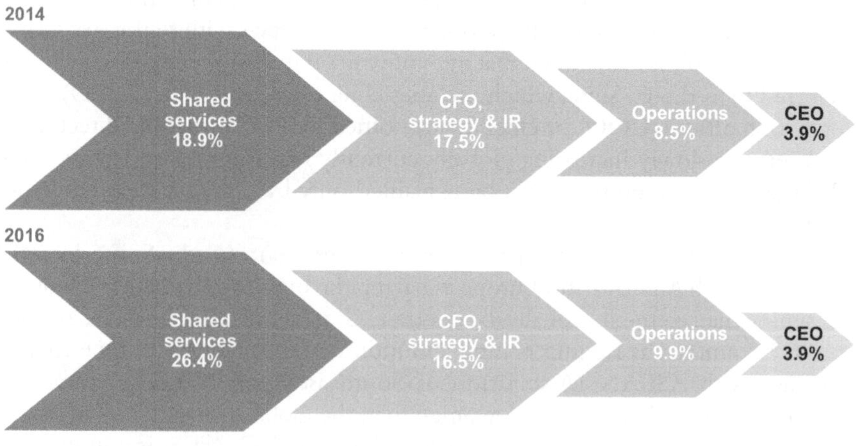

Figure 5.1 The management power line

Source: Credit Suisse, 'The CS Gender 3000: The Reward for Change,' 2016, 14, https://glg.it/assets/docs/csri-gender-3000.pdf.

CEOs: It is agreed according to all the data, as collated by the ILO in 2015, that there is a dearth of women at the very top, at the CEO level. The numbers of female CEOs are extremely low, with research from 2012 to 2018 showing a range of estimates between 4% and 6%, in North America and Europe,[81] and falling to as low as between 0% and 3.6% in developing countries.[82] The odds are stacked against women not only because of glass walls and their dearth in line roles in the corporate pipeline but also because the promotion to CEO is a form of competition in which political manoeuvring outweighs the more objective ways of testing capabilities and, hence, subtle bias with socialisation to regard women's competitiveness as aggressive, rather than successful alpha male behaviour, contribute to pushing women aside.

The dearth of female CEOs adversely affects the gender balance of senior management in general. Far from the Queen Bee syndrome, the data shows that female CEOs are much more likely to surround themselves with other women in senior roles. In fact, according to a Credit Suisse extensive global study in 2016, female CEOs are 50% more likely than male CEOs to have a female CFO, and 55% more likely to have women running business units.[83] This presents convincing evidence that a lack of sponsoring and mentoring in male-dominated senior management is a significant factor in women's failure to reach the top. The 2016 Women in the Workplace Report found that women significantly rely on a network that is mostly female.[84] Moreover, results support the view that women within the management of an organisation are more aware of the barriers to female progression and are therefore more active in addressing them.[85]

Where women do succeed in reaching the pinnacle of corporate power, it may represent an exceptional rather than an evolutionary process. Ryan and Haslam (2005) were the first to identify a phenomenon they named the glass cliff,[86] thus ironically parsing the glass ceiling. Research suggests that women are more likely to achieve leadership positions when their company is in a state of crisis and the job faces a higher risk of failure. A particularly interesting psychological laboratory study showed how gender stereotypes affect the preference for male leaders in conditions of institutional thriving and for female leaders in times of institutional crisis at the brink of the 'glass cliff.' For the success of thriving organisations, researchers found participants adopted a 'think manager-think male' stereotype, rating six characteristics as significantly more needed: independence, competition, dynamic, striving for power, all four of which were rated as descriptive of a typical male leader; fairness descriptive of a typical female leader; and professionality, which was regarded as gender neutral. For the success of companies in times of crisis, participants adopted a 'think crisis-think female' stereotype, judging 11 characteristics as more needed: ability to build confidence in others, cooperation, communication skills, ability to encourage others, ability to work in teams, all five of which were regarded as typical of a female leader; ability to deal with conflict, rationality, ability to motivate others, inspiration, determination and innovative thinking, all six items regarded as gender neutral.[87]

Ending the male monopoly over macroeconomic decision-making

At the pinnacle of macroeconomic policy-making, in leadership participation in both the political and corporate worlds, women have a persistent showing of under 3% in government economic ministries and under 6% at the CEO level, other than in corporate boards which with the help of quotas have reached, according to some surveys, 15%. Hence, the gender gap in economic policy leadership is undeniably more pronounced than it is in women's general leadership in parliaments, governments and the managerial ladder. Moreover, compared to the modest gains women made in prior years, there were signs in 2017 that women's progress in senior management might be stalling.[88] There is nowhere near a critical mass of women in economic policy-making forums in parliaments, governments, financial institutions or corporations, whether international or national. Neo-liberal economic policy has been invented by men, extolled by men and maintained by men.

The negative stereotyping of women is an objective barrier to their opportunities for success in the political and corporate worlds and especially so in the realms of economic power. It blocks their opportunities for promotion and adversely impacts their self-confidence. Although some individual women are breaking through the glass ceiling, they are still a small minority and are liable to be hemmed in by glass walls or run the risk of being precipitated over glass cliffs. Additionally to the identity problems of bias and stereotyping, women in the corporate world are marginalised by a corporate culture which is oriented to the alpha male and blind to the realities of maternity or to caring commitments which are disparately carried by women. The aggregate results show exclusion of women from the bastions of economic power.

The legal policy mechanisms for ensuring the inclusion of women in economic policy making are problematic. Existing IHRL ensures women's right to employment protections regarding maternity, equality in choice of profession and promotion and equal wages. However, economic leadership, political and corporate, is often reached through appointed positions, board membership and self-employment, which are not within the context of an employment relationship and is not systematically covered by protective labour laws, maternity protection, parental care provisions and prohibition of discrimination or sexual harassment by colleagues, customers or suppliers. It is crucial to find ways to apply such standards systematically and effectively in the political and corporate settings.

As regards the political forums, there could be particularisation of political gender quota requirements to include parliamentary committees. Nevertheless, it is hard to envisage effective legal intervention in the task of realigning the topics to which political parties, parliamentary forums and governments designate women members. Change in these respects will have to come largely from greater awareness, cultural transformation and feminist organising pressure within the political hierarchy.

As regards corporations, legal policy frameworks exist. The United Nations General Principles on Business and Human Rights incorporates IHRL obligations,[89] thus requiring states to ensure that business enterprises act in accordance with the CEDAW[90] obligations to eliminate discrimination against women and to achieve equality *de jure* and *de facto*. Accordingly, in the Guidance for National Action Plans (NAP), developed by the Working Group on Business and Human Rights, under the UNGP,[91] business enterprises should be required to respect, protect and promote women's equality of treatment and opportunity. Gender-sensitive analysis should be mainstreamed into all phases of the NAP process, including planning, assessment, monitoring and evaluation. The issue of discrimination against women should be explicitly included in the agenda for each phase and the participation of a critical mass of women experts and professionals, including persons with gender expertise, should be ensured. Baseline studies should include sex-disaggregated data and also intersectional data regarding race, minority status, sex and age, where relevant. This has not been done up till now, either in the Guidance for National Action Plans nor, indeed, in the NAPs so far enacted by states, other than that of Italy. Language counts too: mainstreaming gender does not mean talking about women as one item in a list of vulnerable groups, as is the case in the UNGP guidance to business enterprises on respecting human rights.[92] Women are not a discrete vulnerable group but are a half of the duality of all groups, vulnerable and not vulnerable; the need to gender-mainstream arises as a result of structural disadvantage and discriminatory stereotypes which exclude and silence women in a unique and pervasive way.

The most significant legal policy development in recent years has been, as seen, the introduction of quota requirements for corporate boards in a small number of countries in different regions. In 2014, the WGDAW recommended that states take positive measures to accelerate *de facto* equality for women in leadership positions in corporate, financial and trade institutions and enterprises, including by the introduction of quotas for corporate boards. It is notable that this recommendation, which had been made by the WGDAW for affirmative action in corporate governance, was not included by the Human Rights Council in its 2014 resolution on discrimination against women, presumably because it was considered too radical by the majority of states in the Council.[93] Policy interventions to achieve a greater representation of women in economic policy making is on the drawing board of some UN mechanisms and civil society organisations but in only a preliminary fashion. Examples include the Women's Empowerment Principles for business elaborated by UN Women and the Global Compact, onto which over 1,850 business leaders around the world have signed so far, set principles for business offering guidance on how to empower women in the workplace, marketplace and community.[94] The Maastricht Principles, which represent a consensus view as to the extraterritorial

'The Fearless Girl' was created by Kristen Visbal and commissioned by State Street Global Advisors. It was installed to celebrate 'International Women's Day' and draw attention to women in corporate leadership in March 2017 on the same plaza as the bronze statue 'Charging Bull' by Arturo Di Modica in the Financial District in Manhattan, New York City.

Source: quietbits / Shutterstock.com

obligations of states in the areas of economic, social and cultural rights, require that states observe human rights principles and these include CEDAW, which has been interpreted to guarantee women's right to participate in decision-making, to non-discrimination and to gender equality.[95]

A critical mass of women in economic decision-making would be a force for the emergence of a gender-dualistic economic agenda, which must, on available evidence, necessarily factor in a social agenda, as women are more directly exposed, through their daily care responsibilities, to the realities of welfare needs. It remains essential that the two goals should be pursued simultaneously: both women's equal access to economic leadership and also the promotion of gender-sensitive policy which reduces disadvantage and inequality.

2 Entrepreneurship

Entrepreneurship has become entrenched as a popular social and economic force worldwide, endorsed by such international organisations as the UN, IMF and the World Bank.[96] It is the idol of neo-liberal ideology, putting the burden of success on private initiative, innovation, investment and performance. Women's entrepreneurship melds into this neo-liberal pattern, under which each individual woman is responsible for her own economic fate and must rely on the market, with minimal expectations of support from the state.

Increase in women's entrepreneurial activity

There is a long history of women's entrepreneurship through the ages in different cultures and societies, but the increasing numbers and varieties of women entrepreneurs is a relatively new global phenomenon.[97] Two of the scholars who pioneered research on women entrepreneurs, Buttner and Moore, examining earlier periods of female entrepreneurship, found that in the United States it was mainly from the mid-1970s that women emerged as "modern" entrepreneurs with more professional and managerial experience, stronger professional networks and use of power in business environments, placing greater emphasis on profitability, new market creation and sustainability.[98] Globally, women's economic activity as entrepreneurs has increased. The Global Entrepreneurship Monitor (GEM), which has been tracking women entrepreneurs in the last decade, showed in its 2016/2017 report that, globally, there has been a trend of increase in overall female Total Entrepreneurial Activity (TEA) in most places in the world: in 63 economies (out of 74 in its sample), female TEA rates increased by 17% since 2012.[99]

Nevertheless, women own and manage significantly fewer businesses worldwide than men.[100] ILO data from 2015 showed that they own and manage about 30% of all businesses, ranging from self-employed (or own-account workers), micro and small enterprises to medium and large companies.[101] The GEM 2016/2017 Report found that the gender gap (ratio of women to men participating in entrepreneurship) persists in many regions of the world, and only in five economies women participated at levels equal to or higher than those of men.[102] Nevertheless, GEM also showed that the global entrepreneurship gender gap has narrowed by 11% since 2012, although the decline in some countries is a result of a decline in the male TEA rather than because of an increased female TEA.[103]

The entrepreneurial gender gap

The entrepreneurial gender gap varies substantially both by region as well as by the country's stage of economic development. Analysing the gap in reference to economic development,[104] the GEM Report found that in early stages of economic development with large rural populations, women are 21% less likely than men to start a business; in industrialised economies they are 30% less likely to start a business; and in 'mature economies,' with service-based business as well as industrial sectors based on knowledge intensity, they are 41% less likely than men to start a business.[105] Thus, the entrepreneurial gender gap increases with higher stages of economic development. Some researchers claim that this is probably because many women in lower-income countries start businesses out of necessity.[106] The GEM Report indeed found that globally women are 20% more likely to cite necessity motives compared to men, and that necessity may indeed drive higher TEA rates at lower development levels.[107] On its visits to Peru and Chile,[108] the WGDAW met with women entrepreneurs in favelas and were told by them that entrepreneurship is often a last resort for women with children who have no source of income from spouses, family or social security. Groups of these women support their families from the renovation and sale of scavenged items and are seeking government classification and funding as recycling cooperatives. Their initiative, determination and courage left a lasting impression.

In addition to the gender participation gap in entrepreneurship, women entrepreneurs are, it seems, most often concentrated in micro-businesses and small and medium-sized enterprises (SMEs)[109] and are more likely than men to be in the informal sector, running small enterprises mainly from home. Furthermore, there is gender segregation in entrepreneurship sectors. The GEM 2015 Report found that women's entrepreneurship was concentrated in the consumer, culture and society sector, while men's entrepreneurship was more focused on the transforming sector, which involves manufacturing, construction, transportation and wholesale and is more capital-intensive, and the business sector, which includes finance, insurance and real estate services.[110] The consumer services sector in which women are concentrated is often an overtraded sector populated by low profit-margin businesses; high levels of competition for limited markets; and is particularly vulnerable in periods of economic slowdown, contributing to the generally lower rates of female-established business ownership.[111] Both because of the size of women-owned businesses and the sectors in which they are concentrated, these businesses tend to be far lower down the chain of value-added production, limiting their income and growth.[112]

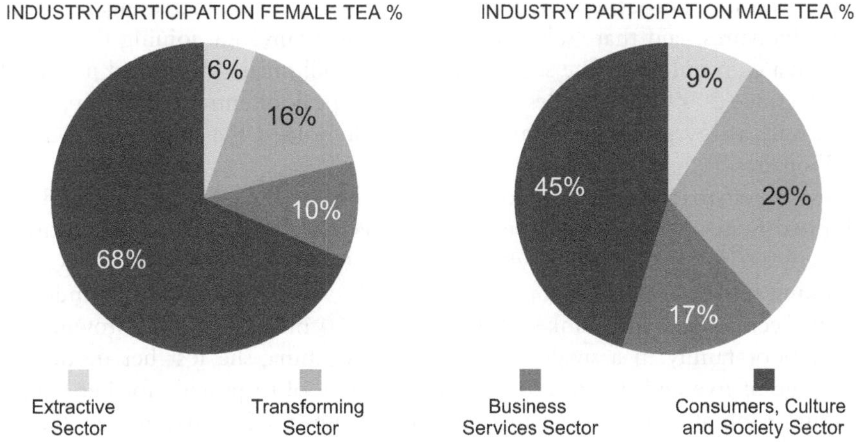

Figure 6.1 Early-stage entrepreneurship activity, by industry, sector and gender

Source: Donna J. Kelley and others, 'Special Report: Women's Entrepreneurship,' Global Entrepreneurship Monitor (GEM), 2015, http://gemconsortium.org/report/49281. Used with permission from the authors and Global Entrepreneurship Research Association.

In the information and communications technology (ICT) sector, fewer than 2% of the entrepreneurs starting businesses are women.[113] This said, there are, of course, many outstanding examples of women who have established highly successful high-tech companies, such as Valrie Grant from Jamaica, who established in 2008 the only female-owned and operated geographic information systems (GIS) company in the Caribbean region, GeoTechVision Enterprises Ltd., which provides clients with high-end IT and geospatial consultancy services, solutions and products. Grant and her business have been recipients of several recognition awards.[114]

At the very top of the entrepreneurial hegemony, taking a look at women billionaires gives an eagle eye view of economic woman. Addressing this issue is not to endorse the desirability of increasing the billionaire club but because the gender ratio of billionaires in general and of self-made billionaires in particular can be viewed as an elitist symbol of gendered inequality in entrepreneurship. While billionaires are very rare, they are becoming a significant item in the rise of extreme inequality. In 2017, *Forbes* commented on its annual billionaires list, that the change in the number of billionaires – up 233 since 2016 – was the biggest in the 31 years that it has been tracking billionaires globally. Furthermore, the total net worth of the billionaires on the list rose by 18% to $7.67 trillion, also a record.[115] Oxfam in 2018 highlighted the place of billionaire wealth in distorting the wealth curve in favour of the super-rich, reporting that billionaire wealth has risen by an annual average of 13% between 2010 and 2017, six times faster than wages of ordinary workers.[116]

Women constitute about 10% of all billionaires[117] and 2.7% of self-made billionaires.[118] Forbes, commenting in 2017 on the fast increasing numbers of billionaires, said that "self-made women billionaires are joining the three-comma club quicker." The self-made women's billionaire group had increased 170% since 2009. Nevertheless, at this absolute peak of entrepreneurship, as we see, only a tiny group of women have actually joined the ranks of self-made billionaires.[119]

Most self-made women billionaires come from China, Hong Kong and the United States. Women billionaires from Asia and North America constitute together 67% of all self-made women billionaires in the world.[120] The top 2017 ranking self-made woman billionaire globally was Zhou Qunfei, founder of Lens Technology, who ranked 186 in the 1,810 billionaires list. Growing up in a poor family in a small village in central China, she lost her mother at the age of five and was forced to leave high school to provide for her family, taking a job at a factory and making watch lenses for $1 a day. At age 22, she started a workshop, making watch lenses for customers. When she converted this business into glass screens for mobile phones she became a highly successful entrepreneur and eventually a self-made billionaire.[121] A famous and powerful self-made woman billionaire, ranked six in the Forbes 2018 list of America's richest self-made women, is the American Oprah Winfrey, who grew up in a low-income family and earned a scholarship to an affluent high school. She started working in babysitting and cleaning homes at the age of 15 and then began a TV career on a small talk show, which later became The Oprah Winfrey Show, the highest-rated American talk show ever, running for 25 years. She made her business career by writing numerous best-selling books, acting in and producing critically acclaimed films and opening her own woman-centric cable network in 2011. At the 75th Golden Globe Awards, Oprah became the first black woman to win the Cecil B. DeMille Award. In her acceptance speech, she talked about the fight for equality, race and the #MeToo movement.[122]

Gender bias in entrepreneurship

Entrepreneurship opportunities are affected by networking, funding, sponsoring, mentoring, credit and access to financial and reproductive resources. Women's access to these essential ingredients for entrepreneurial success are far more limited than men's, and discrimination in training, information and provision of credit and saving facilities may all create barriers for women's entrepreneurship.

Since entrepreneurship is privatised and individualised and the market is regarded as entirely gender neutral or gender blind, it is usually assumed that women's chances to succeed are no different from men's. In particular, it is thought that digital businesses may help level the playing field for women since customers can be reached across the world and cultural gender norms could be avoided.[123] However, this assumption of absolute equality is illusionary. There are barriers to women's entrepreneurship. These include, in some countries, discriminatory laws that restrict women's autonomy and subject them to various forms of male guardianship, with limits on the types of jobs that they are permitted to engage in; and, everywhere, lesser access to credit and start-up funding, as well as to entrepreneurial training and networks.[124] Barriers also include the cross-cutting issues of limited access to ownership of land and other productive resources, unpaid care burdens and gender-based violence.

Some research findings also indicate that gender stereotypes adversely impact entrepreneurial opportunities for women.[125] This kind of stereotyping was exposed in Hila Keren's deconstruction of the successful American TV reality serial 'Shark Tank,'[126] where she analyses the contradiction between the representation of a post-feminist dream world of successful women entrepreneurs in a fully egalitarian business world, ruled by market meritocracy, and the stereotypical characterisation of the women's enterprises as 'mompreneurship,' with feminine life-style products, produced or marketed from home.[127] There is also a study that claims to prove that the pervasiveness of gender stereotyping exists even on the platform economy in the sale of consumer goods.[128]

At the financial institutional level, women are cold-shouldered out of major entrepreneurial support systems and often limited to micro-financing. There is lack of connection to Chambers of Commerce to identify business and trade opportunities.[129] Underinvestment in women entrepreneurs is a phenomenon worldwide.[130] Major financing is frequently conditional on the entrepreneur's ability to post collateral and women own less property. In developing countries, an estimated 70% of women-owned SMEs are not supported by financial institutions.[131] In Africa, female-owned companies in the formal sector in urban areas have two and a half times less start-up capital than male-owned equivalents.[132] Across all EU Member States, women are considerably less likely than men to indicate that they can access the financing needed to start a business.[133] Surveys showed that in the United States, in 2016, companies run by men got more than 16 times more venture capital funding than companies run by women.[134] Interestingly, research shows that venture funds with women managers invest in women entrepreneurs 70% of the time and therefore support the expansion of female-owned businesses, but their impact is limited because women constitute just 10 to 15% of the investment sector.[135]

In government procurement programs, too, women-owned businesses are heavily disadvantaged. In developing countries, governments are the largest buyer of goods and services, accounting for 15 to 20% of gross domestic product, and yet spend only 1% on sourcing from women-owned businesses.[136] Very few countries have initiated programs to tackle this issue.[137]

In response to the difficulties poor rural people, especially women, face in procuring funding or credit, especially in developing economics, schemes of microfinance were developed. Mohammed Yunis pioneered a system of microfinance to provide credit for small business initiatives and was awarded a Nobel Prize for his work in 2006.[138] The microfinance project was greatly celebrated by UN agencies and by civil society.[139] Microfinance usually targets women, in some cases exclusively. Since its inception, the microfinance industry has expanded to become a multibillion-dollar business, and a central feature of foreign aid programs. The optimism regarding its public policy benefits has not however been vindicated. David Roodman argues that, on current evidence, the best estimate of the average impact of microcredit on the poverty of clients is zero. The high repayment rates are not necessarily a result of sustainable business returns. Women may borrow money from poor relatives or choose to forego basic necessities in order to repay the loans. Research has shown that most women were terrified of what might happen if they defaulted.[140]

Entrepreneurial women – the way forward

Entrepreneurship can theoretically provide women with economic opportunities and control over their own economic destiny and time allocation. However, in practice, women's entrepreneurship is far from an equal playing field. Gender gaps in entrepreneurship persist. The widest gender gap in entrepreneurship globally is at the top of the financial pyramid at 97.3%, with only 2.7% of women self-made billionaires, while the narrowest gender gap is in necessity entrepreneurship. Women's entrepreneurial activity is bunched at the lower levels of the economic pyramid, concentrated in household or micro-businesses or small and medium-sized enterprises, which, although they provide the women greater autonomy and economic independence in their families, do not bring commensurate returns on human capital investment. Women entrepreneurs have not broken into a position of influence at the political and macroeconomic policy making level and remain vulnerable to macroeconomic policies over which they have little control and which, especially in times of austerity, have exposed them to economic hardship and insecurity that have been even greater for women than for men.[141]

Women in entrepreneurship have to contend with discriminatory stereotypes and, in some countries, with persistent discriminatory laws, which constitute barriers to their economic opportunities across the board. They are relatively or entirely deprived in many economies of financial resources such as training, funding, credit, government procurement contracts and land or home ownership. Although there have been some policy initiatives to promote women's entrepreneurship, such as microcredit schemes, women entrepreneurs continue to be disadvantaged in access to credit.

Equal entrepreneurship opportunities for women are clearly an essential aspect of their right to economic equality in the economy as it is presently constituted, especially in view of the growing emphasis on entrepreneurship as the way for individuals to achieve economic sustainability. Women's entrepreneurship has been recognised as a component of sustainable development and realisation of human development goals. The World Bank showed that even though women are more limited than men by lack of capital and social constraints, women entrepreneurs contribute substantially to economic growth and poverty reduction. They are also more likely to contribute to their children's education, health and nutrition compared to male entrepreneurs. Goldman Sachs also showed that women entrepreneurs from 43 countries who participated in its program "Goldman Sachs 10,000 Women" mentored other women in their communities in entrepreneurship.[142] These sources, along with others, demonstrate the economic and development cases for women's entrepreneurship.[143]

There are some international and local initiatives to support women's entrepreneurship and facilitate their access to financial resources, such as the ILO Job Creation in Small and Medium Sized Enterprises Recommendation 1998 (No. 189);[144] the Women's Entrepreneurship Development (WED) program;[145] the SheTrades initiative by the International Trade Centre (ITC);[146] the Canadian Business Women in International Trade program;[147] the Global Banking Alliance for Women[148] and the Mann Deshi Mahila Sahakari Bank, founded in 1997, one of the first legally recognised women's cooperative banks provided facilities designed for rural women entrepreneurship banking.[149]

In this context, cooperatives[150] provide an entrepreneurial framework which has proved facilitative for women. Cooperatives are jointly owned and democratically controlled enterprises. In many cases, cooperatives provide a forum to come together to acquire better bargaining power as well as gaining access to markets, credit and important training and services. These are attributes which can compensate for some of the barriers women experience as individual entrepreneurs and, in many countries, women's participation in cooperatives plays an important role in their ability to become successful business leaders. Women are active in most types of cooperatives such as banks, credit societies, market access coops, agricultural producer societies and industrial cooperatives. However, women are significantly underrepresented in leadership and decision-making roles in cooperatives and, in some countries, membership is restricted to male heads of household.[151] Nevertheless, some action to increase women's participation and leadership is being taken. For example, in 2002, the ILO released the Promotion of Cooperatives Recommendation (No. 193), which states that special consideration should be given to women in cooperatives at all levels, particularly in senior management and leadership.[152] The Blueprint for a Co-operative Decade, adopted by the General Assembly of International Cooperative Alliance in 2012, designated a critical area for cooperative development in creating economic opportunities for women and further engaging women members in cooperative democratic processes.[153]

Despite some initiatives to support women's entrepreneurship, attention to entrepreneurship in the context of women's human rights is a barely emerging field. Beyond recognition of the importance of women's entrepreneurship, a whole infrastructure of provisions is required to assure women's equal access. Entrepreneurship opportunities for women need to be facilitated by rights to equality in networking, governmental procurement policies, private investment funding, access to all forms of financial credit and access to resources, including land. Some of these rights have been recognised in international law and policy formulations, such as the call for equal access to land and credit under CEDAW and the Beijing Declaration and Platform for Action.[154] However, the normative mechanisms to implement an agenda for equal entrepreneurship opportunities for women are somewhat vague and their interpretation and implementation are preliminary.

Only in part are the rights requisite for entrepreneurial opportunity guaranteed by express provisions in existing international treaty standards. CEDAW has express provisions regarding women's equal right to "bank loans, mortgages and other forms of financial credit"[155] and right to participate in rural development and development planning, access to agricultural credit and marketing facilities.[156] However, CEDAW does not, outside the context of matrimonial property, have explicit provisions regarding the right to equal access to economic resources and to land ownership and use. These remain to be developed through interpretation of non-explicit provisions of CEDAW, for example the Article 13 right to equality in "other areas of economic and social life," which although it has been interpreted as referring to basic social rights,[157] should also be applied to guarantee equality in access to all economic resources.

The recognition of women's right to equal access to ownership and control of all economic resources was recognised by the Human Rights Council 2014 Resolution calling for states to support women's entrepreneurship, including through training, the dissemination of information and the provision of credit and saving facilities, and by securing women's equal rights over resources to ensure women's equality and well-being.[158] The 2015 Sustainable Development Goals (SDGs) called to target "reforms to give women equal rights to economic resources, as well as access to ownership and control over land and other forms of property, financial services, inheritance and natural resources, in accordance with national laws," with the indicators for achieving this target focusing on collecting sex-disaggregated data regarding ownership and on the legal framework (including customary law) guarantees for women's equal rights to land ownership and/or control.[159] Neither the HRC nor the SDGs have yet been willing to call for government procurement policies that specifically encourage women's entrepreneurship, as had been recommended by the WGDAW,[160] thus indicating that there is still a conservative approach to introducing gender-responsive mechanisms to the allocation of resources in the field of entrepreneurship.

3 Women's economic power deficit

Mapping women's economic decision-making power and entrepreneurial progress systemically on a global scale is a difficult task. The locus of economic power is highly fragmented in political and corporate contexts, and the global data is rudimentary. But there are some road signs regarding trends. While there is evidence, much of it anecdotal, of economic women shattering the glass ceiling and spearheading change, the overall data shows severe gender gaps in all contexts: political forums for economic decision-making, corporate senior management and entrepreneurship.

As regards political forums, women who have gained power in the political world are not well represented in the economic branches of governance at the national and the international levels. Deconstructing the progress women have made in political representation, reaching as we have seen an average of 23.5% in parliaments and 18.3% in governments globally, reveals that, at 3% of the economic portfolios in government ministries, women lag far further behind in areas of economic power than they do in other areas such as welfare, education and health. In senior management of the corporate and financial world, the vast majority of women who are engaged in economic activity do not reach the highest levels of leadership, with regional variations of 0 to 6% women CEOs. And in the corporate pipeline, women continue to be closed in by glass ceilings and glass walls and precipitated towards glass cliffs. In entrepreneurship, women are heavily concentrated at the least profitable levels of micro and small or medium-sized enterprises. Women entrepreneurs are rare at the pinnacle of 'tycoonship' and are concentrated at the middle or lower end of the supply chain, with limited impact only at the micro level.

The importance of women's equal participation in economic policy making cannot be overemphasised. This rests first and foremost on a gender equality imperative as regards democratising the process. It rests also on the need to integrate women's life experience as a pillar of economic policy. Participation of a critical mass of women in the engineering of economic policy is necessary to bring into focus the gender duality of social and economic life. A central example for transformative economic policy making is the economics of unpaid care, which has gone through a process of privatisation and state neglect, flying in the face of some cost-benefit assessments according to which public investment in care services would have actually boosted economies.[161]

Feminist economists and women's organisations have analysed and contested the gender bias of economic policy, which marginalises women's interests and needs. The mechanism which they have developed to address it is gender budgeting. Gender budgeting is based on the view that government budgets are not 'gender neutral,' but rather 'gender blind.' Since their inception about 30 years ago, gender budgeting programs have been introduced in over 80 countries. The purpose of gender budgeting is to systematically incorporate attention to women's needs into fiscal policies and administration and to promote governmental accountability in addressing them. The areas in which gender budgeting has been focused vary in the developing and the developed worlds. In the developing world, gender budgeting has brought attention to issues of girls' access to education, reproductive health, supply of basic utilities to households, such as water, and women's employment, entrepreneurship and agricultural work. In the developed world a focus has been on tax systems which may deter women's economic activity, for example by assessing women's income jointly with the men's.[162]

The IMF observes that "a majority of the gender budgeting efforts seem to have not gone far, reflecting several factors, including a lack of commitment of fiscal policy makers and governmental bureaucracies, and weaknesses in the structure and implementation of the initiative."[163] In a study that included six regional surveys, the IMF observes that gender budgeting efforts appear to have led to meaningful fiscal policy changes only when they had the support of the political centre of fiscal decision-making, such as the finance minister.[164] Other researchers have also noted that, at local government levels in developing countries, women's representation and involvement of women's organisations have been cardinal factors in gender budgeting.[165] Thus, it can be safely concluded that the lack in women's political representation in economic decision-making bodies surely contributes to the poor performance of gender budgeting programs. For success in gender budgeting it is crucial to include women as leaders in those forums which formulate and monitor budgetary allocations.

An increase in women's economic leadership to reach a critical mass is a component of the gender responsiveness of economic policy. Although participation by particular women in economic leadership does not inevitably secure gender-responsive decision-making, an overall pattern of women's participation in economic governance is likely to increase gender responsiveness in policy making. In parliaments, women's lobbies are observed to promote social and equality agendas. Furthermore, researchers have found that companies with more women board directors and corporate leaders show an increased level of commitment to corporate social responsibility.[166] Contrary to commonly held prejudices that women do not promote other women, there is distinct evidence that women in power in politics and the corporate world do promote women in their institutions and, in fact, the advancement of women into leadership roles would create a snowball effect. The data which I have accessed suggests that women in governments, women in corporate governance at the CEO level (although not on boards) and women in venture capital promote women.

The engine for advocating women's corporate leadership has been, primarily, the business case, based on profit profiles or on the ability to cater to consumer identity, which is in many fields dominated by women.[167] Indeed the DNA of corporations is utility and profit. There are researches which suggest a correlation between gender diversity in senior management and improved company performance. However, it has been pointed out that these claims for the business case do not prove causation and indeed they cannot do more than indicate a correlation.[168] However, it should not be considered necessary to show that the inclusion of women actually improves the profits of companies in order to insist on including them in corporate leadership: women should be included wherever they are at the same level of competence and potential as men, as is indeed required to satisfy both the human rights imperative and the equality premise of Pareto efficiency models. Achieving the egalitarian inclusion of women necessitates a massive elimination of the barriers women encounter in competing on a level playing field.

The mechanisms to implement equality requirements in economic decision-making in the political and corporate worlds are at a very preliminary stage of development. Effective guarantee of women's equal access to economic leadership as a legal obligation of states and corporations requires newly developed sets of human rights standards. CEDAW establishes a wide generalised basis for promoting women's economic empowerment: it obliges state parties to take appropriate measures to ensure "the full development and advancement of women," "in all fields, in particular the political, social, economic and cultural fields," "for the purpose of guaranteeing them the exercise and enjoyment of their human rights on a basis of equality with men."[169] This provision, linking as it does development and advancement with enjoyment of human rights, provides a strong conceptual framework for women's empowerment in all areas of economic activity beyond those explicitly covered in the employment, rural life and credit provisions of the Convention.[170] The scope of the article could be applied to cover all issues of women's economic activity and could provide the basis for a transformative approach to women's advancement in both the public and private economic sectors.[171]

Awareness of the need to empower women in economic decision-making is gaining ground in international forums. The Human Rights Council in its 2014 Resolution on discrimination against women called, for

> States to take concrete steps towards eliminating all forms of discrimination against women and girls, directed to achieve gender equality and the empowerment of women at all levels of economic and social decision-making processes, especially during economic and financial crises, and to engage women in State-building.[172]

Its importance was recognised as part of the development agenda in the 2030 Agenda for Sustainable Development,[173] adopted by world leaders in 2015. The goals of the SDGs, expressed in Goal 5 on Gender Equality and Women's Empowerment and in the references to gender throughout the other goals, are that the empowerment of women and human rights of women and girls must be reflected both as a stand-alone goal and also be integrated and mainstreamed into all sustainable development goals in the post-2015 development agenda.[174] As Klaus Schwab, founder and executive chairman of the World Economic Forum, remarked:

> There is another simple and powerful reason why more women should be empowered: fairness. Women represent one half of the global population – they deserve equal access to health, education, influence, earning power and political representation. Their views and values are critical for ensuring a more prosperous and inclusive common future. Humanity's collective progress depends on it.[175]

Equality for women must be both a stand-alone goal and mainstreamed into all economic policies. The need to regard women as a stand-alone goal arises as a result of structural disadvantage and discriminatory stereotypes which exclude and silence women in a unique and pervasive way. Mainstreaming is essential because women are not one more discrete vulnerable group but are a half of the duality of all groups, the vulnerable and the not vulnerable, and hence must be considered in all contexts. Stand-alone equality and gender mainstreaming aims at ultimately ensuring women can be agents of policy-making on equal terms with men.

Up until now, macroeconomic policy has, at the political and corporate levels, both nationally and internationally, been overwhelmingly led by men. The policy adopted and developed by this virtually male monopoly has been global neo-liberalism and austerity policies which have disparately and acutely harmed women. The case for women's empowerment in economic policy making is both a gender equality case and also, in addition to the business case, a clear economic and human development case. Equality for women in economic leadership and gender responsiveness in economy policy are essential elements in ensuring that an economy can function optimally to determine and improve the quality of life for women and men.

Notes

1 Facundo Alvaredo, Lucas Chancel, Thomas Piketty, Emmanuel Saez and Gabriel Zucman, 'World Inequality Report 2018,' 2017, 205, http://wir2018.wid.world/files/download/wir2018-full-report-english.pdf.

2 Ibid. 40.

3 WGDAW, 'Thematic Report on Discrimination Against Women in Economic and Social Life, with a Focus on Economic Crisis,' A/HRC/26/39, 2014, www.ohchr.org/EN/Issues/Women/WGWomen/Pages/ESL.aspx.

4 Human Rights Council, 'Elimination of Discrimination Against Women,' A/HRC/26/L.12, Twenty-sixth session, 23 June 2014, para 16, http://ap.ohchr.org/documents/alldocs.aspx?doc_id=23500.

5 Christina Zander, 'Even Scandinavia Has a CEO Gender Gap,' *The Wall Street Journal*, 21 May 2014, www.wsj.com/articles/SB10001424052702303980004579576074106113980.

6 Avivah Wittenberg-Cox, 'How 6 Countries Compare on Executive Gender Balance,' *Harvard Business Review*, 18 July 2014, https://hbr.org/2014/07/how-6-countries-compare-on-executive-gender-balance.

7 Benxiang Zeng, 'Women's Political Participation in China: Improved or Not?' (2014) 15 *Journal of International Women's Studies* 136, 145–147.

8 Sylvie Fogiel-Bijaoui, 'The Cosmopolitan Future: A Feminist Approach' (2016) 5(3) *Laws* 34.

9 Data regarding single or lower house and upper house combined on the basis of information provided by National Parliaments by 1st December 2017. Inter-Parliamentary Union (IPU), 'Women in National Parliaments,' *Inter-Parliamentary Union*, accessed 16 May 2018, www.ipu.org/wmn-e/world.htm.

10 WGDAW, 'Thematic Analysis: Eliminating Discrimination Against Women in Political and Public Life with a Focus on Political Transition,' A/HRC/23/50, 2013, www.ohchr.org/Documents/Issues/Women/WG/A.HRC.23.50_English.pdf; Souad Abdennebi-Abderrahim, 'Study on Discrimination Against Women in Law and in Practice in Political and Public Life, Including During Times of Political Transitions,' 2013, www.ohchr.org/EN/Issues/Women/WGWomen/Pages/Discriminationinpublicandpoliticallife.aspx; Megan Alexandra Dersnah, 'Women in Political and Public Life: Global Report for the Working Group on the Issue of Discrimination Against Women in Law and in Practice,' 2013, www.ohchr.org/EN/Issues/Women/WGWomen/Pages/Discrimination inpublicandpoliticallife.aspx; International Idea Institute for Democracy and Electoral Assistance, 'Gender Quotas Database,' *International Idea Supporting Democracy Worldwide*, accessed 16 June 2018, www.idea.int/data-tools/data/gender-quotas/quotas; Jennifer Rosen, 'Gender Quotas for Women in National Politics: A Comparative Analysis Across Development Thresholds' (2017) 66 *Social Science Research* 82.

11 UN Women, 'Facts and Figures: Leadership and Political Participation,' *UN Women*, July 2017, www.unwomen.org/en/what-we-do/leadership-and-political-participation/facts-and-figures.

12 WGDAW, 'Report of the Working Group on the Issue of Discrimination Against Women in Law and in Practice on Its Mission to the United States of America,' 2016, A/HRC/32/44/Add.2, paras. 43–44, http://ap.ohchr.org/documents/dpage_e.aspx?si=A/HRC/32/44/Add.2.

13 Some examples include the Republican candidate Donald Trump persistently calling Clinton "crooked Hilary" and "a nasty woman", and the delegates at the Republican National Convention repeatedly breaking into chants of "Lock her up" while vendors outside the hall sold a variety of women-hating pins with slogans such as "don't be a pussy – vote for Trump in 2016"; "Trump 2016: finally someone with balls"; "trump that bitch"; "Hillary sucks but not like Monica." Peter Beinart, 'Fear of a Female President,' *The Atlantic*, October 2016, www.theatlantic.com/magazine/archive/2016/10/fear-of-a-female-president/497564/.

14 In her 2012 'Misogyny Speech' in parliament, Gillard stated: "If he wants to know what misogyny looks like . . . he needs a mirror. . . . I was offended . . . by [his] . . . catcalling across this table at me as I sit here as Prime Minister . . . [and standing] next to a sign that described me as a man's bitch." The Sunday Morning Herald, 'Transcript of Julia Gillard's Speech,' *The Sunday Morning Herald*, 10 October 2012, www.smh.com.au/politics/federal/transcript-of-julia-gillards-speech-20121010-27c36.html. See the speech on YouTube here: www.youtube.com/watch?v=7ziGZCE7fC8. See also Emine Saner, 'Top 10 Sexist Moments in Politics: Julia Gillard, Hillary Clinton and

More,' *The Guardian*, 14 June 2013, www.theguardian.com/politics/2013/jun/14/top-10-sexist-moments-politics.

15 Christine Lagarde, 'Women's Empowerment: An Economic Game Changer,' speech delivered at the Glamour's 2016 Women of the Year Awards, Los Angeles, 14 November 2016, www.imf.org/en/News/Articles/2016/11/14/SP111416-Womens-Empowerment-An-Economic-Game-Changer; Christine Lagarde and Erna Solberg, 'Why 2018 Must Be the Year for Women to Thrive,' *World Economic Forum*, 20 January 2018, www.weforum.org/agenda/2018/01/the-time-has-come-for-women-to-thrive-heres-how; Bérengère Sim, 'In Davos, Pioneering Women Are Chosen to Lead Again,' *The New York Times*, 21 January 2018, www.nytimes.com/2018/01/21/business/davos-world-economic-forum-women-leaders.html. The G8 includes Canada, France, Germany, Italy, Japan, Russia (suspended), United Kingdom, United States and the European Union (non-enumerated).

16 International Monetary Fund, 'Gender Diversity in the Executive Board – Draft Report of the Executive Board to the Board of Governors,' 1 July 2016, 3, 6.

17 Ibid.; The World Bank, 'Past Presidents,' *World Bank*, accessed 14 April 2018, www.worldbank.org/en/about/archives/history/past-presidents; The World Bank, 'Statement by the World Bank Board of Executive Directors on Doing Business – January 16, 2018,' *World Bank*, accessed 14 April 2018, www.worldbank.org/en/about/leadership/directors.

18 WTO, 'Women and the WTO Gender Statistics (1995–2016),' 2017, 5.

19 As of March 2018. See World Economic Forum, 'Leadership and Governance,' *World Economic Forum*, accessed 14 April 2018, www.weforum.org/about/leadership-and-governance.

20 Inter-Parliamentary Union and UN Women, 'Women in Politics 2017 Map,' *UN Women*, www.unwomen.org/en/digital-library/publications/2017/4/women-in-politics-2017-map; UN Women (n 11); UN Women, 'Press Release: Sluggish Progress on Women in Politics Will Hamper Development,' *UN Women*, 10 March 2015, www.unwomen.org/en/news/stories/2015/3/press-release-sluggish-progress-on-women-in-politics-will-hamper-development.

21 Inter-Parliamentary Union and UN Women (n 20).

22 Malliga Och, 'Macron and Trudeau Shouldn't Be So Proud of Appointing Women to Their Cabinets,' *The Conversation*, 29 June 2017, https://theconversation.com/macron-and-trudeau-shouldnt-be-so-proud-of-appointing-women-to-their-cabinets-79990.

23 Anne Vandermey, '7 Female Finance Ministers,' *Fortune*, 6 February 2014, http://fortune.com/2014/02/06/the-next-christine-lagarde-7-female-finance-ministers-fortunes-most-powerful-women-global-edition/; David Smith, 'Ngozi Okonjo-Iweala: A Woman to Make Africa Count,' *The Guardian*, 1 April 2012, www.theguardian.com/theobserver/2012/apr/01/profile-ngozi-okonjo-iweala; Forbes, 'Profile of Ngozi Okonjo-Iweala,' *Forbes*, accessed 14 April 2018, www.forbes.com/profile/ngozi-okonjo-iweala/; Jeremy Clift, 'People in Economics, Second Time Around' (2011) 48(4) *Finance & Development* 2; Forbes Woman Africa, 'The Accidental Economist: Dr. Ngozi Okonjo-Iweala,' *Forbes Africa*, 1 November 2013, www.forbesafrica.com/woman/2013/11/01/accidental-economist-dr-ngozi-okonjo-iweala/.

24 Ngozi Okonjo-Iweala, 'Nigeria Is Defending Our Girls,' *The Guardian*, 9 May 2014, www.theguardian.com/global/2014/may/09/nigeria-our-girls-boko-haram-chibok.

25 Cristina Bodea and Tara Iseneker, 'Exactly How Male-dominated Are Central Banks? Here Are the Numbers,' *The Washington Post*, 8 December 2017, www.washingtonpost.com/news/monkey-cage/wp/2017/12/08/exactly-how-male-dominated-are-central-banks-here-are-the-numbers/?utm_term=.38252a0bbb35. See also Ama Marston, 'Women, Business and Human Rights: Background Paper,' 2014, fn 27, www.ohchr.org/EN/Issues/Women/WGWomen/Pages/ESL.aspx.

26 Heather Long, 'Janet L. Yellen, America's First Female Fed Chair, Finishes to "Standing Ovation,"' *The Washington Post*, 13 December 2017, www.washingtonpost.com/news/wonk/wp/2017/12/13/janet-l-yellen-americas-first-female-fed-chair-finishes-to-standing-ovation/?utm_term=.ec4311186864.

27 As of March 2018. See European Central Bank, 'Executive Board Members – Terms of Office,' *European Central Bank*, accessed 14 April 2018, www.ecb.europa.eu/ecb/orga/decisions/eb/html/ebtimeline.en.html.

28 The female bank governor was Karnit Flug, who was chosen as one of the world's best bank governors by Global Finance Magazine. See Amiram Barkat, '"Global Finance" Again Ranks Flug Among Top Governors,' *Globes*, 6 September 2015, www.globes.co.il/en/article-global-finance-again-ranks-flug-among-top-governors-1001066668.

29 Vered Ramon-Rivlin, 'Women at the Helm of Israel's Financial Institutions,' *Globes*, 10 July 2016, www.globes.co.il/en/article-women-at-the-helm-of-israels-financial-institutions-1001138479.

30 Inter-Parliamentary Union, 'Equality in Politics: A Survey of Women and Men in Parliaments,' Reports and Documents No. 54, 2008, 44, http://archive.ipu.org/pdf/publications/equality08-e.pdf.

31 See Mukesh Eswaran, 'How Did Women Gain Suffrage, and What Are Its Economic Effects' in *Why Gender Matters in Economics* (Princeton University Press 2014) 305. It has been discerned from voting patterns that women and parents of girls tend to give support to political parties with a social agenda.

32 Inter-Parliamentary Union (n 30).

33 WGDAW, 'Report of the Working Group on the Issue of Discrimination Against Women in Law and in Practice Addendum: Mission to Iceland,' A/HRC/26/39/Add.1, 2014, www.ohchr.org/EN/Issues/Women/WGWomen/Pages/CountryVisits.aspx.

34 Gay Flashman, '"A Panel Not a Manel," and Other Top Gender Quotes from Davos 2018,' *World Economic Forum*, 26 January 2018, www.weforum.org/agenda/2018/01/Davos-2018-women-gender-trudeau-malala. See also Sim (n 15).

35 David Callahan, *The Givers: Wealth, Power, and Philanthropy in a New Gilded Age* (Knopf 2017).

36 Marston (n 25) fn 2.

37 While the first nine places were countries, Walmart was ranked 10th, beating the government revenue of major global economies including Australia, South Korea and India. From Walmart down, there were mostly businesses, with only 22 more countries featuring. See Global Justice Now, '10 Biggest Corporations Make More Money than Most Countries in the World Combined,' *Global Justice Now*, 12 September 2016, www.globaljustice.org.uk/news/2016/sep/12/10-biggest-corporations-make-more-money-most-countries-world-combined; Joe Myers, 'How Do the World's Biggest Companies Compare to the Biggest Economies?,' *World Economic Forum*, 19 October 2016, www.weforum.org/agenda/2016/10/corporations-not-countries-dominate-the-list-of-the-world-s-biggest-economic-entities/; Duncan Green, 'The World's Top 100 Economies: 31 Countries; 69 Corporations,' *People, Spaces, Deliberations Blog*, 20 September 2016, https://blogs.worldbank.org/publicsphere/world-s-top-100-economies-31-countries-69-corporations.

38 Joseph Stiglitz, 'Beware of TPP's Investor – State Dispute Settlement Provision,' *Roosevelt Institute*, 28 March 2016, http://rooseveltinstitute.org/beware-tpps-investor-state-dispute-settlement-provision/; The Economist, 'Investor-state Dispute Settlement: The Arbitration Game,' *The Economist*, 11 October 2014, www.economist.com/news/finance-and-economics/21623756-governments-are-souring-treaties-protect-foreign-investors-arbitration.

39 World Bank Group, 'Women, Business and the Law 2016: Getting to Equal,' 2015, 3, Washington, DC: World Bank. © World Bank. https://openknowledge.worldbank.org/

handle/10986/22546 License: CC BY 3.0 IGO. See also World Bank Group, International Finance Corporation, 'Women, Business, and the Law 2014: Removing Restrictions to Enhance Gender Equality,' 2013, London: Bloomsbury. © World Bank. https://openknowledge.worldbank.org/handle/10986/20528 License: CC BY-NC-ND 3.0 IGO.

40 Women senior managers were likely to say that they do more than half of the housework seven times more than men at the same level. Excerpted from 'Women in the Workplace,' 2016, 17, McKinsey & Company, www.mckinsey.com. Copyright © 2018 McKinsey & Company. All rights reserved. Reprinted by permission.

41 Fifty-seven per cent of women versus 38% of men. Excerpted from 'Women in the Workplace,' 2017, 18, McKinsey & Company, www.mckinsey.com. Copyright © 2018 McKinsey & Company. All rights reserved. Reprinted by permission.

42 The Deloitte Global Center for Corporate Governance, 'Women in the Boardroom: A Global Perspective,' 4th edn, 2015, 6, https://www2.deloitte.com/content/dam/Deloitte/global/Documents/Risk/gx-ccg-women-in-the-boardroom-a-global-perspective4.pdf. © 2015. Used with permission. For information, contact Deloitte Touche Tohmatsu Limited.

43 Sara Ashley O'Brien, 'Marissa Mayer on Maternity Leave: "I Understand I'm the Exception,"' *CNN Tech*, 6 May 2016, http://money.cnn.com/2016/05/06/technology/yahoo-marissa-mayer-maternity-leave/index.html.

44 Credit Suisse, 'The CS Gender 3000: Women in Senior Management,' 2014, 34, https://publications.credit-suisse.com/tasks/render/file/index.cfm?fileid=8128F3C0-99BC-22E6-838E2A5B1E4366DF. See also Natalie Bacon, 'Can Millennials in Corporate Jobs Achieve Work-life Balance?' *Forbes*, 11 January 2017, www.forbes.com/sites/nataliebacon/2017/01/11/can-millennials-in-corporate-jobs-achieve-work-life-balance/#2d6ee096216f; Laura Stampler, 'CEO Dads Open Up About Balancing Fatherhood and Work,' *Time*, 15 September 2014, http://time.com/3342431/work-life-balance-fatherhood-ceos/.

45 O'Brien (n 43).

46 ILO, 'Women in Business and Management: Gaining Momentum,' 2015, 95, www.ilo.org/wcmsp5/groups/public/---dgreports/---dcomm/---publ/documents/publication/wcms_316450.pdf.

47 See, for example, Stampler (n 44).

48 Rebecca J. Cook and Simone Cusack, *Gender Stereotyping: Transnational Legal Perspectives* (University of Pennsylvania Press 2010) 28.

49 *Price Waterhouse v Hopkins* 490 U.S. 228 (1989). See also Andrea Sachs, 'A Slap at Sex Stereotypes,' *Time*, 24 June 2001, http://content.time.com/time/magazine/article/0,9171,151787,00.html.

50 Sheryl Sandberg, *Lean In: Women, Work, and the Will to Lead* (Knopf 2013).

51 McKinsey & Company (n 40) 10.

52 Ibid. 13–14. See also McKinsey & Company (n 41) 24–25.

53 McKinsey & Company (n 40) 12.

54 ILO (n 46) 2.

55 McKinsey & Company (n 41) 2.

56 This picture emerges from the available data on women 'at the top' (board chairpersons, board members, senior managers, CEOs, etc.) but, as this data can only be obtained from surveys conducted nationally and globally by different groups and organisations using different company samples which are not corresponding as regards size, sector or region, it constitutes a problematic source for accurate comparison. See ILO (n 46) 12.

57 Catalyst, 'Women on Corporate Boards Globally,' *Catalyst*, 16 March 2017, www.catalyst.org/knowledge/women-corporate-boards-globally; Credit Suisse, 'The CS Gender 3000: The Reward for Change,' 2016, 8, https://glg.it/assets/docs/csri-gender-3000.pdf; Linda-Eling Lee, Ric Marshall, Damion Rallis and Matt Moscardi, 'Women on

Boards Global Trends in Gender Diversity on Corporate Boards,' *MSCI*, 2015, www.msci.com/documents/10199/04b6f646-d638-4878-9c61-4eb91748a82b; The Deloitte Global Center for Corporate Governance, 'Women in the Boardroom: A Global Perspective,' 5th edn, 2017, 3, www.gbaforwomen.org/download/women-boardroom-global-perspective/. © 2017. Used with permission. For information, contact Deloitte Touche Tohmatsu Limited.

58 Credit Suisse 2016 (n 57) 4.

59 Lee, Marshall, Rallis and Moscardi (n 57) 3; Deloitte 2017 (n 57) 79; Credit Suisse 2016 (n 57) 8.

60 Credit Suisse 2014 (n 44) 7–9.

61 Ibid. 9; Credit Suisse 2016 (n 57) 8.

62 ILO (n 46) 37.

63 Lee, Marshall, Rallis and Moscardi (n 57) 3.

64 Ibid.; Catalyst (n 57); Miriam Schwartz-Ziv, 'Gender and Board Activeness: The Role of a Critical Mass' (2017) 52(2) *Journal of Financial and Quantitative Analysis* 751.

65 See discussion of temporary special measures in the Introduction of the book.

66 ILO (n 46) 44; Marston (n 25) 15–18. See also Deloitte 2017 (n 57); Deloitte 2015 (n 42).

67 See Government Companies Law (Amendment No. 7), 1993 (Israel), which requires to appoint an appropriate number of women to the directorates of government companies and see Companies Law, 1999 (Israel), s 239(d); Claire Zillman, 'The EU Is Taking a Drastic Step to Put More Women on Corporate Boards,' *Fortune*, 20 November 2017, http://fortune.com/2017/11/20/women-on-boards-eu-gender-quota/.

68 Deloitte 2015 (n 42) 48, 53; Marston (n 25) 16.

69 ILO (n 46) 42. Denmark is the country with the eight highest number of women on its boards but it drops to the last place in number of women board chairs as not one of the boards had a female chair. See Deloitte 2017 (n 57) 49, 79.

70 Madeline Farber, 'Women and Minorities Serving on Corporate Boards Are Paid Less, Study Finds,' *Fortune*, 11 January 2017, http://fortune.com/2017/01/11/women-minorities-boards-pay-gap/.

71 Marston (n 25) 18; ILO (n 46) 44; Credit Suisse 2014 (n 44) 5, 44–46; Credit Suisse 2016 (n 57) 4–6.

72 Credit Suisse 2014 (n 44) 44. For company initiatives see for example Pui-Wing Tam, 'Join Our Board: Companies Hotly Pursue New Wave of Women in Tech,' *New York Times*, 30 December 2016, www.nytimes.com/2016/12/30/technology/join-our-board-companies-hotly-pursue-new-wave-of-women-in-tech.html.

73 ILO (n 46) 48.

74 Credit Suisse 2014 (n 44) 44; Credit Suisse 2016 (n 57) 6.

75 Credit Suisse 2014 (n 44) 13; Grant Thornton, 'Women in Business: Turning Promise into Practice,' Grant Thornton International Business Report 2016, 2016, 2, www.grantthornton.global/globalassets/wib_turning_promise_into_practice.pdf.

76 Credit Suisse 2014 (n 44) 13; Thornton (n 75) 2, 5. According to Grant Thornton's methodology the G7 includes: Canada, France, Germany, Italy, Japan, United Kingdom and United States.

77 Credit Suisse 2016 (n 57) 16.

78 ILO (n 46) 11, 17–19.

79 Credit Suisse 2014 (n 44) 5.

80 ILO (n 46) 2–3.

81 Credit Suisse, for instance, reported in 2014 that CEO roles remain a male preserve with women representing about 4%. See Credit Suisse 2014 (n 44) 13. In the US, Fortune magazine reported in 2016 that women accounted for only 4.2% of CEO's in Fortune 500 corporations and Catalyst has reported that as of January 2018, women held 5% of CEO positions at the S&P 500 companies. See Valentina Zarya, 'The

Percentage of Female CEOs in the Fortune 500 Drops to 4%,' *Fortune*, 6 June 2016, http://fortune.com/2016/06/06/women-ceos-fortune-500-2016/; Catalyst, 'Women CEOs of the S&P 500,' *Catalyst*, 6 August 2018, www.catalyst.org/knowledge/women-ceos-sp-500. In Europe, according to a 2016 report by S&P Global Market Intelligence, women accounted for 4% of CEOs in the S&P Euro 350 and according to 2016 data from the European Commission only 5.1% of the largest listed companies in Europe have a woman CEO. See Laura Cohn, 'Europe Lags the U.S. When It Comes to Female CEOs,' *Fortune*, 28 September 2016, http://fortune.com/2016/09/28/europe-female-ceo-sp/; Pavle Sabic and David Henslovitz, 'How Times Have Changed? Transatlantic CEO Gender Gap Analysis of the S&P Euro 350 and S&P 500,' *S&P Global Market Intelligence*, September 2016, http://media.spglobal.com/documents/SPGlobal_Market+Intelligence_Article_28+September+2016_How+Times+Have+Changed+-+CEO+Gender+Gap+Analysis.pdf; Věra Jourová, 'Gender Balance on Corporate Boards: Europe Is Cracking the Glass Ceiling,' Commissioner for Justice, Consumers and Gender Equality, fact sheet, July 2016, 4, http://ec.europa.eu/newsroom/document.cfm?doc_id=46280.

82 Data on large corporations in developing countries shows very low figures for female CEOs: in African countries for example, the percentages range from 3.6% in South Africa in 2012 to Cameroon and Ghana where it is rare to find a female CEO of a large company. ILO (n 46) 30.

83 Credit Suisse 2016 (n 57) 34. See also Mark Misercola, 'Higher Returns with Women in Decision-making Positions,' *Credit Suisse*, 3 October 2016, www.credit-suisse.com/corporate/en/articles/news-and-expertise/higher-returns-with-women-in-decision-making-positions-201610.html. See also Harvard Business Review Staff, 'What CEOs Really Worry About,' *Harvard Business Review*, November 2016, https://hbr.org/2016/11/the-best-performing-ceos-in-the-world.

84 McKinsey & Company (n 40) 13.

85 Credit Suisse 2016 (n 57) 34.

86 Michelle K. Ryan and S. Alexander Haslam, 'The Glass Cliff: Evidence that Women Are Over-represented in Precarious Leadership Positions' (2005) 16(2) *British Journal of Management* 81. See also Susanne Bruckmüller and Nyla R. Branscombe, 'The Glass Cliff: When and Why Women Are Selected as Leaders in Crisis Contexts' (2010) 49(3) *British Journal of Social Psychology* 433; Credit Suisse 2016 (n 57) 30.

87 Bruckmüller and Branscombe (n 86). It should be noted that the existence of a glass cliff phenomenon is challenged though not fully refuted by the Credit Suisse 2016 report. See Credit Suisse 2016 (n 57) 30–33.

88 McKinsey & Company (n 41) 2, 4–5.

89 United Nations Human Rights Office of the High Commissioner, 'Guiding Principles on Business and Human Rights; Implementing the United Nations "Protect, Respect and Remedy" Framework,' 2011, HR/PUB/11/04, www.ohchr.org/Documents/Publications/GuidingPrinciplesBusinessHR_EN.pdf.

90 The Convention on the Elimination of all Forms of Discrimination Against Women (entered into force 3 September 1981) 1249 UNTS 13 (CEDAW), www.un.org/womenwatch/daw/cedaw/text/econvention.htm.

91 Frances Raday, 'Embedding Gender in the Business and Human Rights Agenda,' Statement on behalf of the Working Group on the Issue of Discrimination Against Women in Law and in Practice at the 2016 United Nations Annual Forum on Business and Human Rights, Geneva, 14–16 November 2016.

92 Guiding Principles (n 89) 5–6: "how to consider effectively issues of gender, vulnerability and/or marginalization, recognizing the specific challenges that may be faced by indigenous peoples, women, national or ethnic minorities, religious and linguistic minorities, children, persons with disabilities, and migrant workers and their families."

93 WGDAW Report on Economic and Social Life (n 3) para 124; HRC Resolution (n 4).

94 See *Women's Empowerment Principles Website*, accessed 29 April 2018, http://weprinciples.org/Site/.

95 ETO Consortium, 'Maastricht Principles on Extraterritorial Obligations of States in the Area of Economic, Social and Cultural Rights,' 2013, www.etoconsortium.org/nc/en/main-navigation/library/maastricht-principles/?tx_drblob_pi1%5BdownloadUid%5D=23.

96 Benson Honig, 'Compensatory Entrepreneurship: Avoiding the Pitfalls of Global Isomorphic Entrepreneurship Research and Activities' (2017) 6(3) *Iberoamerican Journal of Entrepreneurship and Small Business* 452.

97 Mirjana Radović Marković, 'The Change of Women's Roles Through the Centuries: Confrontation of Tradition and New Challenges' in Mirjana Radović Marković (ed), *The Perspective of Women's Entrepreneurship in the Age of Globalization* (Information Age Publishing 2007) 3; Loza Emile, 'Female Entrepreneurship Theory: A Multidisciplinary Review of Resources' (2011) 1–2 *Journal of Women's Entrepreneurship and Education* 26; Vanita Yadav and Jeemol Unni, 'Women Entrepreneurship: Research Review and Future Directions' (2016) 6(1) *Journal of Global Entrepreneurship Research* 12.

98 Emile (n 97) 36–40.

99 Donna J. Kelley and others, 'Women's Entrepreneurship 2016/2017 Report,' Global Entrepreneurship Monitor (GEM), 2017, 6, 8, 16–22, http://gemconsortium.org/report/49860. See also Donna J. Kelley and others, 'Special Report: Women's Entrepreneurship,' Global Entrepreneurship Monitor (GEM), 2015, http://gemconsortium.org/report/49281.

100 Maria Minniti and Wim Naudé, 'Introduction: What Do We Know About the Patterns and Determinants of Female Entrepreneurship Across Countries?' (2010) 22(3) *European Journal of Development Research* 277–293. See also OECD, 'Policy Brief on Women's Entrepreneurship,' 2016, www.oecd.org/cfe/smes/Policy-Brief-on-Women-s-Entrepreneurship.pdf.

101 ILO (n 46) 51. As the ILO notes, a key challenge in identifying trends on women in business is the lack of a comprehensive data set over time.

102 These high-parity economies are located in two regions: Asia (Indonesia, the Philippines and Vietnam) and Latin America (Mexico and Brazil). GEM 2016/2017 (n 99) 17.

103 Ibid. 8, 16–22. See also GEM 2015 (n 99).

104 As regards the country classification GEM uses, it draws from the World Economic Forum system and includes the following: (1) Factor-driven: recognised as early stages of economic development, usually marked by a largely rural population working primarily in sectors of agriculture and the extraction of natural resources. Population migration from rural to more urban areas drives change in economic activities. (2) Factor-efficiency transition: describes economies in transition from factor to efficiency-driven. (3) Efficiency-driven: reflects changes in increased participation in industrial sectors, including economies of scale leading to advances in productivity. Also includes the development of financial institutions. (4) Efficiency-innovation transition: describes economies in transition from efficiency to innovation-driven. (5) Innovation-driven: describes mature economies, with a distinct shift to more service-based business as well as industrial sectors based on knowledge intensity and innovation. GEM 2016/2017 (n 99) 12–13.

105 Ibid. 27.

106 Minniti and Naudé (n 100) 286.

107 Yet, GEM stresses that there are exceptions to this general rule. GEM 2016/2017 (n 99) 19–20.

108 Medium income countries.

109 David Abney and Arancha González Laya, 'This Is Why Women Must Play a Greater Role in the Global Economy,' *World Economic Forum*, 24 January 2018,

www.weforum.org/agenda/2018/01/this-is-why-women-must-play-a-greater-role-in-the-global-economy.

110 GEM 2015 (n 99) 51–53.

111 GEM 2015 (n 99) 52.

112 Credit Suisse 2014 (n 44) 40. See also OECD 2016 (n 100).

113 GEM 2016/2017 (n 99) 40–41. North America stands out for high female participation in ICT, mostly due to Canada, which reports greatest female activity in this sector across the entire GEM sample.

114 The story is from the GEM 2015 (n 99) 25.

115 Kerry A. Dolan, 'Forbes 2017 Billionaires List: Meet the Richest People on the Planet,' *Forbes*, 20 March 2017, www.forbes.com/sites/kerryadolan/2017/03/20/forbes-2017-billionaires-list-meet-the-richest-people-on-the-planet/#21c9f6e162ff.

116 Oxfam, 'Reward Work, Not Wealth: To End the Inequality Crisis, We Must Build an Economy for Ordinary Working People, Not the Rich and Powerful,' Briefing Paper, January 2018, https://d1tn3vj7xz9fdh.cloudfront.net/s3fs-public/file_attachments/bp-reward-work-not-wealth-220118-en.pdf; Oxfam International, 'Richest 1 Percent Bagged 82 Percent of Wealth Created Last Year – Poorest Half of Humanity Got Nothing,' *Oxfam International: The Power of People Against Poverty*, 22 January 2018, www.oxfam.org/en/pressroom/pressreleases/2018-01-22/richest-1-percent-bagged-82-percent-wealth-created-last-year. See also Dolan (n 115).

117 Oxfam 'Reward Work, Not Wealth' (n 116) 8.

118 Chloe Sorvino, 'It's a Record-breaking Year for Self-made Women Billionaires: Here's Why,' *Forbes*, 21 March 2017, www.forbes.com/sites/chloesorvino/2017/03/21/2017-record-breaking-self-made-women-world-billionaires-list-wealth/#47fe67b358bc. See also Chloe Sorvino, 'The World's 56 Self-made Women Billionaires: The Definitive Ranking,' *Forbes*, 8 March 2017, www.forbes.com/sites/chloesorvino/2017/03/08/the-worlds-56-self-made-women-billionaires-the-definitive-ranking/#6d8760fa68a2.

119 Ibid.

120 Ibid. See also Forbes Corporate Communications, 'Forbes Releases World's Self-made Women Billionaires List,' *Forbes*, 8 March 2017, www.forbes.com/sites/forbespr/2017/03/08/forbes-releases-worlds-self-made-women-billionaires list/#281a51be203f.

121 Ruth Umoh, 'This Former Factory Worker Is Now the World's Richest Self-made Woman,' *CNBC*, 17 July 2017, www.cnbc.com/2017/07/17/meet-zhou-qunfei-the-worlds-richest-self-made-woman.html; Sorvino, *A Record-breaking Year* (n 118); Sorvino, *Self-made Women Billionaires* (n 118).

122 Veronica Quezada, '10 Things You Probably Don't Know About Oprah and Her Money,' *Time Money*, 11 January 2018, http://time.com/money/5098012/how-oprah-made-all-of-her-money/; Alix Langone, 'Oprah Winfrey Is Worth Nearly $3 Billion: Here's How She Made Her Money,' *Time Money*, 8 January 2018 (Updated 9 March 2018), http://time.com/money/5092809/oprah-winfrey-net-worth-billionaire; Luisa Kroll and Kerry Dolan (eds), 'America's Richest Self-made Women,' *Forbes*, 11 July 2018, www.forbes.com/self-made-women/#2b1d26566d96.

123 OECD, 'Policy Brief on the Future of Work: Going Digital: The Future of Work for Women,' 2017, 2, www.oecd.org/employment/Going-Digital-the-Future-of-Work-for Women.pdf.www.oecd.org/employment/Going-Digital-the-Future-of-Work-for-Women.pdf.

124 ILO (n 46) 61. See also OECD 2016 (n 100); International Finance Corporation and Global Partnership for Financial Inclusion, 'Strengthening Access to Finance for Women-owned SMEs in Developing Countries,' 2011, www.ifc.org/wps/wcm/connect/a4774a004a3f66539f0f9f8969adcc27/G20_Women_Report.pdf?MOD=AJPERES.

125 Iiris Aaltio, Paula Kyrö and Elisabeth Sundin, 'Introduction: Women Entrepreneurs – Creators and Creations of Social Capital' in Iiris Aaltio, Paula Kyrö and Elisabeth Sundin (eds), *Women, Entrepreneurship and Social Capital: A Dialogue and Construction*

(Copenhagen Business School Press 2008) 14. The contributors to this 2008 collection of Aaltio, Kyrö, and Sundin observed that there are prevalent gender-biased views as to the capabilities of women candidates for venture capital investments.

126 A reality television format in which entrepreneurs pitch their business ideas to a panel of venture capitalists in order to secure investment.

127 Hila Keren, 'Women in the Shark Tank: Entrepreneurship and Feminism in the Neo-liberal Age' (2016) 34(1) *Columbia Journal of Gender and Law* 75.

128 A study of 1.1 million eBay auction transactions, between 2009 and 2012, showed that women received a smaller number of bids and earned considerably less than men for selling the exact same items: for new products women earned only 80 cents on every dollar that men earned and 97 for used products. According to the researchers, the gender gap existed despite the fact that eBay does not actually declare the gender of its sellers to its buyers but the researchers showed that gender is very often discernible from information gathered from a quick look at the seller's profile, from the range of items that are offered or from the seller's username. Tamar Kricheli-Katz and Tali Regev, 'How Many Cents on the Dollar? Women and Men in Product Markets' (2016) 2(2) *Science Advances* 1.

129 Marston (n 25) 14.

130 Keren (n 127) n 66.

131 The International Monetary Fund, 'IMF Annual Report 2016: Finding Solutions Together,' 2016, 54, www.imf.org/external/pubs/ft/ar/2016/eng/pdf/ar16_eng.pdf.

132 World Bank, 'World Development Report 2012: Gender Equality and Development,' 2012, 203, Washington, DC: World Bank. © World Bank. https://openknowledge.worldbank.org/handle/10986/4391 License: CC BY 3.0 IGO.

133 The gap is substantial in several countries where men were more than one and a half times as likely as women to report that they could access the finances to start a business: Italy (2.3 times), Ireland (1.8 times), United Kingdom (1.7 times), Finland (1.6 times), France (1.6 times), Slovenia (1.6 times) and Germany (1.5 times). See OECD 'Policy Brief on Women's Entrepreneurship' (n 100) 14.

134 Valentina Zarya, 'Venture Capital's Funding Gender Gap Is Actually Getting Worse,' *Fortune*, 13 March 2017, http://fortune.com/2017/03/13/female-founders-venture-capital/.

135 Furthermore, in the United States it was found that fewer than 5% of all venture capital–funded firms have women on their executive teams, and only 2.7% had a female CEO. Sarah Granger, 'A Wave of Angel Investing Organizations Focus on Women,' *Harvard Business Review*, 4 December 2012, https://hbr.org/2012/12/a-wave-of-angel-investing-orga; Wendy DuBow and Allison-Scott Pruitt, 'The Comprehensive Case for Investing More VC Money in Women-led Startups,' *Harvard Business Review*, 18 September 2017, https://hbr.org/2017/09/the-comprehensive-case-for-investing-more-vc-money-in-women-led-startups.

136 Meg Jones, 'The Economic Empowerment of Women Through Trade,' ITC Presentation, Workshop on Business and Gender, Office of the UN High Commissioner for Human Rights, Geneva, 2 October 2013.

137 For example, Kenya put in place Public Procurement and Disposal (Preference and Reservations) Regulations to ensure access to government contracts by enterprises owned by women, youth and persons with disabilities. See Wanjiru Gathira, 'What Should Be Done to Support Women Enterprises to Participate in and Benefit from the Lucrative Public Procurement Market,' Social Impact Institute, June 2013. In the United States in 2011 the federal government had a stated goal of awarding 5% of federal contracts to women-owned businesses, but this goal was reached for the first time only in 2015. See WGDAW Report on the United States (n 12) para 48.

138 The Official Website for Noble Prize, 'Muhammad Yunus – Biographical,' *Nobel Prize Official Website*, accessed 1 May 2018, www.nobelprize.org/nobel_prizes/peace/laureates/2006/yunus-bio.html.

139 See, for example, ILO, 'Small Change, Big Changes: Women and Microfinance,' accessed 1 May 2018, www.ilo.org/wcmsp5/groups/public/@dgreports/@gender/documents/meetingdocument/wcms_091581.pdf.

140 Vivienne Walt, 'Does Microfinancing Really Work? A New Book Says No,' *Time*, 6 January 2012, http://content.time.com/time/world/article/0,8599,2103831,00.html; David Roodman, *Due Diligence: An Impertinent Inquiry into Microfinance* (unknown edn, Center for Global Development 2011). See more information on microfinance in Credit Suisse 2016 (n 57) 36–40. See also Emile (n 97) 45.

141 See the Introduction and Parts II and III of the book.

142 GEM 2016/2017 Report (n 99) 12 and references there.

143 See also 'Strengthening Access to Finance' (n 124); World Trade Organization, 'Removing Barriers to Women's Participation in Trade Critical for Economic Development,' *World Trade Organization*, 12 July 2017, www.wto.org/english/news_e/news17_e/gr17_12jul17_e.htm; Anna Stupnytska, Kathryn Koch, Amy MacBeath, Sandra Lawson and Kathy Matsui, 'Giving Credit Where It Is Due How Closing the Credit Gap for Women-owned SMEs Can Drive Global Growth,' *Goldman Sachs Global Market Institute*, 28 February 2014, www.goldmansachs.com/our-thinking/public-policy/gmi-folder/gmi-report-pdf.pdf; Credit Suisse 2016 (n 57); Elaine Pofeldt, 'Why Women Entrepreneurs Will Be the Economic Force to Reckon with in 2017,' *CNBC*, 28 February 2017 (Updated 6 March 2017), www.cnbc.com/2017/02/28/why-women-entrepreneurs-will-be-economic-force-to-reckon-with-in-2017.html; Lakshmi Puri, 'Women Entrepreneurs Can Drive Economic Growth,' speech delivered at the Global Conference on Women and Entrepreneurship, in Hangzhou, China, 17 July 2017, www.unwomen.org/en/news/stories/2017/7/speech-ded-puri-she-era; Geri Stengel, 'Why the Force Will Be with Women Entrepreneurs in 2016,' *Forbes*, 6 January 2016, www.forbes.com/sites/geristengel/2016/01/06/why-the-force-will-be-with-women-entrepreneurs-in-2016/#2ee75d2f4f8b; Tory Burch, 'Why the World Needs Women Entrepreneurs,' *The Economist*, 18 November 2013, www.economist.com/news/21589133-investing-businesswomen-will-boost-economy-everyone-says-tory-burch-chief-executive-and.

144 ILO, 'Job Creation in Small and Medium-sized Enterprises Recommendation,' 1998 (No 189), www.ilo.org/dyn/normlex/en/f?p=NORMLEXPUB:55:0::NO::P55_TYPE,P55_LANG,P55_DOCUMENT,P55_NODE:REC,en,R189,%2FDocument.

145 See ILO, 'Women's Entrepreneurship Development (WED) Programme,' accessed 16 May 2018, www.ilo.org/empent/areas/womens-entrepreneurship-development-wed/lang--en/index.htm.

146 See ITC, *SheTrades Website*, accessed 18 September 2018, www.shetrades.com/en.

147 Kate Higgins, 'Gender and Free Trade Agreements: Best Practices and Policy Guidance,' *The North-South Institute*, 2012, 15, www.nsi-ins.ca/wp-content/uploads/2013/03/2013-Gender-and-FTAs-Best-Practices-and-Policy-Guidance.pdf. See also The Canadian Trade Commissioner Service, 'Business Women in International Trade (BWIT),' *The Canadian Trade Commissioner Service*, accessed 16 May 2018, http://tradecommissioner.gc.ca/businesswomen-femmesdaffaires/index.aspx?lang=eng.

148 See *The Global Banking Alliance for Women (GBA) Website*, accessed 16 May 2018, www.gbaforwomen.org/.

149 See *The Mann Deshi Mahila Sahakari Bank Website*, accessed 16 May 2018, www.manndeshibank.com/.

150 See Marston (n 25) 17, 22–24. It is important to note that cooperatives generate 20% more salaried jobs than the world's transnational corporations. See Maria Elena Chavez Hertig, '100 Million Jobs: The Contribution of Cooperatives to Employment Creation,' ILO Cooperative Branch, presentation on the role of cooperatives in employment creation the United Nations Department of Economic and Social Affairs (UN DESA) side event, 'Reducing Poverty Through Employment Generation: The Role of

Cooperatives,' which was held during the 46th UN Commission for Social Development, 1 January 2008, www.ilo.org/empent/Publications/WCMS_101313/lang–en/index.htm.

151 Either by law or as part of cooperative bylaws. This includes rules that only one member per family can enjoy membership rights, which in conjunction with cultural norms often means that members selected for households are male. Additionally, many agricultural coops require ownership of land as a prerequisite. Again this disadvantages women given unequal land ownership in inheritance laws and practices. It is important to note however, that in the UK for example, there are twice as many female directors of UK retail cooperatives than of FTSE (Financial Times Stock Exchange) companies. Co-operatives UK, 'Women on Boards of Co-operative Retailers Double Those of FTSE Companies,' *CO-OPS*, 9 March 2016, www.uk.coop/newsroom/women-boards-co-operative-retailers-double-those-ftse-companies.

152 ILO, Promotion of Cooperatives Recommendation, 2002 (No. 193) (entered into force 20 June 2002), www.ilo.org/dyn/normlex/en/f?p=NORMLEXPUB:12100:0::NO::P12100_ILO_CODE:R193.

153 ILO, 'Advancing Gender Equality: The Co-operative Way,' 2015, 3, www.ilo.org/wcmsp5/groups/public/---ed_emp/---emp_ent/---coop/documents/publication/wcms_379095.pdf. India sets a good example in the context of increasing women's participation and leadership: in Maharashtra, local government incorporated gender quotas in legislation governing cooperatives, creating a quota of 30% female representation on their boards of directors. India is also at the forefront of creating a union for women's informal small business owners and workers. Self Employed Women's Association (SEWA) has mobilised and organised women workers into a union and has helped their members form a number of worker-owned and run cooperatives. In 1992, SEWA established the Gujarat State Women's SEWA Cooperative Federation, a state-level organisation of 98 women cooperatives. The Federation provides training courses, cooperative education and management, marketing and design services. See Marston (n 25) 23–24.

154 'Beijing Declaration and Platform for Action,' adopted at the Fourth World Conference on Women at Beijing, China, 4–15 September 1995, para 35 of the Declaration, www.un.org/womenwatch/daw/beijing/pdf/BDPfA%20E.pdf.

155 CEDAW (n 90) art 13(b).

156 Ibid. art 14.

157 Beate Rudolphe, 'Article 13' in Marsha A. Freeman, Christine Chinkin and Beate Rudolf (eds), *The UN Convention on the Elimination of All Forms of Discrimination Against Women: A Commentary* (Oxford University Press 2012) 339.

158 HRC Resolution (n 4) para 9.

159 United Nations Sustainable Development Goals, 'Goal 5: Achieve Gender Equality and Empower All Women and Girls,' *Sustainable Development Knowledge Platform*, Target 5.A and Indicators 5.A.1 and 5.A.2, accessed 1 May 2018, https://sustainabledevelopment.un.org/sdg5.

160 See WGDAW Report on Economic and Social Life (n 3). This recommendation of the WGDAW was not adopted by the Human Rights Council in its 2014 resolution. See HRC Resolution (n 4).

161 Diane Elson, 'Recognize, Reduce, and Redistribute Unpaid Care Work: How to Close the Gender Gap' (2017) 26(2) *New Labor Forum* 52, 57.

162 Janet G. Stotsky, 'IMF Working Paper: Gender Budgeting: Fiscal Context and Current Outcomes,' International Monetary Fund, Research Department and Strategy, Policy, and Review Department, 2016, WP/16/149, 9, 25–27 and references there, www.imf.org/external/pubs/ft/wp/2016/wp16149.pdf.

163 Ibid. 4. See also Rhonda Sharp and Ray Broomhill, 'Budgeting for Equality: The Australian Experience' (2002) 8(1) *Feminist Economics* 25, 42.

164 For example, in Rwanda, Uganda and the Indian state of Kerala. See Stotsky (n 162) 25.

165 Diane Elson and Sharp Rhonda, 'Gender-responsive Budgeting and Women's Poverty' in Sylvia Chant (ed), *The International Handbook of Gender and Poverty: Concepts, Research and Policy* (Edward Elgar 2010) 522; Diane Elson, 'Budgeting for Women's Rights: Monitoring Government Budgets for Compliance with CEDAW,' *UNIFEM*, May 2006, www.internationalbudget.org/wp-content/uploads/Budgeting-for-Women%E2%80%99s-Rights-Monitoring-Government-Budgets-for-Compliance-with-CEDAW.pdf.

166 Catalyst, 'New Catalyst Study Links More Women Leaders to Greater Corporate Social Responsibility,' *Catalyst*, 16 November 2011, www.catalyst.org/media/new-catalyst-study-links-more-women-leaders-greater-corporate-social-responsibility; Rachel Soares, Christopher Marquis and Matthew Lee, *Gender and Corporate Social Responsibility: It's a Matter of Sustainability* (Catalyst 2011); Robert J. Williams, 'Women on Corporate Boards of Directors and Their Influence on Corporate Philanthropy' (2003) 42(1) *Journal of Business Ethics* 1; Corinne Post, Noushi Rahman and Emily Rubow, 'Green Governance: Boards of Directors Composition and Environmental Corporate Social Responsibility' (2011) 50(1) *Business & Society* 189.

167 See, for example, Catalyst, 'Companies with More Women Board Directors Experience Higher Financial Performance, According to Latest Catalyst Bottom Line Report,' *Catalyst*, accessed 16 May 2018, www.catalyst.org/media/companies-more-women-board-directors-experience-higher-financial-performance-according-latest; Francesca Lagerberg, 'The Value of Diversity,' *Grant Thornton*, 29 September 2015, www.grantthornton.global/en/insights/articles/diverse-boards-in-india-uk-and-us-outperform-male-only-peers-by-us$655bn/; Vivian Hunt, Dennis Layton and Sara Prince, 'Why Diversity Matters,' *McKinsey & Company Organization*, January 2015, www.mckinsey.com/business-functions/organization/our-insights/why-diversity-matters; Erica Hersh, 'Why Diversity Matters: Women on Boards of Directors,' *Harvard T.H. Chan School of Public Health*, 21 July 2016, www.hsph.harvard.edu/ecpe/why-diversity-matters-women-on-boards-of-directors/; Mark Misercola, 'Higher Returns with Women in Decision-making Positions,' *Credit Suisse*, 3 October 2016, www.credit-suisse.com/corporate/en/articles/news-and-expertise/higher-returns-with-women-in-decision-making-positions-201610.html; Credit Suisse 2016 (n 57); Vivian Hunt, Lareina Yee, Sara Prince and Sundiatu Dixon-Fyle, 'Delivering Through Diversity,' *McKinsey & Company Organization*, January 2018, www.mckinsey.com/business-functions/organization/our-insights/delivering-through-diversity.

168 As the ILO reports: "While considerable research efforts have been made to examine the impact of gender balance in management on the bottom line, making causal links is still a challenge." See ILO (n 46) 9. See also Alice Eagly, 'When Good Intentions Aren't Supported by Social Science Evidence,' *Northwestern Now*, 10 March 2016, https://news.northwestern.edu/stories/2016/03/opinion-conversation-diversity/; Alice H. Eagly, 'When Passionate Advocates Meet Research on Diversity, Does the Honest Broker Stand a Chance?' (2016) 72(1) *Journal of Social Issues* 199; Kim Elsesser, 'The Truth About Women's Impact on Corporate Boards (It's Not Good News),' *Forbes*, 23 June 2016, www.forbes.com/sites/kimelsesser/2016/06/23/the-truth-about-womens-impact-on-corporate-boards-its-not-good-news/#3bd7950d5ecb; Katherine Klein, 'Does Gender Diversity on Boards Really Boost Company Performance?,' *Knowledge@Wharton Upenn*, 18 May 2017, http://knowledge.wharton.upenn.edu/article/will-gender-diversity-boards-really-boost-company-performance/.

169 CEDAW (n 90) art 3 is particularly important.

170 Christine Chinkin, 'Article 3' in Marsha A. Freeman, Christine Chinkin and Beate Rudolf (eds), *The UN Convention on the Elimination of All Forms of Discrimination Against Women: A Commentary* (Oxford University Press 2012) 101, 121–122.

171 CEDAW (n 90) art 3, in conjunction with art 2(e) which requires states to take all appropriate measures to eliminate discrimination against women by any person, organisation or enterprise, which applies of course to corporations, and art 4 which provides for temporary special measures to accelerate equality.

172 HRC Resolution (n 4) para 13.

173 See 'Transforming Our World: The 2030 Agenda for Sustainable Development,' UNGA Res 70/1, 21 October 2015, UN Doc A/RES/70/1 (2015), https://sustainabledevelopment.un.org/post2015/transformingourworld.

174 WGDAW, 'Post-2015 Sustainable Development Agenda Contributions from the United Nations Human Rights Council's Working Group on Discrimination against Women in Law and in Practice: A Normative Framework for Achieving Development Goals for Gender Equality and the Empowerment of Women,' New York, January 2015, www.ohchr.org/Documents/Issues/Women/WRGS/WGcontributions_to_Post2015DevelopmentAgenda.pdf.

175 World Economic Forum, 'The Global Gender Gap Report 2014,' 2014, v, http://www3.weforum.org/docs/GGGR14/GGGR_CompleteReport_2014.pdf.

Part II

The Sale of Human Capital

Growing up on the legacy of feminist thinking, those of us who were the student generation of the sixties and seventies in European countries, were sure we could have equal economic outcomes given equal economic opportunities and the "rooms of our own" advocated by Virginia Woolf in the 1930s. Telling a lecture hall full of professional women that they would, through their labour and effort, now be able to pay the rent, and have rooms of their own in houses previously owned exclusively by men, Woolf pointed to women's economic independence as their path to a new found autonomy.[1]

This seemed absolutely feasible at the time. An agenda of human rights and equal employment opportunity had been adopted at the international and national levels. After World War II, the sky appeared to be the limit for equal opportunity and social justice, with equal returns for women's investment of their human capital in the workplace. In retrospect, it was not irrational to regard it as feasible, especially in the expanding economies of the developed countries. In Western Europe, social democracy and the welfare state fixed an eight-hour workday, annual holidays, sick leave and protection against arbitrary dismissal, all of which facilitated life-work balance. In the Eastern bloc countries, women were required to work as part of the Communist project and there was a state system of free crèches and childcare in place for working women.

Since then, the post-industrial world has moved into neo-liberal mode and the expectation of gender equality in the sale of human capital has not materialised. The eight-hour day with a tenured job is reality only for a reduced number of employees. In a convergence between developing and developed countries, regular, formal employment is a rarer commodity, leaving women to pursue fragmented working opportunities. There has been individualisation of care responsibilities which now devolve heavily on families, usually on mothers. Concurrently, in both the developed and the developing worlds, individual women's economic role of providing for self and family has been increased in scope and intensity.

Despite this convergence, women and girls are not a homogenous group, and their experience with regard to sale of their human capital varies greatly between regions, countries and socio-economic classes within countries. It varies in accordance with their identities, as members of religious or indigenous communities, minorities or migrant populations, and on account of single parenthood, disability or sexual identity. In some countries and communities within countries, the prevailing cultural norms enforce the confinement of a woman's use of her human capital to home and family. This may take the form of enforced exclusion of women from the public space, for instance in the imposition of male guardianship rules or of religion-based modesty norms; of the imposition of unpaid family work on women, particularly in agriculture or cottage industries; or of paid work whose wages are handed over to male family members. In these contexts, women do not have any real choice as to their economic lifestyle.

Although there are significant differences among women themselves, there are cross-cutting issues which mark out the aggregate of women's economic opportunities differently from men's. No country has closed the gender gap in all aspects of economic and social life, as evidenced by the pervasive gender gap in wages. Women at all economic levels, in high-, middle- and low-income countries, suffer from gender discrimination and infrastructural disadvantage throughout their lives, though this varies across a spectrum between extremely severe and comparatively mild. Women and girls are discriminated against and disadvantaged as a result of social and cultural precepts, expectations, beliefs, stereotypes, values, opportunities, roles and responsibilities associated with being female, which create pervasive barriers to their economic market opportunities.[2] Central to their shared experience is the disparate feminisation of unpaid care responsibilities, which both results from these expectations and stereotypes and perpetuates them.[3] Many women's employment patterns are interrupted, especially in the contexts of childbirth and childrearing and their economic situation varies more extremely than men's at different stages of their life cycle.[4] They are also more exposed to an aggravated impact of poverty because of their gender characteristics. Women also live, to varying degrees, under threat, immediate or remote, of gender-based violence in the public, as in the domestic, sphere. These shared vulnerabilities are discussed in the different parts of this book. These facts are the tip of the iceberg in revealing the gendered influences on women's opportunities and rewards for sale of their human capital.

In the latter half of the 20th century a clear and concerted agenda was adopted in international human rights law and international labour law to guarantee women's equality of opportunity in the workplace. This agenda was clearly articulated in the 1950s regarding equal remuneration for men and women for work of equal value in ILO Convention 100 and prohibition of discrimination in employment in ILO Convention 111.[5] It also rested on the guarantee of equal education for girls and equality for women and girls in the enjoyment of economic and social rights and benefits, articulated in the CESCR in 1966. Thus equal opportunity for women in economic life, including labour markets, became a mandatory rule of international law, imposing an obligation on states to ensure that women and girls are able to enjoy equality in labour rights and in economic and social life.[6]

Indeed, in international human rights law, there is an immediate obligation on states to eliminate sex discrimination in economic and social rights and not merely a gradual obligation to the maximum extent of available resources, as is the case for economic and social rights in general.[7] Women's right to equality requires equal distribution of existing economic and social resources rather than their establishment or extension and hence should be a feasible goal for any economy. In conjunction with the international human rights law initiatives, legal systems in the majority of countries – but not all – have since the last decades of the 20th century, introduced recognition of women's constitutional right to equality and statutory right to elimination of sex discrimination in employment and in education. Hence the formal legal barriers to women's professional and labour force participation, in these countries, have been removed.

This represents a clear global consensus that women should have the right to participate in the labour force on an equal footing with men. A very large majority of states have ratified the ILO's core non-discrimination Conventions Numbers 100 (168 states) and 111 (169 states).[8] ILO Maternity Protection Convention, 2000 (No. 183) and CEDAW both explicitly prohibit dismissal of women on the grounds of pregnancy or maternity leave.[9] The ILO and the European Court of Justice have also called for the prohibition of direct or indirect discrimination on grounds of care functions.[10] However, the mechanisms for implementing this wide consensus are weak. Few systems have succeeded in providing adequate remedies or sufficient administrative enforcement to prevent the violation of their prohibitions of discrimination. The WGDAW has observed that "There is no full equality of results in any labour market. Discrimination in hiring, promotion, conditions and wages and dismissal exists in all countries."[11]

Many countries have enacted equality and non-discrimination laws requiring gender equality in employment conditions.[12] This includes at least 101 countries which have laws prohibiting employment discrimination in hiring practices.[13] We do not have data on the breakdown of the spread of legislative provisions regarding equality in promotion opportunities, non-wage compensation, or vocational or professional development in the workplace. We also do not have a breakdown of positive measures to empower women in the workplace, going beyond mere formal prohibition of discrimination.

Part II explores the adequacy and implementation of the clear and concerted agenda in international human rights and labour law to guarantee women's equality of opportunity in the workplace, articulated in the latter half of the 20th century. It questions whether, in both developed and developing countries, the premise of integration of work in economic markets with care work in the family has become unsustainable, as a result of the changing character of employment in the labour market, on one hand, and disintegration of public care services, as well as community and family support systems, on the other.

Furthermore, just at the moment in time when legal systems and women themselves are starting to cope with the gendered problems of implementing the newly won right to equality in employment, the whole concept of employment is undergoing a seismic change. Hence not only women's current employment realities but also their future opportunities for sale of their human capital need careful reflection and inventive solutions.

1 Female labour force participation (FLFP)

The slice of life between childhood and old age is the period during which people have the opportunity to gain returns on the human capital investment of their preparatory years in order to earn income for their current needs and prepare for their old age.[14] Women's capability to sell their human capital in adult life is restricted, because this period of their lives is characterised by the duality of production and reproduction.[15] Hence their income generating slice of life is marked by the concurrence of economic opportunity with childbearing and caring responsibilities. As discussed in the Introduction and in Part I, women everywhere are still the primary unpaid carers for children and other dependent family members, including elderly parents.[16]

At the same time that women are bearing the main burden of unpaid care work, they also participate, at varying levels in different regions, in the global labour force. Some researchers have presented a U-shaped hypothesis correlating the female labour force participation rate and levels of development in different countries.[17] The ILO assesses that about half of the world's women participate in the global labour force: women's labour force participation rate in 2017 was approximately 49.4% and men's 76.1%, making for a gender gap of about 26%.[18] According to ILO 2017 data, women in developing countries (low income) have the lowest gender participation gap at 12 percentage points; emerging countries (middle income) are facing the largest gender gap, at nearly 31 percentage points; while women in developed countries (high income) have a gender gap of just over 16 percentage points. In the Arab States, Northern Africa and Southern Asia regions, female participation rates are the lowest (less than 30%) and the gaps, exceeding 50 percentage points, are the widest.[19] As these are mainly low-income countries, the wide gap apparently reflects state endorsement of religious and cultural traditionalism in these regions. Also a conservative Christian influence regarding women's role in the family may explain the rather greater LFP gender gap in some Latin American countries, as observed by the WGDAW on its country visits to Peru and Chile, both high middle-income countries.[20] At one end of the spectrum, poor women, other than those in patriarchal theocratic systems, sell their human capital to support subsistence needs. At the other end of the spectrum, highly educated women frequently work in careers which are well paid and well respected.

Table 8.1 Labour force participation rate by sex (per cent) and gender gap (percentage points), 1997–2021

Country/region	1997–2017	2017			2018			2018–21
	Gap	♂	♀	Gap	♂	♀	Gap	Gap
World		**76.1**	**49.4**	**26.7**	**76.0**	**49.3**	**26.7**	→
Developing countries		82.6	70.3	12.3	82.6	70.3	12.3	→
Emerging countries		77.5	46.9	30.6	77.4	46.7	30.7	↑
Developed countries		68.0	51.9	16.1	67.9	51.8	16.1	↓
Northern Africa		**74.1**	**22.9**	**51.2**	**74.1**	**22.9**	**51.2**	↓
Sub-Saharan Africa		**76.3**	**64.6**	**11.7**	**76.4**	**64.7**	**11.7**	→
Latin America and the Caribbean		**78.3**	**52.7**	**25.6**	**78.3**	**52.7**	**25.6**	↓
Northern America		**68.3**	**56.2**	**12.1**	**68.1**	**56.1**	**12.0**	→
Arab States		**76.4**	**21.2**	**55.2**	**76.3**	**21.3**	**55.0**	↓
Eastern Asia		**76.8**	**61.3**	**15.5**	**76.6**	**60.9**	**15.7**	↑
South-Eastern Asia and the Pacific		**81.2**	**58.8**	**22.4**	**81.1**	**58.8**	**22.3**	→
Southern Asia		**79.4**	**28.6**	**50.8**	**79.5**	**28.7**	**50.8**	↓
Northern, Southern and Western Europe		**63.8**	**51.3**	**12.5**	**63.6**	**51.2**	**12.4**	↓
Eastern Europe		**68.1**	**53.0**	**15.1**	**67.9**	**52.9**	**15.0**	↓
Central and Western Asia		**73.5**	**44.1**	**29.4**	**73.5**	**44.1**	**29.4**	→

Source: ILO, 'World Employment and Social Outlook: Trends for Women 2017,' 2017, 6, www.ilo.org/wcmsp5/groups/public/–dgreports/–inst/documents/publication/wcms_557245.pdf.

Labour force participation overall has been decreasing over the last two decades. According to the ILO World Employment Social Outlook: Trends for Women 2017 Report, between 1997 and 2007, the male labour force participation rate declined more than the female one, hence narrowing the gap between the two, which now stands at around 26%.[21] In the past decade, female and male participation rates have remained relatively stable, along with the participation gap, which remains significant.[22] There are various reasons which may explain why women's labour force participation would have been likely to decrease less than men's. The evolution of labour markets in the post-industrial era, with their shift away from the family wage, is generally thought to have introduced an economic exigency for women to enter into the cash economy.[23] The female breadwinner model is on the rise in both developed and developing countries.[24] In fact, in both high and low level income countries, with the exception of some of the theocratic states, there is an increase in the phenomenon of women taking on a role of economic provider for their families. Furthermore, the 2008 economic crisis, as for instance it occurred in North America and Europe, produced the 'added worker' effect, whereby women entered the labour force to provide additional income security to the household.[25] This effect has occurred in previous economic downturns[26] and has again been evident in the era of austerity after the financial crisis of 2008, as Heidi Gottfried observed in "The Great 'He-cession' . . . the economy shed manufacturing and construction jobs, once the primary engines of muscular economic growth and the underpinning of working-class masculinity and the strong male breadwinner family model."[27] There are also various different factors explaining this phenomenon in different regions, as for instance the shift from primary activities to services in the Asia-Pacific region.[28]

There is, however, a contrary assessment by the World Economic Forum (WEF) in 2017 which maintains that the decline in labour force participation has been more accentuated for women than men. There are trends which could also, alternatively, explain this phenomenon: the growing costs of childcare, longer and less regular hours of work, the growth of middle income economies in which more women choose not to work during the child-rearing years; and in some Eastern European countries, women's participation has been declining relative to men's and this can be attributed to a decline in the exceptionally high female participation rate in the prior communist regimes.[29]

Over a longer historical perspective, there are varying assessments as to the changes in women's labour force participation across time and space, which do not necessarily demonstrate a consistent evolutionary trend or a socio-geographic consistency.[30] In order to understand the significance of global trends in labour force participation for women's sale of their human capital, it would be necessary to look at the big data which would show where and under what conditions men and women have been selling their human capital in varied socio-geographic contexts during the periods of reference. The fragmentation and diversity of the modes of work make it difficult to assess the gender distribution of non-traditional forms of employment. This would include work falling outside the employment relationship, whether in informal labour or, more recently, in the growing gig economy. Furthermore, to get the full picture, beyond the gender gap in formal labour force participation, it would be necessary also to relate to the fact that even women who are statistically counted as engaged in the formal labour market are more frequently than men engaged only in part-time employment, as we will discuss below.

The correlation between a high FLFP rate and women's equality of opportunity cannot be taken as a given, as the pressures on women to work or not to work may be coercive, depending on economic, cultural and family contexts. Women's relatively increased labour force participation does not inevitably signify either an agenda of equality for women or increased well-being for women. As regards women who are not working or working part-time, this may be the result of discriminatory barriers;[31] the unavailability of suitable employment which is compatible with care responsibilities; a lack of affordable childcare services; religious or cultural restrictions; or life-style preferences. There is a dilemma to work or not to work in the economic marketplace for those women who are not forced to sell their human capital. Women who do have a choice both debate with each other and agonise within themselves as to the feasibility of combining a career with family responsibilities.

Part-time work is regarded as a compromise solution, allowing the integration of work and unpaid care. Globally, although women constitute less than 40% of total employment, they constitute 57% of those working on a part-time basis, and in a survey of 100 countries covering 87% of global employment, the ILO found that more than one-third of employed women (34.2%) work on a part-time basis of less than 35 hours per week, compared with 23.4% of employed men. Gender gaps in this respect are highest in Northern, Southern and Western Europe; high in Central and Western Asia, in Southern Asia, in Latin America and in the Caribbean; and smaller in Eastern Asia and Eastern Europe.[32]

The advantage of part-time work is in facilitating time management during periods of family life in which care burdens are at their greatest. Part-time work does keep the unpaid carer in contact with economic activities outside the home and hence with some income and a greater potential for a later return to full-time work, sometimes encouraged by the establishment of re-entry programs. Part-time workers are protected in international regulation against discrimination in wages and social security under the ILO Part-time Work Convention 1994 (No. 175) and in regional regulation under the European Directive on Part-time Work 1998,[33] under which employers are required to pay all their wages and social security benefits pro-rata. Nevertheless, there is a high human capital cost in part-time work. Promotion to senior positions, development of expertise, and professional networking are rarely equal for part-time workers. The concentration of women in part-time work aggravates stereotyping at both the individual and the group levels, categorising women as less committed to the career track. Furthermore, the risk of future poverty is considerably increased in the case of termination of economic support for the woman by the primary breadwinner in the household, for whatever reason, death, illness, unemployment or divorce, against which a pro-rata system cannot protect.

It should be the role of policy to provide an infrastructure which will allow women an equal opportunity with men and which will provide equal conditions determining the feasibility of their choices to work or not to work. It should also be the role of policy to allow both women and men a sustainable work-life balance, indeed in real terms this would be the only way to achieve true gender equality in the economy. As Credit Suisse notes in its 2014 report on Women in Senior Management, "there is a generational shift in the expectations of a work-life balance, and what today is seen as a gender issue is set to become an issue across the entire workforce."[34] In almost all countries across the global divide, the necessary infrastructural conditions do not currently prevail.

2 Promotion and gender pay gaps

In 2017, there were extraordinary revelations of gender pay gaps between women and men employed at the highest level of the pay ladder. The pathology of unequal pay for the same job was exhibited in the reshoot of the film 'All the Money in the World,' in which the lead female star, Michelle Williams, was paid $80 a day and the lead male star, Mark Wahlberg, was paid $1.5 million in total. The scandal was doubly ironic in view of the circumstances of the reshooting which took place because the previous male actor Kevin Spacey had been replaced following accusations of his sexual misconduct in the context of the #MeToo campaign.[35] There have been other slightly less dramatic examples, such as the resignation of Carrie Gracie, who after working for the BBC network for 30 years, quit her position as China editor to protest pay inequality within the company[36] and such as the co-host of the E! entertainment channel being paid half of her male colleague.[37]

Equal Remuneration Conventions have been promulgated by the ILO since 1919[38] and there has been extensive domestic legislation establishing the right to equal pay but nevertheless the gender pay gap persists, as is well demonstrated in recent anecdotal stories and in the statistical data. The ILO reported in 2016 that women's wages globally represent 77% of men's wages.[39] The ILO showed that this gender gap varies widely from country to country, from over 30% in the Russia Federation, Korea and Estonia to under 20% in Vietnam and under 10% in Hungary, Spain, Denmark, Norway, Greece, Luxembourg, Belgium and New Zealand.[40] The World Bank estimated the gap as lower than the ILO's 77%, at a 65 to 75% average.[41] The World Economic Forum in 2016 made a far direr assessment of the current gender earnings gap, finding that women's average earnings are "just over 50 per cent of men's," with average global earned income for women and men estimated at $10,778 and $19,873, respectively[42] (57.14% gap), and in 2017 $12,000 and $21,000[43] (54.24% gap). There seems to have been no satisfactory explanation of these significant discrepancies between the ILO, the World Bank and the WEF data and so the trends are hard to understand. The differences in assessment of the current global pay gap may well be a result of methodology.[44]

As regards trends, the ILO sees a reduction in the gender pay gap according to its methodology, and has found signs that the gender pay gap is narrowing, though slowly, and has estimated that given the current rate, without targeted action, gender equality in wage payment will not be achieved before 2086.[45] In strong contrast, the WEF data shows a significant and steady increase in the gap between 2012 and 2016, although, at the same time, without comment or analysis, giving figures which show a decrease between 2016 and 2017.[46]

In general, weekly, monthly or annual wage gap measures tend to be larger than those based on hourly wages. As the ILO observes, this shows that part of the gender wage gap stems from differences between men and women in hours worked.[47] It should also be noted that, in some countries, there is a gender wage gap in net income, which stems directly from governmental tax policy, as a result of assessing spouses' incomes jointly; this policy usually penalises the spouse who is earning the lower income and hence loses the lower rate of tax which would have been applicable on his/her separate income. Generally, the lower income is that of married women and hence the net earnings from their work are further reduced.

Furthermore, mothers earn less than fathers, even when their measured characteristics are the same.[48] Globally, the motherhood gap increases as the number of children a woman has increases; in many European countries, for example, having one child has only a small negative effect, but women with two and especially three children experience a significant wage penalty. In developing countries, evidence suggests the gender of the child may matter as daughters may be more likely than sons to help with household and caring tasks, thereby reducing the motherhood gap.[49]

Women constitute a majority of minimum wage earners,[50] constitute a majority of workers who are working *de facto* beneath the minimum wage, and, in some countries, the minimum wage in jobs more commonly held by women may also be lower.[51] Furthermore, in some countries, the wage gap is wider at the bottom of the wage distribution ('sticky floors').[52] This puts women at higher risk of working poverty as women constitute a majority of the working poor globally. Insofar as the woman's income is in the context of a two-income family, it contributes as a protective factor against poverty[53] but, wherever it becomes the sole or main family income, the fact that it is at a lower level increases the risk of household poverty.

The exploitation of women's labour at the lowest levels of pay has been transnationally institutionalised in the phenomenon of export processing zones (EPZs). EPZs are industrial areas that have been delineated to attract trade and offer exemptions to the normal custom and trade regulations in a country. These EPZs process garments and goods for export and include 5,174 zones in 116 countries. Women account for most of the workforce in EZPs and in some case account for 100% of the workforce. More than 85% of all EPZ workers are in Asia. These zones have flourished in developing countries, which have competed with one another to secure free trade agreements and offer special incentives, including exemptions from normal labour standards, for big business to set up export manufacturing. Record profits in EPZs have been registered. While women have gained an increasing number of jobs through trade agreements for EPZs, their 'competitive advantage' as workers has been in low wages and inferior working conditions.[54]

The wage gap, both monthly and hourly, can be attributed in part to occupational segregation, with women clustered in feminised work in pink ghettos, where there is no direct male wage comparator, with low-level working conditions, little job security and low pay. Existing research on national-level gender-based wage distributions has also pointed to a tendency towards lower pay for occupations that have historically developed as predominantly female and has observed that, when women enter a profession in large numbers, the pay-related benefits of participating in the profession depreciate: this has held true for bank tellers and teachers for instance. The World Bank calculated that, across a sample of 33 low- and middle-income countries, gender differences in occupation and sector of employment accounted for 10 to 50% of the observed wage gap.[55]

Current comparison of the sectoral distribution of employment by sex reveals strong evidence of gender segregation and also shows that the global average segregation across all sectors has increased between 1997 and 2017, from 15.0 percentage points to 20.5 percentage points.[56] Globally, the services sector has overtaken agriculture as the sector that employs the highest number of women and men, but, while just under half of all men work in services (42.6%), almost two-thirds of the world's women are employed in that sector, increasing since 1955 from 41.1% to 61.5% in 2015. In high-income countries, almost one-third of employed women work in the low-paid service sector, primarily in education and health.[57]

In order to address wage gaps resulting from occupational segregation, the CEDAW and the ILO Conventions require employers to give their employees not merely equal pay for equal work but also equal pay for work of equal value,[58] comparable in skill, responsibility, effort and working conditions.[59] While as many as 117 countries have equal pay laws,[60] many fewer, only 59 countries,[61] have laws guaranteeing equal pay for work of equal value. In order to implement equal pay for work of equal value, the ILO has issued a guide to gender-neutral job evaluation which provides an objective evaluation system.[62] The ILO recommended that policies aimed at combating occupational segregation also encourage men to enter occupations traditionally associated with women.[63]

There are examples of court decisions enforcing the right to equal pay for work of equal value. For instance, in 2005, in Iceland, a claim for equal pay between a female manager of the social affairs department of a municipality and a male engineer was successful before the Supreme Court; and in 2011, the Supreme Court of Canada held, relying on an occupational analysis evaluation, that clerical work, performed mostly by women, was of equal value to the higher paying sorting and delivery work (postal operations) which was performed mainly by men.[64] However, there are countries where despite an express legislative right to equal pay for work of equal value, the courts have taken a restrictive view, in effect interpreting the right to comprise only the same or substantially similar work. Hence, Professor Sandra Fredman suggests that legislation should not only refer expressly to work of equal value but also elaborate on the concept, and there should be clear guidance as to how to conduct an objective and independent assessment of the employer job evaluation system, drawing on the ILO guide.[65]

An additional explanation for the wage gap is the positioning of women lower down on the promotion ladder. The WEF found in 2017, "based on an analysis of LinkedIn membership from more than 100 countries and 12 selected industries," that "over the past decade, the proportion of female hiring has increased across all selected industries – as has the tendency to hire women into senior leadership positions." Nevertheless, every industry exhibits a leadership gender gap.[66] Even when women do reach senior positions in management, in many countries or companies, they appear to be receiving far less pay than men although here, too, the comparative data is problematic based as it is on different research methodologies. In China, research shows that a gender compensation gap for executives has persisted.[67] In the United States, too, it has been reported that female executives earned 47% less total compensation than their male counterparts and, even taking into consideration the fact that men usually have more experience, operate larger companies and are more highly concentrated in well-paying industries and occupations, the gender pay gap is still 7% due to gender differences in the portion of variable pay, in particular a different cash payout from stock option exercises.[68] In the United Kingdom, the gender wage gap data for management employees, using the government's 2017 gender reporting requirements, were stunning: the overall gender pay gap for managers was 26.8%, with men earning an average of £11,606 more than women and with male executives receiving an average bonus of £89,230 against £14,945 for women.[69]

The economic implications of this gender promotion and pay gap at the highest levels of the career ladder are significant. Piketty has pointed out that the highest centile of incomes from human capital have managed to obtain "extremely high unprecedented compensation packages for their labour," for example in France since the 1990s and even more so in the United States since the 1980s.[70] Women are not participating in this burgeoning plutocracy in anything like the same percentages as they are entering senior positions in the labour market. More than this, it seems that even when women do reach senior management, they are not likely to partake of the financial rewards that men do. The Eurostat database shows that, in 22 European countries, the greater hiring of women into senior positions has not reduced the gender pay gap but has rather exacerbated it. Within enterprises, the gender pay gap increases gradually as individuals get higher wages: in the bottom centile the gap is 0.7%, whereas in the top centile it is about 45%.[71]

Unlike horizontal segregation in industries and occupations which are lower paid, surprisingly, vertical segregation, the lower promotion rate of women into senior positions, does not seem to constitute a conclusive factor in the overall gender pay gap, since even when women reach those positions their pay is not commensurate with their status. Even when all the factors which may explain the gender pay gap are accounted for, research in different countries shows a residual gap which cannot be explained except by discrimination. In the United States, a Glassdoor Economic Research survey comparing specific job titles in specific companies held by women and men (apples with apples) found a remaining 5.4% 'adjusted' gender pay gap.[72]

Furthermore, the correlation between educational achievement and remuneration does not hold for women. Globally, the gender gap in earnings remains substantial despite women's gains in education, which in many countries equal, and sometimes surpass, the achievements of men.[73] It used to be a mantra that education was the key to women's access to equal employment and wages. However, this has not held to be the case. In 43 out of 53 countries, after controlling for individual characteristics and place of residence, education not only fails to explain the observed gender wage gap but, when taken into account, actually increases it.[74] Across OECD countries, the gender gap in earnings for tertiary-educated women is 27%, which is higher than the gap for those with below upper secondary (24%) and those with upper secondary or post-secondary non-tertiary education (22%).[75] A counter example is China, where researchers have found that the gender employment gap and the gender pay gap are narrower for the better educated.[76]

In an attempt to address the persistent gender wage gap, some European countries, such as the United Kingdom and Germany, have introduced reporting and information requirements for large employers in order to provide a deterrent against wage discrimination.[77] However, it is questionable whether this will be enough to bring about extensive reform or whether it will just meet employer denial tactics as in the case of Google, which when accused by the US Department of Labor of "systematic compensation disparities against women," asserted, relying on its own wages analysis, that it had "confidence that there is no gender pay gap at Google."[78] The most potentially effective policy measure is to be found in Iceland's new legislation, announced on International Women's Day 2017 (and went into effect in January 2018), which requires companies with more than 25 employees to obtain equal pay certification by the end of 2021, which has to be renewed every three years, and if they don't meet the requirements of equal pay they may be fined.[79]

3 Informal work

In the formal labour market, the normative framework, though not properly implemented, has been well established to guarantee equal employment opportunity for women and, as will be discussed, measures for accommodating maternity and, to some extent, childcare, have been introduced. However, these provisions do not, grosso modo, apply to informal work. As there is a shrinking volume of formal employment opportunities for women, unless protective labour law is applied to informal work the system of equal opportunity will be bankrupt.

The ILO coined the term 'informal sector' in the early 1970s to denote those who, despite working, were not recognised, recorded, protected or regulated by the public authorities.[80] In a 2002 resolution concerning decent work and the informal economy, the ILO concluded:

> Although there is no universally accurate or accepted description or definition, there is a broad understanding that the term "informal economy" accommodates considerable diversity in terms of workers, enterprises and entrepreneurs with identifiable characteristics. . . . The term "informal economy" refers to all economic activities by workers and economic units that are – in law or in practice – not covered or insufficiently covered by formal arrangements. Their activities are not included in the law, which means that they are operating outside the formal reach of the law; or they are not covered in practice, which means that – although they are operating within the formal reach of the law, the law is not applied or not enforced; or the law discourages compliance because it is inappropriate, burdensome, or imposes excessive costs.[81]

This wide and vague definition includes both employment and entrepreneurship: "Both persons employed in informal sector enterprises and persons in informal employment outside the informal sector (employees holding informal jobs), as well as contributing family workers in formal or informal sector enterprises and own-account workers engaged in the production of goods for own end-use by their household."[82] However, as protective labour regulation protects workers by imposing standards and obligations on the employer, it can only be effectively applied and enforced where it is possible to identify the entity which uses the worker's investment of his or her labour for profit and is, hence, in loco employer. There is added injury to economic woman in the failure to regulate informal work as women are especially in need of protective labour law to prohibit sex discrimination and to recognise maternity rights. Thus, tolerance for employment practices which are not regulated directly impacts women and leaves them unprotected against discrimination by the entities which are *de facto* employing them.

Economic activities which constitute employment for the profit of others, even though they are not classified as falling under the umbrella of formal labour market employment, contrast with genuine self-employment or entrepreneurship. The earning of an income through employment in the enterprises of others may imposes limits on freedom and autonomy. The employment relationship involves a degree of control by the user and of personal obligation of the service provider. It involves economic dependence of the employee on the employer. It is a relationship which creates a potential for exploitation of more vulnerable members of society, which necessarily targets women. This relationship encompasses not only classical formal employment but also a wide range of current modes of the sale of human capital to identifiable entities which directly profit from the personal performance of the work. The prevalence of informal work has long been a known fact in low- or medium-income countries and the data suggests that informal employment is paired with low-income per capita and high poverty rates.[83] In many low-income countries, formal employment has been and remains scarce and the main economic resource is informal work.[84] It is frequently assumed that the share of women in informal employment outnumbers that of men, but this does not seem to be the case in all developing economies.[85]

Less recognised as informal work than the informal work of women in developing economies has been the growing phenomenon of what is, effectively, women's work outside the protection of labour law in developed economies. Informal employment is growing in the developed economies, even if not usually identified in this way: the workforce is becoming increasingly "flexibilized" as employers attempt to avoid regulation and cut labour costs.[86] Women are disparately concentrated in this growing informal employment sector in developed countries – which is sometimes described as fragmented employment – categorised as freelancers; leased or contract workers; and independent service providers, temporary workers, home workers and telecommuters: the gendered nature of this contingent or precarious work in Western countries has been researched and demonstrated.[87]

The convergence of developed and developing countries as regards the increasing levels of informal labour in general and of women's informal labour in particular poses a worrying threat to the gains made by women in employment law which was developed on the basis of the formal employment model. The International Trade Union Confederation issued a report in 2011 – 'Living with Economic Insecurity – Women in Precarious Work' – that showed an increase in the precariousness of women's work in the wake of the 2008 economic crisis, commenting that the gender inequalities and power imbalances that predated the global crisis resulted in its effects falling disproportionately on women who were already structurally disempowered and marginalised. The report underlined the boom of precarious and informal work in virtually all countries. The 2008 economic crisis accelerated an already rapid process of informalisation of work and women are the most affected by these labour market trends. The ITUC concluded that standard indicators and data used to measure developments on labour markets fail to capture the extent to which women are being driven into increasing economic insecurity.[88] According to the global network 'Women in Informal Employment: Globalizing and Organizing,' nearly 40% of women street vendors interviewed in Africa, Asia and Latin America in 2009 had experienced an overall deterioration of employment and income levels, and 84% of own-account home-based workers reported reduced monthly incomes.[89] The second round of the same study, conducted in 2010, found that although there had been some improvement overall, there was a lag in recovery for women informal workers.[90]

The ILO describes the vulnerability of informal workers:

> By its very nature, the characteristics of the informal economy are largely negative. It can trap individuals and enterprises in a spiral of low productivity and poverty. A coherent national strategy to facilitate transitions to formality needs to recognize that the costs of working informally are high for businesses, workers and the community. From the perspective of unprotected workers, the negative aspects of work in the informal economy far outweigh its positive aspects. They are not recognized, registered, regulated or protected under labour and social protection legislation, and are not therefore able to enjoy, exercise or defend their fundamental rights. Since they are not normally organized, they have little or no collective representation in relation to employers or the public authorities. . . . Workers in the informal economy are characterized by varying degrees of dependency and vulnerability. Women, young persons, migrants and older workers are especially vulnerable to the most serious decent work deficits in the informal economy. They are vulnerable to violence, including sexual harassment, and other forms of exploitation and abuse, including corruption and bribery. Child workers and bonded labourers are also found in the informal economy.[91]

Unlike unpaid care work, informal work is recognised as part of the macroeconomy. The entity which makes a profit from the use of the women's labour is frequently identifiable: traditional concerns, the farmer, the male 'head of the family,' the service provider and the producer or marketer of the products being sold on the street. These entities are profiting from the labour of informal workers, without undertaking employer obligations as regards his or her conditions, wages and social benefits. In order to secure decent work for women, the damaging impact of informal work must be addressed. This requires reduction and reconstruction of informal work.[92]

A conceptual basis for mandating equality in informal employment exists in the ILO's eight fundamental conventions – including those relating to freedom of association, equal remuneration, abolition of forced labour, prohibition of discrimination in employment, minimum age and child labour – apply to all workers, including informal workers. Furthermore, the decent work principles, social security and social protection floors, occupational health and safety and maternity protection should all apply. The ILO has however pointed out the regulatory difficulties of applying these standards in the informal economy.[93]

ILO Recommendation No 204 regarding informal work, adopted in 2015, provides a threefold objective:

> (a) facilitate the transition of workers and economic units from the informal to the formal economy, while respecting workers' fundamental rights and ensuring opportunities for income security, livelihoods and entrepreneurship; (b) promote the creation, preservation and sustainability of enterprises and decent jobs in the formal economy and the coherence of macroeconomic, employment, social protection and other social policies; and (c) prevent the informalization of formal economy jobs.[94]

The WGDAW in its thematic report on economic and social life, in 2014, called states to

> Take measures to reduce and reconstruct informal work. In order to reduce informal work, States should increase job opportunities for women in formal employment, especially in the public sector, and with targeted programmes for women's training, professionalization, reskilling and unemployment programmes. In order to reconstruct informal work, they should redefine the scope of protective labour law, introduce prorata pay and social security benefits for part-time or casual work, and extend paid maternity leave and care rights to workers in both the formal and informal sectors.[95]

These recommendations were only minimally picked up by the Human Rights Council in its 2014 Resolution on discrimination against women, which called for reduction of informal work for women by increasing women's economic opportunities, particularly in formal employment.[96]

Although there is a conceptual basis, specific national policies for implementing protections are sporadic and do not provide a comprehensive cover for labour rights and social protection, including maternity rights, in the informal employment sector.[97] Wherever there is an identifiable entity profiting economically from the hours of work invested by individual service providers in its organisation, that entity should be regarded as having employer obligations under protective labour law. The explosive expansion of informal work is in large part the result of a legal classificatory myth advantageous to capital and enabling the exploitation of labour through leasing or contracting arrangements which avoid classification as a direct employment relationship. Failure to apply protective labour standards and maternity rights in the informal economy has a devastating impact on millions of informal women workers.

4 Sexual harassment at work

Women's equality of opportunity in the sale of their human capital is pervasively undermined by their subjection to sexual harassment, misogyny and violence. Sexual harassment denies women's equality in the workplace and is discriminatory. It humiliates them, jeopardises their well-being and severely violates their dignity. The violence against women (VAW) in the workplace reaches from the highest levels of the career ladder, such as the Hollywood stars who broke the silence in the #MeToo campaign[98] to blue collar workers in the mining industry in the United States, some of whom described the harassment they endured at work as being rougher than any experienced while serving in the military in Iraq.[99]

Much of the focus in international human rights on VAW in the public and economic space has centred on sexual harassment in the workplace, which is a prominent aspect of workers' lives, particularly women workers, around the world.[100] Between 40% and 50% of women in the EU experience "unwanted sexual advances, physical contact, verbal suggestions or other forms of sexual harassment" at work. In Asia-Pacific countries 30 to 40% of women workers report some form of harassment (verbal, physical or sexual).[101] In a South African study, 77% of women reported experiencing sexual harassment at some point during their working lives.[102] Reporting on the situation of women blue collar workers in the United States in 2017, stories emerged of astoundingly brutal behaviour, for example, "A woman on a repair crew was deliberately stranded on top of a 200-foot wind turbine by her male co-workers after enduring months of lewd taunts. . . . Men dropped tools on female co-workers or deliberately turned on electrical power when they began working on lines."[103] Additionally, gender-non-conforming men and women, gay, lesbian, bisexual or trans are frequently subjected to violence and harassment.[104]

ILO research has suggested that the women who are most vulnerable to sexual harassment in the workplace are young, financially dependent, single or divorced or have a migrant status in the community in which they live.[105] In addition, some forms of work create particular vulnerability – for example domestic work, especially for women migrant workers[106] and informal employment, as discussed previously. A 2015 study from Portugal found that the incidence of sexual harassment is higher among those on contracts with "little job security or stability."[107] Nevertheless, women employed in traditionally high-income, male-dominated occupations, such as science, technology, engineering and mathematics, also suffer from high levels of sexual violence and harassment.[108] A 2015 survey in EU countries found that 75% of women in management and higher professional positions and 61% of women in service sector occupations had experienced some form of sexual harassment in their lifetime.[109] In a study of women working in typically male trades in the United States, nearly a third of the women reported that they frequently or always experienced sexual harassment.[110] The documentary 'The Invisible War' (2012) interviewed numbers of women career soldiers and officers in the United States military who gave evidence of their experience of violent rapes by male cohorts in the military and of the failure of the military to prosecute the perpetrators. It is an astounding document even for those who have read the literature on workplace sexual abuse, as it shows women of immense ability, strong personality and career ambition falling victim not only to the violent aggression of the sexual predators but also to the chauvinistic framework of a command hierarchy which, in almost all cases, did not support them by prosecuting the male predators.

Sexual harassment in the workplace was first given a name and prohibited as employment discrimination in the United States in the 1970s. The prohibition against sexual harassment did not find express provision in international treaty law. However, in 1989 the CEDAW Committee, in General Recommendation 12, recognised sexual harassment as a form of VAW and, following this, in General Recommendation 19, the Committee categorised all forms of VAW, including sexual harassment in the workplace, as sex discrimination in breach of the Convention. This has led the way to further development of prohibition of sexual harassment, for instance in the 1993 General Assembly Declaration on the Elimination of Violence against Women, and in the 1995 Beijing declaration and platform for action.[111]

In 2018, the World Bank's 'Women, Business and the Law' report found that 130 states have adopted some form of legislation against sexual harassment in the workplace, while the remaining 59 states do not.[112]

The offence of sexual harassment adds a category of prohibition beyond the criminal offences of rape and indecent acts, outlawing sexually predatory behaviour and aiming to prevent abuse of power in the workplace hierarchy.[113] The harassment may take the form of subtle or explicit threats with job-related consequences (quid pro quo) or of creation of a hostile environment in which women are subjected to humiliation on the grounds of their sexual characteristics, such as derogatory or demeaning 'jokes' about women or display of pornographic materials in shared spaces. A gendered hostile environment may target biological characteristics; socially constructed roles and responsibilities assigned to a particular sex; maternity harassment because of pregnancy, childbirth or a medical condition related to pregnancy or childbirth; or family responsibilities. It can produce a culture of misogyny which physically endangers women, humiliates them and virtually drives them out of the workplace.

In country legislation, unlike in CEDAW Committee's GR19, which is based on the treaty mandate of eliminating discrimination against women, the prohibition of sexual harassment is generally gender neutral and hence applies to male as well as female victims.[114] This gender-neutral approach is reflected in the ILO's 2018 report on 'Ending Violence and Harassment against Women and Men in the World of Work,' which refers to the "rubric of 'violence and harassment'...includ[ing] a continuum of unacceptable behaviours and practices that are likely to result in physical, psychological or sexual harm or suffering." From an 80-country study, the ILO found that 60 countries regulate physical and psychological forms of violence and harassment in the world of work under a variety of terms, such as 'harassment,' 'bullying,' 'mobbing,' 'violence,' 'abuse"' and 'maltreatment,' and 65 countries also specifically regulate sexual violence and harassment in the world of work.[115] The move to regard sexual harassment as part of a wider phenomenon of harassment which affects both men and women conflates VAW in the workplace with other forms of violence and in so doing perhaps undoes some of the hard work done to achieve recognition of sexual violence and harassment as a uniquely pervasive and serious barrier to women's economic empowerment.

In spite of the widespread prohibitions, there is clearly a great enforcement gap.[116] The difficulty of enforcement is in part the fear all employees have of reporting an offence to an enforcement agency because they do not want to risk losing their jobs. This is compounded by insufficient investment in workplace training of employees and managers, lack of proper grievance procedures and lack of support for women to take cases to court.[117] Nevertheless, some women employees have organised effective public protests: there were numerous initiatives taken by women employees, such as the Elephant in the Valley survey in 2017 pointing to sexism in Silicon Valley[118] and Susan Fowler's exposure of the sexist practices at Uber, which resulted in resignations of high-level management.[119] The alternative power of social media is being tested in the #MeToo movement. Women in the movement highlighted how sexual harassment is underreported and the mistrust and disappointment of victims in enforcement by legal or social institutions. It has resulted in high-level male office-holders in the public and private sectors either being dismissed or resigning. These have included leading politicians in the United States and Japan, members of the Nobel Prize Academy, New York's Attorney General, screen stars and top TV presenters.[120]

The challenge of eliminating sexual harassment extends beyond formal places of employment to other forms of the sale of human capital, including informal employment and the gig economy.[121] It also extends beyond the world of work to educational institutions, services, public transport and the street, as was discussed in the Introduction. In all these contexts, there need to be mechanisms in place to deter and punish sexual harassment.

5 The pension gap

Women's quality of life in older age derives from the culmination of the earlier phases in their life cycle and bears their imprint: lower labour force participation, precarious jobs, informal labour, the costs of caring, interrupted career patterns and the gender wage gap. Hence women's situation in retirement can be regarded as a litmus test for the quality of women's entire economic and social life.[122]

There is a gender pension gap in coverage, wealth accumulation and in monthly benefits.[123] Nearly 65% of people above retirement age without any regular pension are women.[124] Evidence from the United Kingdom and the United States suggests that men's total pension assets are substantially larger than women's, even when the percentages of men and women enrolled in a pension system are similar.[125] Many countries have multi-pillar systems, which combine both accumulated occupational pension entitlements from work income and publicly funded social pensions. Whenever pension entitlement depends on wealth accumulation in a contributory scheme, based on wages, women are disadvantaged. Social ('zero pillar') publicly funded schemes, which give basic flat rate citizens' pensions, are non-contributory and do not, as such, differentiate between men's and women's pension entitlement, thus producing equality. Therefore, any trend to increase the share of contributory pensions and base a substantial element of pension entitlement on wages earned – a trend which is being adopted by many countries in all regions – impacts women adversely, increasing the gender pension gap, as women's contribution to these funded pension schemes is lower because of the structural factors in their labour market and unpaid care work discussed earlier.[126]

Discriminatory laws and practice prevail in most countries. Some such laws are self-evident, such as mandatory early retirement for women, decreasing their years of contributory pension accumulation. Some are what has been called 'statistical discrimination,' such as separate annuity tables for women and men based on women's greater longevity, which, at the same level of accumulated wealth in the pension fund, calculate women's monthly benefits at a lower level than men's on the grounds that the same amount of money needs to finance more years of benefit.[127] Others are the result of legislative policy endorsing and perpetuating the economic dependence of women on a husband's income and pension entitlement, as for example in cancelling a widow's pension on remarriage or non-inclusion of the value of a husband's pension rights in the division of property on divorce.[128]

Policy recommendations by international bodies and UN human rights mechanisms include measures regarding both social pensions and accumulated occupational pensions. They urge repeal of all discriminatory legislation. They propose increasing the level of the social pension, which benefits women whose occupational pension benefits are lower than men's. They have proposed gender-specific measures to lessen women's disadvantage in occupational pensions such as mandating continuing pension contributions during maternity and childcare leaves. In order to prevent discrimination against women in contributory pension schemes, they recommend unisex calculation of benefits and equalising mandatory retirement age, so that women are not forced to leave the labour market at an earlier age than men, and mandatory joint annuities.[129]

Some states provide gender-specific compensatory measures, with quite wide margins of difference in the extent of their generosity. Examples are the systems which bestow years of accumulation of pension entitlement during time spent in maternity and childcare. However, they have only a marginal impact in reducing the pension gap.[130] Of the gender-specific measures, the only one that almost closes the gender pension gap is mandatory joint annuities, which is practiced in some Latin American countries.[131] This suggests that the way to rectify women's relative poverty in old age is through mandating joint annuities with their husbands, which is of course another way of saying that women's economic well-being is dependent on the men they marry. Furthermore, this does not solve the problem for single or divorced women and leaves the problem of engineering a system that is both equitable for traditional dependent marriages and yet can still incentivise economically independent women.[132]

International human rights treaty law has not yet proposed practical solutions for the gender gap in pension entitlement. There are no normative rules which require states to take the special measures recommended by international bodies and UN human rights mechanisms to reduce the pensions gap. There is a need for an international convention. However, whatever solutions may be found within the pension framework, the vast majority of older women are still, as I have shown, likely to find themselves with a severe economic deficit in their occupational pension benefits. This will continue to be the case until a systemic solution is found for women's earning disadvantage throughout their productive and reproductive slice of life.

6 The third and fourth industrial revolutions

All the models of formal and informal employment which we have just discussed are relevant to the working relations produced by the first and second industrial revolutions. The first industrial revolution started with the mechanisation of the textile industry and the introduction of factories in the late 18th century. The second industrial revolution took place in the early 20th century, with mass production and the moving assembly line. Following these two industrial revolutions, people became more affluent and more urban.[133] In these models, workers have typically been physically present in the workplace during the time when they are performing their work.

In the third and fourth industrial revolutions, technological developments have, since the 1980s, created new models of work. They have enabled workplace innovations such as remote working and teleconferencing, opening up a range of ways of carrying out occupations in which there is an apparent disconnect between the performance of work and the user's or employer's interaction with the tangible presence of the person performing the work. This disconnect provides a certain anonymity for the personhood of a worker.

In the third industrial revolution, work through digital technology with the personal computer and the internet – work through the modem – does not unseverably attach the performance of the work to a flesh and blood person who is performing it. In the fourth industrial revolution, which is emerging, work is delegated to artificial intelligence, robots and autonomous vehicles and this allows work to be performed by machines, in which personhood is relegated to the planning process of the work and is absent in its performance. The World Economic Forum in 2016 addressed the transformation in jobs and regarded the gender dynamic as crucial to "understanding how the benefits and burdens of the fourth industrial revolution will be distributed." There is a polarisation amongst experts and industry managers between "those who foresee limitless new opportunities and those that foresee a massive dislocation of jobs."[134]

The third industrial revolution is typified by the 'gig economy,' rapidly growing and widely covered in the media.[135] The gig economy is subject to a confusing flurry of terminology,[136] as the 'online platform economy,' 'sharing economy,' 'on-demand economy' or 'crowdsourcing.' Although lacking a unified definition,[137] the gig economy generally describes economic activities involving online intermediary platforms that facilitate the sale of labour services[138] (this amounts to a small but growing percentage of the overall platform economy, which also includes the sale of goods and the renting out of assets).[139] These platforms connect workers directly to customers and facilitate the payment. They also usually endorse the ability to earn money on one's own schedule and often from the vicinity of one's home.[140] Four broad types of platforms that match clients with workers for paid labour can be identified: platforms for relatively high-skill creative and IT tasks (Upwork, for example), platforms for lower-skill repetitive online work (Clickworker), platforms for manual service or domestic work that is carried out on a customer's premises (Taskrabbit) and platforms involving driving or delivery (Uber, Deliveroo).[141] Indeed, the gig economy is occupationally diversified and there is evidence that this model is spreading to more areas, including health services, teaching, legal services and a wide variety of manual and maintenance tasks. While some gig platforms may genuinely be regarded as providing a facility for entrepreneurship opportunities, other of these companies should more properly be defined as quasi employers, who must respect labour law rights and regulations, including those prohibiting sex discrimination and providing accommodation measures for maternity and parenthood.[142]

As regards the gendered aspects of emerging and future work, these new technological work spaces have opened up the apparent opportunity for a gender-neutral work zone. The depersonalisation of work, through anonymous digital platforms or in geographically separated spaces, would seem to facilitate an abandonment of the gender stereotypes which affect face to face contact. There is little research on the extent to which this has proved to be true in practice.[143] However, there is some research which throws up questions as to whether sex discrimination is not in fact pursuing women into these new occupation zones. An extreme example is to be found in the shocking data of wage gaps for women lawyers who constituted 70% of the lawyers in an online platform:

> A study in 2017 carried out a gender analysis of 4,600 online taskers, equally distributed between men and women, on a global online Platform that connects work-seekers of various professional occupations – such as accounting, data analysis, design, engineering and architecture and law – with online tasks to be performed. . . . The researchers found a dramatic gender gap in the Platform facilitated online work, with women's average requested hourly rates, where the tasks, educational level, feedback score and length of experience are similar, 37% lower than men's.
>
> They reported that the hourly rate gap exists in all categories but with significant differences between them. For example, the legal category stood out as the occupational category where the average hourly rate of women makes only 63% of men's.

> The researchers conclude: "... our data set captures the shaping of new dynamics of self-evaluation and self-presentation in the 'gig' economy. Through these interactions, our findings suggest that we are witnessing the remaking of women into devalued laborers."[144]

Furthermore, the pattern of horizontal sex segregation in labour markets may according to some sources persist in the gig economy. McKinsey reports that some platforms are heavily skewed toward one gender: for instance, 86% of Uber's drivers in the United States are men.[145] However, a contrary assessment is to be found in a study undertaken in Europe by scholars from the University of Hertfordshire, who found that female platform workers, or would-be platform workers, tend to step outside the traditional occupational gender roles, offering their services for a wide range of activities, including those generally typed as masculine.[146]

Addressing women's continuing or even increased obstacles to participation and ongoing discrimination in wages in the rapidly changing technologically based job market requires positive policy measures. Legal measures need to be taken to establish gig companies' equal opportunity responsibilities both for access of women to internet platforms for eliminating discriminatory content in profiling or feedback. They must also make sure that information as to hourly rates of men and women is publicly available and introduce pay scales based on qualifications, prohibiting discriminatory deviations based on sex. This can be done similarly to the way that discrimination in the media or in the provision of services to the public should be regulated. Working time regulations (including minimum rest periods and maternity or parental leaves) should be applied wherever relevant.[147]

An additional apparent gender advantage of the third and fourth industrial revolutions is the possibility for the person performing the job to schedule the time and place of performance, which may reduce the care dilemma, which in practice particularly affects women.[148] The ability to work over the modem and the reduction of mechanical housekeeping tasks through machinery and robots have widened the scope for integration of a work-life balance into the home environment and this, in a reality in which women are still the primary carers in all societies, opens economic opportunities for women.[149] Nevertheless, this forecast is perhaps overly optimistic. In an interview survey of Indian IT professionals,[150] the ongoing conflict between work obligations and domestic and childcare responsibilities is clear. The researchers point out that the nature of the IT industry causes challenges such as project work with peak load, working at odd hours and extensive travel that makes the work-life balance difficult to manage for women software professionals. Furthermore, the flexibility and working at home may come at a price. They may result in 24/7 availability, in marginalisation from core organisational activities of the employer and exclusion from a promotion ladder.

As regards job opportunities, the job market for women seems set to shrink in the third and fourth industrial revolutions. According to one assessment, men will face nearly 4 million job losses and 1.4 million gains, approximately three jobs lost for every one job gained, whereas women will face 3 million job losses and only 0.55 million gains, more than five jobs lost for every job gained.[151] This prediction is based on the expected employment growth and decline in the existing horizontally sex-segregated employment market. Women make up low numbers in the STEM (Science, Technology, Engineering and Mathematics) job sector,[152] which is a fast growth area, and high numbers in sectors such as sales, business and financial operations and office and administrative, which are low-growth or declining job sectors. This is not, according to economic projections, offset by women's low numbers in manufacturing and production or construction and extraction, where expected job losses will disproportionately affect men. Overall, these projections point, on current trends, to an increasing gender gap in labour force participation and a possible reversal of some of the gains made in workplace gender parity over the past decade.[153] As opposed to this grim prediction for women's future jobs, the OECD gives a much more sanguine assessment: that the majority of job growth is likely to be concentrated in business, as well as in health, education and social services and therefore most new jobs will not require high-level STEM skills.[154]

On existing evidence, education is a key element in preparing women for the new world of work. Currently, women make up the majority of those enrolled in university in nearly 100 countries,[155] and data has shown that in some countries, more women than men are now tertiary graduates.[156] However, women continue to remain underrepresented among STEM graduates, for which the global gender gap stands at 47%, with 30% of all male students graduating from STEM subjects, in contrast to 16% of all female students.[157] That gap is commonly attributed to negative stereotypes and lack of role models, lowering girls' performance and aspirations vis-à-vis science and technology. It represents a key emerging issue for gender parity, since STEM careers are projected by some economists, though not all, to be some of the most sought-after in the context of the fourth industrial revolution. Gender diversification in academic disciplines and professional training, especially as regards STEM-related jobs, are necessary from school upwards.

State obligation to secure equal education for girls and boys has been a central agenda of both the international human rights and the international development agendas, in treaty provisions and the MDGs and SDGs. The aim of equality in access to education has been widely achieved but there are some remaining countries where girls do not have equal educational opportunity at both the primary and secondary school levels and reform regarding school enrolment and also attendance is urgently required. Career counselling and life skill training should be provided for girls in schools, guiding them to choose study programs that hold greater economic prospects. By one popular estimate, 65% of children entering primary school today will ultimately end up working in completely new types of jobs that don't yet exist[158] and it takes active policy to make sure that girls should not be left behind.

7 Maternity and gendered care responsibilities

There are two aspects of parenting which affect women more intensively than men. The first is the biological aspects of maternity which affects only women and the second is the caring aspect of childrearing, which can be performed by either parent but which empirically speaking is largely performed by women as has been shown in the Introduction. Maternity and the heavier burden of unpaid care impact women's opportunities for labour force participation or other economic activities outside the home. This is reflected in the fact that there is an increased gender gap in the labour force participation rate of mothers during the years of childbearing and rearing, as is substantiated by data from the OECD. In all OECD countries, except Sweden and Iceland, mothers' employment rates are lower than those of non-mothers.[159] Nevertheless, the total time spent by women on work, paid and unpaid combined, is on average 50 minutes a day more than men.[160] Thus it is clear that the unpaid care burden on mothers is not entirely set off by their reduced hours of paid work and they are doing a double shift.

Maternity – pregnancy, birth and breastfeeding – is a biological function in women's lives. Feminist literature has argued that these biological functions should not be regarded as exceptional but as being the very core of human existence. This is true from a societal point of view and CEDAW notes the importance of understanding maternity as a social function.[161] However, in a fragmented economic structure of production and reproduction where production is conducted for profit and reproduction is not factored into profit making, the need to be absent from the productive process for any reason is the exception and not the norm. Even so, when reduced to its essential minimum, the time women spend in these biologically specific aspects of reproduction, which we can identify as maternity functions, is minor compared with the costs in wage and promotion gaps over a working lifetime. This is especially so when women's average fertility has reduced globally from nearly six births per woman in 1960 to less than two and a half in 2015.[162] Normative policy, at the international and state levels, has aimed to facilitate the integration of women's work and maternity functions, by prohibiting pregnancy discrimination and mandating paid maternity leave.

Dismissal on grounds of pregnancy is prohibited under CEDAW and ILO Conventions, and the legislation in many countries prohibits dismissal of women during pregnancy, and, in the better legislative arrangements, for a period after their return to work after childbirth.[163] In some cases, in the absence of express legislation, the courts reversed initial refusals to regard pregnancy discrimination as sex discrimination, holding in their later decisions that it is sex discrimination because only women can become pregnant.[164]

Nevertheless, in practice, discrimination in hiring, promotions and dismissals is especially severe for women who are pregnant or mothers.[165] The ILO has reported on the increase in discrimination against women on grounds of maternity witnessed by several equality commissions worldwide.[166] Most of the cases are related to dismissals for pregnancy, dismissal while nursing, failure to grant time for nursing or non-payment of prenatal and postnatal benefits. Pregnancy-related complaints are a severe problem in the workplace in both the United States and the United Kingdom.

In its report on a country visit to the United States in 2015, the WGDAW noted that although the Pregnancy Discrimination Act established in 1978 that pregnancy discrimination is sex discrimination under Title VII, between 1997 and 2011, the number of pregnancy discrimination complaints filed with the Equal Employment Opportunity Commission increased by 46 percent, while pregnant women largely continued to lose their cases when they looked to the courts for remedy.[167]

In the United Kingdom, based on interviews with 3,034 employers and 3,254 mothers, a 2015 report of the Equality and Human Rights Commission found that 77% of mothers said they had a negative or possibly discriminatory experience during pregnancy, maternity leave and/or on return to work after maternity leave. Around 11% of mothers reported they felt forced to leave their job after becoming pregnant.[168]

That data gave greater impetus to "Pregnant Then Screwed," a British site, founded by Joeli Brearley, inspired by her own experience, where women post stories about their workplace maternity nightmares.[169] The site has developed into a much wider project that also exists in the United States and Spain. One of the movement's activities was the organization of "The march of the Mummies," that took place on October 2017, in 6 cities in the United Kingdom and one city in California where women demanded recognition, respect and change for working mums and dads.[170]

Paid maternity leave: The right of working women to paid maternity leave is required under CEDAW and ILO Conventions,[171] under which states are required to mandate paid maternity leave for a minimum of 14 weeks, six of which must be compulsory, and additional leave for complications arising from pregnancy or birth, and to provide breaks or reduction of hours of work for breastfeeding. Provision of paid maternity leave is almost universal, although some countries give less than the 14 weeks minimum and less than half of them meet the rate of payment required by the ILO at two-thirds of the woman's previous earnings.[172] Maternity leave policies without adequate compensation can lead to financial stress, and research suggests that women who return to work without taking their full maternity leave entitlement usually do so for financial reasons.[173] Despite ILO efforts in 2000 to extend the reach of maternity protections to women in precarious employment, only 34 countries ratified the Maternity Protection Convention, 2000 (No. 183), which covers 'atypical forms of dependent work,'[174] and many working women still do not have these basic maternity rights. The informal economy remains largely beyond the reach of labour regulation and maternity rights.

Only two countries have not legislated for paid maternity leave at all and one of these is the United States. The lack of any mandatory provision for paid maternity leave in United States law, in the world's biggest economy, is appalling. The WGDAW reported on its country visit to the United States:

> The Family and Medical Leave Act, which gives employees of employers who have more than 50 employees the right to take unpaid, job-protected leave of twelve workweeks in a 12-month period, cannot be regarded as in lieu of paid maternity leave and falls far beneath international human rights standards, which require that maternity leave must be paid leave for a minimum of 14 weeks, with best practice being the provision of additional paid leave for fathers too. . . . Attempts by the Obama administration to provide paid maternity leave for federal employees were not successful.[175]

There is a question as to whether maternity leave should be mandatory. For example, the EU Directive on Maternity Leave requires the mother to take only one month of a four-month maternity leave. The benefits of shortened leave for women are debated. On one hand, there are claims by women that they need shorter maternity leaves in order to ensure job security and to counteract stereotypes, but, on the other hand, there have been claims that the longer leave is needed for physiological recovery, including overcoming tiredness, physical and hormonal changes or, in some cases, post-partum depression and, where chosen, establishing breastfeeding. These conflicting claims can only be resolved by truly internalising the legitimacy of women's need for maternity leave and providing the necessary resources and financial incentives to workplaces, through tax or other forms of subsidy, to support their absence. This should ideally go beyond payment of two-thirds or more of the woman's salary by social security and should, through tax relief or subsidy, cover the real costs to employers of finding a replacement worker. Making the maternity leave or any part of it optional is not a good option for women employees as it leaves them vulnerable to pressure from their employers to waive their right to be absent; indeed, this is the reason that protective labour laws in general are mandatory, not optional. Similarly the option of sharing maternity leave (as differentiated from childcare leave) by fathers, which has been introduced by some countries,[176] belies the physiological purpose of maternity leave and also opens up the possibility of employer pressure on the mother to return to work.

The issue of who pays is crucial. By 2013, of 185 countries surveyed, 107 financed benefits through social security, 47 stipulated that payment during leave should be covered entirely by the employer and 25 provided a combination of payments by employers and social security.[177] The ILO Conventions leave a wide margin of discretion to states to decide whether benefits be paid from public funds, social insurance or by the employer but, in contrast, some UN experts have recommended that good practice for payment of maternity leave must be through social insurance or public funds so as not to increase discrimination against women by employers seeking to avoid the burden of paid maternity leave.[178] Employers, even without the additional financial burden of benefits, incur organisational costs as a result of employees' absence during maternity leave. Economic analysis might well regard these costs as in essence social costs because the birthing of a new generation is essential to social survival not to the employer's enterprise. The imposition of the costs on private employers indirectly transfers them onto women themselves who, as a category of employees, are likely to encounter increased discrimination in acceptance to work and bear the eventual costs in reduced appointments, promotions and wages. This indeed has been the experience in China, where a high percentage of employers are reported to avoid employing women of childbearing age.[179]

Childcare: Parenthood functions and the need for childcare clearly do not end after 14 weeks of paid maternity leave. The caring functions continue for children. An essential element for allowing parents to both work in the economy and provide care for their children is not only leave but also childcare services.

Childcare leave should be distinguished from maternity leave for women, with its physiological purpose. CEDAW calls for the recognition of the common responsibility of men and women in the upbringing and development of their children and the ILO conventions refer to workers with family responsibilities in order to counteract the assumption that childcare is a mothers' affair. Parental leave can be divided between the mother and father, whether by regulatory provision assigning a portion of the childcare leave to each parent or, in many systems, according to their preference. To counteract this *de facto* gendering of care leave, an independent paid paternity leave to enable and incentivise men to share childcare functions in the first months of a child's life, was first introduced in the Nordic countries. Iceland has established symmetry for the mother and father in independent paid childcare leave, with three months for each parent individually and three months that can be allocated according to parental choice.[180] Paternal provisions, giving leave to the father independently, are becoming more common around the world and some form of leave which fathers can use around the birth of the child are in force in at least 79 countries.[181]

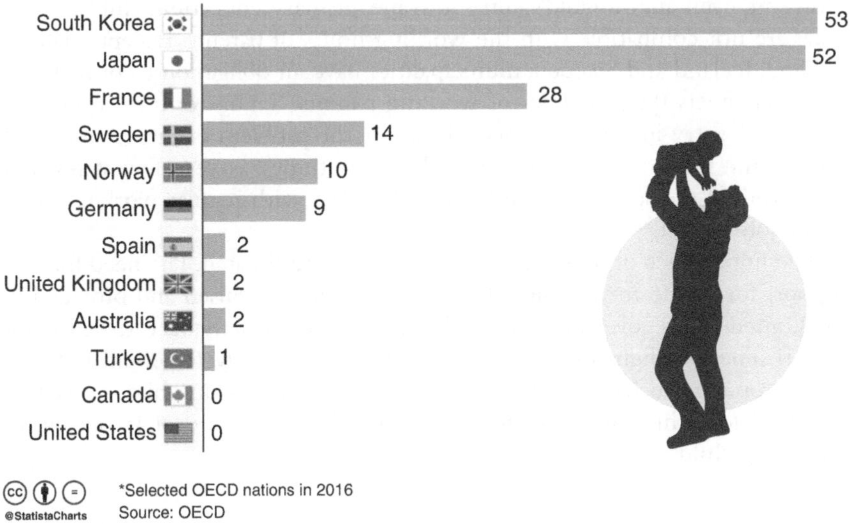

Figure 14.1 Where fathers get the most paid parental leave
Weeks of paid parental leave that can only be taken by the father*

Source: Niall McCarthy, 'Father's Day: Where Fathers Get the Most Paid Parental Leave,' *Statista*, 19 June 2019, www.statista.com/chart/9876/where-fathers-get-the-most-paid-parental-leave/.

Some European countries have various measures of support for parental leave for up to five years. Hungary is a case in point where parents can take parental leave for up to three years with 70% of previous earnings and can take leave and enjoy tax relief for up to five years where the family has a third child.[182] Such extended parental leave programs are ostensibly family friendly and gender neutral. However, in practice, there are pitfalls for women. It is usually women who take the extended parental leave and remove themselves from the labour market, often at a crucial stage in career development.[183] Furthermore, the programs are often structured on an economic basis of parental income, either by providing payment based on a percentage of salary or by giving tax relief on income, and they do not provide a feasible alternative for lower income parents.

The demand for affordable childcare services for children up to three years of age is far from being met, even in the high-income countries of the EU, where only 10 EU member states have met the Barcelona objectives, set in 2002 by the European Council: "Member States should remove disincentives to female labour force participation, taking into account the demand for childcare facilities and in line with national patterns of provision, to provide childcare by 2010 to at least 90% of children between 3 years old and the mandatory school age and at least 33% of children under 3 years of age."[184] In many countries age three is the nominated entrance age for pre-primary education, and in the

EU 86% of children between three and the compulsory school age attend.[185] However, even after a child's entry into pre-primary education, childcare services are not compatible with the working hours of parents. Exceptionally in Finland, Iceland and Sweden, municipalities have an obligation to provide day care that meets the schedules of working parents.[186] Furthermore, even after the age of entry into compulsory education, the problem of integrating work outside the home and care responsibilities continues, as very few states have synchronised the school day and school holidays with regular working hours in the job market.

The importance of state support cannot be overestimated. The need for state support for childcare was, though long forgotten, recognised and provided by the United States government to enable women to 'man' the factories in World War II. The paradigmatic poster image of Rosie the Riveter could not have been promulgated had it not been for the government-run childcare system, the need for which was caricatured in a less known image of Rosie with a screaming child on her back.[187]

Source: Oleksandra Vasylenko / Shutterstock.com

In most societies, four main institutions are involved in the design, funding and delivery of care: households and families, the private sector and the state. Lack of adequate state-supported childcare inevitably drives greater reliance on private sectors in the provision of childcare and ultimately relies on the financial resources of families or the unpaid work of family carers to fill the gap. Developments over the past decades have seen a regression in the provision of state childcare support in many countries. Access to childcare facilities for young children is a significant factor influencing women's participation in the labour market. In the Asian region, surveys have indicated that childcare has been a major barrier to women's labour force participation: in Japan, in 2010, surveys indicated that housework and working hours were the primary reasons that women were not participating in the workforce; in Korea, in 2007, 60% of the women surveyed reported the biggest obstacle to participation was childrearing; and, in Malaysia, it was estimated that 23% of women who stopped working did so for childcare reasons.[188] The price of childcare is considered an obstacle for 53% of EU mothers who do not work or work part-time and 70% in the United Kingdom, Ireland, Netherlands and Rumania.[189] As regards the intensification of the burden of care, there has been a remarkable convergence between the developed and developing worlds. In developing countries, working women have relied on family members, whether grandparents or older daughters, to do the caring.[190] These support systems have been undermined by processes of urbanisation and the loss of extended family support.

The move to a market economy in countries where socialist systems had in the past provided free or heavily subsidised day care, financed either by the state (Russia and China) or by national trade unions (Israel), has resulted in replacing these publicly subsidised care services with for-profit institutions, and the privatisation of services has dramatically increased the costs of childcare.[191] In its country visit to China, the WGDAW reported:

> China established a public childcare system under central planning, which contributed significantly to the high level of participation of women in the labour force. However, the transition from a centrally planned to a market economy has led to a decline in publicly funded childcare and rising childcare costs in private kindergartens. The Working Group notes that, as women bear the burden of childcare, this has a detrimental impact on women's ability to engage in the labour force, particularly for low- and middle-income families, except for those who have parents or grandparents available to take care of the children.[192]

After the financial crisis in 2008, there was a cutback in public services in developed countries which adopted austerity measures, putting the care burden for children, the elderly and the sick back onto families and hence on women. The EU countries united on the implementation of austerity measures and fiscal consolidation programs. In a survey of European countries, findings offer some evidence that the gender gap in the allocation of unpaid work may have widened during the recession. The fall in the supply of social services and joblessness of themselves and other family members was often balanced through women supplying more unpaid labour in the home, including more care services. This ongoing effect was mentioned by Greek and Spanish experts but is likely to exist elsewhere as well.[193] Ex contra, the government in Slovenia increased childcare coverage by 7.5% during the recession, successfully countering the revival of deep-seated gender disparities in unpaid work.[194]

In addition to childcare, there is also a need to care for dependent family members who are old or sick and this aspect of care responsibilities as a barrier to labour force participation is frequently neglected in policy and literature. Encouragingly, the World Economic Forum in 2017, regarding care-related policies as a key element for integrating women into the workforce, included financial arrangements to facilitate care of not only of children but also of elderly relatives or others and direct care service for older people, and senior care services, as well as nursery places for small children. There are, however, only isolated examples of recent increase in state support, as for instance in Hawaii, which introduced an innovative program in 2018 to provide payment to those who provide significant amounts of care services to their elderly family members.[195]

The WEF concludes that the costs and trade-offs associated with care subsidies are often long-term investments for countries as they generate societal and economic returns:

> Public or subsidized childcare can increase the participation of women in the workforce; countries that provide public childcare have been reported to have more than twice the percentage of women receiving wages than those that do not. Similarly, care for older persons is also an important consideration, as women tend to be the primary caregivers for ageing parents.
>
> Investment in the care economy also produces sizeable spillover effects. The International Trade Union Confederation, for example, recently estimated that if 2% of GDP was invested in a country's care industry, there would be corresponding increases in overall employment ranging from 2.4% to 6.1%, depending on the country. This equates to nearly 13 million new jobs in the United States, 3.5 million in Japan, nearly 2 million in Germany, 1.5 million in the United Kingdom, 1 million in Italy, 600,000 in Australia and nearly 120,000 in Denmark.[196]

International legal frameworks provide very little in the way of solutions to the care problem. Even where a strong non-discrimination principle has been dictated for the workplace, this does not seriously address the duality of parents' and particularly women's lives on a structural level. Even in egalitarian families, with shared earning and care work, the burden of care may be unmanageable for both partners.[197] In almost all countries, state and society leave the problem of coping with the clashes between the demands of paid work and unpaid care to the private devices of families.

Diane Elson proposed that the three R's of unpaid care work – Recognition, Reduction and Redistribution – should be integrated into macroeconomic policy.[198] Recognising the economic value of unpaid care work and the economic costs of imposing it on women necessarily requires measures by states to reduce and redistribute it. For example, the recognition of care expenses as deductible for income tax purposes on the grounds that provision of care for dependents is a necessary expenditure to allow an unpaid caretaker to generate income, and there is good practice to this effect in some judicial decisions.[199] The introduction of a social protection floor for care services, can redistribute the cost of care between families and society, as has been recognised at the international level by the HRC.[200] Similarly other agencies can contribute to redistribution of the burden of care, such as trade union or employer initiatives to provide care services. It is also good practice to synchronise children's school hours and holidays with adults' work schedules.[201]

In order to ensure that the burden of care does not disempower women, care must be a public good and, like health services and education, be regarded as a core aspect of the state's economic and social obligations.

Barriers to women's economic opportunities resulting from reproduction and care functions must be removed in order to permit genuine choice by women and men as to how they allocate economic and caring duties. For any real choice to be possible, paid maternity must be available to mothers funded from the public purse and care leave and childcare services must be available to both parents. Solutions have to be sought on the social policy level, in which societies subsidise the cost of care.

8 Domestic workers

The participation of women and mothers in the labour force has produced an increasing demand for domestic and care services. The outsourcing of care functions outside the family has not, however, resulted in their defeminisation as it is carried out almost entirely by women domestic workers: about 83% of the at least 53 million domestic workers are women. Domestic work is hence a major source of wage earning for women, assessed as constituting 7.5% of women's total wage employment worldwide. [202]

Global estimates are that 15.7 percent of all women domestic workers are migrants: in the high-income countries, 66.7% of all female domestic workers are migrants, while in low- and middle-income countries it varies from 2.5% to 6.9%.[203] Global estimations also suggest that 73.4% (around 8.5 million) of all migrant domestic workers are women.[204] Migrant domestic workers caring for children, the disabled and ageing people are a highly vulnerable category of employees. They often encounter long, unregulated hours of work, lack of privacy and exposure to physical and sexual abuse, working as they do in private homes, often beyond the supervisory regulation of public agencies. Typically, they suffer separation from their own families and children.[205]

Maryfe's story:

> I have lived here for the last six years. I have worked as a nanny, a cleaner, a housekeeper, a baby-sitter and a carer for an elderly woman. I am "undocumented"; I do not have a permit to live and work in this country. This is my story. I come from a poor family in the Philippines. . . . I needed to support my children and care for my sick father, and my husband was not much help. I learned that if I went abroad I could earn more money for my children and my family.
>
> In 2004 I decided to look for work outside the Philippines. On 2 October 2004 I went to Hong Kong. . . . When I got there I was given two jobs to do by my employer; I had to care for her disabled child in one house and in the other I had to look after her bedridden father. It was hard work, and my employer was always angry with me. She called me names. She even held a knife to my throat and threatened to kill me. One day I had enough and told her that I wanted to break my contract and return home.

> She got very angry and called the police and told them that I had stolen HK$ 400 from her. They searched my luggage and even strip searched me. I will never forget that. Even though they agreed with me that I hadn't stolen anything the police told me that I would have to leave Hong Kong as I had broken my contract.
>
> . . . I weighed up my duty as a mother to provide my children with a better life against the fact that it would be many years before I could see my children again. That night I called my family and told them I would not see them any more for many years. It was one of the most difficult decisions I have ever made. I miss my children every day.
>
> I have had a few jobs since then in this country. . . . My children and my extended family rely on the money that I send them from here. Everyone at home thinks that because I am working in this country that I should be able to send them back lots of money. They don't know how expensive it is here, and how good work is difficult to find.
>
> . . . I am happy at work, but I miss my children and family. I worry too about my health. . . . I don't have health insurance, and every time I need medical treatment I worry that I will not be able to afford to pay the bill. . . . It is difficult living without papers. I feel scared every time I see the police, even if it is only the transport inspectors. . . . You shouldn't draw attention to yourself. This is the reality of my life.[206]

While on one hand migrant women workers, especially domestic workers are vulnerable to high levels of exploitation and abuse, work migration can also be empowering, as it may bestow additional portable skills, higher self-esteem and increased economic independence.[207] In order to ensure that migrant domestic work empowers women rather than enslaving them it is essential to upgrade domestic work in all contexts. The ILO Domestic Workers Convention (No. 189) called in 2011 for states to guarantee decent work for domestic workers, applying to them the fundamental labour rights of freedom of association, elimination of forced labour and of child labour and elimination of discrimination, equal treatment with other workers as regards minimum wage coverage and monthly payment. It provides for equal treatment with other workers regarding hours of work, overtime pay and rest periods but with the proviso of "taking into account the special characteristics of domestic work."[208] The proviso leaves open a window for draconian exceptions, such as for instance the classification of 24 hours caretaking responsibility for a severely disabled person as hours of work and rest. Despite this loophole, only 25 countries, from different regions have ratified the Convention.[209] Some countries have introduced good practice protections, such as minimum wage, a weekly day of rest, maximum working hours and annual leave, which do not appear to take advantage of the proviso.[210]

It is notable that many of the high-income countries, which are primary destination countries for migrant domestic workers, have not ratified the Convention,[211] and indeed though advanced countries do provide some labour law protection for 77% of domestic workers, only 12% apply their general labour law to them.[212] In contravention of the very concept of decent work for domestic workers, the labour legislation of a significant number of countries wholly or partially excludes domestic workers from its coverage.[213] In the Middle East, where 8% of paid employees are domestic workers (of which women's share is approximately 63%), 99% of them are excluded from the scope of the country's labour laws.[214]

Beyond the searing problem of economic and labour exploitation of domestic workers,[215] there is a strong feminist critique that the whole situation of poor women from the South being employed, instead of caring for their own families, by women in the North in order to free them from the burdens of caring for theirs has produced a kind of inter-feminine women's imperialism.[216] This goes back to critiques of the 1990s, such as Bridget Anderson's 'Servants and Slaves: Europe's Domestic Workers,' which concluded that there is a huge demand for domestic workers in Europe and that affluent European families are employing female domestic workers from the 'third world' often with no official work permits, for long hours and at low wages.[217]

The dilemma is acute. The only way to solve this dilemma is to ensure not only that domestic work be regulated so as to be decent work, as required by the ILO Convention and, further, be professionalised with good pay, but must also be reconciled with the life cycle of both the care service givers and the recipients. Space must be created for the productive and reproductive lives of both. This would require protecting migrant women workers who become pregnant against deportation, before or after the birth, providing employment protections and medical care,[218] and giving residential permits to children born to migrant mothers. The cost implications of this recognition are certainly significant. But these are the true cost implications of factoring the value of care work into macroeconomic calculations. The payment for the long hours of work required by caring has to be assumed by the state, in the form of a widely defined social protection floor providing a decent minimum for both care service givers and recipients and giving both the opportunity to live full productive and reproductive lives. Furthermore, as the WEF has noted, there is ample evidence that recognising and better remunerating work in the care economy could produce significant benefits to economies, societies and individuals.[219]

Looking into the world of the future, robots may take over some caring functions. This is indeed already being introduced for elderly people in Japan, where 26% of the population is over 65. One-third of the government's budget is devoted to developing care robots. There are already robots capable of lifting patients out of bed into wheelchairs or taking them for walks, and there are washing machines to wash and dry elderly people.[220] From my own experience, the future world of childcare could be round the corner. Taking my five-year-old grandson to a museum in Berlin, I found myself replaced by a one-foot-high robot that had him transfixed with interest in its description of all the scientific exhibits and that had a dedicated and obedient little follower who answered its every question: Are you following me? asked the robot and my grandson connectedly replied "Yes I am following you" and trotted happily around after it, with me in tow.

Anecdotes aside, the task of caring will not be mechanised. It is an ongoing essential part of the human experience and it is imperative to integrate the costs of caring into the macroeconomy. Measures must be taken by the state to make sure that women's sale of their human capital is not chained down to unpaid work or exploited in low-paid unregulated work. Care work must be decent work.

9 The unfulfilled promise of equal employment opportunity

There is a strong global consensus in favour of women's labour force participation, freedom from discrimination in the workplace and equal remuneration. Indeed it is almost an axiom of economic thinking to say that the inclusion of men and women in the labour market is indispensable for the welfare of the family, the growth of the economy and women's equality.[221] However what is less clear is that, in current conditions, inclusion of women in labour markets actually achieves the goal of gender equality for most women. Indeed, it may rather, although it increases women's wage earning capacity and potential for economic autonomy, exacerbate certain aspects of gendered inequality.

While there has been a steady increase in the declaratory normative measures intended to provide women with equal employment opportunities and equal wages, the situation on the ground has not greatly improved. Indeed it has even worsened for many women as a result of the financial crisis and austerity measures after 2008 which hit the Western economies and resounded throughout the global economy. Austerity measures, claimed to be in reaction to the financial crisis, reduced public services, on which more women are dependent than men,[222] and cut down public service jobs in which women are more heavily concentrated than men. Following on the crisis, there have been increases in the gender gaps in unemployment in some high and middle income countries,[223] in the movement of women into precarious work[224] and their exposure to trafficking.[225]

Furthermore, the provision of care services which are essential to offset women's disparate burden of unpaid care have been privatised in most developed economies, and public childcare is now the preserve of a select group of countries. As shown throughout Part II, the closing of the gender gap in employment conditions and remuneration requires commitment and investment of significant public resources and these have been lacking under global neo-liberalism and austerity. The continuing relegation of unpaid care responsibilities in the family largely to women takes its toll on economic woman. There has been no normative intervention to compensate the disproportionate imposition of unpaid care on women in a way which can empower the vast majority of women as economic women to participate on an equal footing with men in economic markets. The call for recognition, reduction and redistribution of care work remains inchoate as regards both normative regulation and transformative societal reorganisation.

Part II has taken a global look at women's sale of their human capital. What particularly characterises this form of economic activity is the potential for interpersonal exploitation as the relationship is one which sets the control of the employer above the autonomy of the employee. This control relationship links into the gender stereotypes and sexual harassment which are embedded in culture. Women everywhere are employed at lower rates of return for their human capital than men. Women are vertically segregated, discriminated against in promotion, and horizontally segregated, concentrated in low-wage feminised occupations or industries and are to be found in disparate numbers in the informal economy. Domestic workers are a paradigm case, working in informal work, often as migrants both in developed and developing countries, and expressly excluded in most countries from the full coverage of protective labour law. The expectation that, in the greater anonymity of the third and fourth industrial revolutions, these phenomena would disappear seems to have been premature. Preliminary research results show that discrimination against women is evident in platform services. Assessments of the impact of the robot revolution on women are moot: according to some but not all economists, women's labour force participation will be more drastically reduced than men's because job opportunities will be in STEM occupations, in which women are presently underrepresented.

The evolution of global consensus on equal employment opportunity for women is focused on the removal of discrimination based on gender identity, with equal wages for work of equal value, and accommodation of maternity in formal employment. However, wage and promotion gaps persist in the formal labour market. Attempts to overcome these gaps have had an unsatisfactory success rate. The address for the elimination of discrimination and the provision of accommodation measures for maternity has been the employer or the user of the woman's human capital and it seems that the task of enforcing these requirements through their private agency has not been effective. Furthermore, these efforts do not reach the vast numbers of women who work in informal frameworks both in the developing and the developed economies.

In analysing the contribution of labour income to the rocketing economic inequality globally, Piketty neglects to analyse economic woman. He omits women from his multi-year dynamic analysis of the rise of the supermanager as a greatly increased factor in overall economic inequality as compared with income from capital, both in the Anglo-Saxon countries – the United States, Great Britain, Canada and Australia – and also in the emerging economies – India, South Africa, Indonesia and Argentina.[226] Women do not participate in this top centile's share of national income. It seems clear from the figures of women in senior management and women in high educational achievement brackets that this is a form of discriminatory exclusion from the pinnacle of economic remuneration for sale of human capital. Furthermore, the contribution of gender inequality in work to the malaise of severe income and wealth inequality in general is demonstrable in the situation of the transnational garment industry. The vast majority of employees are women and they are clustered in working poverty, while, at the other end of the scale, the garment industry generates large profits for some of the richest people in the world, such as Amancio Ortega the cofounder and owner of 60% of Inditex, known for its Zara, Massimo Dutti and Pull & Bear fashion chains, who is the world's six richest man, and Stefan Persson, son of H&M establisher and a major shareholder in the company, who is ranked 73 in the Forbes list of the richest people in the world.[227]

Up until now, Part II has discussed the impact of gender differentiation in the workplace and in informal employment on women's experience of economic life. This is, however, just one side of the equation. On the other side is the impact that the exploitation of women's human capital has on the economy itself.

> Eleonora Marx explained the structure of industrial capitalism in plain English. Inequality between men and women in the workplace did not just favour or support capitalism it made capitalism possible.
>
> By dividing workers by gender, the employers kept everyone's wages down. If male workers accepted women's labour as being of less value than their own, they allowed employers to undercut their wages. Net result: lower pay for the entire workforce. The division of labour into men, women and children was simple long-division divide and rule. This was not clever economics or the natural law of markets; it was the unnatural law of patriarchal commodity capitalism.[228]

Eleonora Marx's diagnosis in the late 19th century is valid and can be elaborated on in the 21st century. Women's labour force participation has greatly increased labour supply, thus reducing overall labour costs and increasing the acute income inequality gap, which was analysed by Piketty. Piketty reached his conclusions regarding the income inequality gap without the gender perspective.

Ironically but not unexpectedly, the ethos of equal employment opportunity increases the impact of exploitation of women on industrial capitalism. Women's labour force participation is symbiotic with the move from the male breadwinner wage to the two wage family, thus increasing the pressure on women to work in gainful employment. In this employment, their labour is offered at a lower rate than men's, because of the barriers of structural and stereotypical disadvantage which they face, thus contributing to the numbers of low paid employees. Gary Becker[229] has said that economic efficiency considerations cannot countenance the practice of discrimination, but, though this may be true in theory, we see empirically at the micro-level in countless judicial cases of gender and race discrimination that there is discrimination in practice and women's wages are lower because of sex discrimination in the workplace and structural disadvantage in the society. Women's lower wages brings down all wages, and even if this impact is felt largely in horizontally segregated feminised sectors, the very entry of women to the labour market increases labour supply (Karl Marx's 'reserve army of unemployed') and drives down labour costs.

It is this effect of reducing labour costs which probably explains why, even in the context of neo-liberal opposition to social agendas and the welfare state, the equal employment opportunity agenda for blacks, women and LGBT individuals has thrived almost without objection from conservative economists. While a social agenda increases costs for the wealthier segments of society, an equal employment opportunity agenda decreases them insofar as it increases labour supply. However, although there has been a very significant increase in women's labour force participation, the discrimination gap in promotion and wages has not been closed, either in formal or informal labour markets. Furthermore, there has been a failure to commit to provision of the care infrastructure essential for equal opportunity for women in the sale of their human capital. There is good evidence that both the removal of discrimination and the subsidising of care would benefit economies. They are both certainly an absolute essential if the idea of equal employment opportunity is to be translated into a reality for women everywhere.

Notes

1 Virginia Woolf, 'Professions for Women,' accessed 3 September 2018, http://s.spachman.tripod.com/Woolf/professions.htm.
2 Mayra Gómez, 'Women in Economic and Social Life: Background Paper for the Working Group on the Issue of Discrimination Against Women in Law and in Practice,' 2014, 38, www.ohchr.org/EN/Issues/Women/WGWomen/Pages/ESL.aspx.
3 Sharon Offenberger, 'Reproductive and Care Functions: Background Paper,' 2014, www.ohchr.org/EN/Issues/Women/WGWomen/Pages/ESL.aspx.
4 Nadia Steiber and Barbara Haas, 'Advances in Explaining Women's Employment Patterns' (2012) 10(2) *Socio-Economic Review* 343, 344.
5 ILO Equal Remuneration Convention, 1951 (No. 100) (entered into force 23 May 1953) 165 UNTS 303, http://www.ilo.org/dyn/normlex/en/f?p=NORMLEXPUB:12100:0::NO::P12100_ILO_CODE:C100; ILO Discrimination (Employment and Occupation) Convention, 1958 (No. 111) (entered into force 15 June 1960) 362 UNTS 31, http://www.ilo.org/dyn/normlex/en/f?p=NORMLEXPUB:12100:0::NO::P12100_ILO_CODE:C111. See also ILO, 'ILO and Gender Equality', *International Labour Organization Website*, accessed 10 July 2018, "http://www.ilo.org/gender/Aboutus/ILOandgenderequality/lang-%20en/index.htm" http://www.ilo.org/gender/Aboutus/ILOandgenderequality/lang-en/index.htm.
6 WGDAW, 'Thematic Report on Discrimination Against Women in Economic and Social Life, with a Focus on Economic Crisis,' A/HRC/26/39, 2014, para 8, 4–5, http://www.ohchr.org/EN/Issues/Women/WGWomen/Pages/ESL.aspx. The immediacy of this obligation is in contrast with the notion of progressivity, which as "a necessary flexibility device" applies to the general realization of economic or social rights.
7 Ibid.
8 "The two non-discrimination Conventions are among the five most ratified ILO Conventions. See ILO, 'Equality at Work: The Continuing Challenge', Global Report under

the follow-up to the ILO Declaration on Fundamental Principles and Rights at Work, International Labour Conference 100th Session 2011 Report I(B), 2011, 14, http://www.ilo.org/wcmsp5/groups/public/---ed_norm/---relconf/documents/meeting-document/wcms_154779.pdf."

9 The Convention on the Elimination of all Forms of Discrimination Against Women (entered into force 3 September 1981) 1249 UNTS 13 (CEDAW), art 11(2)(a), www.un.org/womenwatch/daw/cedaw/text/econvention.htm; ILO Maternity Protection Convention, 2000 (No. 183) (entered into force 7 February 2002) 2181 UNTS 253, art 8, www.ilo.org/dyn/normlex/en/f?p=NORMLEXPUB:12100:0::NO::P12100_ILO_CODE:C183.

10 As required under ILO Convention (No. 156) concerning Equal Opportunities and Equal Treatment for Men and Women Workers: Workers with Family Responsibilities (entered into force: 11 August 1983) 1331 UNTS 295 (Workers with Family Responsibilities Convention), and in accordance with the 2013 European Court of Justice ruling that refusal to accommodate a caregiver's request for more flexible working arrangements was unlawful discrimination. See Case 303/06 *Coleman v Attridge Law and Steve Law* (aka the case of Sharon Coleman) [2008] ECR 1-5603. See also WGDAW Report on Economic and Social Life (n 6) fn 204.

11 WGDAW Report on Economic and Social Life (n 6) 10.

12 ILO, 'Equality at Work: The Continuing Challenge', Global Report under the follow-up to the ILO Declaration on Fundamental Principles and Rights at Work, International Labour Conference 100th Session 2011 Report I(B), 2011, 14–15, http://www.ilo.org/wcmsp5/groups/public/---ed_norm/---relconf/documents/meetingdocument/wcms_154779.pdf.

13 The World Bank International Finance Corporation, 'Women, Business and the Law 2012: Removing Barriers to Economic Inclusion,' 2011, 21, Washington, DC: World Bank. © World Bank. https://openknowledge.worldbank.org/handle/10986/27444 License: CC BY 3.0 IGO.

14 This opportunity may be far from realisable in many economies, whether because these economies do not provide sufficient income generating opportunities for individuals to secure decent living standards for themselves and their families or fail to set up an adequate financial infrastructure for future pensions.

15 Heidi Gottfried, *Gender, Work, and Economy: Unpacking the Global Economy* (Polity 2012) 31–32: "Reproductive work involves those activities aimed at social provisioning and daily care for human beings, including 'caring, feeding, clothing, teaching, and nurturing individuals.' . . . A subset of reproductive work specifically centers on care producing affective relations, nurturance and healing that enhance workers' capacities to labor and release labor's productive capabilities (labor power). In essence, these activities are necessary to enable workers to be productive in society."

16 See, for example, ILO, 'Women at Work: Trends 2016', 2016, XV, https://www.ilo.org/wcmsp5/groups/public/---dgreports/---dcomm/—publ/documents/publication/wcms_457317.pdf.

17 ILO, 'Female Labor Force Participation in Developing Countries,' *IZA World of Labor*, September 2014, 2, https://wol.iza.org/uploads/articles/87/pdfs/female-labor-force-participation-in-developing-countries.pdf; Natalija Novta and Joyce Wong, 'Women at Work in Latin America and the Caribbean,' *International Monetary Fund*, 14 February 2017, 8, www.imf.org/en/Publications/WP/Issues/2017/02/14/Women-at-Work-in-Latin-America-and-the Caribbean-44662. The U-shaped hypothesis has been criticised by some economists; see, for example, Isis Gaddis and Stephan Klasen, 'Economic Development, Structural Change and Women's Labor Force Participation: A Reexamination of the Feminization U Hypothesis,' Working Paper, Department of Economics, The New School for Social Research, April 2013, http://citeseerx.ist.psu.edu/viewdoc/download?doi=10.1.1.352.9427&rep=rep1&type=pdf.

18 ILO, 'World Employment and Social Outlook: Trends for Women 2017,' 2017, 5, www.ilo.org/wcmsp5/groups/public/---dgreports/---inst/documents/publication/

wcms_557245.pdf; ILO Women at Work 2016 (n 7) 6. Another assessment by the World Economic Forum in 2016 is that globally, 54% of working-age women take part in the formal economy, on average, as compared to 81% of men. World Economic Forum, 'The Global Gender Gap Report 2016,' 2016, 30, http://www3.weforum.org/docs/GGGR16/WEF_Global_Gender_Gap_Report_2016.pdf.

19 ILO Trends for Women 2017 (n 18) 6.

20 WGDAW, 'Report of the Working Group on the Issue of Discrimination Against Women in Law and in Practice Addendum: Mission to Chile,' A/HRC/29/40/Add.1, 20 May 2015, 9, www.ohchr.org/EN/Issues/Women/WGWomen/Pages/CountryVisits.aspx; WGDAW, 'Report of the Working Group on the Issue of Discrimination Against Women in Law and in Practice Addendum: Mission to Peru,' A/HRC/29/40/Add.2, 26 June 2015, 19, www.ohchr.org/EN/Issues/Women/WGWomen/Pages/CountryVisits.aspx.

21 See ILO Trends for Women 2017 (n 18).

22 Ibid.

23 Gottfried (n 15) 50–53.

24 See discussion in Part IV.

25 Mayra Buvinic, 'Emerging Issue: The Gender Perspectives of the Financial Crisis,' Statement of the World Bank delivered at the Interactive Expert Panel, Commission on the Status of Women, Fifty-third session, New York, 2–13 March 2009, www.un.org/womenwatch/daw/csw/csw53/panels/financial_crisis/Buvinic.formatted.pdf. See also Naoko Otobe, 'Global Economic Crisis, Gender and Employment: The Impact and Policy Response,' Employment Sector: Employment Working Paper No. 74, International Labour Organization, Geneva, 2011, http://wcd1.ilo.org/wcd1/groups/public/---ed_emp/documents/publication/wcms_154198.pdf; ILO, 'Global Economic Crisis, Gender and Work: Key Policy Challenges and Options,' Global Jobs Pact Policy Briefs, Brief No. 15, 2010, www.ilo.org/jobspact/policy/policy-briefs/WCMS_146812/lang--en/index.htm; ILO, 'Global Employment Trends for Women,' International Labour Organization, Geneva, December 2012, www.ilo.org/wcmsp5/groups/public/---dgreports/---dcomm/documents/publication/wcms_195447.pdf; ILO, 'Women at Work: Trends 2016', 2016, XV, https://www.ilo.org/wcmsp5/groups/public/---dgreports/---dcomm/---publ/documents/publication/wcms_457317.pdf. As for the impact of the crisis on developing countries, UN Women have said: "the crisis has had a significantly negative impact on both women and men. Unlike in industrialised countries, the gender-differentiated effects in developing countries are not uniform and depend on the extent to which countries were affected by the crisis and the structure of their labour markets. In some cases, such as in Asia, women's exposure to the export sector, particularly in manufacturing, has led to larger declines in employment for them relative to men; in other cases, the disproportionate loss of men's jobs in the construction sector may have contributed to narrowing gender gaps in employment, achieved mainly through a downward levelling of men's outcomes rather than through progress for women. However, where the recovery is underway, there are concerns that men's employment is recovering faster than women's, leading to further increases in gender gaps. Furthermore, there are also concerns that the crisis has led to increases in informal employment for both women and men, resulting in a further deterioration of their rights at work." UN Women, 'The Global Economic Crisis and Gender Equality,' 2014, 37–38, www.unwomen.org/~/media/headquarters/attachments/sections/library/publications/2014/theglobaleconomiccrisisandgenderequality-en%20pdf.ashx.

26 Buvinic (n 25) 4; ILO Trends for Women 2012 (n 25) 10.

27 Gottfried (n 15) 1–2.

28 ILO Women at Work 2016 (n 16) 6.

29 Hungary for example, see WGDAW, 'Report of the Working Group on the Issue of Discrimination Against Women in Law and in Practice on its Mission to Hungary', 2017, A/HRC/35/29/Add.1, para 4, 35, https://www.ohchr.org/EN/Issues/Women/WGWomen/Pages/CountryVisits.aspx.

30 Marco H.D. van Leeuwen and Richard L. Zijdeman, 'Digital Humanities and the History of Working Women: A Cascade' (2014) 19(4) *The History of the Family* 411, 417. For a review of women's labour force participation development in the United States see Gottfried (n 15) 44–53. However, Catherine Hakim analysed women's work between 1851 and the late 1980s and said that, contrary to widespread belief, there was no substantive change in the overall level of female workforce. Hakim Catherine, ' "https://tau-primo.hosted.exlibrisgroup.com/primo-explore/fulldisplay?docid=TN_sagej10.1177_095001709371005&context=PC&vid=TAU2&lang=en_US&search_scope=Blended&adaptor=primo_central_multiple_fe&tab=default_tab&query=any,contains,The%20Myth%20of%20Rising%20Female%20Employment&sortby=rank&offset=0" The Myth of Rising Female Employment' (1993) 7(1) *Work Employment and Society* 97. In the West for instance, before the first industrial revolution women were involved in the productive economy parallel to men; after the industrial revolution there was a withdrawal of women belonging to higher social groups from the labour market; these women went back into the labour market with the introduction of gender egalitarian values and a rise in levels of education.

31 The World Bank indicates, in its "Women, Business and the Law" 2016 report, that of 173 economies examined, 155 maintain at least one discriminatory barrier for women seeking economic opportunities. However, it should be noted that the nature of the barriers mentioned by the World Bank vary widely, including under the same rubric protective legislation which prohibits night work or heavy manual labour for women, on one hand, and delegation of authority to religious personal law systems which negate women's autonomy in deciding to participate in the labour market or other economic activities, on the other. The countries which adopt personal law systems of this kind are the ones in which women's labour force participation is most severely undermined. See World Bank Group, 'Women, Business and the Law 2016: Getting to Equal', 2015, 3, Washington, DC: World Bank. © World Bank. https://openknowledge.worldbank.org/handle/10986/22546 License: CC BY 3.0 IGO.

32 ILO Women at Work 2016 (n 16) 17.

33 ILO Part-Time Work Convention, 1994 (No. 175) (entry into force 28 February 1998), https://www.ilo.org/dyn/normlex/en/f?p=NORMLEXPUB:12100:0::NO::P12100_ILO_CODE:C175; UNICE, CEEP and the ETUC, The Framework Agreement on Part-time Work, Council Directive 97/81/EC, 15 December 1997, https://eur-lex.europa.eu/legal-content/EN/ALL/?uri=celex%3A31997L0081.

34 Credit Suisse, 'The CS Gender 3000: Women in Senior Management', 2014, 34, https://publications.credit-suisse.com/tasks/render/file/index.cfm?fileid=8128F3C0-99BC-22E6-838E2A5B1E4366DF. See also Natalie Bacon, 'Can Millennials In Corporate Jobs Achieve Work-Life Balance?', *Forbes*, 11 January 2017, https://www.forbes.com/sites/nataliebacon/2017/01/11/can-millennials-in-corporate-jobs-achieve-work-life-balance/#48449617216f.

35 Stephanie Convery, 'All the Money in the World Pay Gap Reports Spark New Hollywood Inequality Row,' *The Guardian*, 10 January 2018, www.theguardian.com/film/2018/jan/10/all-the-money-in-the-world-pay-gap-michelle-williams-mark-wahlberg. Following the public outcry, Wahlberg donated the money to Time's Up Legal Defense Fund, founded to fight pay inequity and the harassment of women across different industries. David Sims, 'The Larger Lessons of Mark Wahlberg's Inflated Salary,' *The Atlantic*, 17 January 2018, www.theatlantic.com/entertainment/archive/2018/01/the-larger-lessons-of-mark-wahlbergs-inflated-salary/550607/.

36 BBC News, 'BBC China Editor Carrie Gracie Quits Post in Equal Pay Row,' *BBC News*, 8 January 2018, www.bbc.com/news/uk-42598775; BBC News, 'Timeline: How the BBC Gender Pay Story Has Unfolded,' *BBC News*, 1 February 2018, www.bbc.com/news/entertainment-arts-42833551.

37 Maggie Astor, 'Catt Sadler Leaves E!,' The *New York Times*, 20 December 2017, www.nytimes.com/2017/12/20/arts/television/catt-sadler-e-equal-pay.html.

38 Martin Oelz, Shauna Olney and Manuela Tomei, 'International Labour Standards Department, Conditions of Work and Equality Department, Equal Pay: An Introductory Guide,' 2013, 2, www.ilo.org/wcmsp5/groups/public/---dgreports/---dcomm/-publ/documents/publication/wcms_216695.pdf.

39 ILO Women at Work 2016 (n 16) 28. See also UN Women, 'Facts and Figures,' *UN Women Website*, accessed 7 September 2018, www.unwomen.org/en/what-we-do/economic-empowerment/facts-and-figures.

40 Jill Rubery and Aristea Koukiadaki, 'Closing the Gender Pay Gap: A Review of the Issues, Policy Mechanisms and International Evidence,' *ILO*, 2016, 2, www.ilo.org/wcmsp5/groups/public/---dgreports/---gender/documents/publication/wcms_540889.pdf.

41 World Bank data as reported by UN Women 'Facts and Figures' (n 39).

42 WEF Global Gender Gap Report 2016 (n 18) 30.

43 Briony Harris, 'What the Pay Gap Between Men and Women Really Looks Like,' *WEF*, 6 November 2017, www.weforum.org/agenda/2017/11/pay-equality-men-women-gender-gap-report-2017/.

44 Rubery and Koukiadaki (n 40). According to the ILO, there are major problems in providing good data on the size of the gender pay gap due to lack of gender disaggregated earnings data, a lack of associated information on working hours and disagreements about whether it is better to present the raw gender pay gaps, to compare median or average earnings between men and women, or to adjust raw gaps for differences in the characteristics of the male and female working populations and/or the employment arrangements under which they work.

45 For example, data that exists for two periods from 37 countries indicate decline from 21.7 to 19.8%. ILO Women at Work 2016 (n 16) 28. The European Commission Report on Progress on equality between women and men in 2013, also brought evidence of an ongoing reduction of the gender pay gap in the European Union countries but it is extremely gradual. See European Commission (Commission Staff Working Document), 'Report on Progress on Equality Between Women and Men in 2013,' 2014. See also Directive 2006/54/EC of the European Parliament and of the Council of 5 July 2006 on the implementation of the principle of equal opportunities and equal treatment of men and women in matters of employment and occupation (recast), OJ L 204, 26.7.2006, 23–36.

46 Harris (n 43).

47 ILO Women at Work 2016 (n 16) 28.

48 Efrat Herzberg Druker, 'The Motherhood Penalty in Labour Markets Across Countries: Background Paper,' 2014, 16, www.ohchr.org/EN/Issues/Women/WGWomen/Pages/ESL.aspx. See also Damian Grimshaw and Jill Rubery, 'Inclusive Labour Markets, Labour Relations and Working Conditions Branch, the Motherhood Pay Gap: A Review of the Issues, Theory and International Evidence,' ILO, 2015, www.ilo.org/wcmsp5/groups/public/---dgreports/---dcomm/-publ/documents/publication/wcms_348041.pdf.

49 Grimshaw and Rubery (n 48).

50 ILO, 'Global Wage Report 2016/17: Wage Inequality in the Workplace,' 2016, 25, www.ilo.org/wcmsp5/groups/public/---dgreports/---dcomm/---publ/documents/publication/wcms_537846.pdf; ILO Women at Work 2016 (n 16) 57.

51 OXFAM, 'An Economy that Works for Women,' Briefing Paper, March 2017, 16–18, https://d1tn3vj7xz9fdh.cloudfront.net/s3fs-public/file_attachments/bp-an-economy-that-works-for-women-020317-en.pdf; Brian Milligan, 'Women More Likely to Be Paid Less Than Minimum Wage,' *BBC*, 18 September 2017, www.bbc.com/news/business-41305033; The Low Pay Commission Press release, 'Low Pay Commission Report on Non-compliance with the Minimum Wage,' 17 September 2017, www.gov.uk/government/news/low-pay-commission-report-on-non-compliance-with-the-minimum

wage; Roger Wilkins and Barbara Broadway, 'The Gender Pay Gap Stretches to Minimum Wage Workers Too,' *WEF*, 7 December 2017, www.weforum.org/agenda/2017/12/the-gender-pay-gap-stretches-to-minimum-wage-workers-too. See also Karen Christopher, Paula England, Timothy M. Smeeding and Katherin Ross Phillips, 'The Gender Gap in Poverty in Modern Nations: Single Motherhood, the Market, and the State' (2002) 45(3) *Sociological Perspectives* 219–242.

52 Tindara Addabbo and Donata Favaro, 'Gender Wage Differentials by Education in Italy' (2011) 43(29) *Applied Economics* 4589.

53 Ana Maria Boudet Munoz, Paola Buitrago, Benedicte Leroy De La Briere, David Locke Newhouse, Eliana Rubiano Matulevich, Kinnon Scott and Pablo Suarez-Becerra, 'Gender Differences in Poverty and Household Composition Through the Life-cycle: A Global Perspective,' Policy Research Working Paper No. 8360, 2018, 33, Washington, DC: World Bank. © World Bank. https://openknowledge.worldbank.org/handle/10986/29426 License: CC BY 3.0 IGO.

54 Ama Marston, 'Women, Business and Human Rights: A Background Paper for the UN Working Group on Discrimination Against Women in Law and Practice,' *Marston Consulting*, 7 March 2014, 31–32, www.ohchr.org/EN/Issues/Women/WGWomen/Pages/ESL.aspx.

55 World Bank data from 2012: see in ILO Global Wage Report 2016/17 (n 50) 31.

56 ILO Trends for Women 2017 (n 18) 10.

57 ILO Women at Work 2016 (n 16) 22–23. More on occupational segregation in UN Women, 'Progress of the World's Women 2015–2016: Transforming Economies, Realizing Rights,' 2015, 89–95, 98, http://progress.unwomen.org/en/2015/pdf/UNW_progressreport.pdf.

58 ILO Equal Remuneration Convention (n 26); CEDAW (n 30) art 11(d). See also Committee on the Elimination of Discrimination Against Women, General Recommendation 13, Equal Remuneration for Work of Equal Value (Eighth session, 1989), UN Doc. A/44/38 at 76 (1990).

59 Sandra Fredman, 'The Right to Equal Pay for Work of Equal Value: Background Paper,' 2014, 18, www.ohchr.org/EN/Issues/Women/WGWomen/Pages/ESL.aspx.

60 By 2011. UN Women, 'Progress of the World's Women 2011–2012: In Pursuit of Justice,' 2011, 24, www.unwomen.org//media/headquarters/attachments/sections/library/publications/2011/progressoftheworldswomen-2011-en.pdf?la=en&vs=2835.

61 By 2014. 'Progress of the World's Women 2015–2016' (n 57) 71.

62 See Marie-Thérèse Chicha, 'Promoting Equity: Gender-neutral Job Evaluation for Equal Pay: A Step-by-Step Guide,' *ILO*, 2008.

63 ILO Trends for Women 2012 (n 25) 28.

64 Oelz, Olney and Tomei (n 38) 33.

65 Fredman's Paper on Equal Pay (n 59) 4–5.

66 World Economic Forum, 'The Global Gender Gap Report 2017,' 2017, 32, http://www3.weforum.org/docs/WEF_GGGR_2017.pdf.

67 Kevin C.K. Lam, Paul B. McGuinness and João Paulo Vieito, 'CEO Gender, Executive Compensation and Firm Performance in Chinese-listed Enterprises' (2013) 21 *Pacific-Basin Finance Journal* 1136.

68 Fernando Monoz-Bullon, 'Gender Compensation Differences Among High Level Executives in the United States' (2010) 49(3) *Industrial Relations: A Journal of Economy and Society* 346, 367. Contrary findings in 2016 found that the 17 female chief executives in 341 S&P companies made nearly $8 million more on average than their 324 male counterparts. See Equilar and Associated Press, 'S&P 500 CEO Pay Study 2016,' 25 May 2016, www.equilar.com/reports/37-associated-press-pay-study-2016.html. See also Margaret Ormiston and James R. Bailey, 'We Know Female CEOs Get Paid More, But We Don't Know Why,' *Harvard Business Review*, 13 March 2017, https://hbr.org/2017/03/we-know-female-ceos-get-paid-more-but-we-dont-know-why.

69 Alexandra Frean and Paul Noellke, 'Bonuses Fuel Pay Gap as Women Bosses Earn 27% Less Than Men,' *The Times*, 25 September 2017, www.thetimes.co.uk/article/bonuses-fuel-pay-gap-as-women-bosses-earn-27-less-than-men-73jb9pmfj.

70 Thomas Piketty, *Capital in the Twenty-first Century* (Arthur Goldhammer tr, Harvard University Press 2014) 290–303.

71 ILO Global Wage Report 2016/17 (n 50) 81.

72 Andrew Chamberlain, 'New Research: Demystifying the Gender Pay Gap,' *Glassdoor Economic Research Blog*, 23 March 2016, www.glassdoor.com/research/demystifying-the-gender-pay-gap/.

73 Angel Gurría, *Education at a Glance 2016: OECD Indicators* (Paris: OECD Publishing 2016) 114–121, https://doi.org/10.1787/eag-2016-en. See also: Michael F. Thompson, 'Earnings of a Lifetime: Comparing Women and Men with College and Graduate Degrees,' *InContext*, March/April 2009, www.incontext.indiana.edu/2009/mar-apr/article1.asp.

74 ILO Global Wage Report 2016/17 (n 50) 31.

75 OECD Education at a Glance 2016 (n 73) 114.

76 Wei Chi and Bo Li, 'Trends in China's Gender Employment and Pay Gap: Estimating Gender Pay Gaps with Employment Selection' (2014) 42(3) *Journal of Comparative Economics* 708.

77 Under the UK legislation from 2017, organisations with more than 250 employees must report on mean gender pay gap in hourly pay, median gender pay gap in hourly pay, mean bonus gender pay gap, median bonus gender pay gap, proportion of males and females receiving a bonus payment, proportion of males and females in each pay quartile, proportion of males and females receiving a bonus payment and proportion of males and females in each pay quartile. As has been widely reported in the UK media, this method has revealed much greater than previously measured wage gaps in leading UK companies. See Regulations No. 353 2017 UK Equality Act 2010 (Specific Duties and Public Authorities); GOV.UK, 'Gender Pay Gap Reporting: Overview,' *GOV.UK*, 22 February 2017, www.gov.uk/guidance/gender-pay-gap-reporting-overview; GOV.UK, 'Gender Pay Gap Reporting: *Make Your Calculations*,' *GOV.UK*, 22 February 2017, www.gov.uk/guidance/gender-pay-gap-reporting-make-your-calculations. As regards Germany, see Tobias Buck, 'German Employers Forced to Reveal Gender Pay Gap,' *Financial Times*, 6 January 2018, www.ft.com/content/e9f618c0-f210-11e7-ac08-07c3086a2625; Philip Oltermann, 'Germany to Require Firms to Publish Data on Gender Pay Parity,' *The Guardian*, 7 October 2016, www.theguardian.com/world/2016/oct/07/germany-to-require-firms-to-publish-data-on gender-pay-parity.

78 Danielle J. Lindemann, 'The UK's Gender Pay Gap Reporting Law Doesn't Go Far Enough,' *Fortune*, 18 April 2017, http://fortune.com/2017/04/18/gender-pay-gap-google-uk-reporting-2016/.

79 ABC Australian Broadcasting Corporation, 'Iceland Equal Pay Law Comes into Effect in Bid to Close Gender Gap,' *ABC News*, 4 January 2018, www.abc.net.au/news/2018-01-04/iceland-law-will-ensure-men-women-paid-equally/9304412; Claire Suddath, 'Can the World's Most Equal Country Finally Kill the Gender Pay Gap? Iceland Has a Plan to Get Women the Same Pay as Men,' *Bloomberg*, 4 January 2018, www.bloomberg.com/news/articles/2018-01-04/can-the-world-s-most-equal-country-finally-kill-the-gender-pay-gap.

80 ILO, 'Decent Work and the Informal Economy,' International Labour Conference 90th Session 2002, Repot VI, Sixth item on the agenda, 2002, 1, www.ilo.org/public/english/standards/relm/ilc/ilc90/pdf/rep-vi.pdf; Sandra Fredman, 'The Role of Equality and Non-discrimination Laws in Women's Economic Participation, Formal and Informal,' 2014, 42, www.ohchr.org/EN/Issues/Women/WGWomen/Pages/ESL.aspx.

81 Resolution and Conclusions Concerning Decent Work and the Informal Economy, The General Conference of the International Labour Organization meeting in its 90th Session, 2002, para 3 of the conclusions, www.ilo.org/wcmsp5/groups/public/---ed_norm/---relconf/---reloff/documents/meetingdocument/wcms_080105.pdf.

82 ILO, 'Key Indicators of the Labour Market,' 9th edn, 2016, 16, www.ilo.org/wcmsp5/groups/public/---dgreports/---stat/documents/publication/wcms_498929.pdf.

83 ILO Department of Statistics, 'Statistical Update on Employment in the Informal Economy,' June 2012, http://laborsta.ilo.org/applv8/data/INFORMAL_ECONOMY/2012-06-Statistical%20update%20-%20v2.pdf.

84 See, for example, ILO, 'Women and Men in the Informal Economy: A Statistical Picture,' 2nd edn, 2013, main findings, www.ilo.org/wcmsp5/groups/public/---dgreports/---stat/documents/publication/wcms_234413.pdf; ILO, 'Transitioning from the Informal to the Formal Economy,' 2013, International Labour Conference, 103rd Session, 2014 Report V(1)), paras 15–17, www.ilo.org/wcmsp5/groups/public/---ed_norm/---relconf/documents/meetingdocument/wcms_218128.pdf; ILO Women at Work 2016 (n 16) 11.

85 ILO Women at Work 2016 (n 16) 11.

86 WGDAW Report on Economic and Social Life (n 6) 15 para 90.

87 See, for example, Judy Fudge and Rosemary Owen, *Precarious Work, Women, and the New Economy: The Challenge to Legal Norms* (Hart Publishing 2006).

88 International Trade Union Confederation (ITUC), 'Living with Economic Insecurity: Women in Precarious Work,' *ITUC*, 5 March 2011, www.ituc-csi.org/living-with-economic-insecurity?lang=en.

89 Zoe Elena Horn, 'The Effects of the Global Economic Crisis on Women in the Informal Economy: Research Findings from WIEGO and the Inclusive Cities Partners' (2010) 18(2) *Gender and Development* 263.

90 Zoe Elena Horn, 'Coping with Crises: Lingering Recession, Rising Inflation, and the Informal Workforce,' Inclusive Cities Study, Synthesis Report, January 2011, http://wiego.org/sites/wiego.org/files/publications/files/Horn-Global-Economic-Crisis-2_0.pdf. For home-based workers there has been some recovery in demand, but for sub-contracted workers, it was not accompanied by any rises in piece rates, despite rising inflation in many study locations and evidence of higher rates for formal workers in nearby factories.

91 ILO Transitioning from the Informal to the Formal Economy (n 84) 9 paras 25–26.

92 As was recommended by the WGDAW, see further below.

93 ILO Transitioning from the Informal to the Formal Economy (n 84) subchapter 2.1: 'The regulatory environment at the international level.'

94 ILO, 'Transition from the Informal to the Formal Economy Recommendation, 2015 (No. 204),' ILO Web page, 15 January 2016, www.ilo.org/employment/units/emp-invest/informal-economy/WCMS_443501/lang--en/index.htm.

95 WGDAW Report on Economic and Social Life (n 6) 17 paras 56–57 and references there.

96 Human Rights Council, 'Elimination of Discrimination Against Women,' A/HRC/26/L.12, Twenty-sixth session Agenda item 3, 23 June 2014, para 8, https://documents-dds-ny.un.org/doc/UNDOC/LTD/G14/061/28/PDF/G1406128.pdf?OpenElement.

97 ILO Transitioning from the Informal to the Formal Economy (n 84) 51 para 169.

98 See, for example, Bonnie Malkin, 'Uma Thurman Breaks Harvey Weinstein Silence, Saying #metoo,' *The Guardian*, 24 November 2017, www.theguardian.com/world/2017/nov/24/uma-thurman-breaks-silence-harvey-weinstein-metoo; Salma Hayek, 'Harvey Weinstein Is My Monster Too,' *The New York Times*, 12 December 2017, www.nytimes.com/interactive/2017/12/13/opinion/contributors/salma-hayek-harvey-weinstein.html; Judith Vonberg, 'Jennifer Lawrence: I Was Treated "In a Way that Now We Would Call Abusive,"' *CNN*, 28 February 2018, https://edition.cnn.com/2018/02/28/entertainment/jennifer-lawrence-amanpour-interview-intl/index.html.

99 Susan Chira, 'We Asked Women in Blue-collar Workplaces About Harassment: Here Are Their Stories,' *The New York Times*, 29 December 2017, www.nytimes.com/2017/12/29/us/blue-collar-women-harassment.html. See also Jody Heymann and Rachel

Vogelstein, 'Commentary: When Sexual Harassment Is Legal,' *Fortune*, 17 November 2017, http://fortune.com/2017/11/17/sexual-harassment-legal-gaps/.

100 ILO, 'Ending Violence and Harassment Against Women and Men in the World of Work,' International Labour Conference 107th Session 2018, 2017, 24, www.ilo.org/wcmsp5/groups/public/---ed_norm/---relconf/documents/meetingdocument/wcms_553577.pdf.

101 UNITE: United Nations Secretary General's Campaign to End Violence Against Women, 'Violence Against Women,' November 2011, http://endviolence.un.org/pdf/pressmaterials/unite_the_situation_en.pdf.

102 ILO Ending Violence and Harassment (n 100) 24.

103 Chira (n 99).

104 ILO Ending Violence and Harassment (n 100) 12.

105 ILO, 'Sexual Harassment at Work,' Fact Sheet, Declaration on Fundamental Principles and Rights at Work, 2007, www.ilo.org/wcmsp5/groups/public/---ed_norm/---declaration/documents/publication/wcms_decl_fs_96_en.pdf.

106 Christine Chinkin, 'Violence Against Women' in Marsha A. Freeman, Christine Chinkin and Beate Rudolf (eds), *The UN Convention on the Elimination of All Forms of Discrimination Against Women: A Commentary* (Oxford University Press 2012) 443, 459.

107 Anália Torres, Dália Costa, Helena Sant'Ana, Bernardo Coelho and Isabel Sousa, 'Sexual Harassment and Bullying in the Workplace in Portugal', Policy brief published in the scope of the project Sexual and Moral Harassment in the Workplace in Portugal, led by CITE (Commission for Equality in Work and Employment) and funded by European Economic Area Financial Mechanism, EEA Grants, Programme PT 07 – Mainstreaming Gender Equality and Promoting Work-life Balance, February 2016, 13, http://cieg.iscsp.ulisboa.pt/images/PDF/Policy%20Brief%20%20Sexual%20Harassment%20and%20Bullyng%20in%20the%20workplace%20in%20Portugal.pdf.

108 ILO, 'Meeting of Experts on Violence Against Women and Men in the World of Work,' Background paper for discussion at the Meeting of Experts on Violence Against Women and Men in the World of Work, 3–6 October 2016, Geneva, 13, www.ilo.org/wcmsp5/groups/public/–dgreports/–gender/documents/meetingdocument/wcms_522932.pdf.

109 Progress of the World's Women 2015–2016 (n 57) 92.

110 Ibid.

111 Frances Raday and Shai Oksenberg, 'The Impact of Violence Against Women on Women's Economic and Social Life: Background Paper,' 2014, www.ohchr.org/EN/Issues/Women/WGWomen/Pages/ESL.aspx.

112 World Bank Group, 'Woman, Business and the Law 2018: Protecting Women from Violence,' accessed 20 September 2018, http://pubdocs.worldbank.org/en/289441522241133897/WBL-fact-sheet-protecting-women-from-violence-FINAL-PDF.pdf.

113 VAW, including rape and indecent acts, when it occurs in the workplace, is often treated under the heading of sexual harassment. In some instances, violent criminal offences, such as rape and even gang rape, when they have occurred in the workplace, have been classified as sexual harassment, as in the 1990s in India when a women social worker, Bhawani Devi, was gang raped and the court found the perpetrators guilty of sexual harassment. This should have been regarded primarily as the crime of gang rape, wherever it occurred. Similarly, the cases reported in the United States military and some of the cases in the #MeToo movement should clearly fall under the general criminal prohibition of sexual violence as well as being sexual harassment in the workplace. The CEDAW Committee addressed VAW in the context of employment in the case of *Vertido v The Philippines* in 1996. Karen Tayag Vertido worked as the executive director of the Davao City Chamber of Commerce and Industry in the Philippines. She alleged that the president of the Chamber had raped her when she accepted his offer of a lift home following a business meeting in the evening. The Philippines Court acquitted. Ms Vertido submitted a communication to the CEDAW Committee, alleging that

the court decision "was grounded in gender-based myths and misconceptions about rape and rape victims," without which the accused would have been convicted. The Committee regarded the national court's grounds for acquittal of the crime of rape as incorporating "references to stereotypes about male and female sexuality and as being more supportive of the credibility of the alleged perpetrator than for the creditability of the victim." See further discussion in Raday and Oksenberg (n 111). See also Chinkin (n 106).

114 See Raday and Oksenberg (n 111).

115 ILO Ending Violence and Harassment (n 100) 6.

116 Progress of the World's Women 2015–2016 (n 57) 94. See also, for example, Mona Chalabi, 'Sexual Harassment at Work: More than Half of Claims in US Result in No Charge,' *The Guardian*, 22 July 2016, www.theguardian.com/money/2016/jul/22/sexual-harassment-at-work-roger-ailes-fox-news.

117 Progress of the World's Women 2015–2016 (n 57) 94.

118 *The Elephant in the Valley Website*, accessed 7 September 2018, www.elephantinthevalley.com/.

119 Deirdre Bosa, Anita Balakrishnan and Todd Haselton, 'Uber Fires More than 20 Workers – Including Some Senior Employees – After Internal Investigation,' *CNBC*, 6 June 2017, www.cnbc.com/2017/06/06/more-than-20-employees-fired-at-uber-in-sexual-harassment-investigation-report.html.

120 See, for example, BBC News, '#MeToo Hits Japan as Junichi Fukuda Quits over Harassment Claims,' *BBC*, 19 April 2018, www.bbc.co.uk/news/world-asia-43819001; Molly Ball, 'Al Franken Is Not Sorry,' *Time*, 9 December 2017, http://time.com/5057462/al-franken-resignation-sorry/; Rick Noack, 'Nobel Literature Prize Canceled This Year, Following Academy's Own #MeToo Scandal,' *The Washington Post*, 4 May 2018, www.washingtonpost.com/news/world/wp/2018/05/04/nobel-literature-price-canceled-this-year-following-academys-own-metoo-scandal/?noredirect=on&utm_term=.532b8381dfad; Sophie Tatum, 'New York AG Eric Schneiderman Resigns over Assault Allegations,' *CNN Politics*, 8 May 2018, https://edition.cnn.com/2018/05/07/politics/eric-schneiderman-violence-allegations/index.html; Doug Criss, 'The (incomplete) List of Powerful Men Accused of Sexual Harassment After Harvey Weinstein,' *CNN*, 1 November 2017, https://edition.cnn.com/2017/10/25/us/list-of-accused-after-weinstein-scandal-trnd/index.html; Madison Feller, 'These High-profile Men Were Brought Down by #MeToo: Now They're Plotting Their Comebacks,' *Elle*, 28 August 2018, www.elle.com/culture/career-politics/a20710282/men-planning-me-too-comebacks-harvey-weinstein/. At the same time, there is a question as to whether sharing stories in the media and on social media platforms is a feasible bypass to a properly handled legal procedure, in which the accused is presumed innocent till proven guilty and the accuser should be protected against retaliatory action by her employer. Furthermore, a backlash is already evolving against #MeToo women, in the form of civil defamation claims by the accused men for large amounts of money, as has already occurred in France and Israel. See Aurelien Breeden, 'Crude, Yes, but Not Like Weinstein: French Man Sues MeToo Accuser,' *New York Times*, 18 January 2018, www.nytimes.com/2018/01/18/world/europe/france-brion-muller-balance-ton-porc.html; Amy Spiro, 'Ex-Keshet CEO Sues Women Who Accused Him of Sexual Harassment,' *The Jerusalem Post*, 10 January 2018, www.jpost.com/Israel-News/Ex-Keshet-CEO-sues-women-who-accused-him-of-sexual-harassment-533393.

121 See below.

122 This section is based on Frances Raday, 'Pension Gender Gap: Background Paper,' 2014, www.ohchr.org/EN/Issues/Women/WGWomen/Pages/ESL.aspx and on the WGDAW Report on Economic and Social Life (n 6).

123 Raday (n 122); World Bank, 'World Development Report 2012: Gender Equality and Development,' 2012, 154–156, Washington, DC: World Bank. © World Bank. https://

openknowledge.worldbank.org/handle/10986/4391 License: CC BY 3.0 IGO; Camila Arza, 'The Gender Dimensions of Pension Systems: Policies and Constraints for the Protection of Older Women,' Discussion Paper for Progress of the World's Women 2015–2016, no. 1, July 2015, 9–12, www.unwomen.org/-/media/headquarters/attachments/sections/library/publications/2015/arza-fin.pdf?la=en&vs=4055; Progress of the World's Women 2015–2016 (n 57) 147.

124 ILO Women at Work 2016 (n 16) 33.

125 World Development Report 2012 (n 123) 154. For data on the gender gap in benefits, see ILO Women at Work 2016 (n 16) 33.

126 The World Bank has identified state-mandated pensions systems as multi-pillar, ranging from flat rate, publicly financed schemes to voluntary, private contribution-based schemes. See Montserrat Pallares-Miralles, Carolina Romero and Edward Whitehouse, 'International Patterns of Pension Provision II: A Worldwide Overview of Facts and Figures. Social Protection and Labor,' Discussion Paper No. 1211, 2012, 34–40, Washington, DC: World Bank. © World Bank. https://openknowledge.worldbank.org/handle/10986/13560 License: CC BY 3.0 IGO; ILO Women at Work 2016 (n 16) 30–34.

127 Ibid. fns 51–53; Arza (n 123) 16–17. This practice was found to be discriminatory by courts in some jurisdictions.

128 Raday (n 122) fns 54–57.

129 WGDAW Report on Economic and Social Life (n 6) paras 101, 134–135; Raday (n 122) fns 58–82. See also Arza (n 123) 29–31; Progress of the World's Women 2015–2016 (n 57) 147–156.

130 Raday (n 122) fns 58–63.

131 Ibid. fns 64–69.

132 Ibid. "Conclusions."

133 The Economist, 'The Third Industrial Revolution,' *The Economist*, 21 April 2012, www.economist.com/node/21553017. See also Klaus Schwab, 'The Fourth Industrial Revolution: What It Means, How to Respond,' *World Economic Forum*, 14 January 2016, www.weforum.org/agenda/2016/01/the-fourth-industrial-revolution-what-it-means-and-how-to-respond/.

134 World Economic Forum, 'The Future of Jobs Employment, Skills and Workforce Strategy for the Fourth Industrial Revolution,' January 2016, v, http://www3.weforum.org/docs/WEF_Future_of_Jobs.pdf.

135 Arianne Renan Barzilay and Anat Ben-David, 'Platform Inequality: Gender in the Gig-economy' (2017) 47 *Seton Hall Law Review* 393, 399.

136 Ursula Huws, 'New Forms of Platform Employment' in Werner Wobbe, Elva Bova and Catalin Dragomirescu-Gaina (eds), *The Digital Economy and the Single Market* (Foundation for European Progressive Studies 2016) 65–82, 65.

137 Barzilay and Ben-David (n 135) 396; Ursula Huws, Neil H. Spencer and Simon Joyce, 'Crowd Work in Europe: Preliminary Results from A Survey in the UK, Sweden, Germany, Austria and the Netherlands,' *FEPS STUDIES*, 2016, 2, http://researchprofiles.herts.ac.uk/portal/files/10749125/crowd_work_in_europe_draft_report_last_version.pdf.

138 Diana Farrell and Fiona Greig, 'Paychecks, Paydays, and the Online Platform Economy Big Data on Income Volatility,' *JPMorgan Chase & Co. Institute*, February 2016, 20, www.jpmorganchase.com/corporate/institute/document/jpmc-institute-volatility-2-report.pdf; Daniel E. Rauch and David Schleicher, 'Like Uber, but for Local Governmental Policy: The Future of Local Regulation of the "Sharing Economy,"' George Mason University Law and Economics Research Paper Series, 2015, 8–10, www.law.gmu.edu/assets/files/publications/working_papers/1501.pdf; Aaron Smith, 'Gig Work, Online Selling and Home Sharing,' *Pew Research Center*, 2016, 8–10, www.pewinternet.org/2016/11/17/gig-work-online-selling-and-home-sharing/; April Rinne, 'What

Exactly Is the Sharing Economy?,' *World Economic Forum*, 13 December 2017, www.weforum.org/agenda/2017/12/when-is-sharing-not-really-sharing/.

139 According to a McKinsey Global Institute survey across Europe and the United States, digital platform utilisation is most common among independent earners who sell goods (60–70%), less common among those who rent assets (25–40%), and much less common among independent workers who offer labour services (8% in the United States and 4% in Europe). Excerpted from 'Independent Work: Choice, Necessity, and the Gig Economy",' October 2016, 37, *McKinsey Global Institute*, www.mckinsey.com. Copyright © 2018 McKinsey & Company. All rights reserved. Reprinted by permission.

140 Farrell and Greig (n 138); Barzilay and Ben-David (n 135) 396.

141 Huws, Spencer and Joyce (n 137) i.

142 Indeed, one of the best known gig companies globally is Uber, which has been held by the United Kingdom labour court to be a fully fledged employer. See Frances Raday, 'Uber, Informal Work and the Expert Working Group on Discrimination Against Women,' *Oxford Human Rights Hub*, 29 November 2016, http://ohrh.law.ox.ac.uk/uber-informal-work-and-the-expert-working-group-on-discrimination-against-women/.

143 Barzilay and Ben-David (n 135) 397.

144 Ibid. While the Platform had not provided a specified field for gender in the work-seeker's profile, the gender was known to people or companies who provide work opportunities through the work-seeker's name or profile picture. The payment is fixed through a process of the work-seeker posting a requested hourly rate, usually an interview with the work-provider, an offer by the work-provider and the signing of a contract.

145 McKinsey Global Institute (n 139) 59.

146 Huws, Spencer and Joyce (n 137) 51.

147 Ibid. 7.

148 See Barzilay and Ben-David (n 135) 400–401.

149 See, for example, ILO Equality at Work (n 12), indicating at page xi of executive summary that: "Flexible and negotiated arrangements on working schedules, job sharing and teleworking are gradually being introduced as an element of more family friendly policies, which can reduce the structural disadvantages experienced by workers with family responsibilities."

150 Reimara Valk and Vasanthi Srinivasan, 'Work–Family Balance of Indian Women Software Professionals: A Qualitative Study' (2011) 23(1) *IIMB Management Review* 39.

151 WEF, The Future of Jobs (n 134) 39.

152 For example, in OECD countries, there is a large gender gap in ICT specialist skills: 5.5% of male workers in OECD countries are ICT specialists but only 1.4% of female workers. OECD, 'Policy Brief on the Future of Work: Going Digital: The Future of Work for Women,' 2017, 5–6, www.oecd.org/employment/Going-Digital-the-Future-of-Work-for-Women.pdf.

153 WEF, The Future of Jobs (n 134) 14.

154 OECD Policy Brief (n 152) 5.

155 WEF, The Future of Jobs (n 134) 35.

156 OECD Policy Brief (n 152) 4.

157 WEF Global Gender Gap Report 2016 (n 18) 29.

158 WEF, The Future of Jobs (n 134) 3.

159 Offenberger (n 3) fn 9.

160 WEF Global Gender Gap Report 2016 (n 18) 31–32. See also the Introduction and Part IV of the book and ILO Women at Work 2016 (n 16) XV.

161 CEDAW (n 30) Preamble and art 5.

162 The World Bank, 'Fertility Rate, Total (Births per Woman),' *The World Bank*, accessed 29 April 2018, http://data.worldbank.org/indicator/SP.DYN.TFRT.IN.

163 As mentioned before, the ILO and the European Court of Justice also called for the prohibition of direct or indirect discrimination on grounds of care functions.

164 See, for example, the *Malaysian Noorfodilla* case from 2010, in Offenberger (n 3) fns 76–78.
165 WGDAW Report on Economic and Social Life (n 6) para 85.
166 ILO Equality at Work (n 12) 25. See also Offenberger (n 3) fns 67–72, 106.
167 WGDAW, 'Report of the Working Group on the Issue of Discrimination Against Women in Law and in Practice on Its Mission to the United States of America,' 2016, A/HRC/32/44/Add.2, para 53 and references there, www.ohchr.org/EN/Issues/Women/WGWomen/Pages/ESL.aspx.
168 IFF Research, 'Pregnancy and Maternity Discrimination Research Findings,' the Department for Business, Innovation and Skills and the Equality and Human Rights Commission, 2016, 6, www.equalityhumanrights.com/en/managing-pregnancy-and-maternity-workplace/pregnancy-and maternity-discrimination-research-findings (the publication is licensed under the Open Government Licence v3.0, see The National Archives, www.nationalarchives.gov.uk/doc/open-government-licence/version/3/).
169 *The 'Pregnant then Screwed' Website*, http://pregnantthenscrewed.com/. See also Sarah Bell, 'How Pregnancy Can Cost You Your Job and Career,' *BBC*, 7 May 2015, www.bbc.com/news/business-32592215; Kristen Bellstrom, 'UK Women Are Telling Their Workplace Discrimination Stories on "Pregnant then Screwed,"' *Fortune*, 27 July 2015, http://fortune.com/2015/07/27/pregnant-then-screwed/.
170 See their website: www.marchofthemummies.com/.
171 CEDAW (n 30) art 11(2)(b); ILO Maternity Protection Convention (n 30). This ILO convention is the most up-to-date international labour standard on maternity protection, although the earlier relevant instruments, the ILO Maternity Protection Convention, 1919 (No. 3) (entered into force 13 June 1921) 38 UNTS 53, www.ilo.org/dyn/normlex/en/f?p=NORMLEXPUB:12100:0::NO::P12100_ILO_CODE:C003, and the ILO Maternity Protection Convention (Revised), 1952 (No. 103) (entered into force 7 September 1955) 214 UNTS 321, www.ilo.org/dyn/normlex/en/f?p=NORMLEXPUB:12100:0::NO::P12100_ILO_CODE:C103, are still in force in certain countries.
172 Offenberger (n 3) 18–19.
173 WGDAW Report on Economic and Social Life (n 6) para 88.
174 ILO Maternity Protection Convention (n 30); ILO, 'Ratifications of C183 – Maternity Protection Convention, 2000 (No. 183),' www.ilo.org/dyn/normlex/en/f?p=NORMLEXPUB:11300:0::NO::P11300_INSTRUMENT_ID:312328.
175 WGDAW Report on the United States (n 167) para 54 and fns there. See also Laur Addati, Naomi Cassirer and Katherine Gilchrist, 'Maternity and Paternity at Work: Law and Practice Across the World,' International Labour Office, 2014, 16, www.ilo.org/global/publications/ilo-bookstore/order-online/books/WCMS_242615/lang--it/index.htm.
176 In Israel for example fathers can replace mothers in the 15 weeks leave or take one week together with them. See National Insurance Institute of Israel Website, 'Paternity Allowance for the Father,' accessed 29 April 2018, www.btl.gov.il/English%20Homepage/Benefits/Maternity%20Insurance/Paternity/Pages/default.aspx.
177 Laur, Cassirer and Gilchrist (n 174) 25.
178 WGDAW Report on Economic and Social Life (n 6) para 88.
179 WGDAW, 'Preliminary Observations and Conclusions of the Working Group on the Issue of Discrimination Against Women in Law and in Practice: End Visit to the People's Republic of China from 12 to 19 December 2013' (Beijing 19 December 2013), http://newsarchive.ohchr.org/EN/NewsEvents/Pages/DisplayNews.aspx?NewsID=14129&LangID=E; The WGDAW, 'Report of the Working Group on the Issue of Discrimination Against Women in Law and in Practice: Mission to China' (2014), A/HRC/26/39/Add.2, paras 39–40, 44, www.ohchr.org/EN/Issues/Women/WGWomen/Pages/CountryVisits.aspx.

180 See OECD Social Policy Division, 'PF2.1: Key Characteristics of Parental Leave Systems' (Updated: 26 October 2017), www.oecd.org/els/soc/PF2_1_Parental_leave_systems.pdf. See also WGDAW, 'Report of the Working Group on the Issue of Discrimination Against Women in Law and in Practice Addendum: Mission to Iceland,' A/HRC/26/39/Add.1,2014, www.ohchr.org/EN/Issues/Women/WGWomen/Pages/CountryVisits.aspx.

181 Laur, Cassirer and Gilchrist (n 174) 51. See also Diane Elson, 'Recognize, Reduce, and Redistribute Unpaid Care Work: How to Close the Gender Gap' (2017) 26(2) *New Labor Forum* 52–61, 57, fns 37–38.

182 WGDAW Report on Hungary (n 20) paras 49, 54; WGDAW, 'UN Working Group on the Issue of Discrimination Against Women in Law and in Practice Finalizes Country Mission to Hungary,' 2016, www.ohchr.org/EN/NewsEvents/Pages/DisplayNews.aspx?NewsID=20027&LangID=E.

183 Laur, Cassirer and Gilchrist (n 174) 65, 67. To counteract this *de facto* gendering of care leave, an independent paid paternity leave to enable and incentivise men to share childcare functions in the first months of a child's life was first introduced in the Nordic countries. Iceland has established symmetry for the mother and father in independent paid childcare leave, with three months for each parent individually and three months that can be allocated according to parental choice. See, for example, WGDAW Report on Hungary (n 20) para 36.

184 Presidency Conclusions, 'Barcelona European Council', 15–16 March 2002, 12, www.consilium.europa.eu/uedocs/cms_data/docs/pressdata/en/ec/71025.pdf.

185 Offenberger (n 3) 49.

186 Ibid. 48, fn 349.

187 Rhaina Cohen, 'Who Took Care of Rosie the Riveter's Kids?' *The Atlantic* 18 November 2015, www.theatlantic.com/business/archive/2015/11/daycare-world-war-rosie-riveter/415650/.

188 Offenberger (n 3) 45.

189 Ibid. 50, fns 364–365.

190 For example, in Kenya. Ibid. 51, fn 371.

191 WGDAW Report on China (n 179) para 48; Expatica, 'Childcare in Moscow,' *Expatica*, accessed 10 April 2018, www.expatica.com/ru/family-essentials/Childcare-in-Moscow_106410.html; Ronald F. Price, *Marx and Education in Russia and China* (Routledge 2012) 109–111; Ruth Halperin-Kaddari, *Women in Israel: A State of Their Own* (University of Pennsylvania Press 2004) 58.

192 WGDAW Report on China (n 179) para 48.

193 Information from interviews conducted on professional missions of the WGDAW to Greece and Spain.

194 Francesca Bettio, Marcella Corsi, Carlo D'Ippoliti, Antigone Lyberaki, Manuela Samek Lodovici and Alina Verashchagina, 'The Impact of the Economic Crisis on the Situation of Women and Men and on Gender Equality Polices: Synthesis Report,' December 2012, 114, www.ehu.eus/documents/2007376/2226923/The+impact+of+the+economic+crisis+on+the+situation+of+women+and+men+and+on+gender+equality+policies%C3%A7.

195 Apolitical, 'Hawaii Is Offering Citizens Money to Care for Their Family – Will They Take It?' *Apolitical*, 19 January 2018, https://apolitical.co/solution_article/hawaii-offering-citizens-money-care-family-will-take/; Agnes Constante, 'Hawaii Passes Law to Ease Responsibility of Elder Care,' *NBC News*, 12 July 2017, www.nbcnews.com/news/asian-america/hawaii-passes-law-ease-responsibility-elder-care-n781941.

196 WEF Global Gender Gap Report 2016 (n 18) 34.

197 Stephen Marche, *The Unmade Bed: The Messy Truth About Men and Women in the 21st Century 2017* (Simon & Schuster 2017).

198 Elson first suggested the three R's framework in 2009 and it has since been used by many international organisations. See Elson (n 181) 52–61, fn 11.

199 WGDAW Report on Economic and Social Life (n 6) para 98; Israeli Supreme Court CA 4243/08 *Pkid Shuma Gush Dan v Peri* (unpublished, 30 April 2009) (in Hebrew), https://supremedecisions.court.gov.il/Home/Download?path=HebrewVerdicts\08/430/042/p17&fileName=08042430.p17&type=4.

200 Human Rights Council, 'Resolution on Protection of the Family: Contribution of the Family to the Realization of the Right to an Adequate Standard of Living for Its Members, Particularly Through Its Role in Poverty Eradication and Achieving Sustainable Development,' A/HRC/RES/29/22, Twenty-ninth session, 22 July 2015, art 20(b), http://ap.ohchr.org/documents/dpage_e.aspx?si=A/HRC/RES/29/22. The HRC in its 2015 Resolution on Protection of the family recognised the principle of shared parental responsibility for the upbringing and development of the child, stressed that it is an essential element of a policy on the family and urged states to take measures to protect and assist the family, including among other things affordable, accessible and quality care services for children and other dependents.

201 WGDAW Report on Economic and Social Life (n 6) para 93.

202 ILO, 'Domestic Workers Across the World: Global and Regional Statistics and the Extent of Legal Protection,' 2013, preface, 19, 95, https://www.ilo.org/wcmsp5/groups/public/@dgreports/@dcomm/@publ/documents/publication/wcms_173363.pdf.

203 ILO, 'ILO Global Estimates of Migrant Workers and Migrant Domestic Workers: Results and Methodology,' 2015, 12, www.ilo.org/wcmsp5/groups/public/---dgreports/---dcomm/documents/publication/wcms_436343.pdf.

204 Ibid. xiii.

205 See Progress of the World's Women 2015–2016 (n 57) 14; Fredman's Paper on the Role of Equality and Non-discrimination Laws (n 80) 57–66.

206 UN OHCHR, 'Behind Closed Doors Protecting and Promoting the Human Rights of Migrant Domestic Workers in an Irregular Situation,' New York and Geneva, 2015, 7, www.ohchr.org/Documents/Publications/Behind_closed_doors_HR_PUB_15_4_EN.pdf.

207 ILO, 'Women and Men Migrant Workers: Moving Towards Equal Rights and Opportunities,' 2008, www.ilo.org/wcmsp5/groups/public/@dgreports/@gender/documents/publication/wcms_101118.pdf.

208 ILO Domestic Workers Convention, 2011 (No. 189) (entered into force 5 September 2013), www.ilo.org/dyn/normlex/en/f?p=NORMLEXPUB:12100:0::NO::P12100_ILO_CODE:C189. See also ILO Press Release, 'Convention 189: Landmark Treaty for Domestic Workers Comes into Force: This Historic ILO Convention Gives Domestic Workers the Same Rights as Other Workers,' 5 September 2013, www.ilo.org/global/standards/information-resources-and-publications/news/WCMS_220793/lang--en/index.htm.

209 As of April 2018. See ILO, 'Ratifications of C189 – Domestic Workers Convention, 2011 (No. 189),' www.ilo.org/dyn/normlex/en/f?p=1000:11300:0::NO:11300:P11300_INSTRUMENT_ID:2551460.

210 See ILO Domestic Workers across the World (n 202).

211 See Ratifications of the ILO Domestic Workers Convention (n 209).

212 ILO Domestic Workers across the World (n 202) 46, 51.

213 See, for example, ILO 'Coverage of Employment Protection Legislation,' 2016, 3, www.ilo.org/wcmsp5/groups/public/---ed_protect/---protrav/---travail/documents/publication/wcms_516125.pdf.

214 ILO Domestic Workers Across the World (n 202) 19, 51.

215 See, for example, documentation in the United Kingdom: Human Rights Watch, 'Hidden Away: Abuses Against Migrant Domestic Workers in the UK,' 2014, www.hrw.org/sites/default/files/reports/uk0314_ForUpload.pdf.

216 ILO, 'Migrant Domestic Workers Across the World: Global and Regional Estimates,' 2016, 2, www.ilo.org/wcmsp5/groups/public/---ed_protect/---protrav/---migrant/

documents/briefingnote/wcms_490162.pdf: "The largest number of migrant domestic workers (almost 80 per cent of the total) are found in high income countries, where they also represent the largest share of all domestic workers (almost 66 per cent)"; Naila Kabeer, 'The Rise of the Female Breadwinner' in Shirin Rai and Georgina Waylen (eds), *New Frontiers in Feminist Political Economy* (Routledge 2014) 62, 69–70; Barbara Ehrenreich and Arlie Russell Hochschild, 'Introduction' in Barbara Ehrenreich and Arlie Russell Hochschild (eds), *Global Woman: Nannies, Maids, and Sex Workers in the New Economy* (Metropolitan Books/Henry Holt 2003) 1–14; Arlie Russell Hochschild, 'Love and Gold' in Barbara Ehrenreich and Arlie Russell Hochschild (eds), *Global Woman: Nannies, Maids, and Sex Workers in the New Economy* (Metropolitan Books/Henry Holt 2003) 15–30.

217 Bridget Anderson, 'Servants and Slaves: Europe's Domestic Workers' (1997) 39(1) *Race and Class* 37.

218 General Recommendation No. 26 of the CEDAW Committee on women migrant workers highlights that discrimination against women migrant workers may be especially acute in relation to pregnancy. See Committee on the Elimination of Discrimination Against Women, 'General Recommendation No. 26 on Women Migrant Workers,' CEDAW/C/2009/WP.1/R, 5 December 2008, para 18, http://www2.ohchr.org/english/bodies/cedaw/docs/GR_26_on_women_migrant_workers_en.pdf. Good practice could be found in the 2011 Israeli High Court ruling in a petition submitted in 2006 against the Interior Ministry and the National Insurance Institute of Israel, submitted by the Association for Civil Rights, the Worker's Hotline and the women's rights organisation Na'amat, in which the court struck down the Interior Ministry regulation requiring female migrant workers to leave Israel three months after giving birth. HCJ 11437/05 *Kav La Oved and others v The Ministry of Interior and others* (unpublished, 13 April 2011).

219 See fn 196 above.

220 Thomas McMullan, 'How a Robot Could Be Grandma's New Carer,' *The Guardian*, 6 November 2016, www.theguardian.com/technology/2016/nov/06/robot-could-be-grandmas-new-care-assistant; Danielle Muoio, 'Japan Is Running Out of People to Take Care of the Elderly, So It's Making Robots Instead,' *Business Insider*, 20 November 2015, www.businessinsider.com/japan-developing-carebots-for-elderly-care-2015-11; Hannah Richardson, 'Robots Could Help Solve Social Care Crisis, Say Academics,' *BBC*, 30 January 2017, www.bbc.com/news/education-38770516; Anna Masui, 'Development of Care Robots Growing in Aging Japan,' *The Japan Times News*, 27 January 2016, www.japantimes.co.jp/news/2016/01/27/national/social-issues/development-care-robots-growing-aging-japan/#.WjTvitIjRdi; Chris Weller, 'IBM Is Working on a Robot that Takes Care of Elderly People Who Live Alone,' *Business Insider*, 28 December 2018, www.businessinsider.com/ibm-pepper-robot-elder-care-2016-12.

221 Nadia Steiber and Barbara Haas, 'Advances in Explaining Women's Employment Patterns' (2012) 10(2) *Socio-Economic Review* 343, 343.

222 Elson (n 181) 55 and fn 21: "Research in a number of countries suggests that cuts to public expenditures have increased women's unpaid work, especially for low-income women, as these women produce caregiving services formerly provided by the public sector, particularly for the elderly and disabled."

223 Michelle Bachelet, 'Critical Perspectives on Financial and Economic Crises: Why Gender Matters,' speech delivered at the Economics Symposium, New York, 21–22 January 2013, www.unwomen.org/en/news/stories/2013/1/speech-by-michelle-bachelet-at-the-economics-symposium. See also Amelita King Dejardin and Jessica Owens, 'Asia in the Global Economic Crisis: Impacts and Responses from a Gender Perspective,' Technical Note, ILO Regional Office for Asia and the Pacific, Bangkok and ILO Policy Integration and Statistics Department, Geneva, Responding to the Economic Crisis – Coherent Policies for Growth, Employment and Decent Work in Asia and Pacific, Manila, Philippines, 18–20 February 2009, www.ilo.org/

wcmsp5/groups/public/---asia/---ro-bangkok/documents/meetingdocument/wcms_101737.pdf.

224 See, for example, UN News Centre Press Release, 'More Women in Cambodia Turning to Sex Trade Amid Financial Crisis – UN Report,' 21 July 2009, https://news.un.org/en/story/2009/07/307372-more-women-cambodia-turning-sex-trade-amid-financial-crisis-un-report.

225 OSCE Press Release, 'Human Traffickers Exploit Economic Crisis, Redoubled Prevention Efforts Urgently Needed, Warns High-level Conference at OSCE,' 14 September 2009, www.osce.org/cthb/51307.

226 Piketty (n 70) 308–335.

227 OXFAM (n 51) 16; Forbes, '#6 Amancio Ortega,' *Forbes*, accessed 7 September 2018, www.forbes.com/profile/amancio-ortega/?list=billionaires#477c4e41116c; Forbes, '#73 Stefan Persson,' accessed 7 September 2018, www.forbes.com/profile/stefan-persson/?list=billionaires#1b2dc3655dbe.

228 Rachel Holmes, *Eleonora Marx: A Life* (Bloomsbury Publishing 2014) 326.

229 Gary S. Becker, *The Economics of Discrimination* (2nd edn, University of Chicago Press 1971).

Part III

Gendered Poverty – Revisiting the Feminisation of Poverty Paradigm

Nelson Mandela, in his speech to the 2005 campaign to end poverty in the developing world, linked massive poverty to obscene inequality and he regarded it as a social evil, to be ranked alongside slavery.[1] Poverty obliterates the right to human dignity and a decent life for both women and men. The eradication of poverty has been repeatedly viewed by UN bodies as "the greatest global challenge and an indispensable requirement for sustainable development."[2] The CESCR Committee stated that poverty is "a human condition characterized by the sustained or chronic deprivation of the resources, capabilities, choices, security and power necessary for the enjoyment of an adequate standard of living and other civil, cultural, economic, political and social rights."[3] The Guiding Principles on Extreme Poverty and Human Rights observe that "Poverty is not solely an economic issue but rather a multi-dimensional phenomenon which encompasses both lack of income and the basic capabilities to live in dignity."[4]

While these destructive characteristics of poverty are shared by women and men, there are additional gendered dimensions of poverty for women. These gendered dimensions encompass both the incidence of poverty and its impact. There has been a widespread claim that the incidence of poverty is higher amongst women than men and, although it is not possible with current survey methods to prove that claim empirically, there is an abundance of secondary evidence which suggests that it may well remain valid. As regards impact, the reproductive and physiological realities of women's and girls' lives expose them to added burdens of exploitation, violence and health hazard beyond the deprivations and social exclusion that they suffer in the same way as men.

A paradigmatic concept of the 'feminisation of poverty' was coined during the 1970s to indicate a phenomenon in which women represent a disproportionate percentage of the world's poor.[5] It was in the 1990s that the term 'feminisation of poverty' became a catch phrase and made a major breakthrough into the development lexicon, with the 1995 Beijing Platform reaffirming it and establishing a strategic goal of eradicating women's poverty.[6] The incidence of poverty amongst women was generally assessed to be 70% of the world's poor.[7] Empirical research has led to rejection of the 70% assessment,[8] but UN agencies have largely continued to assert that a numerical majority of the world's poor are women.[9]

As regards assessing the incidence of women's poverty, existing international measurement is based on surveys of consumption levels in households, which do not reveal the consumption patterns of individual family members.[10] Beyond its incidence, women's poverty is qualitatively different from and harsher than that suffered by men. Although both men and women share the experience of physical deprivation and social exclusion resulting from poverty, women suffer an additional component of abuse and deprivation in a variety of ways, related to their increased vulnerability to gender-based violence, barriers to reproductive health care and denial of conditions of nutrition and sanitation needed in the processes of pregnancy, lactation and menstruation. In all these ways, there is gendered poverty, which must be made fully visible. While various attributes of women's poverty have been identified in the existing literature, they have not been integrated to reinforce the understanding that poverty indeed remains feminised, even if the survey data cannot be used to quantify it.

1 The incidence of poverty

The international poverty line was set by the World Bank, in 2015, at US$1.90 per day in 2011 purchasing power parity terms.[11] Although it is claimed that there has been marked progress on reducing poverty over the past decades, the number of people living in poverty globally remains unacceptably high. According to the most recent assessments, almost 11 people in every 100 in the world, or 10.7% of the global population, live below the international poverty line of US$1.90 per day.[12] The global reduction of poverty has not been evenly spread. Reduction of poverty has been notable in China while the poverty rate has remained high in sub-Saharan Africa and parts of Asia.[13]

Furthermore, this international poverty line has been widely criticised as being a low flat level target that does not reflect the significant impact of poverty on the full enjoyment of human rights,[14] and does not reach the problem of social exclusion associated with poverty. According to one academic research analysis, the current poverty line remains far below subsistence level and, in order to achieve normal human life expectancy of just over 70 years, people need roughly 2.7 to 3.9 times the income at the existing poverty line.[15] Securing the human right to an adequate standard of living[16] can only be addressed if poverty classifications are based on a more generous consumption basket, are defined in terms of relative poverty, as the earning of less than half the country's median income,[17] or include dimensions of poverty other than income.[18] According to a relative criterion for poverty, in 2015, 23.7% of the population in the EU-28 was at risk of income poverty after social transfers, 17.3% at risk of social exclusion and 8.1% were severely materially deprived.[19]

Current international methodology, does not, as said, distinguish between individual household members and so calculation of individual women's versus men's poverty hence remains elusive.[20] The MDGs Report in 2015 stated that women face a greater risk of poverty and refers to a study that used a wealth asset index as a proxy for household poverty to compare the percentage of women and men aged 20 to 59 who live in the lowest wealth quintile of all households. Using this measure, the study found that women are more likely to live in poverty in 41 out of 75 developing countries (with data) and less likely to do so in 17. Furthermore, the report also mentions another study that found, by using conventional national poverty lines, that in Latin America and the Caribbean, the ratio of women to men in poor households increased from 108 women for every 100 men in 1997 to 117 women to every 100 men in 2012.[21] In its 2018 Report on the poverty eradication target of the SDGs, UN Women in partnership with the World Bank acknowledged that there had been no credible global estimates of the number of people living in extreme poverty disaggregated by sex.[22] The various attempts made to assess the extent of the feminisation of poverty remain inchoate.[23]

While the overall data on poverty does not provide decisive evidence of a significant gender gap in the incidence of poverty, there are factors which indicate the probability that such a gap does exist when the dynamics within households are factored in: women's unequal division of power, access to resources, unpaid family labour and care responsibilities.[24] A particularly poignant illustration of the unequal division of resources within families is the greater malnutrition, in some cultures, of women and children than of the males living in the same household. A comprehensive assessment for sub-Saharan Africa reveals that undernourished women and children are spread widely across the distribution of household wealth and consumption.[25] Furthermore, there are stages in women's life cycle, circumstances and contexts in which there may be more significant manifestations of poverty amongst women than men.[26] As regards women's access to resources, unpaid labour in the household and care responsibilities, Sylvia Chant, a leading researcher on poverty and development has said: "The primacy routinely accorded to income in poverty assessments may also minimize other practical and potentially measurable . . . dimensions of poverty such as 'overwork,' 'time-deficiency,' 'dependency' and 'powerlessness.'"[27] She calls for the assessment of poverty to include inputs as well as incomes. [28]

Care responsibilities for children and dependents are an important economic vulnerability factor for households and particularly for women.[29] The UN Women and World Bank 2018 Report found that, globally, 122 women in the 25–34 age group, live in poor households for every 100 men of the same age group.[30]

On one hand, the earning capacity of a primary carer is diminished or entirely preempted and, on the other hand, the costs of maintaining the household are augmented. Social Watch in its policy paper on gender and poverty concludes that there is a strong relationship between unpaid work and the impoverishment of women.[31] The Special Rapporteur on Poverty, analysing the relationship between unpaid care and poverty, inequality and women's human rights, argued that heavy and unequal care responsibilities are a major barrier to gender equality and to women's equal enjoyment of human rights, and, in many cases, condemn women to poverty.[32] Beyond lost opportunity costs, women's care responsibilities for daily provision of food, water and hygiene to children and dependent family members may result in greater personal deprivation, as they share resources, resulting in their increased poverty.

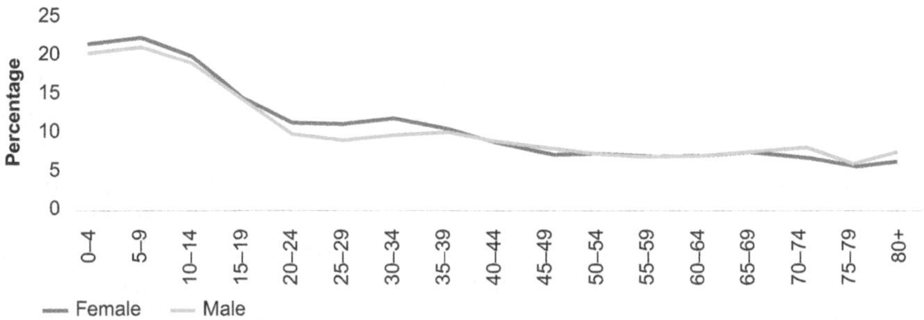

Figure 17.1 Proportion of people living in extreme poverty, by sex and age, 2009–2013

Source: UN Women, 'Turning Promises Into Action: Gender Equality in the 2030 Agenda for Sustainable Development,' 2018, 77, www.unwomen.org/-/media/headquarters/attachments/sections/library/publications/2018/sdg-report-gender-equality-in-the-2030-agenda-for-sustainable-development-2018-en.pdf?la=en&vs=5653 (data refer to the most recent available during the period specified for 89 developing countries).

A woman beggar asking for money in Skopje, Macedonia.

Source: Ljupco Smokovski / Shutterstock.com

Assessments that have focused on single mother families, such as the data on nine Western nations in 2001, revealed that in all the countries, the poverty rates of single mother families are typically much higher than those of other family types.[33] Another more recent assessment indicated that in Canada, Luxembourg and the United States, more than half of single women with young children live in poverty.[34] This is also the case in Japan.[35] A particularly nuanced examination of single parent families, comparing the United States and Japan, accentuates important features of the way in which the data intersects with the assessment of the incidence of women's poverty in general: the increase in the numbers of single parent families, usually headed by women; the increased poverty of single mothers where the social welfare system is not supportive; and the impact of inter-generational residence as a way of mitigating the poverty of single mothers.[36] However, the data on women-headed households has not systematically differentiated between single mothers, widowed women, divorced women and older women-headed households and some research has shown that there was great diversity amongst female-headed households, which are as likely to be present among other income groups as among the poor.[37]

It has been persistently asserted by international bodies and human rights experts that older women are more likely than older men to be poor.[38] Women enter their older years with fewer resources, including property and pensions, than men and this is due to disadvantages that have accumulated over the life course.[39] Furthermore, women have greater longevity and so their share of old-age poverty is numerically greater.

2 Abuse of women's bodies and dignity

A very rich feminist literature has challenged the ways in which the relationship between gender and poverty has been addressed. Researchers have shown how the concentration on income or assets of women in poverty has failed to take account of the diverse influences and experiences of their privation.[40] In addition to the physical deprivation and social exclusion suffered by all those living in poverty, men and women alike, women experience poverty more harshly than men in the dramatic increase of their vulnerability to exploitation and abuse of their bodies. Women in poverty are more exposed to gender-based violence, forced prostitution and trafficking for sexual exploitation. This vulnerability tragically deepens the physical, psychological and social impact of poverty on women. In this respect poverty savagely attacks women's very personhood in a more absolute way than men's. Poverty also imposes an aggravated physiological deprivation on women and girls as it frequently denies them basic medical services for fulfilment of their reproductive rights or needs and access to nutrition, water or sanitation to cope with physiological aspects of reproduction.

Gender-based violence, forced prostitution and trafficking for sexual exploitation

It has been documented that women and girls in poverty are more liable to be subjected to gender-based violence, particularly in situations of migrancy, precarious employment and homelessness.[41] They are targeted, harassed and raped by predators who exploit their vulnerability and lack of a protective shield of any kind. They are also more liable to be the objects of domestic violence by spouses or intimate partners, where the household is poor.[42]

The role of poverty in much of women's and girls' entry into prostitution or vulnerability to trafficking is undeniable.[43] Forced prostitution and sexual exploitation are highly gendered issues, with women's and girls' bodies being exploited by men.[44] The CEDAW Committee, in its General Recommendation no. 19, recognised that poverty and unemployment increase opportunities for trafficking in women and force many women, including young girls, into prostitution and into new forms of sexual exploitation, such as sex tourism and organised marriages between women from developing countries and foreign nationals.[45] The Beijing Platform for Action (1995) recalling the phenomenon of the feminisation of poverty, also indicated that poverty increases the vulnerability of women and girls to sexual exploitation.[46] A 2014 European Parliament Report stated that poverty and bad economic and employment situations are seen as strong push factors forcing women into prostitution.[47]

Prostitution resulting from poverty is forced prostitution, no matter which view is adopted regarding the characterisation of prostitution in general. Where the reason for prostitution is poverty and the woman or girl has no economic autonomy or no alternative survival strategy, the controversy in the feminist literature, as to whether prostitution can be a voluntary act by women who have autonomy to use their own bodies and sexuality as they choose or whether it is invariably an act of coercion which amounts to paid rape,[48] is of no relevance. Prostitution is often an economic survival strategy for women in poverty as a result of the discriminatory barriers to sale of their human capital. Furthermore, within some patriarchal poor households, women and girls may be forced into prostitution in order to support the other members of the family or as a result of widowhood. Women who have been raped may be ostracised and left with no way to support themselves in their home communities. More than all, a high proportion of women in prostitution were sexually abused as children before the age of 18 and their subsequent vulnerability to exploitation, recognised in the psychological literature, is exploited by pimps and predators who then force them from one stage of prostitution to another, usually adding drug addiction as a way of keeping them chained.[49]

Women and children tragically constitute 79% of all detected trafficking victims and women and girls constitute 96% of the persons trafficked for sexual exploitation.[50] Trafficking involves the recruitment, transportation, transfer, harbouring or receipt of persons by means of threat or use of force, coercion, abduction, fraud, deception, abuse of power or vulnerability, or giving payments or benefits to a person in control of the victim; for the purpose of prostitution of others, sexual exploitation, forced labour or services or slavery.[51] The trafficking of women for prostitution and sexual exploitation is the extreme end of the spectrum of abuse of women's dignity and bodies, frequently exposing women and girls to inhuman conditions of sex slavery in which tens of men per day may rape them with impunity. Girls and women may be lured into trafficking with offers of jobs in other countries, sold to traffickers by members of their families or by male partners[52] and, of course, it is poor families and poor women who are most likely to be caught in this net of betrayal. Trafficking for forced labour also more frequently involves sexual exploitation for women than men: the most common forced labour for trafficked women and girls is domestic servitude in which the likelihood of sexual exploitation in the private setting of a home is extremely high. Similarly mail brides may undergo forced or child marriages.[53]

The Special Rapporteur on VAW, Radhika Coomaraswamy, has noted that "trafficking is fuelled by poverty, racism and sexism."[54] An example of the

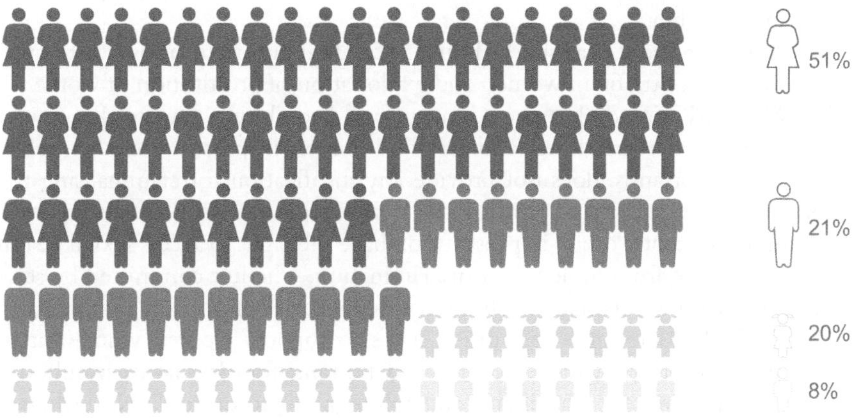

Figure 18.1 Percentages of women, men, girls and boys who are victims of trafficking

Source: United Nations Office on Drugs and Crime (UNDOC), 'Global Report on Trafficking in Persons 2016,' New York, 2016, 7, www.unodc.org/documents/data-and-analysis/glotip/2016_Global_Report_on_Trafficking_in_Persons.pdf.

causative relationship between gendered poverty and trafficking of women became manifest at the time of the fall of the Soviet Union in 1991 and Perestroika with its massive privatisation of the former state-run concerns, the collapse of financial stability and the destruction of the extensive socialist welfare net. Starting off from a base of full employment under the socialist system, subsequently to Perestroika, many women were fired or severely underpaid by employers in the new liberal economy and fell into poverty and these countries became countries of origin of sex trafficking victims.[55]

Poverty is not only a cause but also an effect of prostitution and trafficking. The conditions of women who are in prostitution are particularly harmful to their health and safety and perpetuate their poverty. Surveys conducted amongst victims have found that, in addition to the coercion, threats and violence inflicted on the victims of forced sexual exploitation, one common feature is that the victim is not paid by the client, who instead must pay the pimp or brothel owner directly. The ILO also reports on many instances of debt bondage, especially in the case of migrant victims, where the exploiter retains the victim's earnings, ostensibly to reimburse the travel cost.[56] Furthermore, women and girls in poverty are frequently forced into particularly dangerous and exploitative situations, such as street prostitution,[57] or trapped in underground brothels. The concept of enrichment through prostitution peddled by the media in sensational stories of 'prostitutes turned millionaires' or by Hollywood, as in the film 'Pretty Woman' (1990), was a dangerous manipulation. In those very days, police sources in Poland reported that, while a stolen vehicle could cost DM 15,000, a woman could be bought for a brothel for only DM 3,000–5,000, and only 20 to 40% of her daily earnings were given to her.[58]

CEDAW provides that states should take all appropriate measures to suppress all forms of traffic in women and exploitation of prostitution of women.[59] The WGDAW noted that the Convention's prohibition targets those who are exploiting the prostitutes and not the women in prostitution themselves and thus, importantly, does not provide any justification for criminalising the women who are victims of prostitution, and it recommended that states ensure, at a minimum, that women in prostitution have the right to access sexual health services; are free from violence or discrimination, whether committed by state agents or private persons; and have access to equal protection of the law.[60] The CEDAW Committee has urged states to support women who want to leave prostitution, provide education and training for alternative livelihoods and take measures to rehabilitate and reintegrate prostitutes.[61] Nevertheless, instead, many legal systems continue to penalise the women victims for the act of prostitution, thus trapping women and girls who are living in poverty in a situation of abuse by individual pimps and clients, on one hand, and abuse by the state, on the other.[62]

CEDAW prohibits the trafficking of women and the Trafficking Protocol prohibits trafficking in general and for prostitution or sexual exploitation in particular.[63] The Trafficking Protocol provides that those involved in trafficking, including accomplices, should be liable for a criminal offence. It provides for the assistance to and protection of victims and measures which must be taken to prevent trafficking, including educational, social or cultural measure to discourage the demand that fosters all forms of exploitation of persons, especially women and children, that leads to trafficking.[64] The Council of Europe Convention on Trafficking in Human Beings[65] goes further. It suggests that countries should consider criminalising the use of the services of the victim.[66] And it also adds that the proceeds of the criminal offences relating to trafficking should be confiscated and that the resulting assets might be used to guarantee compensation for victims or measures or programs aimed at social assistance.[67] The number of countries which have criminalised trafficking has increased from 33 in 2003 to 158 in 2016, providing a legal basis for assisting the victims and prosecuting the traffickers. Nevertheless, the average number of convictions remains very low and the numbers of persons trafficked remains horrifically high and on the increase.[68]

Through the lens of women in poverty, approaches to prostitution and trafficking should concentrate on the state's obligation to provide women with economic solutions and proper health and social services.

Lack of access to reproductive services and physiological needs

Women in poverty suffer from multiple discrimination, on combined grounds of sex and socio-economic status, in enjoyment of reproductive health rights and needs. The barriers to reproductive health rights and needs may derive either from restrictive legislation and criminalisation or from a failure to provide essential reproductive services as affordable public goods. Women who have financial resources will often be able to access private medical care services, which provide them with a solution for their reproductive needs in the absence of legal, public health service access. However, poor women are entirely barred from such access by either of these obstacles: criminalisation or lack of affordability.

An estimated 214 million women in developing regions are deprived of access to modern contraception. Providing all women who want it with contraception would prevent 84% of 89 million unintended pregnancies, which occur in developing countries.[69] In spite of the clear economic and social justification for making contraceptive accessible and affordable, a few countries continue to prohibit the sale and many countries fail to ensure the availability and affordability of modern contraceptives.[70]

Although there has been a global trend to decriminalise the use of modern contraceptives,[71] access has, in some cases, been severely undermined by restrictive policies on funding and insurance, such as the United States Supreme Court's Hobby Lobby ruling, which permitted opting out from a statutory obligation to provide health insurance coverage for contraception on grounds of religious conscience.[72] A lack of affordable or free availability of modern contraception prevents women in poverty from exercising their right to decide upon the number and spacing of their children.[73]

Criminalisation of abortion is a measure which targets women in poverty and results in severe and even fatal discrimination against them by the state. Many unsafe abortions are the result of criminalisation of abortion, leaving women to seek out termination of their pregnancy by unauthorised and unqualified providers. The WHO reported in 2018 that around 25 million unsafe abortions were estimated to have taken place worldwide each year, almost all in developing countries. Over half of all estimated unsafe abortions globally were in Asia, and three out of four abortions that occurred in Africa and Latin America were unsafe. Each year, between 4.7% and 13.2% of maternal deaths can be attributed to unsafe abortion.[74] The WHO has demonstrated that, in countries where induced termination of pregnancy is restricted by law and/or otherwise unavailable, the number of abortions is not reduced, safe termination of pregnancy is a privilege of the rich and women with limited resources have little choice but to resort to unsafe providers and practices.[75]

Even where there is no prohibition of abortion, there may be restrictions on access to medical procedures or services, making them inaccessible to poorer women. The restriction of access to abortion services has been a growing phenomenon in the United States, where there has been an erosion of the availability of medical facilities authorised to carry out abortions and imposition of problematic procedural barriers on women seeking abortions. Some limit was placed on these restrictive legislative practices by the United States Supreme Court which regarded them as unduly burdening women's access to their constitutionally guaranteed right of abortion.[76] The restrictive approach of the United States government to abortion has a dire impact on women in developing countries through the 'Global Gag Rule,' which has been repeatedly enacted by Republican presidents in order to deny United States funding for global health assistance to non-governmental organisations, if they provide abortion services, counsel patients about the option of abortion or advocate for liberalisation of abortion laws.[77] The Trump administration is presently proposing to extend the rule to federal funding within the US.[78]

Where countries which prohibit the termination of pregnancy prosecute women whose pregnancy is terminated for murder or manslaughter, these prosecutions are usually directed against poor women who did not have the resources to resort to private medical services, often abroad, where the abortion was permitted. In El Salvador tens of women have been given prison sentences of more than 30 years because they terminated a pregnancy. Some of the women lost their pregnancies in tragic circumstances where there was a miscarriage, danger to the woman's life or a dead foetus. These women are invariably from poor rural communities.[79]

The CEDAW Committee has condemned state violations of women's sexual and reproductive health and rights, such as forced sterilisations, forced abortion, forced pregnancy, criminalisation of abortion, denial or delay of safe abortion and post-abortion care, forced continuation of pregnancy, as forms of gender-based violence that, depending on the circumstances, may amount to torture or cruel, inhuman or degrading treatment.[80] The WGDAW has noted that discrimination against women by states includes the criminalisation of behaviours in which only or mainly women are involved.[81] Much of this discriminatory criminalisation relates to reproduction and sexuality, such as the prohibitions on abortion, prostitution, adultery and fornication. The discrimination is not, however, just against women. It is primarily against women in poverty. The women caught and punished in the net of this gendered penalisation of women's behaviours are overwhelmingly women in poverty who lack the economic resources required to avoid the reach of the criminal law enforcement.

Basic conditions needed in the processes of pregnancy, lactation and menstruation

In the context of women's reproductive life, a lack of availability and affordability of health services puts women in poverty at a heightened level of risk. Ongoing risks of maternal mortality are closely related to the accessibility of health facilities for childbirth and this is affected by regional poverty: while in the developed world a woman's risk of dying during pregnancy and childbirth is 1 in 3,700, in sub-Saharan Africa it is very high at 1 in 38.[82] Risks of maternal mortality affects adolescent girls in particular: pregnancy and childbirth are together the second leading cause of death among 15- to 19-year-old girls globally, putting them at the highest risk of dying or suffering serious lifelong injuries as a result of pregnancy.[83] The MDGs in 2000 targeted reduction of the maternal mortality ratio and the WHO reported in 2013 a global decline of 45% from levels in 1990. The issue of maternal mortality remains on the agenda of the SDGs.[84]

A particularly egregious impact of poverty on women's health[85] and human dignity[86] in the context of their reproductive capacity may be posed by the commercialisation of surrogacy and egg donation, both of which expose women in poverty to exploitation and health risks. The use of the surrogate's services is, furthermore, usually without protective regulation which would ensure full information for the surrogate, extensive health insurance and high minimum payment for the surrogate herself,[87] regulation of all intermediaries, protection of the surrogate's autonomy and psychological needs during and after the pregnancy and birth, including the right to maintain parentage.[88]

In pregnancy and lactation women suffer acute accentuation of any problems in access to food, water and sanitation, the deprivation of which is a violation of the most basic core economic and social rights of all who live in poverty. The failure to secure their supply affects women and girls disparately for both physiological and cultural reasons, which interact to exacerbate the impact of food, water and sanitation poverty.

Women have greater nutritional needs during pregnancy and lactation and hence are more vulnerable to malnutrition. Indeed, CEDAW requires states to ensure appropriate services in connection with pregnancy, confinement and the postnatal period, granting free services where necessary, as well as adequate nutrition during pregnancy and lactation.[89] UNICEF reports that a third of women of reproductive age in India are undernourished. This malnutrition is compounded further in young mothers, especially adolescent girls. Importantly, given the linkages of women's nutrition with poverty alleviation, women's empowerment and food security, nutrition initiatives are being tested with government, civil society and UNICEF cooperation, to improve the nutrient intake of pregnant women and breastfeeding mothers, and reduce the prevalence and severity of maternal anaemia.[90] Furthermore, there are some cultural practices which selectively deprive women of nutritious foods, including during pregnancy and lactation: from infancy, the female child is given a low-nutrition diet; she is weaned at a much earlier age than the male infant, and throughout her life she will be deprived of high-protein food such as animal meat, eggs, fish and milk. As a result, the intake of nutriments by the female population is lower than that of the male population.[91]

Lack of access to water and sanitation creates severe problems for women and girls. The need for sanitary towels or tampons creates a huge and under-recognised problem for women in poverty, resulting in school absenteeism for menstruating girls and desperate situations for homeless women. And, of course, the increased need for toilets and showers becomes crucial in the monthly period of menstruation.[92]

The Special Rapporteur on the human rights to drinking water and sanitation reported in 2016:

> A large and growing body of studies suggests that women and men often have differentiated access, use, experiences and knowledge of water, sanitation and hygiene. Cultural, social, economic and biological differences between women and men consistently lead to unequal opportunities for women in the enjoyment of the human rights to water and sanitation, with devastating consequences for the enjoyment of other human rights and gender equality more generally.
>
> . . . challenges related to inequality include access to sanitation, menstrual hygiene and toilets. . .[93]

Wherever there is a scarcity of food, water and sanitation, women in poverty suffer an added layer of deprivation, beyond that shared with men in poverty, because of their increased need for these commodities in connection with their reproductive rights and physiological needs.

3 Development and human rights agendas for reduction of poverty

An understanding of the disparate incidence and burden of poverty for women and of its differential impact on their sexual, reproductive and physiological rights requires gender analysis of policies to reduce and alleviate poverty in general.

There are two areas of international policy-making for the reduction and alleviation of poverty: the development agenda and the social and economic human rights regime. While these are often dealt with by separate bodies, in different forums and with differing language, they are theoretically overlapping. The Vienna Declaration and Program of Action in 1993 clarified that, while development facilitates the enjoyment of all human rights, lack of development may not be invoked to justify the abridgement of internationally recognised human rights.[94] This means that development exigencies cannot be invoked to justify discrimination against women.

The reduction and alleviation of poverty has been addressed primarily in the context of the development agenda. The UN Development Agenda is an internationally shared framework for action at the global, regional and country levels, engaging key stakeholders: governments, United Nations system organisations, other intergovernmental and non-governmental organisations, civil society and the private sector.[95] It encompasses inter-linked issues ranging from poverty reduction, gender equality, social integration, health, population, employment and education to human rights, the environment, sustainable development, finance and governance.[96]

As methods, the UN Development Agenda has engaged in macroeconomic strategies, international trade regulation, entrepreneurship programs, credit and employment incentives. The MDGs went on to make elimination of poverty a primary goal by 2015 which has been touted to have achieved considerable impact in reducing the incidence of extreme poverty, with the claim being made that the global poverty rate was halved since 1999.[97] The SDGs continued with the poverty elimination goal to be reached by 2030, raising the level, in accordance with the World Bank's poverty line, from $1.25 to $1.90.[98] However, as said before, many commentators point out that the monetaristic income poverty target has been placed far too low, in terms of access to basic resources.

In both the MDGs in 2000 and the SDGs in 2015, the achievement of gender equality and empowerment of all women and girls has been addressed both as a cross-cutting issue for all goals and targets and as a stand-alone goal for the development agenda.[99] Additionally, the poverty eradication goal of the SDGs call for gender-sensitive strategies and the indicators adopted for monitoring implementation of this target require governments to report on the "proportion of their recurrent and capital spending to sectors that disproportionately (sic) benefit women, the poor and vulnerable groups" and on the proportion of men, women and children living below the national poverty line, by sex and age.[100]

Along with the adoption of the MDGs, in 2001, the World Bank started to pay attention to the relevance of women's economic status to development outcomes. One of the strong rationales for doing so was recognition of the impact of women's education on fertility rates and hence on poverty. The bank called for including women's economic status as an indicator in its development projects.[101] In a critique by feminist economists, however, there is a widely spread view that the bank relates to gender in an instrumentalist way, regarding equality for women merely as a way of promoting economic growth under the neo-liberal paradigm and failing to delve into the transformative economics required to facilitate and fulfil women's right to substantive equality.[102] Sylvia Chant, a leading researcher on poverty and development, states: "Since the 'feminization of poverty' came to enjoy the status of global orthodoxy at the Fourth Women's World Conference at Beijing in 1995, women and girls have assumed an unprecedented visibility in development discourse, not only as the principal victims of economic privation, but also as frontline actors in poverty reduction."[103] In the context of the development agenda, the characterisation of women as frontline actors in the reduction of poverty is criticised by Chant as instrumentalising the use of women's human capital. There is certainly an argument to be made that the utilisation of women's human capital in the labour market is not necessarily an indicator for their equality of opportunity, of access to economic resources or fair distribution of unpaid care and this has been discussed in Part II. Nevertheless, the participation of women in the development agenda's economic projects is a legitimate and beneficial aspect of poverty reduction for them and their families. The appropriate guard against instrumentalisation of women's human capital lies in securing the quality and conditions of their work opportunities, the equality of their remuneration and the provision of maternity care and childcare support.

The Development Agenda declares that it is intended to provide a framework for human rights and this perspective of human rights is crucial in understanding the true dimensions of poverty and of gendered poverty. It has become well recognised that poverty is a multidimensional phenomenon that encompasses much more than a lack of sufficient income alone. This multidimensional approach to poverty requires attention to education, health and living conditions. In 2010, the UNDP developed the Multidimensional Poverty Index, which seeks to reflect multiple deprivations at the household level. The assessments of global multidimensional poverty are vague but it seems clear that the numbers of people living in or near multidimensional poverty are far greater than those living under the $1.90 poverty line.[104]

The international human rights regime addresses the issue of poverty from the perspective of social and economic rights. Within the human rights framework, women's right to equality and non-discrimination combines with social and economic rights to provide a normative basis for gender-sensitive policy in poverty alleviation programs. Both the ICESCR and CEDAW require equal rights for men and women in all social and economic rights and, although states only have an obligation to realise economic and social rights progressively to the maximum of their available resources, they have an immediate obligation to end discrimination against women in the allocation of existing social and economic benefits.

Many economic and social rights are directly or indirectly relevant to reducing multidimensional poverty, particularly rights to minimum standards of work, social security, food, education, health, standard of living, housing and water.[105] Of all these social and economic rights it is the right to social security,[106] which most directly focuses on reduction or alleviation of the monetarised elements of poverty.[107] Social security, through its redistributive character, plays an important role, in poverty reduction and alleviation, to prevent social exclusion. Regarding economic woman, it is crucial to question how far women's right to equality has been ensured within social security programs.

Social security includes social insurance, universal benefit schemes and social assistance. Social insurance provides coverage for employees' income during interruptions in continuous employment, such as unemployment, sickness, employment injury and maternity, or after retirement, and is based on employer and employee contributions. Universal benefit schemes are provided for categories of population groups, such as children, persons with disabilities or the elderly, who are entitled to support from public funds and are essentially non-contributory. Social assistance, including non-contributory cash transfer payments, is contingency based, for situations of extreme need, frequently means-tested, and hence largely directed to persons in poverty.

Equality for women in social security is more likely to be achieved in the non-contributory schemes, as the social insurance schemes, based on contributions, penalise women, as a result of their lower lifetime earnings, informal work and unpaid care work, frequently result in their inability to make adequate contributions to the contributory schemes.[108] According to LIS data from 26 high- and middle-income countries in 2016, "income transfers – even with their shortcomings vis-à-vis women's disadvantage – play a key role in reducing women's market-generated poverty."[109] In developing countries, it is said that cash transfers are playing a significant role in the fight against poverty. In 2014, developing countries provided cash transfers to 718 million people to supplement the income of the poorest households, such as child support, pensions, payments to widows or people with disabilities, or cash transfers to particularly poor households.[110] Some of these transfers are directly focused on women, such as the Progresa/Oportunidades program in Mexico[111] or a program in Nigeria which targets pregnant and lactating women, with a view to improving nutrition,[112] and some are paid directly to women.[113] The ILO has produced a policy series, 'Cash Transfer Programs, Poverty Reduction and Empowerment of Women,' that examines cash transfers in developing economies. It reports that there has been a remarkable proliferation of such programs around the world, including, among other countries, Armenia, Bangladesh, Botswana, Brazil, Chile, Columbia, Honduras, India, Indonesia, Jamaica, Mexico, Namibia, Nepal, Panama and South Africa.[114]

Nevertheless, researchers have observed that even non-contributory pillars of social security are not always a panacea for alleviating women's poverty. The payment of social assistance is in some schemes conferred on households or children in ways that do not empower women to break the circle of their own poverty.[115] For example, conditioning social assistance on certain kinds of behavioural compliance often targets mothers and ties them to traditional roles.[116] Non-contributory pillars are, in any case, generally designed with much lower benefits than contributory pillars, which means, of course, that the level of women's coverage from non-contributory systems alone may be inadequate to keep them out of poverty.

There has been a breakaway development in the concept of social security, in the ILO Social Protection Floor Recommendation in 2012, requiring higher levels of protection to as many people as possible, through social protection floors financed by national resources.[117] Philip Alston, the Special Rapporteur on Poverty has said:

> Economic and social rights must become an integral part of human rights programs. A concerted campaign to ensure that every state has a social protection floor in place would signal a transformation in this regard. That concept – initially elaborated by the International Labour Organization, subsequently endorsed by the UN and now even by the World Bank – draws upon the experience of a range of countries around the world that have successfully tackled poverty in terms of programs with universal coverage, formulated in terms of human rights and of domestic legal entitlements.[118]

Social protection is to be funded by public non-contributory systems, which may provide health care, invalidity payments or pensions on a basis of need. A gender dimension has been incorporated in the social protection agenda: the ILO in its preamble recognises social security as an important tool to promote equal opportunity and gender and racial equality, and to support the transition from informal to formal employment.[119] This reference to gender issues is cursory and not further developed,[120] but UN Women notes that the

> Social Protection Floor, according to the context, may comprise a broad range of age and gender-sensitive social security programs: early childhood development programs, pregnancy and maternity benefits, family allowances and parental care services for minors and dependent persons, reproductive health (including maternal and infant health services), food support, access to life-saving medication, health insurance and community assistance services such as water and sanitation, active and passive labour market programs, social and invalidity pensions, education for children with special needs, etc.[121]

Indeed, amongst high-income countries, social protection floors are important to alleviate some of those aspects of poverty which affect women harshly, particularly through the provision of employment support, child support and childcare services. Researchers have noted with regard to the economic vulnerability of households during the child-rearing years that, those with the least developed employment support policies (United States, Australia and the UK) and those with the least developed social transfer systems for families with young children (United States, Australia, Canada) are generally those in which parents have the highest poverty rates compared to nonparents.[122]

Whatever the consensus as to the importance of social security and protection systems for alleviating poverty in general and women's poverty in particular, global neo-liberal trends have since the 1980s been reducing the readiness of states to fund these schemes.[123] The neo-liberal policies encapsulated for the developing world in the 1980s Washington Consensus, which was supported by prominent economists and international organisations, such as the IMF, the World Bank, the EU and the US, visualised social security and social protection as a minimalist notion of 'social safety nets.'[124] This rigid approach was conceptually deconstructed, in what has been called the post-Washington consensus.[125] However, since the 2008 financial crisis, austerity measures have undermined social protection floors, even in regions which have had well-developed welfare systems.[126]

The ILO World Social Protection Report 2017 reveals a bleak picture: the vast majority of people around the world are not covered by comprehensive social protection. Only 45% of the global population are effectively covered by at least one social protection benefit, and only 29% are covered by comprehensive social security. The regional variation is extreme. Europe and Central Asia have relatively comprehensive and mature social protection floors and provide over 80% access to child and family benefits, maternity cash benefits, disability benefits and old-age pensions, with several countries reaching universal coverage. In the Americas, 67.6% of the population are effectively covered by at least one social protection cash benefit, primarily as a result of the extension of social protection systems over recent decades. In the Asia and Pacific region, only

38.9% of the population are effectively covered by at least one social protection cash benefit. In the Arab states, the lack of data allows only a partial assessment of effective social protection coverage and coverage for old-age pensions is limited, estimated at 27.4%. In Africa, despite significant progress in the extension of social protection coverage, only 17.8% of the population receive at least one social protection cash benefit, with significant variation across countries. The situation of women is particularly stark. The ILO reports that there are significant coverage and adequacy gaps in maternity and disability benefits and only 35% of children globally have access to social protection.[127] The deficit for children and persons with disabilities necessarily has an additional rebound impact on women who carry a disparate care burden for children and the disabled. The future does not look rosy. According to one estimation, by 2020, 83% of people in developing countries and 61% in high-income countries will be impacted by public expenditure cuts, due to austerity measures.[128]

Furthermore, trends in tax policy have perpetuated and deepened the neo-liberal impact on poverty alleviation. As the Center for Economic and Social Rights has long emphasised, progressive tax policy is cardinal for the implementation of social and economic rights.[129] Philip Alston, the Special Rapporteur on Poverty, has noted:

> The regressive or progressive nature of a state's tax structure, and the groups and purposes for which it gives exemptions or deductions, shapes the allocation of income and assets across the population. . . . Appropriate redistributive measures through fiscal policies are indispensable for ensuring full respect for human rights.[130]

The redistributive measures through fiscal policies and tax systems, which have been embraced from the 1990s and through to the post-2008 era of austerity policy, have been regressive. Not only has the tax burden for corporations and higher-income individuals been reduced by states but tax collection systems have been undermined by transnational loopholes and tax havens which have facilitated tax avoidance and evasion by economic elites and multinational corporations. This has had a particularly negative impact on the well-being of women in general and women in poverty in particular. It has resulted in cut backs in public services and welfare funding, with a pronounced gender impact as women, as they are the primary carers and are more reliant on these services than men.[131] Neo-liberal tax policy also promotes indirect taxation such as VAT on goods and services, which is regressive since, unlike in systems of progressive income tax, the poorest people pay the same rate of tax as the richest. This too tends to exacerbate gender inequalities because, whether or not women are a significantly greater percentage of the poor, they are most directly hit by the increased cost of food, clothing, housing and health care, as they are the day to day managers of consumption in households.[132]

One of the responses to the growing crisis in social security and protection together with the fear of increased unemployment and social need, is the concept of basic income for everyone in the country, irrespective of employment or income status.[133] Universal basic income proposals have been advocated by social action groups[134] and by hi-tech leaders such as Bill Gates, Elon Musk and Mark Zuckerberg,[135] as a response to the growing trepidation about loss of employment opportunities, especially in the fourth industrial revolution with its automation of jobs.[136] Pilot experiments introducing universal basic income, most notably in Finland (which was cut short) and India, have been inconclusive. The concept of universal basic income has been alternately praised as emancipatory[137] or criticised as being a mere adaptation of extensive existing welfare systems or as creating a disincentive to work. Their viability remains for the time being theoretical.[138]

It has, nevertheless, been argued that universal basic income should be regarded as key to the social support for women whose care responsibilities impede their sale of their human capital, as it would provide an unconditional social safety net:

> Feminists should endorse a basic income, particularly in comparison to other feasible safety-net alternatives, including work-conditioned benefits and a caregiver stipend. A basic income promotes gender equality by creating the social and economic conditions required to reduce the gendered division of labor. Most importantly, a universal, unconditional basic income could greatly reduce the poverty rate of the most vulnerable group in capitalist economies: single women and their children.[139]

This counsel to feminists, based on the idea that universal basic income would address some aspects of women's economic disadvantage, is questionable.[140] It seems inconceivable that a universal support system could be activated at a level which would provide a sufficient level of income compared with that which is feasible on a means-tested basis to those in need. Recent studies support this finding and suggest that well designed mean-tested systems are just as good or better at supporting poor households, including women's, compared to more expensive universal regimes.[141]

The British Fabian Society in its 2016 report on Redesigning Social Security, for the 2020s, assessed that "for the foreseeable future . . . [the UK] should not adopt a fully-fledged basic income, because it brings little or no benefits to low income households,"[142] and it has indeed been suggested that a universal basic income might well drive poverty and inequality upwards:

> It is not affordable, unpalatable to most of the public because of its 'money for nothing' tag and perhaps most importantly – it increases poverty unless modified beyond recognition. It fails to deal with the higher needs that many have because of rent, childcare, children or disabilities. As recently put by the last Secretary of State for Work and Pensions: "An affordable basic income would be inadequate, and a basic income that's adequate for all would be unaffordable.[143]

The Fabian Society concluded that means-tested support remains essential, whether or not a basic universal income is introduced. It advocates a tiered system as optimal, incorporating means-tested non-contributory benefits, contributory benefits, personal accounts and universal benefits: "This new tiered system would itself sit in a broader context of activist government, with economic intervention and public services also playing their part in securing good living standards. No one part of the system would have to do all the heavy-lifting."[144] Interpreting the Fabian report through a gender lens, it seems that women, as low-income households or members of households, benefit most from the means-tested benefits. Women, as lower paid workers and as unpaid carers with less access to economic resources, are more dependent on non-contributory benefits than men, and so the part of the system which remains essential to give women the necessary support to alleviate poverty is the non-contributory means-tested system.

4 Tackling gendered poverty

It is clear that the existing monetarised poverty line does not properly identify the populations whose physical quality of life and social functioning fall beneath the human development indicators for well-being. While poverty is wholly unacceptable for both women and men, it has added implications for women.[145] Revisiting the discredited paradigm of the feminisation of poverty, according to which women constitute 70% of the world's poor, it remains true to say that there is gendered poverty. Though less visible and difficult to measure, there are clear indicators of the higher incidence of poverty for women. These components of poverty include unequal power relations in patriarchal families, unequal access to family resources and property, the disparate burden of providing sustenance to dependent family members and the lower returns on the sale of their human capital. Furthermore, the impact of poverty on women's lives has an additional gendered dimension beyond the deprivations women share with men in poverty. Poverty exposes women to abuse of their physical integrity, increasing their vulnerability to gender-based violence and exposing them to forced prostitution, surrogacy and trafficking for sex. The blocking of access to adequate nutrition, water and sanitation has a particularly harsh physiological impact on women in pregnancy, lactation and menstruation.

The reduction and alleviation of poverty is both a development and a human rights issue. The UN Development Agenda has recognised women in poverty as an essential factor for the reduction of poverty in general and, although there is feminist criticism that the development discourse is instrumentalist aiming to use women's input to economic sustainability rather than addressing their needs, the fact of recognition does create an opening for gender-sensitising of poverty alleviation programs. Under the human rights regime, failure to address poverty of both women and men violates their core economic and social rights. It is additionally, a violation of the requirement to eliminate discrimination against women and to achieve equality between women and men, *de jure* and *de facto*.[146] It is also a breach of the obligation of states to ensure the full development and advancement of women under CEDAW. This obligation, to ensure equality in the distribution of existing resources, is, unlike the realisation of economic and social rights in general, an immediate and not a progressive obligation.

Gendered poverty is the emanation of societal, economic and legal systems' neglect of women's well-being. The roots of women's gendered poverty are so diffuse that addressing them requires a wide-angle lens which includes family, care, workplace, access to economic resources, sexual and reproductive functions and physiological needs. It is indeed only through the multidimensional approach that solutions can be found to the multidimensional nature of gendered poverty. Budgeting for the needs of women in poverty requires ensuring that there is provision of public services essential to their well-being, including primary health care services, contraceptives and legal safe termination of pregnancy, nutrition during pregnancy and lactation, medical services for childbirth, clean water, sanitation, public transport and housing. Such services must be affordable and, in the case of women in poverty, provided free of charge where necessary. Similarly, social protection floors must be provided for care services which are otherwise performed without pay largely by women.[147] Ensuring that women are not disparately denied equal access to resources in the family, in the sale of their human capital, in access to economic resources and in entrepreneurship, discussed in the previous parts of this book, is an integral part of the multidimensional approach to gendered poverty.

Alleviating women's poverty has an increased urgency because of its devastating impact beyond the already tragic realities of poverty as such for women and men alike. Poverty agendas must reflect an understanding that the gendered incidence and abuse associated with poverty in the case of women and girls is a result of women's socially enforced gender roles and relations. Without effectively addressing the root causes and the disparate impact of gender inequality, gendered poverty cannot be fundamentally resolved.[148]

Notes

1 BBC News, 'In Full: Mandela's Poverty Speech,' *BBC News*, 3 February 2005, http://news.bbc.co.uk/2/hi/uk_news/politics/4232603.stm.

2 See, for example, The Future We Want, UNGA Res 66/288(2012), 27 July 2012, UN Doc A/RES/66/288 (2012); Transforming Our World: The 2030 Agenda for Sustainable Development, UNGA Res 70/1(2015), 21 October 2015, UN Doc A/RES/70/1 (2015).

3 Committee on Economic, Social and Cultural Rights, 'Substantive Issues Arising in the Implementation of the International Covenant on Economic, Social and Cultural Rights: Poverty and the International Covenant on Economic, Social and Cultural Rights,' E/C.12/2001/10, twenty-fifth session, 10 May 2001, para 8, http://www2.ohchr.org/english/bodies/cescr/docs/statements/E.C.12.2001.10Poverty-2001.pdf.

4 OHCHR, 'Guiding Principles on Extreme Poverty and Human Rights,' 2012, 2, www.ohchr.org/Documents/Publications/OHCHR_ExtremePovertyandHumanRights_EN.pdf.

5 It was primarily associated with the vulnerability and disadvantage of female-headed households.

6 Carolina Johansson and Wennerholm Kvinnoforum, 'The "Feminisation of Poverty": The Use of a Concept,' *SIDA*, Division for Policy and Socio-economic Analysis, December 2002, www.sida.se/contentassets/cfd458d3a45e41348afd0fe45f1bed5c/the-quotfeminisation-of-povertyquot-the-use-of-a-concept_2621.pdf; Sylvia Chant, 'The Feminisation of Poverty and the Feminisation of Anti-poverty Programmes: Room for

Revision' (2008) 44(2) *Journal of Development Studies* 165, 166; Sylvia Chant, 'Re-thinking the "Feminization of Poverty" in Relation to Aggregate Gender Indices' (2006) 7(2) *Journal of Human Development* 201, 202; 'Beijing Declaration and Platform for Action,' adopted at the Fourth World Conference on Women at Beijing, China, 4–15 September 1995, 18–25, www.un.org/womenwatch/daw/beijing/pdf/BDPfA%20E.pdf.

7 The United Nations Development Programme (UNDP), *Human Development Report 1995* (Oxford University Press 1995) iii; Oxfamblogs, 'Are Women Really 70% of the World's Poor? How Do We Know?' *Oxfamblogs*, 3 February 2010, https://oxfamblogs.org/fp2p/are-women-really-70-of-the-worlds-poor-how-do-we-know/; Johansson and Kvinnoforum (n 6) 31; Chant 2008 (n 6) 166; Chant 2006 (n 6) 202.

8 See, for example, Chant 2008 (n 6) 165; Carolina Sanchez and Ana Maria Munoz, 'No, 70% of the World's Poor Aren't Women, but that Doesn't Mean Poverty Isn't Sexist,' *The World Bank Let's Talk Development Blog*, 3 August 2018, http://blogs.worldbank.org/developmenttalk/no-70-world-s-poor-aren-t-women-doesn-t-mean-poverty-isn-t-sexist; Oxfam from Poverty to Power Blog, 'Are Women Really 70% of the World's Poor? How Do We Know?' *Oxfam from Poverty to Power Blog*, 3 February 2010, https://oxfamblogs.org/fp2p/are-women-really-70-of-the-worlds-poor-how-do-we-know/.

9 For example, in 2012 the Guiding Principles on Extreme Poverty and Human Rights observed that "[w]omen are disproportionately represented among the poor owing to the multifaceted and cumulative forms of discrimination that they endure." Guiding Principles on Extreme Poverty and Human Rights (n 4) 6. In 2015 UN Women maintained there is evidence that women are more likely than men to live in poverty (while commenting that women may also be poor in households which are not poor). UN Women, 'The Beijing Declaration and Platform for Action Turns 20,' Summary Report, 2015, 10–11, https://sustainabledevelopment.un.org/content/documents/1776The%20Beijing%20Declaration%20and%20Platform%20for%20Action%20turns%2020.pdf. Other sources also maintained this, for example, The Oxford Handbook of the Social Science of Poverty commented in 2016 that many scholars studying multiple countries find that, overall, women are more likely to be poor than are their male counterparts. Janet C. Gornick and Natascia Boeri, 'Gender and Poverty' in David Brady and Linda M. Burton (eds), *The Oxford Handbook of the Social Science of Poverty* (Oxford University Press 2016). Oxfam reported in 2017 that rising inequality has slowed down reductions in poverty, and the majority of the world's poor continue to be women. OXFAM, 'An Economy that Works for Women,' Oxfam Briefing Paper, March 2017, 2, 14, www.oxfam.org/en/research/economy-works-women.

10 Razavi Shahra, 'Gendered Poverty and Well-being: Introduction' (1999) 30 *Development and Change* 409.

11 Francisco Ferriera, 'The International Poverty Line Has Just Been Raised to $1.90 a Day, but Global Poverty Is Basically Unchanged. How Is that Even Possible?,' *The World Bank Let's Talk Development Blog*, 10 April 2015, https://blogs.worldbank.org/developmenttalk/international-poverty-line-has-just-been-raised-190-day-global-poverty-basically-unchanged-how-even; Ana Maria Boudet Munoz, Paola Buitrago, Benedicte Leroy De La Briere, David Locke Newhouse, Eliana Rubiano Matulevich, Kinnon Scott and Pablo Suarez-Becerra, 'Gender Differences in Poverty and Household Composition Through the Life-cycle: A Global Perspective,' Policy Research Working Paper No. 8360, 2018, 33, Washington, DC: World Bank. © World Bank. https://openknowledge.worldbank.org/handle/10986/29426 License: CC BY 3.0 IGO.

12 The most recent assessments are from 2013. World Bank Group, 'Poverty and Shared Prosperity 2016: Taking on Inequality,' 2016, 3–4, Washington, DC: World Bank. © World Bank. https://openknowledge.worldbank.org/handle/10986/25078 License: CC BY 3.0 IGO; The World Bank, 'Poverty: Overview,' *The World Bank Website*, accessed 7 September 2018, www.worldbank.org/en/topic/poverty/overview. See also Economic and Social Council, 'Progress Towards the Sustainable Development Goals,' Report of

the Secretary-general, 11 May 2017, E/2017/66, www.un.org/ga/search/view_doc.asp?symbol=E/2017/66&Lang=E.

13 United Nations Department of Economic and Social Affairs, 'Rethinking Poverty: Report on the World Social Situation 2010,' ST/ESA/324, New York, 2009, chapter 2, www.un.org/esa/socdev/rwss/docs/2010/fullreport.pdf; United Nations, 'The Millennium Development Goals Report 2015,' New York, 2015, www.un.org/millenniumgoals/2015_MDG_Report/pdf/MDG%202015%20rev%20%28July%201%29.pdf.

14 OHCHR, 'Special Rapporteur on Extreme Poverty and Human Rights: Introduction,' *OHCHR*, accessed 5 August 2018, www.ohchr.org/EN/Issues/Poverty/Pages/SRExtremePovertyIndex.aspx.

15 Peter Edward, 'The Ethical Poverty Line: A Moral Quantification of Absolute Poverty' (2006) 27(2) *Third World Quarterly* 377, 388.

16 International Covenant on Civil and Political Rights (entered into force 23 March 1976) 999 UNTS 171 (ICCPR), art 11(1).

17 There is however criticism also for the relative poverty measurement; see, for example, OECD Insights: Debate the Issues, 'The Measure of Poverty,' *OECD Insights*, 20 June 2014, http://oecdinsights.org/2014/06/30/the-measure-of-poverty/.

18 As will be discussed later with regard to multidimensional poverty. See also ibid.

19 Eurostat, 'People at Risk of Poverty or Social Exclusion,' *Eurostat: Statistics Explained*, May 2018, http://ec.europa.eu/eurostat/statistics-explained/index.php/People_at_risk_of_poverty_or_social_exclusion.

20 The Beijing Declaration and Platform for Action Turns 20 (n 9) 10.

21 The Millennium Development Goals Report 2015 (n 13) 16.

22 UN Women, 'Turning Promises into Action: Gender Equality in the 2030 Agenda for Sustainable Development,' 2018, 76–77, www.unwomen.org/-/media/headquarters/attachments/sections/library/publications/2018/sdg-report-gender-equality-in-the-2030-agenda-for-sustainable-development-2018-en.pdf?la=en&vs=5653. Stressing the limitations of the available data, the authors attempted a new analysis and went on to assess the female poverty rate by reference to the percentage of women and girls living in poor households (i.e., the female poverty rate) as 12.8%, compared to 12.3% for men and boys. The usefulness of this assessment has to be rated in face of the fact that the authors of the Report acknowledged that the assessment was based on the assumption that all household members enjoy the same standard of living, which in their view may understate the gender dimensions of poverty.

23 Diane Elson, 'Women's Rights and Engendering Development' in Edith Kuiper and Drucilla K. Barker (eds), *Feminist Economics and the World Bank: History, Theory and Policy* (Routledge 2006) 243, 250.

24 Gender Differences in Poverty and Household Composition Through the Life-cycle (n 11) 2–3, 6; The Beijing Declaration and Platform for Action Turns 20 (n 9) 11.

25 Gender Differences in Poverty and Household Composition Through the Life-cycle (n 11) 5; Caitlin Brown, Martin Ravallion and Dominique van de Walle, 'Are Poor Individuals Mainly Found in Poor Households? Evidence Using Nutrition Data for Africa,' Policy Research Working Paper No. WPS 8001, 2017, Washington, DC: World Bank Group, http://documents.worldbank.org/curated/en/427491489094206188/Are-poor-individuals-mainly-found-in-poor-households-evidence-using-nutrition-data-for-Africa.

26 Gender Differences in Poverty and Household Composition Through the Life-cycle (n 11).

27 Sylvia Chant (ed), *The International Handbook of Gender and Poverty* (Edward Elgar Publishing 2010) 3.

28 Chant 2008 (n 6) 176.

29 Gender Differences in Poverty and Household Composition Through the Life-cycle (n 11) 33.

30 Turning Promises into Action (n 21) 77.

31 Social Watch Research Team, 'Gender and Poverty: A Case of Entwined Inequalities' (2010) 6 *Occasional Papers – Social Watch, Beijing and Beyond: Putting Gender Economics at the Forefront – 15 Years After the IV World Conference on Women* 7, www.socialwatch.org/node/11590.

32 UN Women, 'Special Rapporteur Positions Unpaid Care Work as Major Human Rights Issue,' *UN Women News*, 23 October 2013, www.unwomen.org/en/news/stories/2013/10/special-rapporteur-positions-unpaid-care-work-as-major-human-rights-issue.

33 Karen Christopher, 'Caregiving, Welfare States and Mothers' Poverty,' Luxembourg Income Study Working Paper No. 287, November 2001, 11, www.lisdatacenter.org/wps/liswps/287.pdf.

34 Turning Promises into Action (n 21) 137.

35 Sawako Shirahase and James M. Raymo, 'Single Mothers and Poverty in Japan: The Role of Intergenerational Coresidence' (2014) 93(2) *Social Forces* 545, 549.

36 Ibid.

37 Johansson and Kvinnoforum (n 6) 32–33.

38 See, for example, UN Women, 'Progress of the World's Women 2015–2016,' 2015, 147, http://progress.unwomen.org/en/2015/pdf/UNW_progressreport.pdf; Frances Raday, 'Pension Gender Gap: Background Paper,' 2014, www.ohchr.org/EN/Issues/Women/WGWomen/Pages/ESL.aspx. Nevertheless, in apparent contradiction of previous reports, the UN Women and World Bank assess, in their 2018 Report, that by age 55 the percentage of poor women is lower than that of poor men and thus they are not overly represented among the poor. The conclusions regarding older women's poverty are far from conclusive, and the 2018 Report itself advises that more research is required. See Turning Promises into Action (n 21) 77.

39 See Parts I and II. See also Gornick Boeri and (n 9); Progress of the World's Women 2015–2016 (n 38) 147.

40 Johnson-Latham quoted by Chant 2010 (n 27) 3.

41 See, for example, Christine Chinkin, 'Violence Against Women' in Marsha Freeman et al. (eds), *The UN Convention on the Elimination of All Forms of Discrimination Against Women: A Commentary* (Oxford University Press 2012) 443, 459; OHCHR, 'Women and the Right to Adequate Housing,' New York and Geneva, 2012, 38, www.ohchr.org/Documents/Publications/WomenHousing_HR.PUB.11.2.pdf; Mari Kate Mycek, 'Homeless Women Say "Me Too," but No One Listens,' *Huff Post*, 13 March 2018, www.huffingtonpost.com/entry/opinion-mycek-me-too-homeless_us_5aa6c75ee4b03c9edfae87f1; Lauren Kirchner, 'Doubly Victimized: The Shocking Prevalence of Violence Against Homeless Women,' *Pacific Standard*, 22 July 2014, https://psmag.com/social-justice/doubly-victimized-violence-homeless-women-girls-shelter-86458; Gale Holland, 'Attacked, Abused and Often Forgotten: Women Now Make Up 1 in 3 Homeless People in L.A. County,' *Los Angeles Times*, 28 October 2016, www.latimes.com/projects/la-me-homeless-women/.

42 Naila Kabeer, 'Gender, Poverty, and Inequality: A Brief History of Feminist Contributions in the Field of International Development' (2015) 23(2) *Gender & Development* 189.

43 The borderline between forced into prostitution and women trafficked for sexual exploitation is vague, and the boundaries between them are blurred, with women in forced prostitution falling into the trafficking definition of having been recruited or harboured by coercion, fraud, deception or the abuse of power for the purposes of sexual exploitation (the definition is further discussed later). See Janice G. Raymond, 'The New UN Trafficking Protocol' (September 2002) 25(5) *Women's Studies International Forum* 491–502, DOI:10.1016/S0277-5395(02)00320-5.

44 European Parliament Policy Department Citizens' Rights and Constitutional Affairs, 'Sexual Exploitation and Prostitution and Its Impact on Gender Equality,' 2014, 9, www.europarl.europa.eu/RegData/etudes/etudes/join/2014/493040/IPOL-FEMM_ET(2014)493040_EN.pdf.

45 CEDAW, 'General Recommendation No. 19: Violence Against Women,' Eleventh session, 1992, para 14, https://tbinternet.ohchr.org/Treaties/CEDAW/Shared%20 Documents/1_Global/INT_CEDAW_GEC_3731_E.pdf.

46 The Beijing Declaration and Platform for Action (n 6) 19, para 51. Even the highly controversial report of the ILO on what it called the sex sector, in 1998, identified that amongst the motives for women to enter prostitution is the pressure of poverty and dire economic circumstances. ILO, Lin Lean Lim (ed), *The Sex Sector: The Economic and Social Bases of Prostitution in Southeast Asia* (ILO 1998). See also Janice G. Raymond, 'Legitimating Prostitution as Sex Work: UN Labour Organization (ILO) Calls for Recognition of the Sex Industry,' *Coalition Against Trafficking in Women*, 12 July 1999, www.catwinternational.org/Home/Article/61-legitimating-prostitution-as-sex-work-un-labour-organization-ilo-calls-for-recognition-of-the-sex-industry.

47 European Parliament Policy Department (n 44) 7.

48 See, for example, European Parliament Policy Department (n 44); Karni Kissil and Maureen Davey, 'The Prostitution Debate in Feminism: Current Trends, Policy and Clinical Issues Facing an Invisible Population' (2010) 22(1) *Journal of Feminist Family Therapy* 1; Catherine A. MacKinnon, 'Prostitution and Civil Rights' (1993) 1 *Michigan Journal of Gender & Law* 13, 28; Melissa Farley, 'Prostitution Is Sexual Violence,' *Modern Medicine Network*, 1 October 2004, www.psychiatrictimes.com/sexual-offenses/prostitution-sexual-violence.

49 Farley (n 48).

50 United Nations Office on Drugs and Crime (UNDOC), 'Global Report on Trafficking in Persons 2016,' New York, 2016, 1, 27, www.unodc.org/documents/data-and-analysis/glotip/2016_Global_Report_on_Trafficking_in_Persons.pdf.

51 UN Protocol to Prevent, Suppress and Punish Trafficking in Persons, Especially Women and Children, supplementing the United Nations Convention Against Transnational Organized Crime (entered into force 25 December 2003) 2237 UNTS 319.

52 See, for example, stories of women in the U.S. Department of State, 'Victims of Trafficking and Violence Protection Act of 2000: Trafficking in Persons Report,' June 2005, www.state.gov/j/tip/rls/tiprpt/2005/.

53 UNDOC (n 50) 27.

54 United Nations Economic and Social Council, 'Report of the Special Rapporteur on Violence Against Women, Its Causes and Consequences,' Fifty-third session, E/CN.4/1997/47, 12 February 1997, para 72. See also the Special Rapporteur on Violence Against Women (SRVAW), '15 Years of the United Nations Special Rapporteur on Violence Against Women (1994–2009): A Critical Review,' 2009, http://www2.ohchr.org/english/issues/women/rapporteur/docs/15YearReviewofVAWMandate.pdf.

55 Ivan Grishchenko, 'A Study of Relationships Between Socioeconomic Indicators and Rates of Human Trafficking Victimization in Europe and Central Asia,' Senior Project, Social Sciences Department College of Liberal Arts, 2013, http://digitalcommons.calpoly.edu/cgi/viewcontent.cgi?article=1109&context=socssp; Carol Nechemias, 'Women in the Russian Labor Force: A Retreat from Equality?' in Beth English, Mary E. Frederickson and Olga Sanmiguel-Valderrama (eds), *Global Women's Work: Perspectives on Gender and Work in the Global Economy* (Routledge forthcoming).

56 International Labour Organization (ILO), 'Profits and Poverty: The Economics of Forced Labour,' Special Action Programme to Combat Forced Labour (SAP-FL) and Fundamental Principles and Rights at Work Branch (FPRW), 2014, 26, www.ilo.org/wcmsp5/groups/public/–ed_norm/–declaration/documents/publication/wcms_243391.pdf.

57 Jacquelyn Monroe, 'Women in Street Prostitution: The Result of Poverty and the Brunt of Inequity' (2005) 9(3) *Online Journal of Poverty* 69.

58 OHCHR, 'Report of the Special Rapporteur on Violence Against Women: Mission to Poland on the Issue of Trafficking and Forced Prostitution of Women,' E/CN.4/1997/47/Add.1, 10 December 1996, para 53, 66, http://ap.ohchr.org/documents/alldocs.aspx?doc_id=867.

59 The Convention on the Elimination of all Forms of Discrimination Against Women (entered into force 3 September 1981) 1249 UNTS 13 (CEDAW), art 6, www.un.org/womenwatch/daw/cedaw/text/econvention.htm.
60 WGDAW, 'Thematic Report on Health and Safety,' 32th session of the Human Rights Council, A/HRC/32/44, June 2016, paras 84, 85, www.ohchr.org/EN/Issues/Women/WGWomen/Pages/GoodpracticesintheeliminationofDAW.aspx.
61 Janie Chuang, 'Article 6' in Marsha A. Freeman, Christine Chinkin and Beate Rudolf (eds), *The UN Convention on the Elimination of All Forms of Discrimination Against Women: A Commentary* (Oxford University Press 2012) 180.
62 Including many states in the US, see WGDAW, 'Report of the Working Group on the Issue of Discrimination Against Women in Law and in Practice on Its Mission to the United States of America,' A/HRC/32/44/Add.2, 2016, para 82, http://ap.ohchr.org/documents/dpage_e.aspx?si=A/HRC/32/44/Add.2; ProCon, 'US Federal and State Prostitution Laws and Related Punishments,' *ProCon*, 5 April 2018, https://prostitution.procon.org/view.resource.php?resourceID=000119.
63 CEDAW (n 59) art 6; Trafficking Protocol (n 51).
64 Trafficking Protocol (n 51) art 9.
65 Council of Europe Convention on Action Against Trafficking in Human Beings (entered into force 16 May 2005), CETS 197, www.refworld.org/docid/43fded544.html.
66 Ibid. art 19.
67 Ibid. arts 15 and 23.
68 UNDOC (n 50) 12, 27.
69 Guttmacher Institute, 'Adding It Up: Investing in Contraception and Maternal and Newborn Health, 2017,' *Guttmacher Institute*, December 2017, www.guttmacher.org/fact-sheet/adding-it-up-contraception-mnh-2017.
70 See, for example, WGDAW Report on Health and Safety (n 60) paras 75, 90. WGDAW, 'Report of the Working Group on the Issue of Discrimination Against Women in Law and in Practice Addendum: Mission to Chile,' A/HRC/29/40/Add.1, 20 May 2015, para 59, www.ohchr.org/EN/Issues/Women/WGWomen/Pages/CountryVisits.aspx; WGDAW, 'Report of the Working Group on the Issue of Discrimination Against Women in Law and in Practice Addendum: Mission to Peru,' A/HRC/29/40/Add.2, 26 June 2015, para 65, www.ohchr.org/EN/Issues/Women/WGWomen/Pages/CountryVisits.aspx; WGDAW Report on the United States (n 62) paras 65–66.
71 In the Philippines, the wide ban on the sale of contraceptives, supported by the Pope, was only lifted in 2017: Human Rights Watch, 'Philippines Lifts Ban on 51 Contraceptives Fully Implement and Enforce the Reproductive Health Law,' *Human Rights Watch*, 20 November 2017, www.hrw.org/news/2017/11/20/philippines-lifts-ban-51-contraceptives.
72 *Burwell v Hobby Lobby* 573 US 22 (2014).
73 CEDAW (n 59) art 16(e).
74 World Health Organization (WHO), 'Preventing Unsafe Abortion,' *WHO*, 19 February 2018, www.who.int/en/news-room/fact-sheets/detail/preventing-unsafe-abortion.
75 WGDAW, 'Women's Autonomy, Equality and Reproductive Health in International Human Rights: Between Recognition, Backlash and Regressive Trends,' October 2017, 2, www.ohchr.org/Documents/Issues/Women/WG/WomensAutonomyEqualityReproductiveHealth.pdf.
76 *Roe v Wade*, 410 U.S. 113 (1973); *Whole Woman's Health v Hellerstedt*, 579 US 136 (2016).
77 U.S. Department of State, 'Protecting Life in Global Health Assistance,' fact sheet, Office of the Spokesperson, Washington, DC, 15 May 2017, www.state.gov/r/pa/prs/ps/2017/05/270866.htm.
78 The Bmji Opinion, 'Bringing the Gag Rule Home: The Trump Administration Wants to Infringe Women's Rights to Abortion Counselling,' *Thebmjiopinion*, 13 June 2018, https://blogs.bmj.com/bmj/2018/06/13/bringing-the-gag-rule-home-the-trump-administration-wants-to-infringe-womens-rights-to-abortion-counselling.

79 Sarah Spiller, 'Life at Any Price,' *Aljazeera*, 8 August 2013, www.aljazeera.com/programmes/peopleandpower/2013/08/2013841542313541.html.
80 CEDAW, 'General Recommendation No. 35 on Gender-based Violence Against Women, Updating General Recommendation No. 19,' CEDAW/C/GC/35, 14 July 2017, para 18, https://tbinternet.ohchr.org/Treaties/CEDAW/Shared%20Documents/1_Global/CEDAW_C_GC_35_8267_E.pdf.
81 Women's Autonomy, Equality and Reproductive Health in International Human Rights (n 75).
82 WHO, 'MDG 5: Improve Maternal Health,' *WHO*, May 2015, www.who.int/topics/millennium_development_goals/maternal_health/en/.
83 For example, up to 65% of women with obstetric fistula, which is a severely disabling condition and often results in social exclusion, develop this condition as adolescents. WGDAW Report on Health and Safety (n 60) para 34.
84 United Nations Millennium Goals, 'Goal 5: Improve Maternal Health,' *Millennium Development Goals and Beyond 2015*, accessed 4 August 2018, www.un.org/millenniumgoals/maternal.shtml. See also WHO (n 82); United Nations Sustainable Development Goals, 'Goal 3: Ensure Healthy Lives and Promote Well-being for All at All Ages,' *Sustainable Development Knowledge Platform*, Target 3.1, accessed 1 August 2018, https://sustainabledevelopment.un.org/sdg3.
85 Claire de La Hougue and Caroline Roux, 'Surrogate Motherhood and Human Rights: Human, Legal and Ethical Issues,' a report issued in September 2015, www.nomaternitytraffic.eu/wp-content/uploads/2015/09/2015-Contribution-HCCH-No-Maternity-Traffic-EN.pdf.
86 European Centre for Law and Justice, 'Surrogate Motherhood: A Violation of Human Rights,' report presented at the Council of Europe, Strasbourg, 25 April 2012, www.ieb-eib.org/en/pdf/surrogacy-motherhood-icjl.pdf.
87 Raywat Deonandan, Samantha Green and Amanda van Beinum, 'Ethical Concerns for Maternal Surrogacy and Reproductive Tourism' (2012) 38 *Journal of Medical Ethics* 742.
88 OHCHR, 'Report of the Special Rapporteur on the Sale and Sexual Exploitation of Children, Including Child Prostitution, Child Pornography and Other Child Sexual Abuse Material,' A/HRC/37/60, 15 January 2018.
89 CEDAW (n 59) art 12.
90 The United Nations Children's Fund (UNICEF), 'India: Introduction,' *UNICEF*, accessed 4 August 2018, http://unicef.in/Whatwedo/6/Women-Nutrition.
91 OHCHR, 'Harmful Traditional Practices Affecting the Health of Women and Children,' Fact Sheet No. 23, August 1995, 9–10, www.ohchr.org/Documents/Publications/FactSheet23en.pdf.
92 WGDAW Report on Health and Safety (n 60) paras 67–70; Eleanor Goldberg, 'For Homeless Women, Getting Their Period Is One of the Most Difficult Challenges,' *Huff Post*, 14 January 2015, www.huffingtonpost.com/2015/01/14/homeless-women-tampons_n_6465230.html.
93 UNGA, 'Report of the Special Rapporteur on the Human Right to Safe Drinking Water and Sanitation,' 26 July 2016, UN Doc A/HRC/33/49, 2016, paras 1–2, 20, https://digitallibrary.un.org/record/847923/files/A_HRC_33_49-EN.pdf.
94 Vienna Declaration and Programme of Action, A/CONF.157/23, 12 July 1993, art I(10).
95 UNGA, Res 1161(XII)(1957), 26 November 1957, UN Doc. A/3716 (1957).
96 United Nation Department of Economic and Social Affairs, 'The United Nations Development Agenda: Development for All,' UN Doc ST/ESA/316, 2007, III, www.un.org/esa/devagenda/UNDA_BW5_Final.pfd.
97 United Nations Millennium Goals, 'Goal 1: Eradicate Extreme Poverty & Hunger,' *Millennium Development Goals and Beyond 2015*, Target 1.A, accessed 4 August 2018, www.un.org/millenniumgoals/maternal.shtml; OHCHR, 'Human Rights and the Millennium Development Goals in Practice: A Review of Country Strategies and

Reporting,' New York and Geneva, 2010, 9, www.ohchr.org/Documents/Publications/HRAndMDGsInPractice.pdf; The Millennium Development Goals Report 2015 (n 13) 15.

98 United Nations Sustainable Development Goals, 'Goal 1: End Poverty in All Its Forms Everywhere,' *Sustainable Development Knowledge Platform*, accessed 1 August 2018, https://sustainabledevelopment.un.org/sdg1.

99 United Nations Millennium Goals, 'Goal 3: Promote Gender Equality and Empower Women,' *Millennium Development Goals and Beyond 2015*, accessed 22 September 2018, www.un.org/millenniumgoals/gender.shtml; United Nations Sustainable Development Goals, 'Goal 5: Achieve Gender Equality and Empower All Women and Girls,' *Sustainable Development Knowledge Platform*, accessed 22 September 2018, https://sustainabledevelopment.un.org/sdg5; High-level Political Forum on Sustainable Development, '2017 HLPF Thematic Review of SDG 5: Achieve Gender Equality and Empower All Women and Girls,' 2017, 4, https://sustainabledevelopment.un.org/content/documents/14383SDG5format-revOD.pdf.

100 United Nations Sustainable Development Goal 1 (n 98) Target 1.B and Indicator 1.B.1.

101 Andrew D. Mason and Elizabeth M. King, 'Engendering Development Through Gender Equality in Rights, Resources, and Voice,' a World Bank policy research report, 2001, Washington DC: World Bank, http://documents.worldbank.org/curated/en/512911468327401785/Engendering-development-through-gender-equality-in-rights-resources-and-voice.

102 E. Kuiper and D.K. Barker (eds), *Feminist Economics and the World Bank: History, Theory and Policy* (Routledge 2006).

103 Sylvia Chant, 'Addressing World Poverty Through Women and Girls: A Feminised Solution' (2016) 30(2) *Sight and Life Magazine* 58, 58.

104 According to UNDP's Human Development Report from 2014, over 2.2 billion people are either near or living in multidimensional poverty. See UNDP, 'Sustaining Human Progress: Reducing Vulnerabilities and Building Resilience,' Human Development Report 2014, 2014, 3, http://hdr.undp.org/sites/default/files/hdr14-report-en-1.pdf. In 2016, the Multidimensional Poverty Index found that in the developing world, 29% were living in multidimensional poverty. See UNDP Human Development Reports, 'Multidimensional Poverty Index (MPI),' *UNDP*, accessed 1 August 2018, http://hdr.undp.org/en/content/multidimensional-poverty-index-mpi.

105 These social and economic rights address the infrastructure which produces poverty and their gender dimensions have been addressed previously.

106 International Covenant on Economic, Social and Cultural Rights (entered into force 3 January 1976993 UNTS 3 (ICESCR), art 9; CEDAW (n 59) art 11(e).

107 ICESCR (n 108) art 9.

108 See Part II of the book.

109 Gornick and Boeri (n 9).

110 The Institute of Chartered Accountants of India (ICAI), 'The Effects of DFID's Cash Transfer Programmes on Poverty and Vulnerability,' an impact review, *ICAI*, 12 January 2017, https://icai.independent.gov.uk/html-report/effects-dfids-cash-transfer-programmes-poverty-vulnerability/.

111 Gender Differences in Poverty and Household Composition Through the Life-cycle (n 11) 6.

112 ICAI (n 110).

113 Luisa Natali, Sudhanshu Handa, Amber Peterman and David Seidenfeld, 'Making Money Work: Unconditional Cash Transfers Allow Women to Save and Re-invest in Rural Zambia,' WP-2016-02, UNICEF, Office of Research – Innocenti Working Paper, GelsonTembo on behalf of The Zambia Cash Transfer Evaluation Team, March 2016, www.unicef-irc.org/publications/pdf/IWP_2016_02.pdf; Ana Paula de la O Campos, 'Empowering Rural Women Through Social Protection,' Food and Agriculture

Organization of the United Nations, Rome, 2015, 11, www.fao.org/3/a-i4696e.pdf. Some observers have criticised the practice of making transfers to the woman as a mother or carer as essentialising this role.

114 Elaine Fultz and John Francis, 'Cash Transfer Programmes, Poverty Reduction and Empowerment of Women: A Comparative Analysis: Experiences from Brazil, Chile, India, Mexico and South Africa,' ILO Working Paper 4/2013, Social Protection Department, 2013, 1, www.ilo.org/wcmsp5/groups/public/–dgreports/–gender/documents/publication/wcms_233599.pdf.

115 See Beth Goldblatt's research into social security programs in Australia, India and South Africa. Beth Goldblatt, *Developing the Right to Social Security – A Gender Perspective* (Routledge 2016).

116 Beth Goldblatt, 'Developing the Right to Social Security from a Gendered Perspective,' a thesis in fulfillment of the requirements for the degree of Doctor of Philosophy, School of Law, University of New South Wales (September 2014), 232.

117 ILO, Social Protection Floors Recommendation, 2012 (No. 202), Recommendation concerning National Floors of Social Protection Adoption, Geneva, 101st ILC session, 14 Jun 2012, www.ilo.org/dyn/normlex/en/f?p=NORMLEXPUB:12100:0::NO::P12100_ILO_CODE:R202.

118 Committee on Economic, Social and Cultural Rights (n 3) para 7.

119 See Part II of the book.

120 Goldblatt thesis (n 116).

121 Rebeca Torada Máñez and Larraitz Lexartza Artza, 'Fighting Inequality from the Basics: The Social Protection Floor and Gender Equality – Executive Summary,' International Labour Organization, United Nations Entity for Gender Equality and the Empowerment of Women and United Nations Development Programme, 2012, 5, www.unwomen.org/-/media/headquarters/attachments/sections/library/publications/2013/1/combatiendo-desigualdad-summary%20pdf.pdf?la=en&vs=1453. Cf Beth Goldblatt who criticises this formulation for failing to include a right to basic income for those dimensions of women's poverty which result from their responsibility for the care of others, as had been proposed by a coalition of NGOs during the drafting process of the SPFs. Beth Goldblatt and Lucie Lamarche (eds), *Women's Rights to Social Security and Social Protection* (Hart 2014).

122 Karen Christopher, Paula England, Timothy M. Smeeding and Katherin Ross Phillips, 'The Gender Gap in Poverty in Modern Nations: Single Motherhood, The Market, and the State' (2002) 45(3) *Sociological Perspectives* 219, 223.

123 Elson (n 23) 253.

124 OHCHR, 'Report of the Special Rapporteur on Extreme Poverty and Human Rights,' A/HRC/35/26, 22 March 2017, para 4, http://ap.ohchr.org/documents/dpage_e.aspx?si=A/HRC/35/26.

125 By the late 1990s increasing criticism shifted the focus away from a view of development as simply economic growth and toward poverty reduction and the need for participation by both developing country governments and civil society. That change of direction came to be known as the post-Washington Consensus. See Stephen R. Hurt, 'Washington Consensus,' *Encyclopedia Britannica*, accessed 2 August 2018, www.britannica.com/topic/Washington-consensus.

126 Kate Donald and Nicholas Lusiani, 'The IMF, Gender Equality and Expenditure Policy,' Bretton Woods Project, September 2017, http://socialprotection-humanrights.org/wp-content/uploads/2017/10/Gendered-Costs-of-Austerity-2017.pdf.

127 ILO, 'World Social Protection Report 2017–19: Universal Social Protection to Achieve the Sustainable Development Goals,' 2017, www.ilo.org/wcmsp5/groups/public/–dgreports/–dcomm/–publ/documents/publication/wcms_605078.pdf.

128 Isabel Ortiz, Matthew Cummins, Jeronim Capaldo and Kalaivani Karunanethy, 'The Decade of Adjustment: A Review of Austerity Trends 2010–2020 in 187 Countries,'

Extension of Social Security (ESS) Working Paper No. 53, ILO, Columbia University and the South Centre, 2015, 3, www.social-protection.org/gimi/RessourcePDF.action?ressource.ressourceId=53192.

129 The Center for Economic and Social Rights (CESR), 'Human Rights in Tax Policy,' *CESR*, accessed 4 August 2018, www.cesr.org/human-rights-taxation.

130 Philip Alston, 'Extreme Inequality as the Antithesis of Human Rights,' *Open Global Rights*, 27 August 2015, www.openglobalrights.org/extreme-inequality-as-the-antithesis-of-human-rights.

131 Donald and Lusiani (n 126) 9.

132 OXFAM (n 9) 20.

133 Karl Widerquist, *Independence, Propertylessness, and Basic Income: A Theory of Freedom as the Power to Say No* (Palgrave Macmillan 2013); Philippe van Parijs and Yannick Vanderborght, *Basic Income: A Radical Proposal for a Free Society and a Sane Economy* (Harvard University Press 2017); Rutger Bregman, *Utopia for Realists: How We Can Build the Ideal World* (Bloomsbury Publishing 2017); Andy Stern, *Raising the Floor: How a Universal Basic Income Can Renew Our Economy and Rebuild the American Dream* (Public Affairs 2016). It should be noted that this idea is not new and was proposed by prominent neo-liberal thinkers: Milton Friedman in 1962, in the form of negative income tax. It has been remarked that Negative Income Tax scheme is coherent with the libertarian idea of distributive justice, while Basic Income follows egalitarian thought. See Davide Tondani, 'Universal Basic Income and Negative Income Tax: Two Different Ways of Thinking Redistribution' (2009) 38(2) *The Journal of Socio-Economics* 246.

134 Anthony Painter and Chris Thoung, 'Creative Citizen, Creative State: The Principled and Pragmatic Case for a Universal Basic Income,' *RSA*, 2015, 32, www.rexsresources.com/uploads/6/5/2/1/6521405/rsa_basic_income_20151216.pdf.

135 Catherine Clifford, 'What Billionaires and Business Titans Say About Cash Handouts in 2017 (Hint: lots!),' *CNBC*, 28 December 2017, www.cnbc.com/2017/12/27/what-billionaires-say-about-universal-basic-income-in-2017.html; June Javelosa and Kristin Houser, 'Bill Gates: The World Isn't Ready for Universal Basic Income Now, but We Will Be Soon,' *Futurism*, 28 February 2017, https://futurism.com/4-bill-gates-thinks-countries-arent-ready-for-basic-income-yet/.

136 See Part II of the book.

137 Guy Standing, 'How Cash Transfers Promote the Case for Basic Income' (2008) 3(1) *Basic Income Studies*, www.degruyter.com/view/j/bis.2008.3.1/bis.2008.3.1.1106/bis.2008.3.1.1106.xml.

138 Report of the Special Rapporteur on extreme poverty and human rights (n 124) paras 34–38.

139 Almaz Zelleke, 'Institutionalizing the Universal Caretaker Through a Basic Income?' (2008) 3(3) *Basic Income Studies*, www.degruyter.com/view/j/bis.2008.3.3/bis.2008.3.3.1133/bis.2008.3.3.1133.xml.

140 It has been argued that the existing debate over a citizens' basic income disturbingly focuses on labour markets and has an androcentric bias, void of any comprehensive treatment of women. See Ailsa McKay, 'Rethinking Work and Income Maintenance Policy: Promoting Gender Equality Through a Citizens' Basic Income' (2011) 7(1) *Feminist Economics* 97.

141 Dimitri Gugushvili and Donald Hirsch, 'Means-tested and Universal Approaches to Poverty: International Evidence and How the UK Compares,' CRSP Working paper 640, 2014, www.lboro.ac.uk/media/wwwlboroacuk/content/crsp/downloads/reports/Means-tested%20and%20universal%20approaches%20to%20poverty_Working%20Paper.pdf.

142 Andrew Harrop, 'For Us All: Redesigning Social Security for the 2020s,' *Fabian Society*, 2016, 149–150, www.fabians.org.uk/wp-content/uploads/2016/08/FAB_J4556_For_Us_All_Social_Security_Report_V5_08-2016_WEB-002.pdf.

143 Chris Goulden, 'Universal Basic Income – Not the Answer to Poverty,' *Joseph Rowntree Foundation (JRF)*, 25 April 2018, www.jrf.org.uk/blog/universal-basic-income-not-answer-poverty.
144 Harrop (n 142) 151.
145 Shahra (n 10).
146 Meghan Campbell, *Women, Poverty, Equality* (Hart 2018). Campbell has proposed that it is under the equality norms of CEDAW that the harms of gendered poverty should be addressed to activate international accountability mechanisms and inform the domestic interpretation of human rights. It should be noted that, although CEDAW does not have an express provision as regards poverty, in the preamble poverty is referred to: "in situations of poverty women have the least access to education, food, health, training for employment and other needs," and both the CESCR and the CEDAW guarantee women equality in all the social and economic rights which are so relevant to both the incidence of women's poverty and the disparate harshness of its impact on women and girls.
147 As recommended by the WGDAW in its report to the HRC on women's social and economic life. WGDAW, 'Thematic Report on Discrimination Against Women in Economic and Social Life, with a Focus on Economic Crisis,' A/HRC/26/39, 2014, paras 97, 128, 131, www.ohchr.org/EN/Issues/Women/WGWomen/Pages/ESL.aspx.
148 UN Women, 'Gender Mainstreaming in Development Programming,' 2014, 13, http://www2.unwomen.org/-/media/headquarters/attachments/sections/library/publications/2014/gendermainstreaming-issuesbrief-en%20pdf.pdf?v=1&d=20150220T190747.

Part IV
Family Economics

All the various aspects of economic woman's opportunities and realities start out from the family. Women's and girls' economic lives are greatly influenced by the type of family in which they are situated. The kinds of family women live in are largely determined by the normative framework of law, religion and culture, as well as by the urban or rural setting. There remains room for significant variation between specific families and between individual women but the family structure established by law, religion and culture will heavily impact women's and girls' level of economic autonomy and empowerment.

Most women live in families and almost all girls grow up in families. Even if no one form of family can be described as global, the work that the family does can be described in that way. Care and dependency relations exist in all communities and all communities want to ensure safe and reliable reproduction.[1] Universally and pervasively, the imperatives of care and reproduction are carried out primarily in the private context of the family. Inevitably, these care and reproductive relations attract measures of regulation and protection by cultures, religions and legal systems both locally and internationally.[2] It is also on this basis, empirical and ideological, that there is a wide global consensus which regards the family as the natural and fundamental unit of society and entitled to protection by the state.[3]

Perception of the family is primarily in this caring and reproductive role. The family frequently fulfils many of these care and reproductive expectations, in nuclear families nurturing children and in vertical inter-generational families fulfilling mutual obligations and interdependence of grandparents, children and grandchildren.[4] The conjugal relationship may be created with a romantic celebrative aura, in Western nuclear family with a bridal white wedding, adopted also in weddings in Japan, while in India brides are in glorious red. But marriages are an economic transaction. Traditionally and still in some cultures, marriages have been openly arranged to create various kinds of alliances between families. The global trend, however, is for marriages to be rooted in choice by the spouses themselves with a move from alliances to relationships.[5]

The entry into marriage in reality establishes an economic unit, which determines the range of investment and returns on the human capital of individual family members, whether by legal dictate or by agreement between the parties.

As an economic unit, the family may be considered to have on its balance sheet the property, income and investment of individual members on the credit side and the rights to ownership and the proceeds of the investment on the debit side. Investment in the family by individual members includes transfers of property or income to the family unit, encompassing earnings, agricultural and investment assets, insurance and social benefit rights. Furthermore, allocating the burden of providing unpaid care is an economic transaction and women are usually the bearers of this burden, physically and psychologically. Women's caring role has, indeed, been codified by traditionalist cultures into the family DNA.

The idea of equality between women and men in the family requires women's equal autonomy, equal access to resources and division of responsibilities on an equal basis. The international human rights system and secular legal systems at the national level have fully endorsed this vision of equality. There is a strong economic component to this idea of equality in the family. As the CEDAW Committee has observed, "Despite women's contributions to the economic well-being of the family, their economic inferiority permeates all stages of family relationships, often owing to their responsibility for dependents."[6]

1 Women's right to equality in the family – historical development

The family is the site of a transformative late 19th- to 20th-century conceptualisation of women's equality. It is also the site of the most regressive patriarchal norms and practices. The right of women to equality in the family was not even visualised in traditionalist religious and in classical legal systems, which uniformly entrenched the patriarchal family. Furthermore, feminist literature has demonstrated that in the philosophy of political justice women's situation in the family was persistently invisible up until our times. Social and political philosophers have, as perceptively analysed by Susan Okin, failed to include relations within the family in their concepts of justice.[7] Perception of the family as a primary social unit not divisible into individual members, with the preservation of privacy within the home, served to keep the family from any intrusive gaze by philosophers or law enforcement agencies.[8]

That said, Okin's analysis overlooked 19th-century economic philosophy analysis of the exploitation of women in the family, by Engels who did recognise the existence of gender hierarchy in the family, analysing it as an aspect of economic exploitation of labour in society, the demise of which would be conditioned on the elimination of class differences.[9] Further overlooked has been the stunningly advanced feminist analysis, writing and political activism of Eleanor Marx in the 19th century, later followed by Emma Goldman in the US, which fully revealed the gender and class dimensions of the exploitation of women's labour in the family. In 'The Woman Question,' responding to a political attack made on suffragettes, Eleonor Marx wrote: "It is the Sex Question and its economic basis that I propose to discuss with you. . . . I propose to deal with the Sex Question from the point of view of the working class and the class struggle."[10] As regards women's place in the family, she co-wrote the lampoon "A Doll's House Repaired." Henrik Ibsen's play, which had presented, in 1879, a highly critical study of marriage, portraying Nora as a wife who behaved in a totally infantilised way in order to live up to the expectations of society and her apparently benign but actually tyrannical husband. The outcome of this traditional marriage was Nora's flight from home abandoning husband and children in order to have a life of her own. British critics, like their European peers, lambasted the play as heralding the end of decent morality founded on hearth and home, where women knew their place as subordinate to husband and children.

In Eleanor Marx's lampoon, in order to mockingly satisfy the critics' demands of morality and decency, she produced a sarcastic rewrite of the ending of the play: Nora stays on her husband's terms, resolves to mend her willful ways and admits to her error in having worked to earn money.[11]

Finally, Okin's analysis failed to relate to the transformative guarantee of women's right to equality in the family in the 1948 Universal Declaration of Human Rights, endorsed by countries from all regions and all religious and cultural affiliations, and then reiterated in a series of international instruments, including the ICCPR, CEDAW and the Beijing Declaration and Platform for Action.[12] On this firm IHRL basis, the human right of women to equality in the family is an inalienable, integral and indivisible part of universal human rights.[13] Accordingly, any regime of gender hierarchy in the family should clearly be considered anathema.

In 1980, Article 16 of CEDAW called for specific measures to eliminate economic discrimination against women in marriage and family relations: mentioning specifically the right to choose a family name, a profession and an occupation; and the same rights for both spouses to in respect of the ownership, acquisition, management, administration, enjoyment and disposition of property.[14] A preliminary basis was thus laid in CEDAW for securing women equal rights as fully fledged members of the economic unit of family and it is clear that a start was made in converting economically invisible wife and mother into economic woman in the family. The World Bank has shown that over half of the constraints on women's and girls' equal rights to property and restrictions on their legal capacity that were on the books in the 1960s were removed by 2010 and in some regions these reforms represented radical change. Interestingly, the World Bank found that the ratification by states of the CEDAW was linked to legal reforms within a short-term period, positively affecting property rights for unmarried women, as well as inheritance rights for both daughters and surviving spouses.[15]

However, the question for economic women in families is how far has this legal dictate of equality been translated into their realities. The World Bank, in its 'Women, Business and the Law' 2016 report, found that there are many laws that still restrict married women from taking certain actions, on an equal basis with men: to apply for a passport, become head of household, choose where to live, get a job without permission, travel outside the home or the country, obtain a national identity card, register a business, open a bank account or sign a contract. It should be noted, from the data itself, that these restrictions on married women currently apply to a limited number of countries, thus, for example 32 countries do not allow married women on an equal basis to apply for a passport, 30 countries do not recognise them as head of household and only two countries do not allow them to sign contracts. Furthermore, the countries which have these restrictions are traditionalist countries, whose legal systems give deference to religious codes, and not countries with modern secular family law systems.[16]

In the dichotomy between the religious and the secular, the right of women to equality in the family has become the focus of retrogression and backlash in women's human rights at both the global and the national levels. There may be no other facet of women's right to equality which is so fragmented in law and so rifted in practice. Women's right to equality in the family is currently the site of a backlash, motivated by a traditionalist religious agenda, led by a lobby of the Russian Federation and OIC states and supported by some of the non-aligned states.[17] This lobby has gained a majority in the Human Rights Council for resolutions which call for the reinterpretation of human rights in the light of traditional values and for protection of the family. In its 2014 Resolution calling for protection of the family, as the natural and fundamental group unit of society entitled to protection by society and the state, the Human Rights Council omitted to include the crucial 20th-century gain of women's right to equality in the family.[18] As chair of the expert WGDAW, I brought the issue of this egregious and intended omission before the annual meeting of the independent experts of the Human Rights Council's Special Procedures and the experts unanimously agreed to call on the Council to expressly guarantee women's and girls' right to equality in the family. Following on this, the Council, in its 2015 Resolution on protection of the family, modified its position: "recognizing that equality between women and men and respect for all the human rights and fundamental freedoms of all family members are essential to family well-being and to society at large."[19] Nevertheless it stopped short of guaranteeing women's right to equality in the family and, on this ground, has been yet again criticised by the independent experts. The states in the Council divide primarily but not solely on religious grounds. Some wholly secular states, such as China, which itself provides strong directives in its own legislation for women's equality in the family, are nevertheless included amongst the supporters of the resolutions on traditionalism and protection of the family.[20]

2 A spectrum between traditionalist and modernist families

For the purpose of analysing economic gender relations in families, it is the divergence between traditionalist and modernist families and the spectrum between them that is the most central. These family frameworks range from the 'traditionalist,' in which the functions of the family members and their rights and obligations are defined by status and are usually nonnegotiable, to the 'modernist,' in which family relations are constructed and shifted according to individual choice, and are contractually binding. Traditionalist families tend to be rigidly formulated into hierarchical patriarchal units, often justified or even 'sacralised' by religious edict, while the modernist family is amorphous and based on a conception of autonomous choice.[21] Both of these types of family and the variations between them exist concurrently in different countries and societies and within them.

In traditionalist regulation of families, the male hegemony is the religious and cultural norm, while, in modernist secular regulation, gender equality is the legal norm. Women are hence dramatically differently situated in terms of rights and recognition as regards their economic status and opportunity in these different types of families, although even the modernist equality guarantees have not necessarily resulted in women's equal income and property in practice.

The spectrum of traditionalist to modernist approaches is also highly relevant to the increasingly diverse forms of family structure, currently recognised in the human rights regime. Diverse families are often described in terms of same sex partnerships or marriages, and their regulation is of great significance for the social and economic situation of members of those families. Traditionalist approaches almost uniformly oppose recognition of diversity in the constitution of families, insisting that families should be restricted to the model of a male and female union and hence either preempting the application of regulatory norms to the relationships within non-traditional families or prohibiting them altogether with punitive impact on their members. Modernist systems, in contrast, have uniformly repealed all prohibitions of same sex relationships and a growing number have recognised same sex marriages.

Traditionalist systems for regulating families

Unmodified traditionalist regulation of families is patriarchal. The formation of the family as a gendered hierarchy is fundamental to the legal codes and the representations of the sacred in the three monotheistic religions.[22] In patriarchal tradition determined by cultural and religious norms, the ownership and proceeds from property, income and investment will frequently be allocated to the male heads of family and males have preferred rights in inheritance.[23] Women's role is predetermined and typically restricted to provision of care and subsistence labour. Patriarchal hierarchy in families sets a psychological mind set of girls and boys, of men and women that capabilities are gendered, thus acting as a primary breeding ground for gender stereotypes. The vesting of property and income in the male head of family obviously negates women's economic potential. Under these norms, woman's economic fate will be entirely determined by her relationship with male members of the family. Traditionalist cultures and religions are the hard core preservers of the patriarchal family which inculcates gender hierarchy from a child's first perception of self and limits girls' imagination of holding economic power. Indeed, research into female students from traditionalist families has shown that a major factor in a girl's educational success and independence has been active encouragement by their fathers.[24]

There are claims in the traditionalist religions that the refusal to recognise women's right to equality in the family is because women are complementary to men in the family and are benefited by male protection and responsibility. These claims, however, can only point to charity or compassion and cannot replace women's right to equality. This conceptualisation of women's complementary status and dependence is in direct conflict with CEDAW's requirement of formal and substantive equality for women on the same terms as men and its call for transformative redistribution of resources and power between women and men. In international human rights instruments, in the General Comments and Concluding Observations of the treaty bodies and in the reports of Special Procedures of the Human Rights Council, it has been constantly reiterated that freedom of religion cannot be used to justify discrimination against women. The Vienna Declaration and Programme of Action in 1993, prioritised and guaranteed women's universal right to equality:

> While the significance of national and regional particularities and various historical, cultural and religious backgrounds must be borne in mind, it is the duty of States, regardless of their political, economic and cultural systems, to promote and protect all human rights and fundamental freedoms.... The human rights of women and the girl-child are an inalienable, integral and indivisible part of universal human rights.[25]

Under theocratic legal systems, traditionalist religious codes are the law which governs the personal law and the family lives of all the women in the state. In plural legal systems, a secular legislative system may delegate power to determine the regulation of family life to religious or customary communities in the state. Thus, either in theocratic or plural legal systems, traditionalist religious codes still determine the status of women in the family in many countries. As the WGDAW noted:

> Several States have no secular family code and regulate personal status either by integrating religious laws on the family into constitutional or legislative provisions or by granting religious authorities or religious tribunals jurisdiction over personal status so that they may apply the family codes derived from the sacred texts. Currently, a large number of States that have Islam as their State religion, such as the Islamic and Arab republics, regulate the personal status of all citizens by applying Islamic law from the Koran and the Sunna. Some States that recognise the legal competence of a majority religion in the State also grant non-majority religions jurisdiction over their own communities of faithful, such as Lebanon (Muslim majority), India (Hindu majority) and Israel (Jewish majority).[26]

In this context, there are states that continue to allow polygamous marriage, early and/or forced marriage and temporary marriage, which have dire economic consequences for women and are condoned in the majoritarian religious codes of the countries concerned. Polygamy, which is legal in almost all of the approximately 57 Muslim states other than Tunisia and Turkey,[27] has serious emotional and financial consequences for women and grave ramifications regarding their economic well-being.[28] Child marriage allows slavery and slavery-like practices to occur with apparent impunity.[29] Girls are robbed of their childhood, deprived of their right to education, at great risk of domestic violence and marital rape, and also exposed to the problem of early pregnancy with its high level of threat to their health or life. Child and early marriages, which were the norm in traditionalist family regimes and are still practiced in a considerable number of countries today, create a major barrier to the economic as well as social, physiological and psychological development of girls. Early marriage exists in developed as well as developing countries: in the US, more than one in ten of all women surveyed between 2001 and 2002 had married before age 18, and in 2010, more than 500,000 teens were married, divorced, separated or widowed. Researchers pointed out that girls who marry early are more likely to discontinue their formal education prematurely, earn low wages and live in poverty.[30]

A worst-case scenario of women's total economic disempowerment and its impact on the welfare of families and societies is one that has actually been played out by the Taliban in Afghanistan, which insisted that women and girls, who had previously been in a situation of relative equality and autonomy, stay at home, unless fully covered by a burqa and accompanied by a male relative, thus relegating them to economic impotency. Still today, Afghanistan is one of the worst places for women in the world. The global Women, Peace, and Security Index ranking 153 countries on measurements of peace and security, women's inclusion and justice, ranked Afghanistan in the lowest place, with disastrous indicators for women's economic and social welfare.[31] Data on Afghanistan showed very high levels of maternal and infant mortality, with one out of ten children dying before their fifth birthday; life expectancy for women 51; 85% of women with no formal education; almost 60% of girls married by 16.[32]

Human rights mechanisms have called for the non-recognition of all those forms of marriage that discriminate against women and girls, including polygamy and child, early and forced marriage. CEDAW has repeatedly called for the abolition of polygamy.[33] The UN Resolution on Child, Early and Forced Marriage,[34] is a landmark resolution calling for a ban on child and early marriage. In the recommendations of the WGDAW, it is pointed out that the ban on all these discriminatory forms of marriage must protect the rights of women and girls, who are the victims of these harmful marriages. Their rights to subsistence, to property, including land and inheritance, to a place of residence, to custody of children and to remarry must be guaranteed.[35] Other practices allowed by state legal systems, which have been condemned by human rights mechanisms, include the prosecution of women for adultery, which in a few countries has resulted in stoning of women by Sha'ri courts or by community practice;[36] a husband's absolute power to veto a wife's right to divorce in Jewish law;[37] and the power of unilateral divorce by husbands under Islamic law.[38]

Where family law has been based on religious law, reforms to introduce a measure of equality for women in the family have come about in two different ways. The first involves reform based on religious interpretation (hermeneutics). Reforms of religious family codes, based on interpretations of sacred texts that favour equality, have taken place in some Muslim-majority countries, which have carried out legislative reforms founded on progressive interpretations of sharia, for example, Tunisia where polygamy was prohibited and Morocco where polygamy was subjected to significant restrictions.[39] While the extent of hermeneutic reform has been limited in scope, its successes provide an important tool for religious women's organisations, such as Sisters in Islam, to seek change. The second way to reform patriarchal religious family law involves the replacement of religious family law with secular law. This sort of legal reform started to take place from the end of the 19th century, when many states reformed their laws on the family by separating religion from the state and introducing measures to promote women's equality within marriage and the family, including the right of married women to conclude contracts, own property, divorce and have guardianship and custody of children, on an equal basis with men. In Turkey, Ataturk secularised family law in 1926 and in traditionally Christian states, civil family codes were introduced to replace religious personal laws most recently in Italy in 1970 and Greece in 1982–1983.[40]

Modernist systems for regulating families

In progressive modernist families, there is more flexibility and the legal designation of a male head of family has been removed. In theory, the modernist family is not hierarchically gendered and women have the right to equality as regards marriage, divorce, property, income and work outside the family. Despite the conceptual equality for women and men in marriage in secular legal systems, there are persistent cultural pressures which militate against the actualisation of women's free choice and autonomy in modernist families. In view of these persistent cultural stereotypes and social pressures,[41] modernist families are considered by many feminist observers to be as patriarchal as traditionalist families, giving power over family decision-making and over the allocation of economic resources to the male, while gendered division of labour continues.[42]

Indeed, women's enjoyment of equality in modernist families has not translated into a universal reality in any society. Domestic violence perpetrated by men persists even in the most egalitarian legal systems and is the pathology of a patriarchal reality which has not been eliminated. Thus, for instance, in Iceland, which is at the top place in the Gender Gap Index, the figures for domestic violence against women remain very high.[43] Furthermore, as Part II of the book showed, the gender wage gap persists globally and, even in the most egalitarian countries, lower remuneration for women's market work is an ongoing reality,[44] constituting a discriminatory push factor for women to opt for unpaid childcare, part-time work and contingent employment. The combination of lower pay and the costs of childcare may make it economically unviable for women to sell their human capital at its full value outside the home and pay from the net proceeds for the outsourcing of care services in the family.

Furthermore, gender stereotypes persist. Where women do work and develop careers, this is often subtly condemned even in the modernist western world. Working women as portrayed in Hollywood movies usually feature overly ambitious career women who sacrifice their chance to find love in the arms of a man or betray their relationships as wife or mother and, as careerists, end up losing out on 'the truly important things in life,' in their own eyes and hence those of the viewer.[45] Television series are no exception. The Danish Borgen, celebrated as a welcome feminist series, is a case in point. Although the heroine is a woman prime minister with a family, Statsminister Birgitte Nyborg Christensen (actress Sidse Babett Knudsen), who is doing quite well at keeping her Moderates-led coalition government together, is not a success at married life; her husband, Philip Christensen (actor Mikael Birkkjær), portrayed as an ever-patient, supportive and feminist partner, has left her and is now waiting for her to sign their divorce papers. There are signs of a counter-trend genre in a number of American series, such as 'Commander in Chief' (2005) and 'The Good Wife' (2009), which though they may be complex from a feminist angle, do portray women maintaining families and highly successful careers. The American series 'Madame Secretary' shows for example the United States Secretary of State as able to fulfil her functions in a supremely feminist mode accompanied by an ever-supportive professor husband and the understanding of her teenage children. Another example is the Nigerian 'Nollywood,' in which women are presented in a highly positive light as successful career women and the integration of family and career is not part of the genre.[46] The film and television industries, as a mirror to popular culture, seem to be responding only partially to the shift in modernist family culture which regards it as a fact of life that many women are integrating careers and family life.

The potential for equality in the modernist family is far greater than in the traditionalist family. A normative foundation for the egalitarian modernist family has been well established in international human rights law and in secular legal systems. This normative potential for a gender equal partnership model may not yet have been fully realised but it is imminent in modernist families. The rise of the modernist egalitarian family, while not universal, is a significant phenomenon. Esping-Andersen & Billari[47] posit a return to "more family" as gender egalitarianism gains increasingly dominant normative status: after decades of decrease in fertility rates, there has been some "recovery" and in some countries an increase can be detected. They suggest that while in the late 1980s in countries that were more gender egalitarian there were higher rates of unmarried women, since the late 2000s, the trend has changed and is now described as an inverted U-shaped curve – the highest rates of unmarried women can be found in the middle of the gender equality scale and lower rates of unmarried women can be found not only in the less gender equal but also in the highest gender equal countries. Thus, a model of modernist families with children, based on an ethos of gender equality, seems to be emerging. Furthermore, the growing recognition of the diversity of modernist families, with same sex and transgender marriages or partnerships, do much to deconstruct the hierarchically gendered prototype of family.

As an aside, it is interesting to note that this modernist alternative to the patriarchal family is a gender equal partnership model and that the possibility of a matriarchal option is not even conceived of in policy or practice. The matriarchal option is almost extinct. It is, however, demonstrated by small Himalayan tribes in China that have changed little in centuries. These seem to be the last matrilineal societies on earth, where power lies in the hands of women. In the Mosuo tribe, all decisions and rights related to money, property, land and the children born to them rest with the women, who live completely independently of husbands, fathers and brothers, with the grandmother as the head of each family.[48] In the Na tribe, brothers and sisters live together their entire lives, sharing household responsibilities and raising the women's children.[49] In both tribes, the woman's lovers, whom they choose from men within the tribe, frequently more than one, bear no economic responsibility for her or her children.

3 Women's investment in the family and women breadwinners

Investment in the family can derive from property, from earned income or from unpaid care work. The prevalent perception has been of a gender division of labour in the family, according to which men earn the major part of cash income and women carry out most of the unpaid care work. As regards women's earning of income through work outside the home, the assumption that there is a prevailing gendered division of labour in the family does not accurately describe families, whether in modernist or even in all traditionalist environments. In the modernist family, although the gendered division of labour is considered by some to be a rational economic choice for the family,[50] women are increasingly cast in the role of breadwinner.[51] The rise in women's labour force participation rate (LFPR) is not actually as new a global phenomenon as often thought since poor women in pre-industrial societies and rural communities have always worked in various forms of agricultural, service or cottage industries, which brought income to the family.[52] Nevertheless, it is significant in the era of industrialisation and urbanisation, where work in the cash economy usually involves lengthy separations from home and children, thus exacerbating the work and care dichotomy in the lives of worker-carers. Hence, women's high LFPR represents a dramatic change in urbanised high-income countries, such as the United States.[53]

The trends and significance of women's labour force participation are discussed in Part II of the book and it can be said that on average women are participating in income generating activities outside the home at two-thirds the rate of men. These numbers are revealing given the common assumption that the division of labour in families is pervasive and especially so in traditionalist families. The high LFPR of women is, exceptionally, however not evident in states which incorporate traditionalist customary laws or religious codes in their legal systems, mandating traditionalist norms which keep women out of the labour market, forfeiting economic opportunities in favour of traditionalist family roles.[54]

To quantify the way in which women's LFPR results in women's cash investment in the family we need to take a look at the income earned by women who do participate in the labour force as compared with men. Different models of female breadwinning are typified on a scale between part-time worker and unpaid carer in the context of a two parent family; dual career earner; or sole breadwinner. One indicator of the level of women's investment through earned income is the number of women who are primary or equal breadwinners in families. As early as 1995, the Beijing Declaration and Platform for Action observed that one-fourth of all households worldwide are headed by women and many other households are dependent on female income even where men are present.[55]

In the developed world, the transition to female breadwinners represents a radical change over the past century. In the world's leading economy, the US, research by economist Heather Boushey in 2009 empirically illustrated that mothers are more likely to provide significant financial support to their families than ever before.[56] In more recent assessments, the trend toward female breadwinning continued – nearly two-thirds of mothers are primary or co-breadwinners for their families, including more than half of married mothers, 52.9%, who bring home at least 25% of their families' incomes.[57] In the United Kingdom, almost 30% of working mothers equalled or out-earned their husbands or as single mothers provided sole income for their families.[58] Women are frequently primary breadwinners not only in developed countries but also in developing countries. Research shows a growing trend for women to become breadwinners in developing countries, with marriage rates tumbling, fertility rates declining and divorce initiated by women on the rise, as women celebrate their hard-won financial autonomy.[59] The sole female breadwinner model in female-headed households takes a wide variety of forms: female-headed extended households; lone, single-sex, female dominant households; and grandmother female-headed households.[60] The rise of the female breadwinner in the developing world has been described as the 'feminization of survival,' as households and whole communities become dependent on women's income, including, with its harsh implications for economic woman, as migrant workers.[61] There is nevertheless, according to United Nations Department of Economic and Social Affairs data, wide regional variation: households headed by women (not only lone-mothers) are most common in Northern America (with a median proportion of 47%), followed by Europe (37%), Latin America and the Caribbean (34%) and Oceania (33%). The median prevalence of female-headed households is much lower in Africa (27%) and lowest in Asia (19%).[62]

Women who are earning an income are becoming dominant breadwinners not only because of the income they generate but also for an additional reason, because of the percentage of that income which they devote to family needs. The rather dramatic finding attributed to the World Bank is that where women do have earned income they invest, on average, 90% of it in family needs,[63] and some sources contrast this with men who invest only 30 to 40% of their earned income on family needs.[64] The World Bank and the IMF conclude, on the basis of evidence from a range of countries in different regions, that increasing the share of household income controlled by women, either through their own earnings or cash transfers, influences household spending in ways that benefit children.[65]

Explanations for this may range from the existence of a patriarchal family structure in which women's wages 'belong' to the male head of family or it may be because of different gendered understandings of responsibility for care of family members. It is a phenomenon which requires research and analysis and should become a salient consideration in economic and welfare policy.

4 Family caregiving

Women everywhere are still the primary unpaid carers for children and other dependent family members, including elderly parents. Empirical studies clearly show that globally, women bear the heavier share of unpaid care work. In 2017, The World Economic Forum assessed that globally men do only 37% of the unpaid work that women do (originally reported as 34% for OECD countries).[66] Additionally, the ILO showed that, when both paid work and unpaid work are taken into consideration, women work longer hours per day than men with a gender gap of 73 minutes per day in developing and 33 minutes per day in developed countries.[67] Veerle Miranda, in 2011, found an average gender gap in unpaid work at home of 2 hours and 28 minutes per 24-hour day, with a significant divergence across countries. The time men and women devote to unpaid work is to some extent related to the country's level of economic development, although the correlations are rather weak: women's unpaid working time is negatively correlated with GDP per capita, while that of men is positively correlated with GDP per capita.[68] There is evidence of some convergence in Europe and North America between the amount of housework done by men and women.[69] Nevertheless, the extra burden of unpaid care on women operates in high income as well as poor countries and does not disappear with economic growth.[70] Even in the high-income country with the highest average unpaid working time among men, Denmark, men still devote less time to unpaid care work than women devote in Norway, the country with the lowest female unpaid working time (Figure 24.1).[71]

Women's disparate burden of unpaid care holds true for both traditionalist and modernist settings.[72] It is true, whether the woman works in the cash economy or not. Furthermore, single parent families are predominantly headed by women.[73] Even outsourcing of care retains the female paradigm: frequently domestic workers are migrant women whose own family caring roles are suspended as a result of distance and typically they suffer negative psychological and long-term repercussions as a result of the separation from their own families and children.[74] Other outsourcing relies on grandmother help, whether in the developed or the developing world. The allocation of care to women is in some part physiological, at the stage of birthing and breastfeeding, but in larger part based on gender stereotypes and on an economic premise which allows

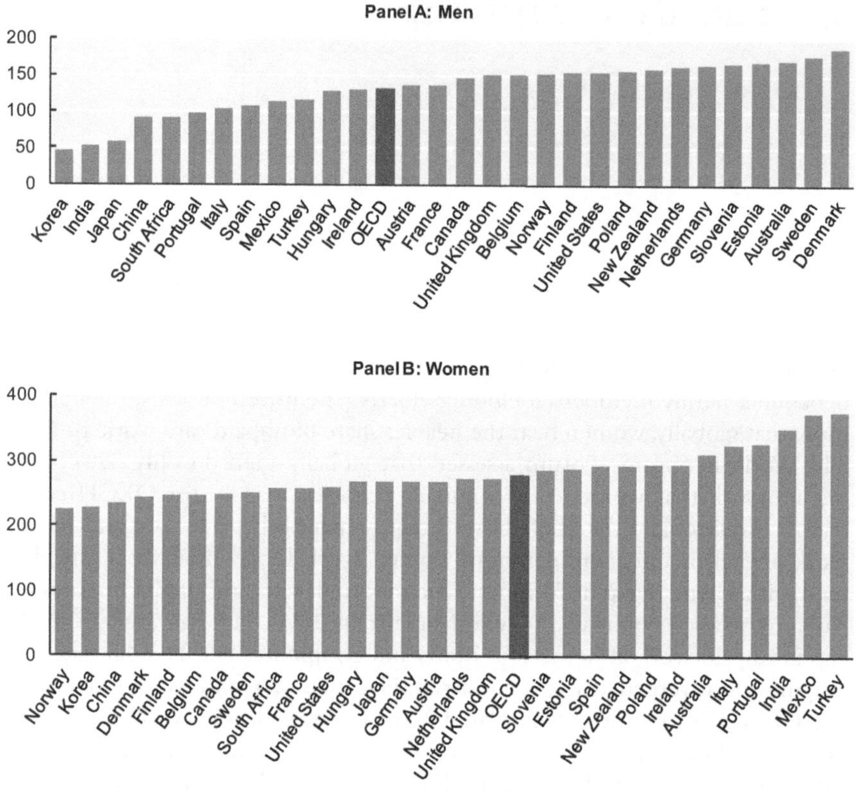

Figure 24.1 Minutes of unpaid work per day for the population aged 15–64, over the period 1998–2009

Source: Miranda V., 'Cooking, Caring and Volunteering: Unpaid Work Around the World', OECD Social, Employment and Migration Working Papers, No. 116, OECD Publishing, Paris, 2011, https://doi.org/10.1787/5kghrjm8s142-en.

the use of women's unpaid labour. Unlike women's reproductive function, care functions do not necessarily have to fall on women but, as the data in the Introduction shows, in fact they largely do so.

The overall data on time spent by women and men on unpaid care work encompasses variations between individual families and it is clear that there are families at both ends of a spectrum between those in which one partner, almost always the woman, does all the unpaid care work and the other, still a small minority, in which the care work is equally shared or largely performed by men.[75] In gay marriages all the unpaid care and domestic work is performed by men and the increase in the adoption or surrogacy of children in marriages of gay men[76] appears to be an exceptionalist break away from the female care paradigm, though there is research which indicates that gay spouses are themselves falling into divided care patterns necessitated by the lack of infrastructure for a different work-life balance.[77]

Indeed, the pressures of combining work with childrearing are infinitely increased in the age of Capital, where the demands of the economic market are unrelenting, requiring long hours at work, daily travel from home, long distance travel for work, relocation and rescheduling in accordance with the needs of the employing enterprise and job insecurity which may entail constant readjustment of home management. Families are under increasing stress in attempting to bring in adequate income for family units, in the light of the decline of the family wage for one breadwinner and the economic exigency of two-earner families,[78] while at the same time providing the caring facilities essential for dependent family members.

CEDAW requires states to ensure that family education includes a proper understanding of maternity as a social function and the recognition of the common responsibility of men and women in the upbringing and development of their children.[79] The concept of gender equality propagated in CEDAW has clearly been that women like men should work in an income earning capacity and men should share the care work. The CEDAW Committee has said that the persistence of male breadwinner models and the lack of sharing of care responsibilities represents a discriminatory stereotype, based on the idea of a male head of household. The Committee rejects the encouragement of women's part-time work as a solution to the problem of their combining care and paid work.[80] Similarly, the Beijing Declaration and Platform for Action calls for harmonisation of work and family responsibilities for women and men.[81] In this vision, the feasibility of equal market activity of women is inextricably linked to the equal sharing of care functions by men.

All forms of care, including childcare, are amenable to social reconstruction, and indeed in the Nordic countries, which have long pursued a policy of gender equality in the division of work and childcare functions, the distribution of care work has been said to come close to parity.[82] Good practice regarding the allocation of care responsibilities, pioneered in the Nordic countries, with paid maternity and parental leave, 'daddy leave,' publicly funded childcare and cash payments for home-based care, assumes a 'dual-earner/dual-career' family and encourages men to enter traditionally women's worlds, both in the family and in the workplace.[83] It is nevertheless clear that even in the Scandinavian model women still spend considerably more time on domestic work than men and prolonged part-time work is associated with women.[84]

The complexities of families on the spectrum of individualised social, psychological, health and economic circumstances, requires us to visualise a system in which there are variations in the division of care in the family and of work outside the family. The important task for gender equality goals is to make sure that these variations are not dictated by discriminatory cultural, religious or legal barriers or by gender stereotypes regarding the rights to equality and equal autonomy of family members. Secular legal systems which have developed the concept of the right of women to equality in all aspects of family life provide the normative basis for this scenario. However, they have not been widely realised in practice or fully internalised in attitudes. Indeed, change on the ground cannot materialise without a transformative change in infrastructure, with provision of affordable care services and synchronisation of school days to facilitate a proper work-life balance. Furthermore, as we saw in Part II, IHRL does not mandate the provision of such services and they have not been provided except exceptionally in a tiny minority of states.

Even in the many countries which have introduced legal equality rights in the family, the playing field has not been fully equalised in any society. It cannot be overlooked that market pressures affect the economic assessment of the optimal division of roles between partners, in equal autonomous choice situations: as the returns on a women's market investment is invariably, across all societies, lower than that of a comparable man,[85] the likelihood remains that it is women who will continue to take on the unpaid care. Hence, solutions have to be sought on the social policy rather than the individual level, through third party care arrangements, in which domestic work is outsourced as decent work and in which societies subsidise the cost of care through social protection floors. This would solve the problem of dual careers for most families.

Even if the economic option for equal division of all roles by women and men in the family becomes truly available and the choice is made on a basis of equality in both family hierarchy and income potential, the economic outcome will not in, the reality of the age of capital when there has been no renegotiation of "space for non-market values of solidarity"[86] be equal for a partner who chooses to stay at home rather than take the market role. The partner who takes the market role accumulates skills and the capability to earn a living. The partner who stays at home develops an economic dependency, which can lead to poverty in the case of loss of support by the earning partner, for whatever reason.[87] It has not, as discussed in Part III, been feasible for the social safety nets of the welfare state or of universal basic income to adequately replace the unpaid time investment of a carer (usual a woman) and convert it into economic viability and earning capacity over the span of a lifetime.

5 The economics of biological motherhood

Along with the emotional experience and social importance of having children, the advent of parenthood has major economic implications and those economic implications are of course gendered as regards the biology of pregnancy and birth. The biological aspects of motherhood entail a time and money investment in pregnancy, childbirth and breastfeeding. The time consumption elements of these biological functions are less cumulatively onerous in societies which have low birth rates but nevertheless even one or two pregnancies may be economically disruptive during women's formative years of adulthood. For some women, health complications, in their pregnancies or in their newborns, may result in total dislocation from all other activities for longer periods of time. Even routine breastfeeding, especially where this is strongly recommended for health of the newborn, may be a longer term barrier to economic activity where facilities are not available in the public or work space. The health and nutrition costs of biological motherhood may also be far from negligible. If the birth is in childhood or adolescence it will have a crucially damaging impact on the mother.

The economics of motherhood are often viewed on an individual basis but there are macroeconomic forces at play in women's fertility. Indeed, women's fertility is a major battlefield for opposing socio-economic interests. There is a pendulum between, on one hand, the advocates of population control in the face of the escalating global population affecting environmental sustainability and advocates of increasing the birth rate, on the other, in view of the rise in the proportion of countries with low fertility rates, bringing about shifting age demographics in which the percentage of older people compared to those of working age is expected to rise rapidly.[88]

At the Rio Conference on Environment and Development in 1991, the need for population control as a measure to achieve environmental sustainability in the face continuing deterioration of the environment and serious degradation of global life-support systems was raised by science groups but assiduously kept off the agenda because of opposition from various interest groups, including religious institutions. The result was that Principle Eight of the Rio Declaration refers only to promotion of "appropriate demographic policies."[89] Traditionally, the world's major religions have encouraged and continue to encourage women's fertility and have done so through opposition to contraception and abortion which, in many countries, has resulted in prevention of access to affordable medical contraception and termination of unwanted pregnancy. A deconstructive approach could reveal the economic implications of increasing the population size of sectarian communities.

A commercialised aspect of women's reproductive capacity, especially of women in poverty, being subjected to market economics is the trade in surrogacy creating for instance in India, which has had one of the most notable reproductive tourism sectors, an industry estimated to be worth as much as $2.3 billion annually, and where the government intervened to prohibit this international trade.[90] The renewed interest in the highly popular television series of Margaret Atwood's 1985 prophetic novel *The Handmaid's Tale*, in which women were farmed to produce babies for men whose wives were not fertile, indicates that this commercialisation of women's reproductive capacity in an age of growing problems of infertility, is a matter of widespread concern.

In contrast, China provides a unique example of restricting fertility for macroeconomic reasons. China introduced its one-child policy in 1979, aiming to limit mothers and fathers to one child in order to reduce population growth and thus eliminate poverty and increase the GDP more quickly. This policy was largely enforced by economic penalties. It was a gender-neutral policy affecting fathers as well as mothers though where, in some cases, it was enforced through forced abortion, it constituted a severe violation of women's human rights.[91] In 2015, again motivated by macroeconomic policy, the Chinese government decided to allow an increase in the number of children per family in order to address the severe demographic imbalance which had developed between the working population and the elderly.[92]

Macroeconomic policy has, thus, at one end of the spectrum supported population control and at the other has aimed to maintain or increase the birth rate. In both cases motherhood is not merely a matter of individual choice but is instrumentalised for economically oriented population policies. Under international human rights law, men and women have the right to control the number and spacing of their children. To fulfil their obligation to ensure this right, states must provide access to affordable family planning services including modern contraceptives and medical abortion services. In pursuance of economic population agendas, states can use economic incentives and disincentives but clearly must not use coercive measures of any kind.

6 Matrimonial property

In ancient Egypt, 3100 BCE and after, women held equal rights with men to acquire, own and dispose of property (both real and personal) in their own name. Also, in Jewish law, in ancient Rome, in Islam and in Anglo-Saxon laws, married women could own property.[93] However, under modern legal systems based on Roman civil law, which influenced most of continental Europe, or those based on English common law, like the majority of British and American colonies, women who married lost, if not ownership then, at a minimum, control over their property.[94] In the famous words of Blackstone in 18th-century England, "[b]y marriage, the husband and wife are one person in law."[95] This in fact signified that women lost their separate legal personhood, disappearing into the legal persona of their husbands, and hence married women did not have the capacity to manage property, even such property they owned or earned themselves. In England, a 20-year campaign by women's groups supported by some men led to the passing of The Married Women's Property Act of 1870 which protected a woman from her husband gaining control of her property. It is interesting to note that women's right to own and manage matrimonial property thus predated their right to vote in the Western world.[96]

Since the late 19th century, there has been a global trend to bring about universal legal recognition of married women's right to own and manage property, thus restoring the position which existed in some ancient legal systems. This right was not specifically mentioned in the Universal Declaration of Human Rights but could clearly be subsumed under the provision that "men and women . . . are entitled to equal rights as to marriage, during marriage and at its dissolution." The CEDAW further spelled out that states must secure the same rights for both spouses in respect of the ownership, acquisition, management, administration, enjoyment and disposition of property.[97] The Human Rights Committee, in its General Comment No. 28 (2000) on equality of rights between men and women, has also stated that "the capacity of women to own property . . . may not be restricted on the basis of marital status or any other discriminatory ground" and that state parties must ensure that the "matrimonial regime contains equal rights and obligations for both spouses with regard to . . . the ownership or administration of property, whether common property or property in the sole ownership of either spouse."[98]

International human rights law provisions for equality in matrimonial property provide a normative basis for a transformative change in married women's potential for capital acquisition and property management. There is however, no systemic global data available to show how this is being implemented. From such data as available, it seems that while many countries have adopted equal rights legislation as regards control and ownership of matrimonial property, there remain regions and countries in which this has not been achieved. In this context, the SDG Goal 5.A which sets out to undertake reforms to give women access to ownership and control over land "in accordance with national laws," is not transformative but rather preserves the legal status quo.[99]

The World Bank's 'Women, Business and the Law' reports examine, in a section on 'using property,' women's ability to access and use property based on their ability to own, manage and control it. The reports analyse indicators of equality for married women, such as: ownership rights over property, administering marital property and legal recognition for non-monetary contributions to marital property.[100] The World Bank's findings in 2018 indicate that, as regards many of these rights, there are still countries which maintain discriminatory marital property regimes.[101] The OECD Development Centre's Social Institutions and Gender Index (SIGI), covering 160 countries worldwide, provides some regional indications as regards women's right to equality in matrimonial property. In 2014, it found that in the OECD countries, women and men have equal rights in law in respect to land, property and financial services, although customary practices persist in Mexico and Korea.[102] In East Asia and the Pacific, there is a mixed picture, mainly due to conflict between customary, religious and civil laws (e.g. Indonesia, Malaysia, the Philippines and Singapore).[103] In Latin America and the Caribbean, out of the 22 countries covered by SIGI, 19 show no discrimination on non-land assets, as compared with only 10 which show no discrimination on rights to land, and 11 show no discrimination in inheritance rights.[104] In the Middle East and North Africa, SIGI found that family codes are based on customary and religious laws, which assign unequal inheritance rights to girls and restrict women's resources and assets.[105] The South Asia region has some of the highest levels of discrimination in the family code.

Even where there is gender equality at the national legislative level, as regards the implementation of women's right to own property, there is country information which provides fragmented data indicating that, married women may actually own only a small share of matrimonial property. This discrepancy is the result of the ongoing prevalence of patriarchal family customs.

In China, until the promulgation of the Republic of China's Civil Code in 1930, when women married, they left their natal families and lost any rights to their birth family's property. In 1930, a gradual process of reform began, culminating in the Marriage Law as amended in 2001, which states that marriage is to be based on equality between men and women, including in matters of matrimonial property, and the rights and interests of women must be protected.[106] Nevertheless, only 13.2% of married women have homes in their own names, compared with 51.7% of married men. Moreover, although over 70% of women contribute to the marital home purchase, only 30% of marital home deeds include the woman's name. Women often transfer all of their assets to their husband or boyfriend to finance the purchase of a home, which is then registered in the man's name alone. The reasons are complicated, but include deeply entrenched attitudes that the man must be the official homeowner. Such attitudes are leading to a new gender wealth gap in China's transition to an intensified market economy. Chinese women have largely missed out on what is arguably the biggest accumulation of residential property wealth in history, estimated by HSBC at more than £17.5 trillion at the end of 2013.[107]

The World Bank reported that, although in most East European and Central Asian countries, women and men have the same formal legal rights to own land and other property, experience gathered from over two decades of land projects and recent analytical work in this region suggests that women face barriers to property rights, particularly in rural areas. Titles and deeds to land are often solely in the name of a head of household, who is usually male and, although privatisation or restitution of farmland has been applied to whole families, the male head of household is often listed formally on the title or registered deed, thereby reducing the *de facto* rights of other family members.[108] SIGI also reports that while, as regards Central Asia, patterns of discrimination exist, such as son bias and early and forced marriages, in Eastern Europe, gaps in laws or poor implementation are the challenge.

7 Dissolution of marriage

The ownership of property is crucial for determining women's economic situation on dissolution of the marriage. Division of matrimonial property on dissolution of the marriage, whether as a result of separation, divorce or death of one of the spouses, has to be regulated against a backdrop of diverse spousal property regimes. There are common default marital property regimes:[109]

1 Separation of property – all property acquired by the spouses before they marry, as well as all property acquired during the marriage, remains separate property also on dissolution of the marriage.
2 Partial community of property – assets acquired before marriage are considered the property of the acquirer. Assets and income acquired by either spouse during marriage, apart from inheritance or gifts to one spouse, are considered joint property during the marriage or, in deferred systems of community property, may be under the control of each spouse and then divided equally on dissolution of the marriage.
3 Full community of property – all assets and income brought into the marriage, as well as those acquired during it, apart from inheritance or gifts to one spouse, are considered joint property.

The possibility of realising women's equal right to property in the family, recognised in principle, depends on which of these legal regimes for division of matrimonial property is adopted. In general, community property regimes will secure a greater part of the property for the less economically active partner and will factor in the contribution of unpaid care as an economic value. This is evident in a study on gender asset and wealth gaps in Ecuador, Ghana and the Indian state of Karnataka, that used household asset surveys to estimate married women's share of couples' wealth. The study found that in Ghana, married women owned 19% of couples' wealth and in Karnataka they owned 9%. Surprisingly, in Ecuador married women owned 44% of couples' wealth. The much larger share of couples' wealth held by married women in Ecuador was explained by the country's partial community property regime, where most assets are owned jointly by wives and husbands. Married women's smaller share of couples' wealth in Ghana and Karnataka was largely explained by their separation of property regimes, whereby assets are not jointly owned.[110]

Even in the case of community property regimes, many complex issues need to be regulated in order to achieve equality between women and men in division of the matrimonial property. How should property be defined – does it include and by what calculation accumulated future rights, such as pensions and insurances? Does it include shared liability for debts incurred by a property owning spouse securing credit in the joint names of the couple? How free should the spouses be to condition the division of property between them in prenuptial agreements? The legal method for ensuring equality in economic division of property, income and investment between spouses is, as said, a highly complex issue. The family is an economic unit and its members are potentially both investors and beneficiaries. They may invest both in cash (property or earned income) and in kind (care functions and unpaid work). The issue to be resolved is how the investment in family by individual members is to be evaluated and how to achieve a correlation between an individual's investment and his or her entitlement to a share of the property and the earned income of both spouses.

An attempt to achieve universal principles for regulation was made by the CEDAW Committee in its 2013 General Recommendation 29 on the economic consequences of marriage, family relations and their dissolution:

> The guiding principle should be that the economic advantages and disadvantages related to the relationship and its dissolution should be borne equally by both parties. The division of roles and functions during the spouses' life together should not result in detrimental economic consequences for either party.
>
> State parties are obligated to provide, upon divorce and/or separation, for equality between the parties in the division of all property accumulated during the marriage. State parties should recognize the value of indirect, including non-financial contributions with regard to the acquisition of property acquired during the marriage.
>
> State parties should provide for equal formal and de facto legal capacity to own and manage property. To achieve both formal and substantive equality with respect to property rights upon the dissolution of marriage, State parties are strongly encouraged to provide for: . . . Valuation of non-financial contributions to marital property subject to division, including household and family care, lost economic opportunity and tangible or intangible contributions to either spouse's career development and other economic activity and to the development of his or her human capital.[111]

The two main thrusts of CEDAW's guiding principle are equality in the division of property accumulated during the marriage between the spouses and the inclusion of unpaid care work in the assessment of the investment of the spouses in the acquisition of property. The recognition of the value of unpaid care work is in and of itself a great stride forward in understanding an ignored economic contribution made generally by women.[112] Looking at families as economic and social units, the principle of equality in division of the property after dissolution of the marriage or death of one of the spouses should reflect the investment made by each member. The basic presumption is of a partnership where the investments in cash and in kind are of equal value for the flourishing of the family unit and its members. The work of caring is not severable from the flourishing of the family and thus should not be assessed by the market value of the care work but rather by the economic unit value of the sharing of partnership roles. Hence the care work should not be regarded as merely giving a right to compensation or to valuation, as stated by the CEDAW Committee, but rather there should be a basic presumption that care work earns the right to an equal share in family income and property accumulated as a result of the partnership. This is true whichever partner, male or female, is the caregiver.

For some families the automatic cutting of the property down the middle may not always serve justice and may even act as a boomerang, as where one spouse, usually the woman, is both the sole or primary wage earner or financial supporter and the primary caregiver.[113] However, any exception to the presumption of equal division of the matrimonial property, must be carefully restricted to avoid weakening the presumption of equal financial partnership in both income and property acquired during the marriage.

From the data it is clear that for the majority of women a principle of equal financial partnership has not in practice resulted in equal sharing of the family assets on dissolution of the marriage. The figures show that women usually suffer a significant loss of income after divorce. The CEDAW Committee noted that research has shown that women suffer a substantial decline in household income after separation or divorce, while men suffer either no decline or a smaller decline.[114] Indeed, early research in the United States showed that after divorce, men actually experience an increase in income, while women experienced a severe decline.[115] A more recent research from 2008 in the United Kingdom also showed that in the years following the marital split, separating husbands' incomes appear to rise almost continuously on average, while for separating women, although the sharp fall in income experienced immediately after the marital split is followed by a gradual improvement in the subsequent four years, it doesn't reach pre-split levels. The poverty rate among separating wives was found to be 27%, almost three times that of separating husbands.[116] As regards developing countries, UN Women and World Bank found, based on data for 89 countries, that divorced women aged 15 and older are two times as likely to be poor than divorced men in that same age group.[117] Hence the greatest policy priority in order to reduce inequality for economic woman is to extend the financial partnership principle globally and to apply it effectively.

8 Inheritance

Another path to property or poverty for women and girls is through inheritance. Women have traditionally been excluded from the inheritance route to wealth by pervasive religious and customary discrimination depriving them of rights to equal inheritance. In religious, civil and common law systems, preference in inheritance has traditionally been given to sons over daughters and usually over widows as well, along with partial exceptions such as the reform of Islamic law which entitled women to a (still discriminatory) half of the male share of the inheritance.[118] Development of equal inheritance rights for women has been sporadic. In 1791, Revolutionary France gave women equal inheritance rights (although they lost them later, when the monarchy was restored). In 1850, Iceland introduced unconditional equal inheritance rights. In 1922, the United Kingdom allowed equal inheritance. In Turkey, in 1926, and in Albania, in 1928, legislation secured equal rights to women in inheritance.[119] Many secular legal codes have by now introduced equality between women and men and between girls and boys in inheritance.

Treaty law has not yet specifically addressed the right of women to equal inheritance as widows and as daughters. CEDAW is silent as to women's and girls' inheritance rights. Nevertheless, the CEDAW Committee recommended equality in inheritance for spouses.[120] Although the Beijing Declaration and Platform for Action requires the girl-child's equal right to inherit, it does not include the right of widows to equality in inheritance as a strategic objective.[121] A specific call for equality for both women and girls in intestate succession was made by the WGDAW.[122] The SDGs have also called for reforms to give women and girls equal inheritance rights however, they have circumscribed this with a proviso recognising that the right may be regulated in accordance with national laws.[123]

SIGI reported in 2014 that only 55 countries of the 160 countries it covered accorded women the same inheritance rights as men, both in law and in practice.[124] In 36 of the 189 economies covered by 'Women, Business and the Law' in 2018, female surviving spouses still do not have the same inheritance rights as their male counterparts and in 39 of them daughters are prevented from inheriting in the same way as sons.[125] Furthermore, such provisions for women's inheritance rights as there are have not, in all cases, been very effective for women. In inheritance under Shari'a law, women, who are entitled to half the inheritance of a male, frequently waive the inheritances to which they are entitled.[126] Attempting to eliminate this practice, in 2010, Jordan passed a law preventing women from waiving their inheritance and requiring any property they inherit to be registered in their name when the will is executed. It also requires that relatives challenging the bequest go to court to demonstrate valid reasons for nullifying a woman's inheritance.[127] This law both evidences the existence of the problem of waiver of inheritance rights and provides an instance of good practice to put an end to it.

Exclusion of women from inheritance has a devastating impact on girls and widows. The stark reality produced by the exclusion of women in many religious and customary systems from a share or an equal share in family property through inheritance is particularly evident in land ownership. Women's access to land as a productive resource is frequently barred by custom, which regards land given to women as 'lost to another family' in the event of marriage, divorce or (male) death, justifying the deprivation of rights from the woman by arguing that men will provide for women's financial security.[128]

The exclusion of widows from family inheritance, both in their own and in their marital families, has been tragically and forcefully expressed in the film 'Water' (2005), which shows the situation of widows in traditionalist Hindu culture, with an eight-year-old widow being torn from her family home to be confined to a widows' hostel in which the widows become virtually 'untouchables' and their only source of livelihood is through provision of cleaning services. Against this background, in 2005, the government of India amended the Hindu Succession Act to ensure daughters enjoy equal rights to inherit their parent's land and property. The reforms were found to have had a positive impact on the total value of asset transfers to women, the share of household land they received, and their level of land ownership.[129] Women who inherited under the reform were more likely to have bank accounts, twice as much was invested in their daughters' education and their households were more likely to have sanitary latrines, "suggesting that legal empowerment gives women more bargaining power within the household and leads to better educational and financial outcomes for families."[130] Nevertheless, a 2014 survey of more than 1,400 women and 360 men in agricultural districts with large numbers of women farmers in three Indian states found that just one in eight women whose parents own agricultural land inherit any of it.[131]

In those regions and countries in which legal equality in regard to inheritance has been achieved, we can, in the absence of systematic sex-disaggregated data on the ownership of family property, only draw upon anecdotal evidence. The *Forbes* list of the world's billionaires show that most of the women who became billionaires did so on the basis of wealth inherited as daughters or widows.[132] Thus, a tiny group of women are entering the realms of the super-rich, largely through inheritance. The impact of equality in inheritance is almost inevitably increasing women's wealth at all levels of families which own property. However data is needed to show the way the extent of the increase in practice.

9 Maintenance and custody[133]

The connection between women's economic status in the family and their care functions may become particularly acute after the dissolution of the marriage where there are children. Different models of child custody have varying outcomes for women. Models of custody allocation, such as joint or shared custody or allocation of custody without a tender years presumption granting mothers preference in the case of custody of younger children, which are open to negotiation between the parents will generally disadvantage women who want to have custody as they have lesser bargaining power in contested proceedings. On the other hand, sole custody allocation to mothers or to primary carers can result in time burdens and economic hardship for single mothers.

Parents are obliged under the Convention on the Rights of the Child to secure, within their abilities and financial capacities, the conditions of living necessary for the child's development. This applies to non-custodial as well as custodial parents and has strong gender implications. The majority of custodial parents are single mothers who are as a group highly vulnerable to poverty and the non-custodial fathers are required to pay maintenance. However, child maintenance and support systems are, in almost all countries and contexts, inadequate to provide single mother families with the income required to maintain a suitable standard of living for themselves and their children and this contributes to gender-based poverty. The systems of calculation do not sufficiently take into account the discriminatory realities of women's lesser economic opportunities, especially after the dissolution of a marriage in which there was a gendered division of roles, with women devoting their time to unpaid care and not developing income earning capabilities.

Furthermore, the failure to enforce the payment of maintenance obligations by non-custodial fathers results in a high percentage of custodial mothers who do not receive maintenance payments at all. In case of default by the non-custodial parent, public support systems, in which the state advances the payment of support to the custodial parent, are the most viable solution. These systems should improve enforcement mechanisms against the non-custodial parent and, interrelatedly, provide high levels of public support to the custodial parent in the case of default. These measures are essential to reduce the poverty of single mother families.

10 International human right to equality in the family – transformation and backlash

Starting with the UDHR and continuing in the human rights treaties, there has been a gender equality transformation in the concept of family in international human rights law, recognising the right of women and girls to equality in marriage and family relations. This transformative recognition came against a background of the paradigm of the patriarchal family in political philosophy and in legal systems, both religious and secular. At the same time, many women in the world remain subject to religious legal systems or to cultural norms which preserve the patriarchal family and its allocation of economic assets to its male members. The legal transformation is still globally a work in process: the World Bank reported in 2018 that of 189 economies 40% have at least one legal constraint on women's property rights.[134]

The equality transformation in the family is the most ideologically contested aspect of the international human rights system. It is the site of a clash between the secular order, which conceptually regards the modernist family as an egalitarian unit, in which all members have equal economic opportunities, autonomy and rights, and the traditionalist religions and cultures, under which the family remains patriarchal. CEDAW has a large number of state reservations to the Article 16 right to equality in the family, on grounds of religious exceptionalism, but the human rights mechanisms have regarded these reservations as incompatible with the Convention's guarantee of equality for women.

Nevertheless, the backlash against women's right to equality in the family has continued at the international level. The challenge to the universality of human rights on grounds of traditionalism, religion and conservatism has found expression over the past decade at the heart of the international human rights system: the Human Rights Council. A series of resolutions passed by a majority of the Council's 47 member states have attempted to redraw the boundaries of human rights. Amongst them, one set of resolutions called for the interpretation of human rights in accordance with traditional values; later resolutions called for protection of the family without inclusion of a guarantee for women's right to equality in the family.[135] These resolutions throw into question, centrally, women's right to equality in the family. Paradoxically, the Human Rights Council has been not only an author of this backlash as discussed previously, but also condemned it in its 2017 Resolution on Elimination of Discrimination against Women and Girls, following the annual report of the WGDAW.[136] The anti-universalist moves at the international and local levels, are taking place in the context of and in tension with a thriving international legal culture which maintains and preserves the human rights regime. The UN human rights experts in the treaty bodies and the Special Procedures of the Human Rights Council have parried the political backlash by states in the Council with reassertions of the universality of human rights, the inability to justify discrimination against women on grounds of freedom of religion, the right to freedom of expression and the rights of women and LGTB to equality in the family.[137]

Under secular legal systems, women have gained the right to shared economic resources and opportunities and this is resulting in significant numbers of women having economic power both within the family and in the public economic space. Nevertheless, even in the context of the egalitarian modernist family, division of power and roles remains in practice patriarchal for many families, at varying levels of intensity, with domestic violence remaining a litmus test for the continued oppression of many women. Despite the ongoing manifestations of patriarchy, the potential for women's equality of autonomy and choice in the secular context is considerably greater than in traditionalist religious marriage systems and indeed there are 'new families' in which the traditional roles have been abandoned or even reversed.

Women's investment of earned income in their families through FLFP has increased, with the rise of the female breadwinner noted in both developed and developing economies. Only in traditionalist theocracies have women lagged behind in FLFP. Furthermore, as regards investment of unpaid care work in families, largely performed by women, there has been an unprecedented shift of perception and its economic value has been recognised as part of family income for the purposes of division of matrimonial property. However, women's increased investment from both these sources has frequently not translated into an increased share of the matrimonial property. Reality lags behind across countries, with women, in practice, having a low share of the matrimonial property, with for example demonstrable disadvantage for women after divorce, and an extremely low share of rural property.

The IHRL matrimonial property revolution, in which women's right to own and control property has been fully recognised, has not expressly encompassed inheritance rights, but in secular legislation, a move has been made to secure equal inheritance rights for women and girls, which had been traditionally denied in legal systems, customary, religious and secular. Women's newly acquired inheritance rights opened the way to women being dispersed along the inequality scale as are men. However, for many women, the promise of equal inheritance has not yet materialised and is obstructed by cultural and religious barriers.

The equality transformation in families has subjected women to a world of extremely pressurised expectations. They are expected to function and earn in economic markets, while still being the primary carers in their families. The reliance of families on the earned income of women has been necessitated by changes in the world economic order, such as urbanisation, undercutting of the family wage and unemployment.[138] The change has been lopsided, with economies forcing families to rely on women's earned incomes without establishing the infrastructure for making this feasible along with performance of the care functions still disparately placed on women. While women's paid employment and contribution to family income is significant, with a growth in female breadwinners in developed countries and in the developing world and while there are some families in which men are sharing the care work, there has not been a global breakthrough in equalising the unpaid work of men and women in the family.[139] In fact, the progress towards women's economic participation in paid work in the current economic and social constellation, usually exacts a heavy burden on women, disparately increasing their combined hours of work in the market and at home, the latter long labelled as "the second shift" by feminist researchers.[140] Clearly, workforce participation together with a disparate part of the unpaid care work at home may encumber many women rather than liberating them.

A transformative path to equality would ensure that both men and women have equal opportunity to develop their caring responsibilities within the family alongside fulfilling their potential as economic actors. This would require the elimination of all legal, religious or customary regulation of the family which discriminates against women or imposes patriarchal hierarchies in the family. It would involve the removal of gender stereotypes regarding proper division of roles in the family together with a strong social protection floor to provide care services. It would need education and awareness raising to make sure that women share equally in family resources in law and practice. It is essential both to defend the gains made in the modernist secular family regimes and to preempt the conservative and fundamentalist backlash which focuses on protection of the family at the cost of women's hard-won right to equality.

Notes

1 Dorothy O. Helly, 'Introduction: The History of the Family and the History of Family History' in *Family History* (The Haworth Press 1985) 1, 1–7.
2 Alison Diduck and Frances Raday, 'Introduction: Family – an International Affair' (2012) 8 *International Journal of Law in Context* 187.
3 The Universal Declaration of Human Rights, UNGA Res 217A(III), 10 December 1948, UN Doc A/810 (1948) (UDHR), art 16(3).
4 Jui-Shan Chang, 'Encumbered Womanhood,' *Australian Review of Public Affair*, 21 May 2003, www.australianreview.net/digest/2003/05/chang.html.
5 UDHR (n 3) art 16(2).
6 CEDAW, 'General Recommendation No. 29 on art 16 of the Convention on the Elimination of All Forms of Discrimination Against Women: Economic Consequences of Marriage,

Family Relations and Their Dissolution,' CEDAW/C/GC/29, 30 October 2013, para 4, http://docstore.ohchr.org/SelfServices/FilesHandler.ashx?enc=6QkG1d%2fPPRiCAqhKb7yhsldCrOlUTvLRFDjh6%2fx1pWDn3WHqqJ3IVTSBdup3cNv3DQC%2fGcQdgTzvPZJiBl3Uvy2%2fdGCrYDfjaxHtk2Xa0GOPds69ZKD4rX0xgLCmpw%2fA.

7 Susan Moller Okin, *Justice, Gender, and the Family* (Basic Books 1989).

8 Reva B. Siegel, '"The Rule of Love": Wife Beating as Prerogative and Privacy' (1996) Faculty Scholarship Series, paper 1092, http://digitalcommons.law.yale.edu/fss_papers/1092.

9 Friedrich Engels, *The Origin of the Family, Private Property and the State* (Ernest Untermann tr, Charles H. Kerr and Company 1908).

10 Rachel Holmes, *Eleonor Marx: A Life* (Bloomsbury Publishing 2014) 390.

11 Israel Zangwill and Eleanor Marx, 'A Doll's House,' *Time*, March 1891, www.marxists.org/archive/eleanor-marx/1891/dolls-house-repaired.htm.

12 UDHR (n 3), art 16(1); International Covenant on Civil and Political Rights (entered into force 23 March 1976) 999 UNTS 171 (ICCPR) art 23(4); The Convention on the Elimination of all Forms of Discrimination Against Women (entered into force 3 September 1981) 1249 UNTS 13 (CEDAW), art 16, www.un.org/womenwatch/daw/cedaw/text/econvention.htm; 'Beijing Declaration and Platform for Action,' adopted at the Fourth World Conference on Women at Beijing, China, 4–15 September 1995, www.un.org/womenwatch/daw/beijing/pdf/BDPfA%20E.pdf. In addition to these, the SDGs include, under Goal 5 of Gender Equality, targets relevant to achieving women's equality in the family, especially as regards sexual and reproductive autonomy to make decisions, recognition of unpaid care and domestic work, inheritance and equal rights to ownership and control of land. United Nations Sustainable Development Goals, 'Goal 5: Achieve Gender Equality and Empower All Women and Girls,' *Sustainable Development Knowledge Platform*, accessed 1 May 2018, https://sustainabledevelopment.un.org/sdg5.

13 Vienna Declaration and Programme of Action, A/CONF.157/23, 12 July 1993, art I(18).

14 CEDAW (n 12) arts 16(1)(g)-(h).

15 See Mary Hallward-Driemeier, Tazeen Rusu, Hasan and Bogdana Anca, 'Women's Legal Rights over 50 Years: Progress, Stagnation or Regression? Policy Research Working Paper No. 6616, Washington, DC: World Bank. © World Bank. https://openknowledge.worldbank.org/handle/10986/21474 License: CC BY 3.0 IGO.

16 World Bank Group, 'Women, Business and the Law 2016: Getting to Equal,' 2015, Washington, DC: World Bank. © World Bank. https://openknowledge.worldbank.org/handle/10986/22546 License: CC BY 3.0 IGO. Similar results were found in 2018: World Bank Group, 'Women, Business and the Law 2018,' 2018, 30, Washington, DC: World Bank. © World Bank. https://openknowledge.worldbank.org/handle/10986/29498 License: CC BY 3.0 IGO. See also WGDAW, 'Thematic Report on Family and Cultural Life,' A/HRC/29/40, presented at the 29th session of the HRC, 2015, www.ohchr.org/EN/Issues/Women/WGWomen/Pages/FamilyAndCulturalLife.aspx.

17 Human Rights Council, 'Human Rights Council Adopts Texts on Enhancing the Efficiency of the Council, Rohingya Muslims, the Protection of the Family, and Ukraine,' *Human Rights Council*, 3 July 2015, www.ohchr.org/en/NewsEvents/Pages/DisplayNews.aspx?NewsID=16196&LangID=E.

18 Human Rights Council, 'Protection of the Family,' A/HRC/26/L.20/Rev.1, Twenty-sixth session, 26 June 2014, http://ap.ohchr.org/documents/dpage_e.aspx?si=A/HRC/26/L.20/Rev.1. See also Frances Raday, 'Recent Developments in the UN Human Rights Council: Traditional Values and Women's Right to Equality in the Family,' *Oxford Human Rights Hub*, 2 September 2015, http://ohrh.law.ox.ac.uk/recent-developments-in-the-un-human-rights-council-traditional-values-and-womens-right-to-equality-in-the-family/.

19 Human Rights Council, 'Resolution Adopted by the Human Rights Council on 3 July 2015, Protection of the Family: Contribution of the Family to the Realization of the Right to an Adequate Standard of Living for Its Members, Particularly Through Its Role

in Poverty Eradication and Achieving Sustainable Development,' A/HRC/RES/29/22, Twenty-ninth session, 22 July 2015, art 20(b), http://ap.ohchr.org/documents/dpage_e.aspx?si=A/HRC/RES/29/22.

20 *See further* Frances Raday, 'Culture, Religion and Women's International Human Rights' in Fareda Banda and Lisa Fishbayn Joffe (eds), *Women's Rights and Religious Law: Domestic and International Perspectives* (Routledge 2016) 13.

21 Diduck and Raday (n 2).

22 Frances Raday, 'Sacralising the Patriarchal Family in the Monotheistic Religions: "To No Form of Religion Is Woman Indebted for One Impulse of Freedom"' (2012) 8 *International Journal of Law in Context* 211; Diduck and Raday (n 2).

23 See full discussion in Frances Raday, *Culture, Religion, and Gender* (Vol. I, Oxford University Press and New York University School of Law 2003) 663.

24 Naomi Weiner-Levy, 'Patriarchs or Feminists? Relations Between Fathers and Trailblazing Daughters in Druze Society' (2011) 11(2) *Journal of Family Communication* 126: the life stories of trailblazing Druze women, reveal unique relationships between fathers and their daughters and showed that the father's active encouragement was an essential element in shattering gender roles in a highly traditionalist society.

25 Vienna Declaration and Programme of Action (n 13) art I (5) and art I (18).

26 WGDAW Report on Family and Cultural Life (n 16) para 48.

27 Ibid. para 50.

28 CEDAW GC 29 (n 6) para 27.

29 Catherine Turner, 'Out of the Shadows: Child Marriage and Slavery,' *Anti-slavery International*, 2013, www.antislavery.org/wp-content/uploads/2017/01/child_marriage_final-1.pdf.

30 Vivian E. Hamilton, 'The Age of Marital Capacity: Reconsidering Civil Recognition of Adolescent Marriage' (2012) 92 *Boston University Law Review* 1817.

31 As of June 2018, Afghanistan and Syrian Arab Republic shared the same average index rating and were ranked together at the lowest place of 152 out of the 153 countries. See Afghanistan Country Profile, accessed 9 May 2018, https://giwps.georgetown.edu/country/afghanistan/. See also BBC, 'Poll Says Afghanistan "Most Dangerous" for Women,' *BBC News*, 15 June 2011, www.bbc.com/news/world-south-asia-13773274; Amnesty International UK, 'Women in Afghanistan: The Back Atory,' *Amnesty International UK*, 25 November 2014, www.amnesty.org.uk/womens-rights-afghanistan-history.

32 Trust in Education, 'Life as an Afghan Woman,' *Trust in Education: Providing Educational, Economic and Health Care Assistance to Afghan Families,* accessed 6 June 2018, www.trustineducation.org/resources/life-as-an-afghan-woman.

33 CEDAW GC 29 (n 6) para 27.

34 United Nations, General Assembly Sixty-ninth session, Agenda item 65(a) Resolution adopted by the General Assembly 69/XX. Child, Early and Forced Marriage, 19 December 2016, www.un.org/en/ga/search/view_doc.asp?symbol=A/RES/71/175&referer=www.un.org/en/ga/71/resolutions.shtml&Lang=E.

35 WGDAW Report on Family and Cultural Life (n 16) para 26.

36 WGDAW, 'Adultery as a Criminal Offence Violates Women's Human Rights,' Position Paper, 1 October 2012, www.ohchr.org/Documents/Issues/Women/WG/AdulteryasaCriminalOffenceViolatesWomenHR.pdf.

37 See, for example, CEDAW, 'Concluding Observations on the Sixth Periodic Report of Israel,' CEDAW/C/ISR/CO/6, Adopted by the Committee at its sixty-eighth session, 23 October–17 November 2017, http://tbinternet.ohchr.org/_layouts/treatybodyexternal/Download.aspx?symbolno=CEDAW/C/ISR/CO/6&Lang=En.

38 See, for example, CEDAW, 'Concluding Observations on the Combined Second and Third Periodic Reports of Oman,' CEDAW/C/OMN/CO/2-3, 22 November 2017, http://tbinternet.ohchr.org/_layouts/treatybodyexternal/Download.aspx?symbolno=CEDAW%2fC%2fOMN%2fCO%2f2-3&Lang=en.

39 See Human Rights Council, 'Report of the Working Group on the Issue of Discrimination Against Women in Law and in Practice Addendum Mission to Tunisia,' A/HRC/23/50/Add.2, 2013, paras 7–8, 31, www.ohchr.org/Documents/HRBodies/HRCouncil/RegularSession/Session23/A.HRC.23.50.Add.2_ENG.pdf; Human Rights Council, 'Report of the Working Group on the Issue of Discrimination Against Women in Law and in Practice Addendum Mission to Morocco,' A/HRC/20/28/Add.1, 2012, paras 18–22, https://documents-dds-ny.un.org/doc/UNDOC/GEN/G12/142/19/PDF/G1214219.pdf?OpenElement.

40 June Starr, 'The Role of Turkish Secular Law in Changing the Lives of Rural Muslim Women 1950–1970' (1989) 23(3) *Law & Society Review* 497, 498; Annalisa Rosselli, 'The Policy on Gender Equality in Italy: In-depth Analysis,' Document Requested by the Committee on Women's Rights and Gender Equality, 2014, 9, www.europarl.europa.eu/RegData/etudes/note/join/2014/493052/IPOL-FEMM_NT(2014)493052_EN.pdf; Achilles G. Koutsouradis, 'Grounds for Divorce and Maintenance Between Former Spouses: Greece,' Faculty of Law, University of Thessaloniki, September 2002, 1.

41 Rebecca J. Cook and Simone Cusack, *Gender Stereotyping Transnational Legal Perspectives* (University of Pennsylvania Press 2010).

42 Diduck and Raday (n 2).

43 WGDAW, 'Report of the Working Group on the Issue of Discrimination Against Women in Law and in Practice Addendum: Mission to Iceland,' A/HRC/26/39/Add.1, 2014, www.ohchr.org/EN/Issues/Women/WGWomen/Pages/CountryVisits.aspx.

44 See, for example, in Iceland: Claire Suddath, 'Can the World's Most Equal Country Finally Kill the Gender Pay Gap? Iceland Has a Plan to Get Women the Same Pay as Men,' *Bloomberg*, 4 January 2018, www.bloomberg.com/news/articles/2018-01-04/can-the-world-s-most-equal-country-finally-kill-the-gender-pay-gap; Jon Henley, '"Equality Won't Happen by Itself": How Iceland Got Tough on Gender Pay Gap,' *The Guardian*, 20 February 2018, www.theguardian.com/world/2018/feb/20/iceland-equal-pay-law-gender-gap-women-jobs-equality.

45 See, for example, Souha R. Ezzedeen, 'Portrayals of Career Women in Hollywood Films: Implications for the Glass Ceiling's Persistence' (2015) 30 *Gender in Management: An International Journal* 239, 250–252.

46 Leslie de Oliveira, 'Women on and off Screen in Nollywood,' *Dispatch*, accessed 21 May 2018, www.dispatchfmi.com/single-post/2016/12/14/WOMEN-ON-AND-OFF-SCREEN-IN-NOLLYWOOD. See also the works of Nigerian female film directors featured in Tope Oshin's documentary 'Amaka's Kin: The Women of Nollywood' (2016); and Tara Brady, 'Hooray for Nollywood: How Women Are Taking on the World's Third Largest Film Industry,' *The Irish Times*, 16 November 2016, www.irishtimes.com/culture/film/hooray-for-nollywood-how-women-are-taking-on-the-world-s-third-largest-film-industry-1.2870650.

47 Gøsta Esping-Andersen and Francesco C. Billari, 'Re-theorizing Family Demographics' (2015) 41 *Population and Development Review* 1.

48 Choo Wai Hong, *The Kingdom of Women: Life, Love and Death in China's Hidden Mountains* (I.B. Tauris and Co Ltd 2017).

49 Cai Hua, *A Society Without Fathers or Husbands: The Na of China* (Zone Books 2008).

50 Gary S. Becker, *A Treatise on the Family* (Harvard University Press 1981).

51 That said, it is an illusion to think that the work of women outside the home is an entirely modernist phenomenon. There have long been notable exceptions to this traditional approach, as for instance in the ultra-orthodox Jewish community in which women have for generations been the breadwinners while the men studied in seminaries: Donna Shai, 'Working Women/Cloistered Men: A Family Development Approach to Marriage Arrangements Among Ultra-orthodox Jews' (2002) 33 *Journal of Comparative Family Studies* 97.

52 According to the ILO, in low-income and lower middle-income countries agriculture is still the most important source of employment for women, for example: "In Southern Asia and sub-Saharan Africa, over 60 per cent of all working women remain in agriculture, often concentrated in time and labour-intensive activities, which are unpaid or poorly remunerated." See ILO, 'Women at Work: Trends 2016', 2016, XV, https://www.ilo.org/wcmsp5/groups/public/---dgreports/---dcomm/—publ/documents/publication/wcms_457317.pdf.

53 According to United States Bureau of Labor Statistics, from a starting point of extremely low LFP up to World War II, in 2013, almost 70% of women, compared with 90% of men, with children under 18 were in the labour force. Working full time is the ideal situation, according to 32% of working mothers compared to 20% in 2007. More than 40% of mothers in 2014 were the primary breadwinners for households. It should be noted that this change has occurred in the absence of supportive childcare policies as the United States is one of the few nations which have no mandatory paid maternity leave. See Bureau of Labor Statistic U.S. Department of Labor, 'Employment Characteristics of Families – 2013,' Press Release, 25 April 2014, www.bls.gov/news.release/archives/famee_04252014.pdf.

54 Ida Mirzaie, 'Females' Labor Force Participation and Job Opportunities in the Middle East,' ASSA Annual Meeting at Boston, January 2015, www.researchgate.net/publication/277707654_Females'_Labor_Force_Participation_and_Job_Opportunities_in_the_Middle_East.

55 Beijing Declaration and Platform for Action (n 12) 11.

56 The Center for American Progress has first released 'The New Breadwinners,' as a chapter in the 2009's Shriver Report 'A Woman's Nation Changes Everything.' See Sarah Jane Glynn, 'Breadwinning Mothers, Then and Now,' *Center for American Progress*, June 2014, 1, https://cdn.americanprogress.org/wp-content/uploads/2014/06/Glynn-Breadwinners-report-FINAL.pdf.

57 Ibid. 14.

58 IPPR, 'Who's Breadwinning? Working Mothers and the New Face of Family Support,' 2013, 2, www.ippr.org/files/images/media/files/publication/2013/08/whos_breadwinning_August2013_11082_11082.pdf?noredirect=1.

59 Naila Kabeer, 'The Rise of the Female Breadwinner: Reconfigurations of Marriage, Motherhood, and Masculinity in the Global Economy' in Shirin M. Rai and Georgina Waylen (eds), *New Frontiers in Feminist Political Economy* (Routledge 2014) 62, 65–75.

60 Chant Sylvia, *Women-headed Households: Diversity and Dynamics in the Developing World* (Macmillan Press 1997).

61 Saskia Sassen, 'Women's Burden: Counter-geographies of Globalization and the Feminization of Survival' (2000) 53 *Journal of International Affairs* 503.

62 United Nations, Department of Economic and Social Affairs, 'Household Size and Composition Around the World 2017 – Data Booklet,' Population Division, ST/ESA/SER.A/405, 2017, 7, www.un.org/en/development/desa/population/publications/pdf/ageing/household_size_and_composition_around_the_world_2017_data_booklet.pdf.

63 Tae Yoo, 'Why Women Make the Best Tech Investments,' *World Economic Forum Website*, 20 January 2014, www.weforum.org/agenda/2014/01/women-technology-world-economy/. See also Clinton Global Initiative, 'Empowering Girls and Women,' accessed 17 May 2018, www.un.org/en/ecosoc/phlntrpy/notes/clinton.pdf.

64 Clinton Global Initiative (n 63); Plan UK, 'Because I Am a Girl: The State of the World's Girls 2009 – Girls in the Global Economy: Adding It All Up,' Executive Summary, 2009, 9, www.ungei.org/resources/files/BIAAG_Summary_ENGLISH_lo_resolution.pdf.

65 World Bank, 'World Development Report 2012: Gender Equality and Development,' 2012, 5 and references there, Washington, DC: World Bank. © World Bank. https://openknowledge.worldbank.org/handle/10986/4391 License: CC BY 3.0 IGO; David E. Bloom, Michael Kuhn and Klaus Prettner, 'Invest in Women and Prosper' (2017) 54 *Finance and Development* 50.

66 World Economic Forum, 'The Global Gender Gap Report 2016,' 2016, fn 27, http://www3.weforum.org/docs/GGGR16/WEF_Global_Gender_Gap_Report_2016.pdf.
67 ILO Women at Work 2016 (n 52) XV. See also the Introduction of the book.
68 V. Miranda, 'Cooking, Caring and Volunteering: Unpaid Work Around the World,' OECD Social, Employment and Migration Working Papers, No. 116, OECD Publishing, Paris, 2011, https://doi.org/10.1787/5kghrjm8s142-en.
69 Evrim Altintas and Oriel Sullivan, 'Fifty Years of Change Updated: Cross-national Gender Convergence in Housework' (2016) 35 *Demographic Research* 455.
70 Kabeer (n 60) 65–75.
71 Miranda (n 68).
72 See ILO Women at Work 2016 (n 52) XV.
73 According to a 2017 UN Department of Economic and Social Affairs data on 124 countries, 21% of households are lone-mother while only 3% are lone-father. See UN Department of Economic and Social Affairs (n 63).
74 See discussion in Part II. See also Kabeer (n 60) 69.
75 Gayle Kaufman, *Superdads: How Fathers Balance Work and Family in the 21st Century* (NYU Press 2013).
76 See for example, Nara Schoenberg, 'Gay Men Increasingly Turn to Surrogates to Have Babies,' *Chicago Tribune*, 23 November 2016, www.chicagotribune.com/lifestyles/health/sc-gay-men-having-babies-health-1130-20161123-story.html; Sally Hayden, 'More LGBT Couples and Fewer Heterosexual Couples Are Applying to Adopt Children in the UK,' *Independent*, 23 November 2017, www.independent.co.uk/news/uk/home-news/lgbt-couples-uk-adoption-applications-more-heterosexual-gay-lesbian-a8071316.html.
77 Claire Cain Miller, 'Equality in the Age of Modern Parenting,' *The New York Times International Edition*, 28 May 2018, 8.
78 Fully discussed in Part II of this book.
79 With the proviso that the interest of the children is the primordial consideration in all cases. CEDAW (n 12) art 5(b).
80 Rikki Holtmaat, 'Article 5' in Marsha A. Freeman, Christine Chinkin and Beate Rudolf (eds), *The UN Convention on the Elimination of All Forms of Discrimination Against Women: A Commentary* (Oxford University Press 2012) 158.
81 Beijing Declaration and Platform for Action (n 12) strategic objective F.6.
82 Manisha Desai, 'Hope in Hard Times: Women's Empowerment and Human Development,' United Nations Development Programme Human Development Reports Research Paper 2010/14, July 2010.
83 Arnlaug Leira, *Working Parents and the Welfare State: Family Change and Policy Reform in Scandinavia* (Cambridge University Press 2012). See also Deborah Brennan, 'Balancing Work and Family: A Scandinavian Perspective,' Symposium: The Contemporary Family, *Australian Review of Public Affairs*, 21 May 2003, www.australianreview.net/digest/2003/05/brennan.html.
84 Miranda (n 68); Nordic Council of Ministers, 'Nordic Gender Equality in Figures 2015,' 2015, www.diva-portal.org/smash/get/diva2:790696/FULLTEXT02.pdf.
85 See discussion in Part II.
86 Kabeer (n 60) 79.
87 Furthermore, economic dependency of women is pointed to be one of the main indicators of structural gender inequality which affects the odds of leaving a violent relationship. See Directorate General for Internal Policies, 'Policy Department C: Citizens' Rights and Constitutional Affairs,' Women's Rights & Gender Equality, the Issue of Violence Against Women in the European Union: Study, 2016, www.europarl.europa.eu/RegData/etudes/STUD/2016/556931/IPOL_STU(2016)556931_EN.pdf.
88 See, for example, United Nations, Department of Economic and Social Affairs, Population Division, 'Policies to Influence Fertility and Promote Work-family Balance,' 2017, www.un.org/en/development/desa/population/publications/pdf/policy/Infochart_work-family_balance.pdf.

89 Geoffrey Palmer, 'The Earth Summit: What Went Wrong at Rio?' (1992) 70 *Washington University Law Quarterly* 1005, 1018. The Rio Declaration on Averment and Development, UN Doc. A/CONF.151/26 (Vol. I) 31 ILM 874, 1992, www.unesco.org/education/pdf/RIO_E.PDF.

90 Roli Srivastava, 'Indian Surrogate Mothers Grab Last Chance to Make Babies Ahead of Impending Ban,' *Reuters*, 19 January 2017, www.reuters.com/article/us-india-women-surrogacy/indian-surrogate-mothers-grab-last-chance-to-make-babies-ahead-of-impending-ban-idUSKBN1530FL; Sneha Banerjee, 'Emergence of the "Surrogacy Industry"' (2012) 47 *Economic and Political Weekly* 27. *See also Part III. The ethics of surrogacy are* a burning feminist issue but lie beyond the scope of this book.

91 Susan E. Short and Zhai Fengying, 'Looking Locally at China's One-child Policy' (1998) 29 *Studies in Family Planning* 373. The one-child policy has resulted in a sex ratio distortion in China, as millions of newborn female babies are evidently 'missing' (were either murdered or aborted). See Avraham Ebenstein, 'The "Missing Girls" of China and the Unintended Consequences of the One Child Policy' (2010) 45 *The Journal of Human Sources* 87.

92 Wang Feng, a sociologist and demographic expert from the University of California, Irvine has said: "The low fertility rate is here to stay." The fertility level is 1.1 and this low fertility rate is being driven by the postponement of marriage age. It seems that Chinese couples no longer have small families because of a one-child governmental policy but because of social and economic factors such as the cost of urban life and education and uncertainty in the job market. See Feng Wang, 'The Implications of China's Demographic Profile,' Lecture at the 6th Annual NYU Conference on Chinese Capital Markets -China's Future Economic Growth at Greenberg Lounge, NYU School of Law, 9 December 2016, www.youtube.com/watch?v=yLNPJWWNM48. See also Ana Swanson, 'Why Many Families in China Won't Want More than One Kid Even If They Can Have Them,' *The Washington Post*, 30 October 2015, www.washingtonpost.com/news/wonk/wp/2015/10/30/why-many-families-in-china-wont-want-more-than-one-kid-even-if-they-can-have-them/.

93 Suzanne McGee and Heidi Moore, 'Women's Rights and Their Money: A Timeline from Cleopatra to Lilly Ledbetter,' *The Guardian*, 11 August 2014, www.theguardian.com/money/us-money-blog/2014/aug/11/women-rights-money-timeline-history.

94 Raquel Fernandez, 'Women's Rights and Development,' Working Papers 2011-029, Human Capital and Economic Opportunity Working Group, 2010, 1, http://siteresources.worldbank.org/EXTLACOFFICEOFCE/Resources/870892-1265238560114/Fernandez_WomensRights.pdf.

95 William Blackstone, *Commentaries on the Laws of England 1765–69* (Vol. I, University of Chicago Press 1979) 431.

96 This apparent anomaly has been attributed by some historians to the interest men had in endowing property on their wives and thus removing it from the reach of their creditors and, by others, to the interest men had, with reduced numbers of children, to making sure their daughters retained property rights as in the US. See Fernandez (n 94) 5 and references there.

97 CEDAW (n 12) art 16(h).

98 UN Human Rights Committee, CCPR General Comment No. 28: Article 3 (The Equality of Rights Between Men and Women), CCPR/C/21/Rev.1/Add.10, 29 March 2000, paras 19, 25, www.nichibenren.or.jp/library/ja/kokusai/humanrights_library/treaty/data/HRC_GC_28e.pdf.

99 United Nations Sustainable Development Goal 5 (n 12) Target 5.A.

100 World Bank, 'Women, Business and the Law: Methodology,' accessed 22 May 2018, http://wbl.worldbank.org/en/methodology#a. It should be noted that the World Bank also examines under this indicator girls' equal rights to inherit assets from their parents, in addition to female surviving spouses' equal rights to inherit assets.

101 World Bank Group 2018 (n 16) 7–8, 11–13.
102 OECD, 'SIGI Social Institutions and Gender Index 2014 Synthesis Report,' 2014, 26, www.oecd.org/dev/development-gender/BrochureSIGI2015-web.pdf.
103 Ibid. 31.
104 Ibid. 38.
105 Ibid. 42–43. From other sources it is of note that in Tunisia in the wake of the Arab Spring, hundreds of women took to the streets in 2018 to demand equal inheritance rights with men, demanding an end to inheritance laws based on Islamic law. Tarek Amara, 'Tunisian Women March for Equal Inheritance Rights,' *Reuters*, 10 March 2018, www.reuters.com/article/us-tunisia-women/tunisian-women-march-for-equalinheritance-rights-idUSKCN1GM0OT.
106 However, the disadvantage of women is exacerbated by an amendment to the Marriage Law, which for purposes of division of property in divorce, attributes the matrimonial home to the registered owner. The WGDAW in its country report on China remarked on the need to reformulate the amendment in order to restore the equality impact of the law. See Jonathan K. Ocko, 'Women, Property, and Law in the People's Republic of China' in Rubie S. Watsonand Patricia Buckley Ebrey (eds), *Marriage and Inequality in Chinese Society* (California University Press 1991); WGDAW, 'Report of the Working Group on the Issue of Discrimination Against Women in Law and in Practice: Mission to China,' A/HRC/26/39/Add.2, 12 June 2014, para 17, www.ohchr.org/EN/Issues/Women/WGWomen/Pages/CountryVisits.aspx.
107 WGDAW Report on China (n 106); Leta Hong Fincher, 'China's Growing Gender Gap: Women Are Not Just Leftovers' but Left Out,' *The Guardian*, 12 May 2014, www.theguardian.com/lifeandstyle/2014/may/12/china-leftover-women-property-boom; Leta Hong Fincher, *Leftover Women: The Resurgence of Gender Inequality in China* (Zed Books 2014).
108 Victoria Stanley, Tony Lamb, and Samantha De Martino, 'Property Rights for Women in The ECA Region: Results from Recent World Bank Projects,' Land Policy and Administration Notes No. 1, 2013, Washington DC: World Bank. http://www-wds.worldbank.org/external/default/WDSContentServer/WDSP/IB/2013/03/18/000442464_20130318170327/Rendered/PDF/750280BRI0REPL00AES0Note0100PUBLIC0.pdf.
109 World Bank Group 2018 (n 16) 47; World Bank Group 2015 (n 16) 13–14, 52; World Bank Group, 'Women, Business, and the Law 2014: Removing Restrictions to Enhance Gender Equality,' 2013, 52, London: Bloomsbury. © World Bank. https://openknowledge.worldbank.org/handle/10986/20528 License: CC BY-NC-ND 3.0 IGO.
110 World Bank Group 2018 (n 16) 31.
111 CEDAW GC 29 (n 6) paras 45–47. The legal method for ensuring equality in economic division of property, income and investment between spouses is, however, a highly complex issue. The family is, as said, an economic unit and its members are potentially both investors and beneficiaries. They may invest both in cash (property or earned income) and in kind (care functions and unpaid work). The issue to be resolved is how the investment in family by individual members is to be evaluated and what kind of correlation there should be between an individual's investment and his or her entitlement to a share of the property and the earned income of both spouses.
112 See also United Nations Sustainable Development Goal 5 (n 12) Target 5.4.
113 Frances Raday, 'Is Contractual Egalitarianism Equitable?' (1992) *Israel Law Review Special Volume: Equity and Contemporary Legal Developments* 659.
114 CEDAW GC 29 (n 6) para 4.
115 Lenore J. Weitzman, *The Divorce Revolution: The Unexpected Social and Economic Consequences for Women and Children in America* (Free Press 1985). See also Darlena Cunha, 'The Divorce Gap,' *The Atlantic*, 28 April 2016, www.theatlantic.com/business/archive/2016/04/the-divorce-gap/480333/.

116 Stephen P. Jenkins, 'Marital Splits and Income Changes over the Longer Term,' ISER Working Paper Series, No. 2008-07, ISER, Colchester, 2008, www.econstor.eu/bitstream/10419/92067/1/2008-07.pdf; Amelia Hill, 'Men Become Richer After Divorce,' *The Guardian*, 25 January 2009, www.theguardian.com/lifeandstyle/2009/jan/25/divorce-women-research.
117 UN Women, 'Turning Promises into Action: Gender Equality in 2030 Agenda for Sustainable Development,' 2018, 137, www.unwomen.org/-/media/headquarters/attachments/sections/library/publications/2018/sdg-report-gender-equality-in-the-2030-agenda-for-sustainable-development-2018-en.pdf?la=en&vs=5653.
118 Haim Sandberg and Adam Hofri-Winogradow, 'Arab Israeli Women's Renunciation of Their Inheritance Shares: A Challenge for Israel's Courts' (2012) 8 *International Journal of Law in Context* 253.
119 Suzanne Desan, '"War Between Brothers and Sisters": Inheritance Law and Gender Politics in Revolutionary France' (1997) 20 *French Historical Studies* 597, 598–599; Thora Kristin Thorsdottir, 'Iceland in Crisis: Gender Equality and Social Equity' in Maria Karamessini and Jill Rubery (eds), *Women and Austerity: The Economic Crisis and the Future for Gender Equality* (Routledge 2014) 102; Thalia Dragonas and Faruk Birtek (eds), *Citizenship and the Nation-state in Greece and Turkey* (Routledge 2009); McGee and Moore (n 93).
120 CEDAW GC 29 (n 6) para 52; Marsha A. Freeman, 'Article 16' in Marsha A. Freeman, Christine Chinkin and Beate Rudolf (eds), *The UN Convention on the Elimination of All Forms of Discrimination Against Women: A Commentary* (Oxford University Press 2012) 435. In concluding observations to states, the Committee recommended legislative reform to provide women with equal rights in inheritance without specifically differentiating between widows and daughters.
121 Beijing Declaration and Platform for Action (n 12) 112.
122 WGDAW Report on Family and Cultural Life (n 16) para 73(d)(iii).
123 United Nations Sustainable Development Goal 5 (n 12) Target 5.A.
124 SIGI (n 102) 9.
125 World Bank Group 2018 (n 16) 13.
126 Sandberg and Hofri-Winogradow (n 118).
127 World Bank Group 2015 (n 16) 13.
128 See the discussion in the Introduction.
129 Aparajita Goya, 'Importance of Equal Inheritance Rights for Female Empowerment,' *The World Bank Let's Talk Development Blog*, 14 May 2012, http://blogs.worldbank.org/developmenttalk/importance-of-equal-inheritance-rights-for-female-empowerment.
130 World Bank Group 2015 (n 16) 13.
131 Ashok Sircar and Diana Fletschner, 'The Right to Inherit Isn't Working for Indian Women, Says U.N. Study', *The Wall Street Journal*, 2 March 2014, http://blogs.wsj.com/indiarealtime/2014/03/02/the-right-to-inherit-isnt-working-for-indian-women-says-u-n-study/.
132 Jennifer Wang, 'Rags to Riches 2016: Wealthiest Self-made Billionaires,' *Forbes*, 1 March 2016, www.forbes.com/sites/jenniferwang/2016/03/01/rags-to-riches-2016-wealthiest-self-made-billionaires/#5ec0bbe93290; Chloe Sorvino, 'The World's 56 Self-made Women Billionaires: The Definitive Ranking,' *Forbes*, 8 March 2017, www.forbes.com/sites/chloesorvino/2017/03/08/the-worlds-56-self-made-women-billionaires-the-definitive-ranking/#6d8760fa68a2. This is further discussed in Part I of the book.
133 This section is based on Frances Raday, 'Gender Equality and Women's Rights in the Context of Child Custody and Child Maintenance: An International and Comparative Analysis,' paper for UN Women, 2018 to be published in the Annual Report of UN Women (on file with author).

134 World Bank Group, 'Woman, Business and the Law: Methodology' (n 100); World Bank Group 2018 (n 16) 7–8. This includes the issue of equal inheritance rights of daughters to inherit assets from their parent, as well as those of female surviving spouses to inherit assets.

135 Raday (n 18). See also the Introduction of the book.

136 Human Rights Council, 'Elimination of Discrimination Against Women and Girls,' Human Rights Council Thirty-fifth session, A/HRC/35/L.29, 19 June 2017, http://ap.ohchr.org/documents/dpage_e.aspx?si=A/HRC/35/L.29; WGDAW, 'Report of the Working Group on the Issue of Discrimination Against Women in Law and in Practice,' A/HRC/35/29, 19 April 2017, para 21, www.ohchr.org/Documents/Issues/Women/WG/A_HRC_35_29_AEV.docx. See also the Introduction of the book.

137 See further Raday 'Culture, Religion and Women's International Human Rights' (n 20).

138 See discussion in the Introduction and Part II.

139 See ILO Women at Work 2016 (n 52) fn 65.

140 Arlie Hochschild and Anne Machung, *The Second Shift: Working Families and the Revolution at Home* (Viking Penguin 1989).

Concluding Chapter – Economic Woman at a Crossroads

1 Reflections

This book has been a quest to explore the interplay between economic inequality and gender inequality. My quest to elucidate this interplay has been strewn with unexpected realisations and numerous questionings, which make up an inherent part of my 'conclusions.' The journey itself has for me and my wonderful chief researcher and academic editor, Shai Oksenberg, been a fascinating one.

I start my conclusions with a number of caveats. The first is that my call to address extreme economic inequality through the reduction of gender inequality is relevant only for those who regard extreme economic inequality as an undesirable result of economic policy choices, which are amenable in some measure to policy change. The second, my call for equality for economic woman is not a dictate of lifestyle, insisting on women and men following the same template for participation in the economic marketplace but is rather a call to states and corporate institutions to remove all the discriminatory and infrastructural gendered barriers to economic choices. The third is that data regarding the situation of economic woman in economic markets, the corporate world, poverty and the family is at best fragmented, not harmonised across countries or surveys and less available in developing than in developed countries. While acknowledging these limitations, there is enough literature, research and survey information to make it possible to try and understand how economic woman is faring in a global neo-liberal economy, to bear witness to successes and good practices and to be aware of threats to equality achievements.

The intersectional diversity in women's and girls' starting point, dramatically affects their economic opportunity, amongst other things, on the basis of culture, religion, socio-economic status, racial minority status and family situation. Women and girls nevertheless, despite dramatic intersectional diversity between and within countries, share in experiencing cross-cutting barriers of lesser access to resources, a disparate unpaid care burden and exposure to gender-based violence. Even in those countries which hold out a greater legal guarantee of equal opportunity and non-discrimination, the realities of economic woman are in flux: her achievements are polarised and the barriers she faces are pervasive, affected by discriminatory stereotypes, lesser resources, failure to provide an infrastructural framework for integrating work outside the home with care responsibilities and VAW.

In this book, I have examined economic woman's situation in four contexts: economic power, sale of human capital, poverty and family.

Part I on economic power showed that women's economic power deficit is startling. The overwhelming picture that emerges from the saga in search of economic woman in the corridors of economic power is one which demonstrates just how near to invisible she is.

Despite significant advances in equality for women and girls in education, employment and political representation, women lag severely behind in all forums where the power to determine economic policy is situated. This holds true for political, corporate and financial forums. Women's representation in positions of power, in international and national economic forums, which stand at less than 6% across the board whether they be in political ministries or corporate firms, is far lower than women's general parliamentary representation (at 23.5%) or governmental portfolios (at 18.3%). One may perhaps speculate that the economy is the last bastion of power in the 21st century and women have not yet broken in.

The few but growing number of highly successful women political and corporate leaders are proof that there are cracks through which women can enter but these cracks have not yet opened to facilitate a full participatory process in which women join in formulating economic policy with men. In the corporate world, women face formidable odds, their advancement into the C-suite and up to CEO hemmed in by glass ceilings, glass walls and glass cliffs. In entrepreneurship, women have much less access to venture capital funding or credit and to mentoring. They are concentrated in micro-businesses or in small and medium-sized enterprises with low profit margins. There is considerable advocacy in corporate forums for advancing women into business leadership, usually based on the justification of the business case according to which gender diversity in business management increases profits. This clearly does not tally with the equality case, as it assumes that the reason for accepting women should be that they are better, while being just as good is all that is required for equality.

The need for a critical mass of women in economic leadership is not merely process oriented, though that in itself is important. It is aimed to ensure that the duality of humanity, which stems from women's and men's differing life trajectories and experiences, resulting along a spectrum, from various combinations of gender stereotypes, cultural environment and socialisation, gender hierarchies in the family, patriarchal edicts of religious communities and sexual and reproductive characteristics, is integrated into economic policy-making itself.

In Part II on the sale of human capital, it becomes clear that economic woman has, in contrast to her position in the corridors of power, become highly visible on the roads of work. Female labour force participation (FLFP) has greatly increased and the gender participation gap decreased. However, participation does not necessarily signify equality or power.

FLFP is important for improving GDP, as consistently claimed by major international economic institutions. However, this is an instrumentalist argument for women's participation in the labour force and not a satisfactory measure of an equal playing field for sale of women's human capital. Although women's employment in the labour force, giving them both an occupation outside the home and earned income, may empower them within the family, it does not necessarily bring equality in the labour market, and may, in some circumstances, even involve severe exploitation.

Though there is, in IHRL, International Labour Conventions and in most countries' legislation, protective labour law in formal labour markets, with prohibition of employment discrimination and sexual harassment and mandating of paid maternity leave, equality for women has proved delusional: gender pay and promotion gaps, sexual harassment and discrimination on grounds of pregnancy persist everywhere. In spite of equal education, which has been achieved in most countries, at least in part because of international commitment to the MDGs, women's lower earnings persist across every level of education.

Furthermore, the global south and north converge in the concentration of women in informal work, traditional in developing countries and proliferating in developed economies with the growth of precarious work, to which protective labour provisions do not extend. Women globally are under increasing pressure with growing responsibility for breadwinning together with widespread failure to accommodate maternity and childcare responsibilities. There is *de facto* discrimination against women on grounds of maternity and there has been an increased reduction of affordable care services, in the developed countries because of austerity measures, in post-communist countries because of privatisation and in developing countries because of the decline of extended family grandmother care in urbanised settings.

The third and fourth industrial revolutions promise greater anonymity and flexibility, which has been claimed to offer a solution to employment discrimination for women, but there is evidence that, unless effective measures are taken, discrimination and the pay gap will not disappear, the gender care gap will not evaporate and women's labour force participation is likely to be adversely affected more than men's.

In Part III on poverty, I revisited the contested paradigm of feminisation of poverty. Reviewing the situation of women in poverty demonstrates that, although international surveys of poverty do not reveal the situation of women as individual members of households and hence do not substantiate the claim that more women are poor than men, the feminisation of poverty remains a valid concept. In patriarchal households, which exist *de jure* in theocracies and plural legal systems and *de facto* in many families under secular family law, women have lesser access to resources and are charged with more of the burden of care for dependent family members. Poverty remains feminised because, in addition to the tragic impact shared by both women and men of injury to health and social exclusion, women and girls in poverty suffer additional deprivation and humiliation. They are exposed to increased gender-based violence.

Their reproductive health and lives are at risk, where the state does not provide affordable or free obstetric care, modern contraceptives and medical abortion services. Women and girls in poverty are frequently victims of forced prostitution, surrogacy and trafficking. Deprivation of nutrition, water and hygiene products is aggravated for women and girls because of their physiological needs in menstruation, pregnancy or lactation.

An understanding of the harsh dimensions of women's poverty indicates that women and girls are primary losers in the extreme inequality and austerity which prevail in global neo-liberalism. This understanding should be fully integrated into the development and human rights agendas for the reduction of poverty.

Part IV investigated the economics of the family. Economic woman is forged in a family context and this has traditionally meant, in all legal, religious and customary systems, that women have been subjected to a gendered hierarchy of male power. IHRL recognition of women's right to equality in the family, in all matters relating to marriage or family relations, represents a radical shift of paradigm away from patriarchy. Currently, regulation of family lies along a spectrum between modernist equality norms in secular states and traditionalist patriarchy under theocracies and plural legal systems, affecting reproductive freedoms, division of labour, recourse to remedies for domestic violence and access to resources, including the right to own or manage property such as land.

The percentage of women breadwinners in families has increased but, nevertheless, women in almost all families continue to assume a greater part of nurturing and unpaid care. In international human rights norms and in some legal systems, there has been transformative recognition of unpaid care as giving entitlement to a share of matrimonial property in the case of dissolution of a marriage. Recognition of women's right to ownership and management of family property has been mandated by CEDAW. The impact of the legal right on the actual property holdings of women has not been systematically measured and quantified but data showing women's relative economic deprivation subsequent to divorce and, women's significant exclusion from land ownership, indicate that women still own far less property than men.

Economic woman's level of autonomy or entitlement within the family and capability to undertake economic activity outside the home varies dramatically in different contexts of law, custom and religion, mandating equality in secular systems and patriarchy in traditionalist systems. The regulatory framework is a crucial key to the freedom and autonomy of women and girls, including in their economic potential (although there are variations in individual families along a spectrum between oppressing and liberating women and girls).

Applicable to all these aspects of economic woman's life discussed in the four Parts of the book, IHRL has established a strong universalist normative regime requiring states to guarantee equality and prohibit discrimination on grounds of sex whether by the state or by private actors. This regime in its essence should, in addition to being a treaty obligation for state parties under CEDAW, be regarded as customary international law, binding on all states. The constitutional, legislative and judicial systems in almost all states have incorporated women's right to equality but there is a derogation from the right to equality in theocratic and plural legal systems, which relegate aspects of the legal system, particularly family law, to patriarchal religious jurisdictions. The IHRL equality regime extends in principle to women's social and economic rights and hence embraces economic woman. However, it has been most fully developed and elaborated in treaty law as regards only certain aspects of women's economic rights, as elucidated in the various chapters of this book, particularly equal opportunity in the workplace, which has been legislated by a majority of states, and the right to equality in family relations and property ownership and management, which have not been realised in the legislative framework of theocratic and plural legal systems. Remaining issues such as equal participation in forums which determine economic policy, a social protection floor for care, many of the gendered impacts of poverty and equal inheritance have not been fully formulated in the international treaty provisions and are not yet mandated in most states.

The implementation of the equality rights of economic woman, including to equal opportunity, equal remuneration, accommodation of maternity and freedom from VAW, has to be achieved not only in state institutions but also in labour markets, formal and informal, in political forums, in corporate hierarchies, in social security and poverty alleviation programs and in the family. Unlike the universality of the right to vote and to stand for office, the implementation of the right to equality in these institutions cannot be achieved by direct state action alone. It must be achieved through a combination of legal edict and policy measures directed to private as well as public actors. In the economic sphere, the diversity of protagonists, public and private, requires a more complex set of rules and enforcement to eliminate discrimination against women. Legal edict must include prohibition of discrimination and access to justice for the victims of discrimination. It must include a wide scope of remedies for discrimination, direct or indirect; for non-payment of equal pay for equal work or for work of equal value; for enforcing rights to maternity leave against employers; for VAW or sexual harassment in the workplace, the street, services or educational institutions; and for domestic violence.

In addition, however, to the legal edicts, an entire change of infrastructure is essential to eliminate the barriers to advancement for economic woman and to even the playing field. While unpaid care burdens cannot be eliminated, they can be recognised, reduced and redistributed. Social protection floors for child and dependent care services and synchronisation of school time and regular working hours, which have existed in socialist countries in the past and continue to exist in a few countries today, give both women and men a realistic way of combining family with work outside the home, whether in the labour market, the corporate world or entrepreneurship. Temporary special measures, such as quotas, can be used to ensure representation of qualified women in economic policy-making forums, as has been applied in some countries' quota requirements for company boards. There should be monitoring of credit facilities, venture funding and procurement policies to ensure proper representation of women amongst the recipients, together with penalties for institutions which do not meet the required levels. Social security and pension rights need to be adjusted to compensate for different gendered employment patterns. Poverty alleviation programs must integrate special requirements for women in poverty, arising from their reproductive and physiological characteristics and their vulnerability to VAW.

Infrastructural change requires allocations from state budgets and hence gender mainstreaming has to be a part of the whole budgetary process. It has, however, been shown that gender mainstreaming does not bring about change unless it is promoted by critical leadership figures in the process. It is therefore only through the development of women's economic leadership that headway will be made.

The process of creating women's economic leadership needs a jumpstart in order to create a dynamic of change. Contrary to commonly held prejudices that women do not promote other women, there is evidence that women in power in politics and the corporate world do promote women in their institutions and, in fact, the advancement of women into leadership roles would (and will) create a snowball effect.

Individual women in leadership cannot achieve transformative change alone and indeed not all women leaders are committed to this goal. What is essential is the involvement of women's organisations, national human rights institutions and other civil society actors, men as well as women, including public interest lawyers and scholars, to monitor, publish and take action to promote policies and people which further a gender equality agenda throughout societies and institutions. The input of women's civil society organisations is essential to the conceptualising, planning, realisation and sustainability of transformative change for women's economic empowerment.[1] As an OECD paper on women's economic empowerment noted, women's organising at global and national level is crucial for economic empowerment.[2] Women's organisation is taking place amongst women workers: in the book, "Global Women's Work: Perspectives on Gender and Work in the Global Economy," the editors highlight women's agency and the worldwide mobilisation of women in the global north and the global south, particularly women workers, to resist conservative backlash in the globalised neo-liberal economy.[3] The Self Employed Women's Association (SEWA) set up in the early 1970s in India is an early and outstanding example of empowerment led by poor women working in the informal economy, achieving significant progressive governmental measures on social security for informal workers and protections for street vendors.[4] There are, however, increased governmental restrictions, in numerous countries, on the activities of human rights defenders in general and women human rights defenders in particular. On its country visits to both China and Hungary, the WGDAW expressed its consternation at the growing repression of women's rights organisations and, in its 2017 annual report, emphasised the global scope of the problem, citing ongoing attacks on women's movements and human rights defenders by state actors as well as private parties, in which these key actors are criminalised, defunded and sometimes killed.[5] Women human rights defenders working on rights contested by fundamentalist groups, such as women's reproductive rights, and those denouncing the actions of extractive industries and businesses face a heightened risk of violence, including murder.[6]

The IHRL universal norm of gender equality is a core resource for the civil society organisations and human rights defenders who are working in diverse national contexts to apply and advance universal human rights standards, whether through the legislatures, the courts or the media. The work of UN mechanisms, the treaty bodies and the special rapporteurs of the Human Rights Council is to hold states to account in maintaining their obligation to respect, protect, fulfil and promote IHRL norms. In carrying out this function of monitoring of state obligation, the independent experts of the UN are informed by governments, research and civil society organisations. The dissemination of IHRL norms and the advocacy for implementation within states is the crucial function of civil society organisations and human rights defenders. The UN and its independent experts, in their work of communicating, reporting and recommending ways of implementing state human rights obligations, provide a normative basis for the advocates and defenders of human rights, including women's organisations, national human rights institutions and other civil society actors, men as well as women, including public interest lawyers and scholars.

We must end on a note of sobriety, optimism and hope.

For sobriety, the near male monopoly on economic power has produced global neo-liberalism, austerity and escalating economic inequality in wealth and incomes, which affect women even more harshly than men. Gendered inequality is an aggravated offshoot of economic inequality. It is also the engine which augments it. The barriers for economic woman of less access to resources, disparate burdens of unpaid care and VAW are universally apparent. If the IHRL imperative and the much vaunted policy of equal gender opportunity is to be fully and universally enforced, the only way the mass of economic women can achieve equality in all spheres of life is by revolutionising the infrastructure of the economy, as has been attempted by very few countries in the neo-liberal era, so that the infrastructure is one in which the gendered barriers are removed and the market and care functions of family and society are integrated.

For optimism, there is a universalist IHRL obligation on states to guarantee equal economic opportunity for women in the workplace, in the corporate world and in the family. The beginnings of implementation *de facto*, whether fuelled by the quest for gender equality and justice or by instrumentalist aims such as the business case, the human development case or the 'economic' case, have opened the door to women's participation in economic life in the labour market, in corporations and in entrepreneurship. The move of economic woman from participation to power has yet to be achieved but cracks in the glass ceiling and the glass walls of power are visible as some exceptional women are making their way through them, and not all of them are falling over glass cliffs.

For hope, the mainstreaming of women's life experience into macroeconomic policy would prioritise social agendas and equality goals and, as such, promote the well-being of women, men, families and communities. Economic equality and gender equality would merge. The stagnation in implementation and the ideological backlash threatening the commitment to the universal human right of economic woman to equality must be contested and reversed. Women economic leaders, women's movements, international human rights mechanisms and male allies are at the forefront of this ongoing fight to secure equality gains made and to move forward to greater empowerment for economic woman.

Notes

1 Indeed, the critical role that women must play, recognised in Security Council Resolution 1325, in 2000, and seven subsequent Resolutions calling to integrate women into conflict prevention, management and resolution, is a basis for recognition of the importance of including women in the negotiation and dialogue for bringing about transformative change. See UN Women, 'Poster: Security Council Resolutions: Women Peace and Security,' *UN Women Website*, accessed 11 October 2018, www.unwomen.org/en/digital-library/publications/2017/1/poster-security-council-resolutions.
2 OECD, 'Women's Economic Empowerment,' Issues Paper, DAC Network on Gender Equality (GENDERNET), April 2011, 28, www.oecd.org/dac/gender-development/47561694.pdf.
3 Beth English, Mary E. Frederickson and Olga Sanmiguel-Valderrama, 'Introduction: Perspectives on Gender and Work in the Global Economy' in Beth English, Mary E. Frederickson and Olga Sanmiguel-Valderrama (eds), *Global Women's Work: Perspectives on Gender and Work in the Global Economy* (Routledge forthcoming).
4 OECD (n 2) 30.
5 WGDAW, 'Report of the Working Group on the Issue of Discrimination Against Women in Law and in Practice: Mission to China,' A/HRC/26/39/Add.2, 12 June 2014, paras 66–67, www.ohchr.org/EN/Issues/Women/WGWomen/Pages/CountryVisits.aspx; WGDAW, 'Report of the Working Group on the Issue of Discrimination Against Women in Law and in Practice on Its Mission to Hungary,' 2017, A/HRC/35/29/Add.1, paras 33–34, 97–98, www.ohchr.org/EN/Issues/Women/WGWomen/Pages/CountryVisits.aspx; WGDAW, 'Report of the Working Group on the Issue of Discrimination Against Women in Law and in Practice,' A/HRC/35/29, 19 April 2017, para 21, www.ohchr.org/Documents/Issues/Women/WG/A_HRC_35_29_AEV.docx.
6 WGDAW, 'Strengthening Protection Networks for Women Human Rights Defenders to Combat Discrimination: Challenges and Opportunities in the Current Context,' *OHCHR Website*, 18 May 2017, www.ohchr.org/EN/Issues/Women/WGWomen/Pages/WomenHumanRightsDefendersGender.aspx.

Index

Note: **Boldface** page references indicate photographs. *Italic* references indicate figures. References to authors and organisations cited in endnotes but not named in the text are not indexed.

2030 Agenda for Sustainable Development 72
2666 (Bolanyo) 24

Abbott, Tony 46
abortion 157–158, 200, 228; *see also* poverty; reproduction
Afghanistan 188–189
Africa 104, 158, 166; *see also specific country*
Albania 207
Alston, Philip 12, 164, 166
Anderson, Bridget 124
Asia 43, 203; *see also specific country*
Atatürk, Mustafa Kemal 189
Atkinson, Anthony B. 8
Atwood, Margaret 200
austerity: 22, 26, 48, 92
autonomy: of breadwinners 193; economic 51–52, 87, 126, 181, 228; employment relationship 101, 127; entrepreneurship 66; in family 182, 186, 188, 190, 197–198, 210, 228; feminism 11; legal barriers to 51–52, 64; liberalism 6;in modernist system 190, 210–211; in politics 4; prostitution 154; Woolf and 87

backlash to equality 16, 28, 210–212, 232
Balakrishnan, Radhika 12
banks 47; *see also specific name and topic*
Becker, Gary 128
Beijing Declaration and Platform for Action (1995) 4, 13, 67, 105, 147, 154, 184, 193, 197
Billari, Francesco C. 191
billionaires 64, 208
biological motherhood 199–200
birth rate 200; *see also* fertility
Blackstone 201
Bolanyo, Roberto 24
Boushey, Heather 193
breadwinners 192–194, 228
Brearley, Joeli 114
Brooks, Rosa 13

Canada 67, 97
capitalism 3–6, 8, 26–27, 128
Capital in the Twenty-First Century (Piketty) 7–8, 98, 127
care responsibilities: European Court of Justice 89; corporate world and 52; cross-cutting issues 20–22; economic vulnerability factor of 150; family 195–198; in gay marriage 196–197; gender equality in 197–198; humanity and 23; individualisation of 21–22; outsourcing 195; reproduction and 21; sale of human capital and 167; stereotypes of women and 20, 195–196; unpaid 20–22, 102, 113, 195; *see also* childcare; parenthood
cash transfers 164
CEDAW Committee 14–16, 24, 46, 105–106, 153, 156, 158, 182, 188–189, 197, 205–207
CEOs 27, 57, 71
CESCR 88

Chant, Sylvia 150, 162
childcare: adoption of children 196; affordable, 117–118; CEDAW 116; in China 22, 119; custody and maintenance of 209; employment and 111, 116–121, *117*, 197; family economics 197, 209; financial crisis of 2008 and 119; Indian IT industry and 111; parental leave for 116–117, *117*; policy 120–121; Scandinavian model 22, 197; socialist model 22, 119; in Russia 22, 119; state obligation, 118–119; child custody 209
child marriage 188–189
China 22, 25, 56, 98, 119, 149, 191, 200, 202–203
Christensen, Birgitte Nyborg 190
Christensen, Philip 190
civil society organisations 20, 230–231
Clinton, Hillary 46
'Commander in Chief' (US television series) 190
company boards 54–55; *see also* corporate world
contraception 157, 200, 228; *see also* reproduction
Convention on the Elimination of All Forms of Discrimination Against Women (CEDAW): childcare 116; *de facto* equality and 46; divorce 205–206; economic empowerment of women 71; economic leadership 59; entrepreneurship 67–68; equality in family 184, 210; equal rights for men and women 165, 169, 187, 228; inheritance 207; International Bill of Rights 13; international human rights law 12–16; maternity 113–114, 197; matrimonial property 201; paid maternity leave 114; pay gap 97; polygamy 189; pregnancy 159; prohibition of discrimination against women 12; reproductive health and rights 158; sexual harassment 105–106; substantive equality 14; trafficking 153–154, 156; transformative equality 15; violence against women 24; see also Working Group on Discrimination Against Women
Convention on the Rights of the Child 209
Convention on Trafficking in Human Beings 156
Coomaraswamy, Radhika 154
cooperatives 67
corporate leadership 17, 98 *see also* corporate world
corporate world: advocating for women's leadership in 70–71, 226; care responsibilities and 52; CEOs 57, 71; company boards 54–55; C-Suite and 55; *de facto* equality and 51; *de jure* equality and 51; economic leadership 51–60, **60**; glass ceiling 57, 69; glass cliff 57, 69; glass walls 53, 56, 69; international human rights law and 51–52, 58; leadership 17, 46; leadership gaps in 98; legal policy frameworks and 59–60; occupational segregation 56; overview 27; Pareto efficiency model and 73; political power 51; profit 17; senior management 55–56, *56*; stereotypes of women 52–54, 58
cosmopolitanisation of feminism 45
Council of Europe 156
Credit Suisse 55–57, 94
cyber violence 25

Danish Borgen feminist series 190
Deere, Carmen Diana 19
de facto equality 14–15, 46, 51, 59, 96, 101, 169, 203, 231
de jure equality 14, 51, 169
Denmark, 195
discrimination 107; *see also* gender inequality; stereotypes of women
dismissal 87, 89, 114
divorce 189, 204–206, 209
'Doll's House Repaired, A' (Eleanor Marx) 183
domestic work/workers 122–125, 127
duality: male-female 15, 29, 48, 59, 69, 72, 226; production and reproduction 21, 91

economic equality 17, 29, 66–67, 232
economic inequality 3–4, 7–10, 29, 225; *see also specific type*
economic leadership: banks and 47; CEDAW and 59; European Central Bank (ECB) 47; CEOs 57, 71; company boards 54–55; corporate world and 51–60, **60**; economic policy-making and 48–49; economic power and 45–60, 70–71; international institutions 46–47; male monopoly and 58–60; need for critical mass of women in 226; overview 45; parliamentary representation and 45–46, 48; politically based economic power 45–50; prime minister and

47; private finance 47–48; senior management 55–56, *56*; stereotypes of women and 46; World Economic Forum 45, 47, 49–50, **50**
economic man 3–4
economic policy 11, 26, 44, 48, 69–70, 72; *see also specific policy*
economic power: CEDAW and 71; deficit of, women's 69–72; economic leadership and 45–60, 70–71; entrepreneurship 61–68; gender bias and 70; gender budgeting and 70; Human Rights Council 71–72; male monopoly on 231; overview 27–28, 43–44, 226; progress of women and 69; Sustainable Development Goals and 68, 72; 2030 Agenda for Sustainable Development and 72; World Economic Forum and women's acquisition of 49–50, **50**
economic woman: concept of 3–4; at crossroads 223–232; economic inequality and 8; economic man versus 3–4; empowering 71, 230–231; entrepreneurship 63; equality and, right to 4–5, 229–231; family economics 181, 184, 206; female breadwinners 193; feminism and 11; informal work 100; international human rights law and 12–17; intersectionality and 10–11, 225–226; neo-liberalism 5–7, 9–11, 28, 72, 126, 228, 231; overview 27–29; Piketty an 127; poverty and 165; right to equality and to 4–5, 229–230; socialism 5–7; unpaid care and 20–22, 126; violence against women and 22–26; *see also specific topic*
Ecuador 204
education: achievement in and corporate power 54; barriers to 93; in China 56; correlation with remuneration 99; earnings of women and 227; equal access to 47; fertility rates and 162; Guangzhou Gender and Sexuality Education Centre (China) 25; sexual harassment and 106; STEM and 112; school day and working hours 118; in traditionalist system 187–189; violence against women 25
Einarsdóttir, Thorgerdur 49
electoral process 45–46
El Salvador 158
Elson, Diane 12, 20–21, 120
employment: autonomy of individuals and relationships with 101, 127; childcare and 111, 116–121, *117*, 197; depersonalisation of work 110; domestic workers 122–125, 127; equal employment opportunity, unfulfilled promise of 126–129; equal opportunity 126–129; EU Directive on Maternity Leave 115; export processing zones (EPZs) 96–97; female labour force participation 91–94, **92**; fourth industrial revolution 109–112; gender inequality in 127–128; in gig economy 109–110; horizontal occupational segregation, 98–99; informal work and 100–103, 227; 'Living with Economic Insecurity—Women in Precarious Work' (2011 report) 101–102; maternity leave 93, 113–117, *117*; migrant working woman 23, 122–125; motherhood gap 96; non-discrimination laws in 89–90; part-time work 93–94; paternity leave 116–117, *117*; pension gap 107–108; pregnancy and 89, 114; protective labour law 227; sectoral distribution of, by sex 97; sex-segregated 56, 98–99, 112; sexual harassment in 24, 104–106; 'sticky floors' concept 96; third industrial revolution 109–112; vertical occupational segregation in 56, 98–99; *see also* corporate world; entrepreneurship
Engels, Friedrich 183
Enlightenment 4
entrepreneurship: autonomy of women and 66; Beijing Declaration and Platform for Action and 67; Blueprint for a Co-operative Decade 67; Canadian Business Women in International Trade program 67; CEDAW 67–68; concentrations of women in 62–63, *63*; cooperatives 67; economic equality 66–67; economic opportunities for women 66; economic power 61–68; financial resources 67; future of women in 66–68; gender bias 64–66; gender gap 62–64, *63*; Global Banking Alliance for Women 67; Global Compact 59; Global Entrepreneurship Monitor 61–62; Goldman Sachs 10,000 Women program 67; Human Rights Council 68; ILO 61; Job Creation in Small and Medium Sized Enterprises Recommendation 67; Mann Deshi Mahila Sahakari Bank 67; microfinance 65–66; overview 27–28, 61; Promotion

of Cooperatives Recommendation 67; SheTrades initiative 67; stereotypes of women 66; Sustainable Development Goals 68; women's, increase in 61–62; Women's Entrepreneurship Development program 67
equal pay: court decisions on 97–98; Equal Remuneration Conventions 95
Esping-Andersen, Gøsta 191
essentialism 14–15
EU Directive on Maternity Leave 115
Europe 43; *see also specific country*
European Central Bank (ECB) 47
European Court of Justice 89
European Parliament's Women's Rights Committee (2004) 26
export processing zones (EPZs) 96–97

Fabian Society (UK) 167–168
family economics: backlash to equality 210–212; biological motherhood 199–200; caregiving 195–198; childcare 197, 209; child custody 209; divorce 204–206; economic unit of family 182; equality in family 182–185, 212; fertility 199–200; gender equal partnership 191; historical perspective 183–185; inheritance 207–208; maintenance payment 209; matriarchy 191; matrimonial property 201–203, 228; modernist system 186, 189–191, 228; overview 28–29, 181–182, 228; patriarchy 28, 183; single parent 151–152; state obligation 5–6; traditionalist system 91, 183, 186–189, 228–229; women as breadwinners 192–194
'Fearless Girl, The' (Visbal) **60**
female labour force participation (FLFP) 28, 91–94, **92**, 192, 227
feminism 11, 13–14, 45
feminisation of poverty 28, 147, 169, 227–228
fertility 113, 162, 191, 193, 199–200
financial crisis (2008) 119, 126
financial resources access 18, 46, 67–68
Finland 167
Folbre, Nancy 9
Forbes 63, 208
fourth industrial revolution 28, 109–112, 227
Fowler, Susan 106
France 98, 207
Fredman, Sandra 98

Gates, Bill 167
gay marriage 196–197
gender-based violence 153–156, *155*; *see also* violence against women (VAW)
gender bias 64–66, 70
gender budgeting 70
Gender and Development (GAD) field 9
gendered poverty: abuse of women's bodies and dignity 153–160, 228; development agendas for alleviating 169–170 human rights agendas for reduction of 161–168; incidence 149–152; overview 28, 147–148; patriarchy 28, 154, 169; Perestroika in Soviet Union 155; proportion of people living in extreme poverty *151*; prostitution and 25–26, 153–156; roots of 170; single mother families 151–152; taxation and 166; unemployment and 166–167; World Bank 161–162; *see also* poverty
gender equality: care responsibilities and 197–198; CEDAW 197; economic equality 232; economic policy 48, 69, 71–72; equal employment opportunity 126; formal equality 14; in families 186, 191, 197; GDP impact on 17, 120, 195, 227; in Iceland 48–49; income and, basic 167; international human rights law 16, 232; Maastricht Principles 60; matrimonial property 202; in modernist system 186, 191; in Nordic countries; overview 27; transformation 210; universal human right 13, 72, 989, 162, 228; in wage payment 96; women in labour market and 126; women parliamentary leaders championing 48; work-life balance and 94; *see also* equality; *see also specific topic*
gender gaps: academic 112; entrepreneurial 62–64, *63*; female labour force participation 91; Gender Gap Index 190; land ownership 18–20; leadership 98; pay 95–99, 110–111; pension 107–108; political 5; poverty 150; promotion 95–99; STEM field 112, 127; taxation and 166; unpaid work *196*; wage 95–99, 110–111; World Bank 66; *see also specific topic*
gender inequality: economic growth and reduction of 17; economic inequality and 4, 225; in employment 127–138; feminism in eliminating 11; gendered

poverty and 170; *see also* inequality; *see also specific topic*
gender stereotypes *see* stereotypes of women
gender trolling 25
Ghana, wealth in marriage in 204–205
gig economy: depersonalization in 110; sexual harassment in 106; work in 109–112
Gillard, Julia 46
glass ceiling 57, 69
glass cliff 57, 69
Glassdoor Economic Research survey 99
glass walls 53, 56, 69
Global Banking Alliance for Women 67
Global Compact 59
Global Entrepreneurship Monitor (GEM) 61–62
Global Gag Rule 158
globalisation 3, 9
Global Justice Now 51
Global Women's Work 230
Goldman, Emma 183
Goldman Sachs 10,000 Women program 67
'Good Wife, The' (US television series) 190
Google 99
Gottfried, Heidi 92
Gracie, Carrie 95
Grant, Valerie 63
Great 'He-cessation,' The 92
Guangzhou Gender and Sexuality Education Centre (China) 25
Guiding Principles on Extreme Poverty and Human Rights, The 147

Handmaid's Tale, The (Atwood) 200
hard porn commercialisation 26
Haslam, S. Alexander 57
Heintz, James 12
Hobby Lobby ruling 157
hooks, bell 11
Hopkins, Ann 53
horizontal occupational segregation 98–99
human capital *see* sale of human capital
Human Rights Council (HRC) 16, 59, 68, 71–72, 103, 185, 187, 210–211; *see also* Working Group Committee on Discrimination Against Women
Hunting Ground, The (documentary) 25

Ibsen, Henrik 183
Iceland 48–49, 54, 97, 99, 113, 116, 118, 190, 207
ILO (International Labour Organization): cash transfers in developing economies 164; Domestic Workers Convention 123; 'Ending Violence and Harassment against Women and Men in the World of Work' 106; entrepreneurship 61; equal opportunity in the workplace 94, 97; Equal Remuneration Conventions 95; female labour force participation 91–92, **92**, 93; financial resources for women 67; informal work 100–103; Maternity Protection Convention 89, 115–116; paid maternity leave 114–116; Part-time Work Convention 94; quotas 55; sexual harassment 104, 106; social protection coverage 165–166; Social Protection Floor Recommendation 164–165; stereotypes of women 53–54; wage gaps and 97; work hours 20; Women in the Workplace Report 53, 57; World Employment Social Outlook 92; World Social Protection Report 165
income inequality 43; *see also* pay gaps; wage gaps
India 24, 159, 167, 204–205, 208
industrial revolutions, third and fourth 109–112
inequality *see specific topic*
Inequality (Atkinson) 8:
inequality, economic: capitalism 8; economic woman 7–10; gendering 3–4, 7–20, 29, 225; income 43; international economic actors 12; macroeconomics15, 43–44; neo-liberalism 6–7, 9, 11; wealth 7, 43, 203–204; *see also* gender inequality
informal work 9, 100–103, 227
Informal Employment network 102
inheritance 207–208
International Association of Feminist Economics 9
International Bill of Rights 13; ICCPR 184; ICESCR 165; *see also specific topic*
International Cooperative Alliance Blueprint for a Co-operative Decade 67
international human rights law (IHRL): backlash to 16, 210–212; CEDAW 12–16; corporate world 51–52, 58; economic woman 12–17; gender equality 16, 231; international economic actors 12; matrimonial property 202, 211; overview 12–13; pension gap 108; right to equality in family 184; state's obligation to ensure women's right

to equality 13–16; women's right to equality 93 228–229; *see also specific topic*
International Monetary Fund (IMF) 46, 50, 61, 70, 193–194
International Trade Centre (ITC) 67
International Trade Union Confederation (ITUC) 101–102
Inter Parliamentary Union (IPU) 47–48
Intersectionality 10–11, 14, 225–226
Invisibile Heart, The (Folbre) 9
'Invisible War, The' (2012 documentary) 105
Israel 47–48

Job Creation in Small and Medium Sized Enterprises Recommendation 67
Jordan 208

Keren, Hila 65
Krugman, Paul 7

Lady Globes 47–48
Lagarde, Christine 5, 46, 55
land ownership and management 18–20, 65–66, 189, 191, 202–203
Latin America 20, 108; *see also specific country*
Lean In (Sandberg) 53
Leon, Magdalena 19
LFPR 211
liberalism 5–7, 13; *see also* neo-liberalism
LIS income transfer data 165
literary woman 4

Maastricht Principles 59–60
macroeconomics: decision-making in 5, 44, 48, 58–60; economic woman 5, 28, 58–60; fertility 199–200; inequalities 15, 43–44; informal work 100; male-female duality 15; male monopoly in 28, 58–60; monetary economy 21; neo-liberalism 3; non-monetary economy 21; political leadership 45–50; women's participation in, importance of 29
'Madame Secretary' (US television series) 190
male-female duality 15, 29, 48, 59, 69, 72, 226
male monopoly 3, 5, 15, 28, 46, 58–60
Mandela, Nelson 147
Mann Deshi Mahila Sahakari Bank 67
Marcal, Katherine 3
marriage: child 188–189; dissolution of 189, 204–206, 209; gay 196–197; polygamous 188–189; property and 201–204; rates, declining 193; wealth in 203–204
Marx, Eleonora 8, 128, 183–184
Marx, Karl 8
maternal mortality 158–159, 189
maternity: economics of 199–200; failure to accommodate 227; gendered care responsibilities 113–121 leave 89, 114–117, *117*, 197; Maternity Protection Conventions (ILO) 89, 115–116; reproduction and 21
matriarchy 191
matrimonial property 201–203, 211, 228
McKinsey reports 17, 111
MDGs Report (2000) 158–159
MDGs Report (2015) 149–150, 161
Meir, Marissa 52
menstruation, basic conditions needed 158–160
Merkel, Angela 5, 45
#MeToo campaign 95, 106
Mexico: Progresa/Oportunidades program in 164; violence against women in Cuidad Juarez 24
microfinance 65–66
Middle East 43, 124, 202; *see also specific country*
migrant working woman 23, 122–125
Miranda, Veerle 195
misogyny, culture of 105–106
monetary economy 21
Moore 61
Morocco 189
Mosuo tribe 191
motherhood gap 96
Moyan, Samuel 13
Musk, Elon 167
Muslim states 188–189

Na tribe 191
neo-liberalism: capitalism 3; challenge of, ideological 6; economic woman and 5–7, 9–11, 28, 72, 126, 128, 231; global embrace of 6; historical perspective 6, 11; inequality of 6–7, 9, 11; macroeconomics and 3; male monopoly in 3, 58; market conditions created by 9; policy 9; privatisation and 10; public services and 10; stereotypes of women and 9; tax policy 166; transformation from socialism 5–7; *see also specific topic*
'Nigerian Nollywood' series 190
non-monetary economy 21
Nordic countries 197; *see also specific country*
Norway 54–55, 95, 195

occupational segregation 56, 98–99
OECD countries 99, 112, 202
Okin, Susan 183–184
Okonjo-Iweala, Ngozi 47
Ortega, Amancio 128
Oxfam 7, 63

parental leave *see* maternity leave; paternity leave
parenting 113; *see also* childcare
Pareto efficiency models 71
parliamentary representation 45–46, 48
part-time work 93–94
Part-time Work Convention 94
paternity leave 52, 116–117, *117*, 197
patriarchy: capitalism and 8, 128; cyber violence and 25; economic autonomy of women and 51–52, 228–229; economic woman and 10–11; equality transformation and 210–212, 229; family economics and 28, 183; gendered poverty and 28, 154, 169; household resources and, women's share of 28; inequality of women and 4, 44, 183, 228–229; intersectionality 10; male-female duality 15; manifestations of, ongoing 10–11; prevalence of, ongoing 202, 211; re-entrenching, efforts to 16, 128; shift from 228; traditionalist system systems 186–187, 189–190
patrimonial capitalism 8
pay gaps 55, 95–99, 110–111
pensions/pension gaps 107–108. 164
Persson, Stefan 128
Peru 20, 23
Pétursdóttir, Gyða Margrét 49
Philippines 23
physiological needs 15, 156–158
Pickett, Kate E. 8
Piketty, Thomas 7–8, 98, 127
political leadership 5, 45–50, 69, 226; *see also specific leader's name*
political woman 5, 45–50
polygamy 188–189
pornography 25–26, 105
Portugal 104–105
poverty: abuse of women's bodies and dignity and 169; in China 149; feminisation of 28, 147, 169, 227–228; gender gaps 150; Global Gag Rule 158; human rights and 147, 149; incidence of 148–152, 161; international line of 149; lactation, basic conditions needed 158–160; Mandela and 147; maternal mortality 158; multidimensional issues of 147; Multidimensional Poverty Index and 162–165; overview 28, 147–148, 227–228; proportion of people living in extreme *151*; social insurance in reducing 165; social security in reducing 165; unpaid work and 150; World Bank and 149–150; *see also* gendered poverty
precarious work 21, 28, 101–102, 153, 227; *see also* employment
pregnancy 89, 114, 158–160
Pretty Woman (1990 film) 155
Price of Inequality, The (Stiglitz) 8
privatisation 3, 10, 22, 50, 69, 119, 183, 203, 227
'productive' economy 20–21, 28
Progresa/Oportunidades program (Mexico) 164
Promotion of Cooperative Recommendation 67
promotion/promotion gaps44, 49, 52–55, 95–99, 127, 129, 227
prostitution 25–26, 153–156
public services, reduction in 10, 119
public transport 23–24, 26, 38, 48, 170

quotas, mandatory gender 33, 46, 54–55, 58–59; *see also* temporary special measures

Report on Women, Business and Law (2016) 51
reproduction 15, 21, 28, 64, 70, 148, 156–158, 165, 200, 228
'reproductive' economy 21, 28
Resolution on Elimination of Discrimination against Women and Girls (HRC) 211
Resolutions of the Human Rights Council 16
resources, access to: credit facilities 18, 65–66; cross-cutting issues 18–20; to financial resources 18, 46, 65–68; to general resources 18–20, 159–160; to land ownership 18–20; to reproductive services 28, 64, 70, 148, 156–158, 165; *see also specific topic*
retirement 107–108; *see also* pensions
Rio Conference on Environment and Development (1991) 199–200
robots 127
Roodman, David 66

Rosie the Riveter 118, **118**
Russia 19, 22, 119
Ryan, Michelle K. 57

sale of human capital: care responsibilities and 167; domestic workers 122–125; economic impact of 128; equal employment opportunity 126–129; female labour force participation 91–94, **92**; fourth industrial revolution 109–112; historical perspective 87; informal work 100–103; intersectionality 10–11; maternity 113–121; motherhood gap 96; overview 28, 87–90, 227; pay gaps 95–99; pension gap 107–108; promotion gaps 95–99; sexual harassment 24, 104–106; third industrial revolution 109–112
Sandberg, Sheryl 5, 53
Schwab, Klaus 72
Self Employed Women's Association (SEWA) 230
Sen, Amartya 7
senior management 55–56, *56*, 94; *see also* corporate leadership
'Servants and Slaves' (Anderson) 124
sex industry 25–26, 153–154
sexism 106; *see also* stereotypes of women
sex-segregated employment 56, 98–99, 112; *see also* employment
sexual harassment 24, 104–106; *see also* violence against women (VAW)
Sha'ri law 189, 208
SheTrades67
Sigurðardóttir, Jóhanna 48
Silicon Valley 106
single parent families 151–152; *see also* family economics
Sisters in Islam 189
Slaughter, Anne-Marie 22
Smith, Adam 3
social assistance 164; *see also* social protection
Social Institutions and Gender Index (SIGI) 202–203, 207
social insurance in reducing poverty 165
socialism 5–7, 22
social protection coverage 164–166; *see also* social security
social security: basic income 167; LIS income transfer data 165; in poverty reduction 165; Social Protection Floor Recommendation (ILO) 164–165
Social Watch 150
South Africa 104
Spacey, Kevin 95
Special Investigation Commission (SIC) 49
Special Procedures of Human Rights Council 16, 185, 187, 211
Special Rapporteur on Human Rights and Drinking Water 160
Special Rapporteur on Poverty 150
Special Rapporteur on VAW 154–155
Spirit Level, The (Pickett and Wilkinson) 8
statistical discrimination 107
STEM, gender gaps in field of 112, 127; *see also* third and fourth industrial revolutions
stereotypes of women: care responsibilities 20, 195–196; corporate world 52–54, 58; economic leadership 46; entrepreneurship 66; ILO 53–54; in modernist system 190; neo-liberalism and 9; reverse gender stereotypes 53; roles and unpaid care and 20
'sticky floors' concept 96
Stiglitz, Joseph E. 7–8
substantive equality 6, 13–15, 162, 187, 205
surrogacy 159, 196, 200
Sustainable Development Goals (SDGs) 68, 72, 161–162, 207

Taliban 188–189
taxation and gender gaps 166
temporary special measures 33 229; *see also* quotas
Thatcher, Margaret 50
'think crisis-think female' stereotype 57
third industrial revolution 28, 109–112, 227
Thomson Reuters Foundation 19
Thornton, Grant 55
tokenism 55
Total Entrepreneurial Activity (TEA) 61–62
traditionalist system 91, 183, 186–189, 228–229
trafficking 25–26, 153–156, **155**
transformative equality 15
trickle-down effect of wealth 7
Trump administration 158
Tunisia 189
Turkey 189, 207

Uber 106, 111
UN Broadband Commission 25
UN Department of Economic and Social Affairs data 193

UN Development Agenda 161–162, 169
UN Food and Agriculture Organization (FAO) 19
UN General Assembly Declaration on the Elimination ofViolence against Women 105
UN General Principles on Business and Human Rights 59
UN Protocol to Prevent, Suppress and Punish Trafficking in Persons, especially Women and Children (Trafficking Protocol), 156
UN Resolution on Child, Early and Forced Marriage 189
UN Women 38, 46–47, 59, 150, 165, 206
UN Women and World Bank Report (2018) 150
unemployment 166–167
UNGP 59
UNICEF 159
United Kingdom: divorce in 206; Fabian Society in 167–168; inheritance in 207; pay gap in 98; pension gaps in 107; pregnancy-related complaints in 114; women as breadwinners in 193
United States: abortion access in 157–158; divorce in 206; pay gap in 98; pay gaps in 55, 98–99; pension gaps in 107; pregnancy-related complaints in 114; sexual harassment at work in 105–106; violence against women on college campuses in 25
Universal Declaration of Human Rights (UDHR) 4, 6, 13, 184, 201
unpaid work: for care responsibilities 20–22, 102, 113, 195; in Denmark 195; GDP per capita and women's 195; gender gap *196*; in Norway 195; poverty and 150; three R's of 120
U.S. Federal Reserve 47

vertical occupational segregation 56, 98–99; *see also* promotion
Vienna Declaration and Program of Action (1993) 13, 161, 187
violence against women (VAW): Convention on the Elimination of All Forms of Discrimination Against Women 24; cross-cutting issues 22–26; in Cuidad Juarez (Mexico) 24; cyber 25; domestic violence 190; economic opportunities and 23–26; education 25; European Parliament's Women's Rights Committee and 26; hard porn 26; migrant working woman 23, 122–125; poverty and 230; sexual harassment 24, 104–106; trafficking 25–26, 153–156, **155**
Visbal, Kristen 60
voting rights for women 45

wage gaps 55, 95–99, 110–111
Wahlberg, Mark 95
Washington Consensus (1980s) 165
Water (2005 film) 208
wealth 7, 43, 203–204
welfare 5–6, 165
West, Robin 3–4
WGDAW *see* Working Group on Discrimination Against Women (Human Rights Council Special Procedures) (WGDAW)
Who Cooked Adam Smith's Dinner? (Marcal) 3
'Why Women Still Can't Have It All' (Slaughter) 22
Wilkinson, Richard G. 8
Williams, Michelle 95
Winfrey, Oprah 64
'Woman Question, The' (Eleanor Marx) 183
'Women, Business and the Law' (World Bank report, 2016, 2018) 24–25, 51, 105, 184, 202
Women's Empowerment Principles 59
Women in Senior Management report 94
Women's Entrepreneurship Development (WED) program 67
women's right to equality: backlash 16, 28, 210–212, 232; *de facto* 14–15, 46, 51, 59, 96, 101, 169, 203, 231; *de jure* 14, 51, 169; economic 29, 66–67, 232; economic justification for 16–17; economic policy and 72; economic woman 4–5, 229–230; feminism 11; formal 14; human well-being 17; in informal work 103; progress of economic woman 5, 69, 226; state's obligation 13–16; substantive 14–15; transformative 15; *see also* economic woman; gender equality; *specific topic*
Women's World Conference in Beijing (1995) 162
Women in the Workplace Report (2016) 53, 57
Women's World Studies Conference (2005) 9
Woolf, Virginia 87

Working Group on Discrimination Against Women (Human Rights Council Special Procedures) (WGDAW) 14–16, 20, 46, 59, 62, 91, 103, 114, 115, 119, 156, 158, 188, 189, 207, 211, 230
Working Group on Business and Human Rights 59
World Bank: divorce and 206; entrepreneurial women and 66; equality of women and 17, 184; gendered poverty and 161–162; matrimonial property and 202–203; poverty and 149–150; property rights and 210; wage gaps and 96; woman as president of, nonoccurrence of 46; women as breadwinners and 193–194; 'Women, Business and the Law' 24–25, 51, 105, 184, 202
World Economic Forum (WEF): childcare responsibilities and 120; economic empowerment of women and 49–50, **50**; economic leadership 45, 47, 49–50, **50**; family caregiving and 195–198; female labour force participation and 91; fourth industrial revolution and 109; gender gaps and 5; Iceland's gender equality and 49; pay gap and 95; unpaid care and 20
World Employment and Social Outlook (2017 ILO report) 92, **92**
World Health Organization (WHO) 23–24, 157, 159
World Inequality Report (2018) 7
World Social Protection Report (2017 ILO report) 165
World Trade Organization (WTO) 46–47

Yellen, Janet 47
Yuen, Betty 52
Yunis, Mohammed 65

Zhou Qunfei 5, 64
Zuckerberg, Mark 52, 167